D1238640

Violence, Civil Strife and Revolution in the Classical City

750-330 BC

Andrew Lintott

THE JOHNS HOPKINS UNIVERSITY PRESS
BALTIMORE, MARYLAND

Published in the United States of America, 1981,
by the Johns Hopkins University Press,
Baltimore, Maryland 21218

Library of Congress Cataloging in Publication Data

Lintott, Andrew.
    Violence, civil strife, and revolution in the
classical city, 750-330 B.C.

    Bibliography: p. 274
    Includes index.
    1. Greece — Politics and government — To 146 B.C.
2. Violence — Greece — History. 3. Revolutions —
Greece — History. 4. Social conflict - Greece —
History. 5. Social classes - Greece — History.
I. Title.
DF82.L56   1981   938   81-48181
ISBN 0-8018-2789-2   AACR2

Printed and bound in Great Britain

CONTENTS

FOR MY FRIENDS IN SCOTLAND

PREFACE

This book is intended for all those with a serious interest in the history of the ancient world, whether they know classical languages or not. Greek and Latin words are only used in the text when they are technical terms hard to translate, and all Greek is transliterated. Translations of most of the ancient literary sources are available; papyri are published with translations into a modern language; only inscriptions tend to be out of reach of those with no Greek or Latin. I have therefore included, where possible, references to books of translated sources by C.W. Fornara and by M.M. Austin and P. Vidal-Naquet.

My publishers could not allow me unlimited space for notes, and so I have concentrated on giving source-references and citations of those modern works which I have found most helpful (according to the Harvard system). My failure to cite a modern work does not necessarily mean that I have not read it, but I cannot pretend that I have read everything that I should or might have. In particular I must apologise to anyone whose views I appear to reproduce without acknowledgement (I know from my own experience how galling this can be): any failure to acknowledge is the result of ignorance rather than malice.

A more agreeable duty than apology is to thank those who have helped in the production of this book. Howard Scullard first suggested that I should write it; Tony Andrewes, Peter Brunt and George Forrest provided much helpful and forthright criticism of the whole work; David Lewis lent me works not easily accessible; Edward Raven gave me advice on numismatics; Bettie Loraine Farmer helped me in preparing the typescript. My thanks are due to them and finally to Richard Stoneman and Croom Helm Ltd for accepting it for publication. The completion of this book marks the end of a happy and profitable stay in Scotland. It is perhaps a pawky but genuine token of gratitude that I dedicate the book to my friends north of the border.

A.W.L.

King's College, Aberdeen
and Worcester College, Oxford

ABBREVIATIONS OF MODERN WORKS USED IN THE NOTES

APF   J.K. Davies, *Athenian Propertied Families*, Oxford, 1971.

ATL   B.D. Meritt, H.T. Wade-Gery and M.F. McGregor, *The Athenian Tribute Lists*, Cambridge, Mass./Princeton, N.J., 1939-53.

ATPW   C.W. Fornara, *Archaic Times to the Peloponnesian War*, Baltimore/London, 1977.

DK   H. Diels and W. Kranz, *Die Fragmente der Vorsokratiker*, Berlin, 1934-7.

FGH   F. Jacoby, *Die Fragmente der Griechischen Historiker*, Berlin/ Leiden, 1923- .

FIRA   S. Riccobono, *Fontes Iuris Romani Anteiustiniani*, Florence, 1968.

GHI   M.N. Tod, *Greek Historical Inscriptions*, Oxford, 1946-8.

HCT   A.W. Gomme, A. Andrewes and K.J. Dover, *A Historical Commentary on Thucydides*, Oxford, 1956-81.

Hill   G.F. Hill, R. Meiggs and A. Andrewes, *Sources for Greek History between the Persian and Peloponnesian Wars*, Oxford, 1951.

IC   F. Halbherr and M. Guarducci, *Inscriptiones Creticae*, Rome, 1935-50.

IG   *Inscriptiones Graecae*.

ILS   H. Dessau, *Inscriptiones Latinae Selectae*, Berlin, 1892-1916.

LGS   D.L. Page, *Lyrica Graeca Selecta*, Oxford, 1968.

ML   R. Meiggs and D.M. Lewis, *Greek Historical Inscriptions to the End of the Fifth Century B.C.*, Oxford, 1969.

NC   *Numismatic Chronicle*.

OP   *Oxyrhynchus Papyri*.

P. Ryl.   A.S. Hunt *et al.*, *Catalogue of the Greek Papyri in the John Rylands Library*, Manchester, 1911-15.

RE   Pauly-Wissowa-Kroll, *Real-Encyclopädie der klassischen Altertumswissenschaft*.

Schmitt   H.H. Schmitt, *Die Vertrage der griechisch-römischen Welt von 338 bis 200 v.Chr.*, Munich, 1969.

SEG   *Supplementum Epigraphicum Graecum*.

SGDI   H. Collitz, F. Bechtel *et al.*, *Sammlung der griechischen Dialekt-Inschriften*, Göttingen, 1884-1915.

Sherk   R.K. Sherk, *Roman Documents from the Greek East*, Baltimore, 1969.

Syll.   W. Dittenberger, *Sylloge Inscriptionum Graecarum*, 3rd ed., Leipzig, 1915-24.

Welles   C.B. Welles, *Royal Correspondence in the Hellenistic Period*, New Haven, Conn., 1934.

INTRODUCTION

The subjects of this book have an important place in most modern books about the ancient world, whether they deal with political, socio-economic or cultural history. What is the point then of a special study? In a previous book about violence in the Roman Republic I argued that violence played such an important part in late Republican politics that it became more than a symptom of other disturbances, but rather a disease itself which made its own contribution to the fall of the Republican government. This was the ultimate justification for picking out this violence for analysis, although the subject in itself raised sufficient historical problems to merit special investigation. In the wider field of the history of the ancient world as a whole, apart from individual problems of interpretation, there are important relationships and similarities between this phenomenon in different lands and historical periods. One aim of this book is to make a conspectus of these possible. Beyond this, it would perhaps be overambitious to assign civil violence a prime place among the causes of decline of the world of the city-state. Such a claim would be vulnerable to the charge of superficiality. However, it may be fairly argued to have been an extremely revealing symptom of the failings of that form of society.

The subject is topical. I see no need to defend the undertaking of a subject which may be relevant in the modern world, whatever the dangers of importing prejudices from one's own period. However, it is worth pointing out that the thesis, which was the germ of my first book, was complete before President Kennedy was assassinated, and the writing of that book largely preceded the era of urban guerrilla warfare, hijacking, campus conflict, not to mention civil war in Ireland, Cyprus, Chile and elsewhere. This is an instance of a historian of the past being overtaken by his own subject in the present. What has happened recently has not inclined me to change my basic views about the Roman Republic.

Inevitably, a work like this must be selective, if it is to be manageable by author and reader. I have concentrated on the best attested occasions of civil strife, provided they have an exemplary value or a bearing on the course of history. We possess accounts of Egyptian and Mesopotamian rulers faced with revolt and conspiracy,[1] but the isolated sources are not very informative and we lack the background to understand the facts that they relate. The divisions of the people of Israel in Old Testament times form a subject in themselves. I have confined my- self to the Greco-Roman world. As a starting-point I have taken the emergence of Greece from the 'Dark Age' about 750 BC, when it begins to be possible to separate history from legend.

Note

1. E.g. A. Gardiner, *Egypt of the Pharaohs*, 288, 307; D.W. Luckenbill, *Ancient Assyrian Records*, II, 257, 501, 642, 789.

1 VIOLENCE IN ARCHAIC SOCIETY AND ITS LEGACY

Ancient philosophers had two main views about the formation of human society, first that it occurred through a love of association in man, secondly that it was the result of men's weakness and fear of harm. The first is the well-known view of Aristotle, which was adopted by Cicero among others. The second was already current in the fifth century BC; it was held by the sophist Protagoras, according to Plato, the politician Critias and the author of a pamphlet praising philosophy. It seems also to have been adopted by the Epicureans, since it is the foundation of Lucretius' explanation of the growth of society. This second evolutionary view posited an era of lawlessness after the initial development of primitive technology. It was in reaction to this that men were thought to have founded communities such as cities. Even if the creation of a state in embryo and some form of law was not required by conditions within the community, it was necessary as a response to outside attack. Thus Plato in *Republic* II argues that the needs of his ideal city, which is 'luxurious' (i.e. lives above subsistence level), will require it to fight with neighbours over territory: therefore it will require military guardians and a political organisation to control them.[1]

The myth of the five ages of man, found in Hesiod, is the first quasi-historical explanation of human development in Greek literature. This begins with man in Paradise in the Golden Age, but the third, Bronze, Age is an age of violence from whose effects humanity has not yet recovered: in spite of the ensuing age of heroes, the grim Iron Age follows. Of the historians proper, Herodotus says little about this period in Greek history, although he is impressed by the way that the Spartans through Lycurgus achieved *eunomia*, a well-ordered society, after a long period of lawlessness (Greek tradition about divinely inspired lawgivers must have encouraged belief that before their intervention life was intolerable).

Thucydides, however, in the review of early Greek history with which he opens his work, combines a critical summary of existing tradition with a more theoretical account of social evolution. In his view, Greece was originally occupied by unsettled peoples, who were unremittingly expelled from their land by more powerful neighbours or split by faction, especially when they occupied highly fertile land. Attica was

13

an important exception, and a haven for fugitives. There was brigandage, moreover, and piracy, as seafaring developed. People nevertheless became sufficiently confident in face of piracy to found walled cities by the shore. After the temporary unity during the Trojan War enforced by the superior power of Mycenae, the delay in the return of the Greeks led to further revolutions, migrations and the founding of new cities. It thus took a long time for Greece to be peaceful, secure and free from upheavals.[2]

As evidence for this account Thucydides used the nature of society in one of the less developed parts of Greece in his own day, the northwest region — where brigandage and piracy were a respected way of life until centuries later. He also drew on the Homeric poems and more generally on the heroic myths, as they had come down to him in a variety of literature. These must have influenced his conception of primitive Greek society as much as his inferences about probable historical development, although he justifiably insists that the second factor made his own account superior to preceding ones. Two of the most popular cycles of saga, the Theban cycle and that of the family of Atreus, have usurpation of kingly power as one of their major themes, while enforced migrations and attempts to return to one's native land are found throughout mythology. Indeed, both Herodotus and Thucydides accept the return of the descendants of Heracles, expelled from Argos by Eurystheus, as historical events. Assuming that there is a kernel of historical truth in the sagas, we cannot build too much on them in themselves, since the stories of the royal houses of Argos and Thebes, for example, may have survived because they were unusual and striking. Nevertheless, anthropological studies show that the usurpation of the power of the chief is common in tribal societies, as is the secession of tribes or clans from a community.[3]

However, my concern at the present is not so much with individual political struggles, about which any degree of certainty is unattainable, as with the extent and function of violence within the more regular workings of society. With this aim I wish to examine more closely two kinds of evidence that Thucydides used — the Homeric poems and the survival of customs. A reservation must be made at the start about the implications of the second kind of evidence. Much of it is of procedures commonly embraced under the term 'self-help', that is, the use of force by individual or group as a result of an offence allegedly committed against them, with or without the sanction of a higher political authority. The proved existence of such procedures does not necessarily imply that the societies concerned were continually torn by the violence of feuding groups. Granted that in many societies, whether or not they possessed a central authority with powers of enforcement, self-help was the ultimate sanction available to a wronged party in order to obtain restitution or compensation, in practice many disputes may have tended towards reconciliation, simply because the ensuing violence would have been intolerable. This is particularly true where kinship links are manifold or there exist other forms of political association which cut across kinship links.[4]

The Evidence of the Homeric Poems

Declining to join in the controversy over the exact post-Mycenaean date of the 'World of Odysseus',[5] I assume that the type of society described in the Homeric poems is one which existed in the Dark Age, and that many of the features of this society were still present, particularly in the more backward communities, about 700 BC, when the poems were being composed. These societies have a chief, whose position may be violently usurped and whose security is often only positively maintained by his own strength and by that of his kindred, as by Odysseus himself and Telemachus. Nevertheless, appeal may be made to an assembly in self-justification, and the approval of the assembly, if not much direct help to the vulnerable chief, is at least an insurance policy against support being afforded to a usurper from that quarter. One may compare this to the situation obtaining recently among the Tswana in southern Africa. This tribe was unusual in having a regular assembly, and a chief paid respect to the views expressed there in an endeavour to keep his tribe's loyalty. Otherwise his leading opponents might use his unpopularity in order to remove him, not by attempting assassination but by general revolt. This would not happen without leadership from among the magnates in the tribe, but a really unpopular ruler was an incitement to his rivals. The importance of popular sentiment up to a point in such a society was appreciated by the Greek tragedians. Clytemnestra and Aegisthus at the end of Aeschylus' *Agamemnon* have to confront a chorus which is trying to voice public resentment. At the beginning of Sophocles' *Oedipus Tyrannus* the hero has an uneasy meeting with his plague-stricken people, which makes him all the more ready to suspect a plot to unseat him from the throne when he is accused by Teiresias.[6]

The Homeric chief may himself have judged disputes between his subjects, but more probably he kept himself aloof from quarrels which were likely to make him unpopular and diminish his authority with one of the parties. Instead we find arbiters appointed and for important cases a council of elders, such as were depicted on the shield of Achilles hearing a case arising from a homicide. One may compare the Hottentot custom of using a council of clan-heads as a supreme court. In the scene on the shield the precise issue being presented and the background to the trial are both significant. The question is whether compensation for blood-guilt has been duly paid and the aim of the process is to settle what satisfaction, if any, is still due and so to reconcile the parties. Each party has brought his supporters who are cheering him on, and it is probable that the poet is imagining a confrontation between two 'sibs' or kinship groups, who might be embroiled in violence, should the dissatisfied party resort to self-help. Their presence adds to the pressure on the judges to settle the case fairly.[7]

Settlement was thus possible, particularly if the offender had kinsmen to support him and there was constraint on the injured party to accept compensation, since the alternative was a serious feud involving many people. This principle was accepted by the Germanic tribes later. The killer would pay heavy compensation and remain in the community, the kinsman of the dead man would have his passion and pride soothed, as Ajax reminded Achilles. The importance of protecting the status of the victim's kinsmen accords well with anthropologists' conclusions about the attitudes of African tribes, among whom it appears that the aim of revenge and compensation is to restore an equilibrium between the two groups involved.[8] However, the injured party could only expect to get a settlement if he had a claim to respect in the community and in the last resort a force of supporters to back this claim.

Blood-vengeance was none the less a praiseworthy act: Orestes was a hero. As for the man with blood-guilt, he might be unequal to facing the kinsmen of the victim. So the child Patroclus was taken from Opus to the house of Peleus after killing another boy, and the seer Theoclymenos fled from Argos and the many kindred and siblings of his victim, because the murdered man was of his own clan and thus he would have against him those who would normally be for him. After Odysseus and Telemachus had killed the suitors, Odysseus ordered it to be concealed for the moment, pointing out the danger that faced even the killer of a single man who had many avengers. Such a man, says Odysseus, will be forced to leave his own kin and go into exile. But clearly this would depend on the strength of his own physical support; Odysseus himself was not contemplating retreat. In the end it was only with divine help that Odysseus and his family resisted the vengeance of a combined force of relatives of the dead suitors, who attacked the house after a protest meeting in the *agora*.[9] We shall find many later parallels to what was for the suitors' relatives a communal attack on a common enemy.

The group violence of the Homeric world was not, however, confined to blood-feuds. Thucydides drew the obvious inference from the question Nestor put to Telemachus and Mentor in the Odyssey, that there was nothing disgraceful in piracy. The first action of Odysseus' fleet on its return from Troy is to sack Ismarus in Thrace, city of the Kikones. When Odysseus pretends to be a Cretan to Eumaios, he gives a fine character sketch of the man who prefers war and piracy to household management and agriculture. Plundering by land was as common as piracy, cattle-rustling in particular being an accepted form of adventure then, as more recently. Achilles, describing how everything except a man's life can be got for the seeking, remarks that cattle and fat sheep can be looted, but a man's life cannot be seized and brought back by force.[10] The most famous description of a cattle raid is retailed by Nestor in *Iliad* XI. This shows cattle-raiding as a recognised form of border warfare between whole communities, which is profitable in itself but also a means of righting other wrongs. If the passage is a late insertion in the epic, it may even be taken to represent a typical war in Greece at the beginning of the Archaic Age. A particularly interesting feature is the assembly, which was proclaimed after the return of Nestor's force with their loot, for all those who were owed a debt (*chreios*) in Elis. The word 'debt' here means, as the context shows, 'requital for previous loss'. Neleus himself wanted reparation for the stealing of four chariot horses, and it may even be implied that the kindred of men killed by the Eleans in previous years sought compensation from a share of the spoil. The flexibility of the concept of 'debt', which can cover a wide range of torts and delicts, has been noted in present-day African tribes.[11]

Thucydides implies that brigandage and piracy had diminished in importance in many parts of Greece by his time. To some extent this was the result of direct action by Athens herself and Persia. Moreover, the satisfaction and profit deriving from private plundering could be sought in public wars. The original programme of the Delian confederacy was to seek compensation for past wrongs as Nestor's men had done, by raiding the territory of the Persian king. During the Peloponnesian War the Athenians backed Messenian raiding from Pylos, while the Spartans encouraged privateers in wholesale piracy against the merchant fleets of Athens and her allies.[12] However, the peoples of north-west Greece and Crete, for example, continued to make a profession of plundering down into the Hellenistic Era. Ironically, this is implied in particular by treaties made by the Aetolians and Cretans, in which the parties agree to prohibit plundering and kidnapping by their nationals of the nationals of their new ally. Moreover, border-raiding was continued by cities which were not habituated to robbery, especially when the borders themselves were disputed. The quarrel between Magnesia-on-the-Maeander and Priene was only finally settled under the supervision of the Roman senate about 143 BC.[13]

I will discuss later how a person or property might be forcibly seized by an individual as part of legal procedure. It should be mentioned here, however, that such activities could take place on a broader international scale, either by agreement between cities or in default of such an agreement. When a city as a whole or members of it had an unresolved dispute with another city or with individual citizens from it, the city might encourage the seizure of any person or property belonging to its antagonist as a reprisal, perhaps with a view to forcing negotiations. This might take the form of detaining foreign visitors or arresting and bringing to shore foreign ships as well as border-raiding. Such seizures were called *rusia* or *sula* (hence the prohibition of *sula* was *asulon*/asylum). The fact that *sula* can refer both to such *démarches* in international relations and to unprovoked plundering seems to be a reflection of the facts: what was regarded by the victim as brigandage was for the plunderer frequently self-help to remedy a previous wrong.[14]

Community Defence — 'Hue and Cry'

The corollary of raiding and piracy was that communities, however primitive, had to have some means of collective self-defence. While Odysseus' men after their raid on Ismarus spent their time feasting and drinking, the Kikones went and cried out to the neighbouring Kikones, who soon took vengeance on Odysseus' men. Similarly, though with less provocation, the Laistrygonian Antiphates raised an outcry (*boē*) throughout the town which mobilised his gigantic fellow townsmen. Even the Cyclops' neighbours, hearing his scream as he was blinded, gathered from all sides round the cave in response to this cry.[15]

Boē is the equivalent of the medieval English 'hue and cry' (with its Anglo-Saxon ancestry) and the German *Gerücht*.[16] Such cries are a feature of closely knit societies without professional defence forces or proper police; they are made in the expectation of effective help and receive a regular, universal response. Although in medieval European society the custom was to some extent an inheritance from earlier times, it may be fairly regarded as a natural response to the problems of primitive society. So, in the ancient world, it is found in Old and New Testament Palestine, in many different Greek communities, in Italy and in Punic Africa. In a small village an undifferentiated cry for help may have been used to rouse the whole community in situations varying from attack by human or animal enemies to theft or rape. However, the cry of 'wolf' in Aesop's fable both reminds us of the importance of animal enemies to primitive societies and shows us that people soon learnt to categorise the trouble in order to get the right response.[17] Later, the cries took two main forms, those which summoned the aid of neighbours or passers-by to deal with a personal or family matter and those which roused the whole community against outside attack.

Custom and the moral code originally enjoined that those summoned should go to assist. By the fifth century BC it was even required by law. In Aeschylus' *Suppliants* the Argive assembly is portrayed protecting the Danaids by decreeing that they should live inviolate in Argive land; anyone who does not help, if they suffer violence, is to be banished. In practice, the Thebans penalised in 404 anyone who failed to defend an Athenian exile, if he was carried off by those working for the then oligarchic government of Athens. People were supposed to run in response to a cry for help, *boē-thein* or *boē-dromein*, and the verb *boēthein* (with its corresponding noun, *boētheia*) became one of the standard Greek words for giving assistance. We even find in a fourth-century decree conferring protection on an Athenian friend of the Bithynian city of Cius: 'If anyone should do wrong to Athenodorus or Athenodorus' descendants, the people of Cius are to assist him (*boēthein*) with the greatest strength they can muster, and it will be better for them if they do so running quickly.'[18] The conventional cries used in Greek communities were '*Io, polis*' or something similar, meaning roughly 'Ho there! members of the city', or a cry for 'help' combined with an address to neighbours or kinsmen.[19]

The earliest known example in Greek history of appeal to the whole community when a city was in danger is the occasion of Cylon's *coup d'état* at Athens about 630, when the whole people 'ran to the shout' after the acropolis was seized. The shout was also raised during an attack on a tyrannical junta at Rhodes in 395. We still find evidence in the Roman period which shows the persistence of such customs in vulnerable communities. During Verres' governorship of Sicily the people of both Agrigentum and Assorum gathered to drive away Verres' men when these tried to loot their shrines. The men of Assorum were even summoned by a regular trumpet signal (the 'hu' of the English 'hue and cry').[20]

The Individual Calls for Help

There is much more evidence for the cries raised by individuals in trouble, both from imaginative literature and life. The first allusion may be discerned in a metaphor of Hesiod, when he says: 'There is an uproar when Justice is dragged off, wherever bribe-eating men shall take her.'[21] The image seems to be that of a debtor or other delinquent being dragged off to slavery and appeal for help being made by himself and his kin. In tragedy both Oedipus and the children of Heracles are portrayed successfully appealing to the people of Athens for protection against seizure by their enemies, while the Danaids call on the assistance, which the Argive people promised them. We have noticed an historical Theban attempt to protect Athenian exiles in danger. A passage in Polybius shows the people of Megalopolis offering similar help to Boeotian horse-stealers, who had taken a white horse belonging to the Spartan tyrant Nabis and, in spite of yielding up their booty, had been seized by the tyrant's men who pursued them. The Boeotians first asked to be taken before a local magistrate. No one paid any attention: so one of them cried '*boētheia*', and all the inhabitants rushed to the spot and demanded that official approval should be obtained for the arrest.[22]

Apart from the Cian decree for Athenodorus, considered earlier, the most precise piece of evidence for the requirement of such assistance by law is in the recently published gymnasium law from Beroea. This document, although it originated in Macedonia under Roman rule, perhaps during the early Principate, is avowedly based on earlier gymnasium laws. In the gymnasium, whereas the gymnasiarch had power to beat boys or slave *paidagogoi* who infringed discipline, severe penalties were laid on anyone who struck him.

> If any one shall strike the gymnasiarch in the gymnasium, let those present prevent and not allow it, and let him likewise fine the assailant one hundred drachmai, and let that man be separately liable to him under the general laws. And whoever of those present shall not run to his aid, when he can, let that man be fined fifty drachmai.

Another way of enforcing such mutual assistance is probably indicated by a comment of Aristotle on the constitution of Cyme, that neighbours contributed towards loss by theft. The reason behind this is surely not that the theft was likely to have been committed by one of the neighbours (a dangerous act in a small community), but that they were collectively responsible for the integrity of the neighbourhood's property and were expected to act themselves to prevent or take reprisals for theft.[23]

From the earliest times, however strong one's kinship group, it was desirable to have good neighbours as well. As Hesiod remarked, 'If any trouble happens in your place, neighbours come as they are, but relatives dress for the journey.' We find this theme exploited in Aristophanes' comedies. When Strepsiades is assaulted by his son, who has recently graduated from Socrates' academy, he cries out to his kinsmen, neighbours and demesmen. But Aristophanes gives a twist to the idea too. Cleon, attacked by the chorus of Knights, calls on the 'old jurymen, brethren of the three obols [jury pay]', while the old juror, Philocleon, in the *Wasps*, appeals to his fellow jurors and Cleon.[24]

When a man was assaulted in the street, any by-stander or passer-by might help, as when the young boyfriend of a client of Lysias' was dragged out of a cleaner's shop, where he had taken refuge, by Simon and his cronies. A running battle ensued in which the cleaner and others joined in on the side of the young man and Lysias' client, and these subsequently bore witness to what had happened in court. In another case when Pancleon was claimed as a slave, a force of his friends went to battle on his behalf and prevented him being taken off on two successive occasions by those who claimed to be his owners. When a woman was being stripped of the family furniture by force in consequence of a judgement, her neighbours' slaves called the passers-by as well as men of the neighbourhood to protect her.[25]

The crowd of supporters were gathered for two basic reasons, firstly to provide physical force, should it be needed, secondly as witnesses to the justice of the action taken by him who summoned them. This second function acquired greater importance as law developed. Although self-help was later given considerable scope in Greek law codes, as we shall see, it had to be self-help in pursuit of a right recognised by the law. This is why Lysias' client summoned his neighbours before he broke in on Eratosthenes, the adulterer of his wife and, catching him in the act, killed him. This was technically legitimate, it seems, according to Solon's law, if Eratosthenes was caught 'with his limbs on her limbs', though there may have been special conditions.[26]

Incidents as drastic as these had become sufficiently unusual under the rule of law by the fourth century BC for this killing to lead to a lawsuit. However, in classical Athens the summoning of neighbours or passers-by as witnesses was a common response to minor assaults or theft, as we find from a number of references in Old and New Comedy. Similarly, they would be invoked by someone employing what he believed to be legal self-help, in order to secure something adjudicated to him by a court, whether real estate, moveable property (including slaves) or money — in the last contingency he would frequently seize other goods belonging to the delinquent as a pledge.[27] Outside Athens self-help in the Classical and Hellenistic periods extended to the seizure of free persons and the need of either party for the support of a crowd would consequently have been more urgent. The importance of outside intervention on behalf of the person assaulted is especially attested by manumission inscriptions, which declare the released slave to be free from seizure and grant to anyone who appears on the scene the right to carry him off back into freedom (the word normally used for this, *sulan*, is also a common word for making an initial seizure, legal or illegal).[28] Similar provisions to these are found in the treaties we have already mentioned, which limit border-raiding and piracy between the nationals of the contracting states.

Parallel Developments in Roman Society

Collective assistance by the community in response to a cry for help was also a feature of Roman and Italian society. It existed before the earliest laws in Rome and was regulated by them, but it can still be seen as a living tradition in the late Republic. It appears from a number of texts in Livy that the Romans were originally summoned to defend themselves against outside attack by the cry 'To arms!' (*ad arma*). Later, when as a result of Rome's increasing territory earlier warning was possible, a more formal procedure was evolved for an emergency levy of troops. Yet the cry of '*ad arma*' or '*arma*' seems to have survived and reappears later in the medieval laws of the Franks.[29]

Individuals in trouble might summon the aid of their fellow citizens by shouting '*Pro (fidem), Quirites*', which means 'Out here, by your good faith, fellow-Romans!' The Latin word for to cry for help, *plorare*, is probably etymologically *pr(l)o-orare*, i.e. 'to cry "Out here!"' The two earliest examples of this word are in a law attributed to Servius Tullius, where it describes the cry raised by a parent struck by a son,

and in the Twelve Tables, where the compound form *endo plorare*
(= *implorare*) is used for the cry required from a man who was about
to kill a thief. As we have seen, in situations of this kind in the Greek
world one regularly summoned those nearby and this is precisely the
interpretation that Cicero places on the clause from the Twelve Tables.

A particular form of this summons to fellow citizens developed a
special function recognised by law. This was *provocatio ad populum*
(*pro-vocare*, like *pr(l)o-orare*, had the basic meaning 'to cry "Out!"')
— the shout by which the plebeian, threatened by a magistrate or a rich
creditor, called on the mass of his fellow plebeians to protect him. It
was later associated with, and to some extent replaced by, appeal to the
tribunes. They could intervene safely as representatives of the plebs as
a whole, since their persons were treated as physically inviolable, originally by virtue of a sworn guarantee by the plebs to take vengeance on
an assailant, later according to statute.[30]

The Importance of the Family Group

The kinship group was the mainspring of justice in the society portrayed
by Homer. It remained an important source of support in the period
when the city constitutions and law codes were developing. Something
about its function then can be learnt from the legal procedure used
when death or serious injury occurred. In Athens the earliest homicide
laws included a provision for reconciliation by ritual after accidental
homicide. According to the code attributed to Draco, the culprit had to
be banished but could be readmitted to the community by a decision of
the *phratria*, the sib-group, of the victim.[31] This probably stabilised what
had previously been custom, the blood-kinsmen of the victim being
responsible, as in the Homeric poems, for ratifying the settlement of the
dispute. In Rome an important provision was attributed to Numa, whereby anyone who killed a free man deliberately was declared a *paricidas*,
which probably means 'killer of an equal' in the sense of 'killer of a
person of his own standing within his group'.[32] This law seems to have
meant that the kinship groups were to treat a murder of someone outside the group by one of their own members as if the victim had come
from within their group. This would no doubt have involved some ritual
atonement and the killing or banishment of the murderer. This law, if
our interpretation of it is correct, was an ingenious way of limiting
blood-feuds. It also suggests that the leaders of kinship groups exercised
some jurisdiction over their members at the time when it was enacted.

The principle of 'life for life, eye for eye, tooth for tooth' in ancient Jewish law is not, as far as we can tell, a common one in the ancient world. It is attested at Thurii and at Italian Locri but is best known in the Roman *lex talionis*, referred to in the Twelve Tables. The clause there prescribed reciprocal injury in cases where some person had been deprived of the use of a bodily organ, unless some agreement was reached. For minor injuries specific financial penalties were laid down. *Talio* was probably a survival from a time when the eye was demanded for the eye to satisfy a desire for equalisation, a primitive sense of rightness depending on a balance in the community. It implies a stage in social development when the relative standing of the kinship groups, who were the component parts of the community, was all important. The man who tried to execute *talio* in any period, after losing the use of an organ of the body, would have required the backing of a group of supporters. If a bargain was successfully concluded, in the absence of precise recommendations in law much would have necessarily depended on the relative strengths of the opposing parties.[33]

Popular Justice

Although private vengeance and mutually arranged compensation took the place in primitive societies of much of the state-inflicted punishment which is customary today, there is also some evidence for the collective exaction of punishment from enemies of the community, especially those who had by their actions alienated themselves and become, as it were, outlaws. The Greek tragedians seem to have regarded stoning as the regular form of public execution for traitors or those who had polluted the land with some other crime. This is the punishment decreed by Creon for the burying of Polyneikes. It is also specified as the punishment that awaited Iolaos for assisting the escape of Herakles' children, Creousa for attempted murder at Delphi, and Orestes and Electra for their matricide. It is even the death that Oedipus longs for. I need hardly mention the parallels in ancient Jewish law.[34]

In Greek historical writing of the Classical and Hellenistic periods we find references to a number of genuine instances of stoning, the majority of which seem to have been examples of lynch justice arising from the passion of a crowd. So, the Athenians stoned to death Lycidas in 479 for bringing to Salamis Mardonius' proposals; the Mytileneans killed Coes, the deposed tyrant; the Argives attacked Thrasylos for his armistice with King Agis of Sparta in 418; the Agrigentine assembly stoned to

death four generals for failing to make a sortie against the Carthaginian
camp in 406; the Theban politician Ismenias was almost killed by exiles
in Chalcis in 172. It seems to have been particularly common for an
army, or an assembly which represented an army in time of war, to
express their anger and revulsion in this way against their own leaders,
perhaps because tradition and discipline restrained them from using
their military arms.[35]

However, the stoning might also be more formal and ceremonial. It
was the recognised form of execution by the Macedonian army and
people, after the king had investigated a capital crime before an assembly. We find the Athenians in 479 stoning (in cold blood, it seems, this
time) the son of Artauktes in front of his crucified father, as a reprisal
for the plunder of a shrine. The Arcadians stoned those who improperly
entered the Lykaion shrine. The stonings which Paul met with from the
Jews at Iconium and Lystra (one may compare the pursuit at Perge
which drove him over the city boundary) seem to have been not so
much spontaneous actions by a crowd as deliberate traditional acts of
popular justice against the impious. There might also be the aspect of
human sacrifice. In 183 BC, after the Achaean league had brought back
the ashes of their leader, Philopoemen, from Messene to Megalopolis for
burial, with Polybius the later historian heading the procession, they
stoned to death Messenian captives over his grave, as a reprisal or an
offering to their dead hero. The people of Caere in Etruria once treated
Phocaean captives, probably in the early fifth century, in the same
way.[36]

Stoning might be combined with fire-raising. Such were the means by
which the Greeks of Lampsacus attacked Verres after he had used violence on his host in an attempt on the honour of the latter's daughter.
According to Cicero, Verres nearly suffered the same fate during the
scandal over his repression of piracy at Syracuse, after a crowd had
collected at his door. However, it is also possible to detect a tradition of
making such attacks which was not influenced by politics. Strepsiades
gets revenge on Socrates in Aristophanes' *Clouds* by firing the roof of
his house. In one of Herondas' *Mimes*, the brothel-keeper Battaros
describes how Thales, another alien living in Cos, attacked his house
after a row over a girl, breaking down the door and burning the lintel.[37]

In Plautus' comedies we find two references to attacks on the doors
of houses with fire which are associated with the Italian custom called
occentare — the loud rhythmic chanting of insulting songs (in two parts)
in order to bring a man into public infamy. Like the character in Herondas, the imagined victims of this are men regarded as lechers or pimps.

Such an attack seems to have been intended either to drive the victim physically from the community or to turn him into a social outcast.

It is difficult to find a close equivalent of this complex Italian tradition in Greek society, although the elements may have existed separately. In Aristophanes' *Ploutos* there is a scene in which Chremulos and Carion impress on Ploutos (Wealth) the conclusion that everything depends on him. This takes the form of an antiphonal chant by two people who are probably standing on either side of Ploutos. Yet it is tame by comparison with what we find in Plautus. Nor, to my knowledge, is there any parallel anywhere in the ancient Mediterranean world to the mutual abuse which is sometimes used ritually in primitive societies to take the heat out of disputes. At most, we may suspect that something of this kind may lie behind the formalised abuse of the *agōn* in Old Comedy.[38]

Self-help by the Individual

It is legitimate to believe, given the importance in developed Greek and Roman society both of group support in defence of the community and individual and of popular justice, that these traditions were even more important when these societies were comparatively in embryo. The same argument should apply to the need for self-help by the individual in order to obtain what he believed to be his rights. This is attested in cities during the Classical and Hellenistic eras, whose societies were ruled by written law and where the element of kinship had diminished in importance. We have already seen some evidence for it in connection with the mobilisation of support and eye-witnesses from among neighbours. In the following section I wish to demonstrate further its scope under the rule of law in order to indicate its probable importance in earlier society. It seems likely that many of the procedures known to us would have been taken for granted in the primitive societies of, for example, the early Archaic age in Greece, especially as the support of a crowd would nearly always be available to a man by virtue of his domicile or kinship group.

In general, in Greek and Roman society a man was expected to execute through private means many acts which are now done for him by the state. As we have seen, he had to defend himself, with the aid of his neighbours, against those who violated his household. If a man wished to bring his adversary before some judge or arbitrator in order to get redress for a private wrong, it was up to him to get his opponent there, however serious the offence. This remained true in principle even during the Roman Principate. In classical Athens procedure was comparatively civilised. Private summons was made with a witness or witnesses. Imprisonment before trial for citizens only occurred after special procedures (*apagoge*, *ephegesis*, *endeixis*, *eisaggelia*) and in most cases could be avoided by the provision of sureties. The prime sanction against non-appearance was that failure to appear would make one liable to lose a case.[39] In other parts of Greece we find that defendants, if foreigners, were liable to be seized and only released if they gave security. In Rome, according to the Twelve Tables, the plaintiff making the summons called the by-standers to witness, if his opponent was reluctant; then, if he continued to be obstructive, he seized him, as we still find happening in Cicero's time.[40]

Private force was also required to execute a judgement or to assert other rights. A person alleged to be a fugitive slave in both Greek and Roman society was arrested with little ceremony, and release from this arrest, at least for the time being, depended on rescue from a passer-by who was prepared to act as *prostatēs* or *vindex*. A typical Delphic manumission decree includes the clause: 'Let the passer-by who champions Soterichus and carries him off to assure him freedom be licensed to do so without penalty and without liability to any judgement or penalty.' Thus rescue from slavery required the physical intervention of an outsider who by himself laying hold of the alleged slave challenged the current possessor's right to this person. In some cases the possessor immediately acceded to the challenge; in others, as with Pancleon at Athens, the challenge initiated further proceedings in or out of court.[41]

We shall be dealing in Chapter 2 with social unrest caused by creditors' seizure of debtors in Archaic Athens. It was the law generally in Greece and Rome until the Roman Principate that a creditor could distrain on the possessions of a debtor as security, and distraint on the person of a debtor was also commonly allowed. At Athens after Solon's legislation it was only possible to take security from property, either directly if some property had been specifically pledged for the debt by *hypothēkē* or *prasis epi lysei*, or, after a judgement, on any property. Similar provisions are attested elsewhere.[42] However, Athens may have been unusual in forbidding debt servitude of any kind. It is found in the fifth century law of Gortyn; its existence outside Athens is implied by Lysias and Isocrates; it is found at Delphi, in Egypt, and in the Peloponnese in the Hellenistic period, and was still a feature of the cities of the Achaean League when they made their last attempt to free themselves from Roman domination in 147-6 BC.[43] In early Rome creditors seem to have distrained on the persons of debtors without further ado, if we believe the tradition of the background to the first secession of the plebs. After the Twelve Tables, the creditor had to obtain judgement first, and the debtor was then allowed a delay to obtain a vindicator (*vindex*) who would take responsibility for his debts. However, after this, he could legally be led off into private debt servitude, which was virtual slavery, this remaining the law in the late Republic and early Principate.[44]

What was true of debtors was also true of those condemned by a court to pay a sum of money. So, according to the inter-city judicial agreement between Athens and Boeotia, Stratophanes' father in Menander's *Sicyonian* had been *agōgimos*, liable to be led away into detention, for a judgement of many talents. An extant example of this kind of judicial treaty is that between Aigeira and Stymphalos in Arcadia, partially preserved in an inscription. This specifically allows the seizure of a person or property in consequence of either a debt or some other judgement. However, and this bears on the importance of community participation in self-help, citizens of both cities had to be present when that occurred.[45]

Was Archaic Society Dominated by Violence?

The account that I have just given is inevitably one-sided, in so far as it suggests that life in the cities of Italy and the Greek world was a continuous physical struggle both before and for some time after the earliest written law codes. One cannot justify so generalised a conclusion. There is no doubt that rights ultimately depended for protection on the strength of the group to which a person belonged. On the other hand, the threat of force was not necessarily incompatible with settlement based on some kind of compensation, except in cases of deliberate murder. It is also worth making the point that much of the physical force was used in pursuit of what were believed to be rights. This violence was thus viewed by its users not as a negation of law and order but its reinforcement.[46]

I have cited earlier many passages showing the survival of violent methods of settling quarrels and complaints. It is appropriate by contrast to cite one showing an informal meeting to discuss a legal dispute. There is a scene, partially preserved in the fragments of Menander's *Sicyonian*, in which a more or less spontaneous meeting of the demesmen of Eleusis takes place by the gateway to the temple of Demeter in order to discuss the claim of a girl, bought as a slave in Asia, to be an

Athenian citizen. Procedure is informal, but arguments on both sides are heard and a temporary solution is reached. The importance of these local centres of community life is attested as far back as the time of Peisistratus and the scene probably has a long tradition of district meetings behind it. This is a factor in society which must be set beside the pursuit of justice by self-help.[47]

Nevertheless, the general impression given by our evidence may not be entirely misleading. One of the chief arguments used by the anthropologists to show the forces tending towards reconciliation rather than violence both in stateless societies and those whose central judicial system is of limited importance, is the complexity of blood and social ties. In particular, kindred may be spread over more than one local community, and a man may belong as well to some other kind of association, for example as a warrior or through co-operative economic activity. When a dispute occurs in such a society, a man's loyalties are pulled in more than one direction and the best way to remove this tension is to calm the dispute with a minimum of offence to either side.[48]

The evidence for the development of such complex social relationships in the archaic Greek world is largely lacking. At best, we know that in Hesiod's Boeotia that neighbours were as important a source of assistance as kindred. On the other hand, there is evidence for polarisation in society. We hear of racial divisions being maintained, for example those between the Dorians and the previous inhabitants in the Peloponnese and Crete which seem to have resulted in the depressed group having the status of serfs.[49] We know that those kinship groups called in Greece *phratriai* or *patrai* were considered such an obstacle to political unity in Attica as late as 510 BC that Cleisthenes, following the example of his grandfather in Sicyon, completely reorganised the subdivisions of the citizen body in order to minimise the political importance of the old blood-ties.[50]

Nor can one disregard the original political fragmentation of the Greco-Roman world. Even tiny communities often appear isolated among hostile neighbours. This is the atmosphere of the law regulating the settlement of new land by the Ozolian Locrians about 500 BC. The community might be unable to defend itself and so might need in the future to bring in 200 more fighting men. The background of insecurity and suspicion can be seen in the treaties made by states in north-west Greece from the fifth century onwards, which limited the right to plunder. This is the central provision of the earliest of these treaties between Oianthea and Chaleion.[51] Later this safeguard is associated with the exchange of citizenship rights. So the Aetolians granted to

Trikka in Hestiaeotis, citizenship, freedom from tax, freedom from seizure (*asulia*) and personal security (*asphaleia*). Indeed the treaties which created exchange of citizenship rights between communities, *isopoliteia* — common in the fourth century BC and later — are particularly interesting because of the depth of the pre-existing divisions which they imply. Associated with the exchange of citizenship are intermarriage (*epigamia*) and the ownership of land and a house in the other community (*gēs enktēsis*).[52] This shows the lack of ties between communities which were often in themselves very small.

In early times the strife and insecurity which derived from political fragmentation was not confined to these backward areas of the Greek world. We hear that in the Megarid the five villages (*kōmai*) used to conduct a permanent war on each other for profit, albeit with gentlemanly rules: men were taken captive for ransom but were entertained properly as guests during the time of their detention. Moreover, insecurity would create suspicion. In 495, when the survivors of the Chian fleet, returning home overland after their defeat at Lade, entered Ephesian territory at the time of the Thesmophoria festival, they were assumed to be bandits out to steal the local women and consequently killed.[53]

It is difficult to summarise the implications of this evidence, but let me set out some general propositions, which may at least form a working hypothesis about the nature of the societies, whose political developments we are about to study. Many settled homogeneous communities probably maintained peace and order over long periods with a minimum of friction. However, there are important instances of communities which were not homogeneous, even among those newly founded in the archaic age of colonisation. Within communities there is some evidence for divisions caused by caste and mutually exclusive kinship groups. In external relations every community was threatened by raiding and piracy, probably far more than by formally declared war, and tended to be on its guard against strangers for this reason. Moreover, the Greek world was a patchwork of jealously independent communities and it took time for their suspicions of each other to be overcome.

There is a further possible cause of tension and conflict in early Greek and Italian society, by contrast with some existing primitive societies. In tribal African societies a holding of land is guaranteed to every subject of the king, for him to work as an individual but not to have free disposition of, inasmuch as reversionary rights over it belong to the head of household, head of village and ultimately to the king himself. A man's landholding corresponds to his status in society.[54] In the ancient world land distribution by the state to members of the community as of right is attested in specific contexts, at the initial founding of colonies and in certain established communities, notably the nine or ten thousand lots of the 'equals', the dominant caste at Sparta. However, it was on our evidence rare for the permanence of such holdings to be guaranteed or free disposition of them to be totally forbidden. Such provisions seem to be the exception, and the rule seems to be that land was owned by individuals and was alienable, though disposition by will was frequently limited. Hesiod's *Works and Days* shows about 650 BC a system of individual tenure, where a division of land between brothers is settled outside the family by a lawsuit and the reward of piety is that you may buy another's land, not he yours. Buying and selling of property may have led to the mingling of kinship groups within localities and thus introduced a complexity of social relationships conducive to public peace. On the other hand, it may also have led to fiercer struggles as men sought to keep landholdings intact or improve them. Hesiod, though angry over the division of his father's land between Perseus and himself, preferred to see Perseus increase his holding at the expense of others than to lose it.[55]

Notes

1. Ar., *Pol.* 1253a; Cic., *Rep.* I.39; Plato, *Prot.* 322b; Critias DK B.25; Anonymus Iamblichi DK, pp. 402-3; Lucr. 5.1109; Plato, *Rep.* II.373d.

2. Hesiod, *WD* 110; Hdt. I.65.2; Thuc. I.2-12.

3. Thuc. I.5, 12.3, 21.1; Hdt. VII.204 (cf. IX.26-7); Schapera, 1956, 152, 164.

4. Schapera, 1956, 78, 84, 116; Gluckman, 1967, 107.

5. Finley, 1974(= 1977, 142) with references to earlier work.

6. *Od.* II.40, IV.740 (cf. II.244, IV.669 for the threats of the suitors), XVI.375, 425; Aesch., *Agam.* 1612; Soph., *OT* 1-299; Finley, 1977, 74; Schapera, 1956, 152.

7. *Od.* XIX.109, a vague reference to a good king maintaining *eudikiai* ('righteous dealings') is the only evidence in Homer for a king judging. Cf. Gluckman, 1967, 88 on the king keeping aloof. Arbiters – *Od.* XII.439; *Il.* I.238, XVI.386; Schapera, 1956, 124, cf. 80, 141. Shield scene – *Il.* XVIII.497, on which see Wolff, 1946 (though he fails to allow for a weaker party bringing a lawsuit).

8. Tac., *Germ.* 21.1; *Il.* IX.632; MacCormack, 1973, 79 with further references.

9. *Il.* XXIII.85; *Od.* III.193, XV.223, 272 (cf. XIII.256), XXIII.117, XXIV.420; Walcot, 1970, 78; Finley, 1977, 100.

10. Thuc. I.5.1; *Od.* III.71, XIV.199; *Il.* IX.406; cf. *Od.* XIII.470; Walcot, 1970, 97.

11. *Il.* XI.670; cf. OP XXX.2508 (? Archilochus) on cattle-raiding in Euboea c. 700-600 BC. For *chreos* as what is owed after a delict has been committed, Schmitt, no. 511.8; cf. Gluckman, 1967, 209. Division of booty – cf. Livy V.28.3.

12. Thuc. I.5.3; Hdt. VI.42.1; Plut., *Cim.* 8.3, 17.1. Contrast Thuc. I.96.1, II.67.4, 69.1, IV.41.2.

13. Pol. XVIII.4.8-5.2. Cf. IG IX^2.1.1., nos. 3, 4, 136, 169, 189, 192, 193, 195a, IX^2.1.3., no. 717 (= GHI 34, ATPW 87); SGDI 5100, 5165, 5170, 5172, 5176. For wrecking see Xen., *Anab.* VII.5.12. Border-raiding – *Hell. Oxy.* 18.3; Welles, no. 7; Sherk, nos. 7, 10; Pouilloux, 1960, no. 4.

14. Lys. 30.22; Ps. Ar., *Oec.* 1347b; Pol. IV.53.2, XXII.4.13; *Olympia* V, no. 16.8; GHI I.34; ML 42B.2; IG V.2.357 (=Schmitt, no. 567), 91, IX^2.1.1.189, 192.9; G. Pugliese-Carratelli in Oliviero, 1961-2, 278; Wilhelm, 1911, 195-200.

15. *Od.* II.47, X.118, IX.399.

16. Pollock and Maitland, 1952, II.578; Brunner and von Schwerin, 1906, II.627; Schulze, 1933; Lintott, 1974, 232.

17. Deuteronomy 22.27; Job 19.7; Habakkuk 1.2; Acts 21.28; Livy XXIX.28.6-9; Aesop, 353b; and see the following notes.

18. Aesch., *Supp.* 609; Diod. XIV.6.3 (cf. Plut., *Lys.* 27.3); GHI II, 149.9. *Boē* – see e.g. Aesch., *Supp.* 730; Soph., *OC* 887; Eur., *Troi.* 999; *Heraclid.* 121; Longus, *Daphnis and Chloe*, 14.2.

19. Soph., *OC* 833, 884; Aesch., *Supp.* 908; Eur., *Hec.* 1091; *Heraclid.* 69; *Hipp.* 884; Arist., *Clouds* 1322.

20. Thuc. I.126-7; *Hell. Oxy.* 15.2; Cic., *Verr.* IV.94-6; cf. Verg. *Aen.* VII.513; Livy I.7.7.

21. *WD* 220; cf. West, 1978, 211 for the translation (he believes, however, the dragging to be rape).

22. Soph., *OC* 822; Eur., *Heraclid.* 69; Aesch., *Supp.* 905; Pol. XIII.8.5-6 (Livy XXXIII.28.3 is probably a translation of a similar description in Polybius).

23. J.M.R. Cormack, *Ancient Macedonia* (Thessaloniki, 1977), 139, Face B, 41, cf. 21; Ar., fr. 611.39.

24. Hesiod *WD* 344; Arist., *Clouds* 1321; *Knights* 255, cf. 725; *Wasps* 197; also Men., *Dysc.* 594, 620; Hdt. VI.138.2 (a rally of Athenian children on Lemnos).

25. Lys. 3.15, 23.9, 12; Dem. 47.60; cf. Lys. 13.23; Isoc. 18.6 for interventions by by-standers in physical struggles.

26. Lys. 1.23; cf. Latte, 1931.

27. Arist., *Clouds* 495, 1297; *Peace* 1119; *Birds* 1031; *Plutus* 932; Men., *Samia* 576; Lys. 23.9; Dem. 47.34, 64; IG V.2.357 (= Schmitt, no. 567), 94-5. Note also the publicising of past wrongs as a preliminary to legal action – Lys. 119, fr. 75 Thal.

28. Syll.^{3} 841, 843 (= SGDI 1541, 1545); SGDI 1684ff., esp. 1690, 1701, 1724-6, 1740, 1938, 1951, 2145; Schmitt, no. 482 for general regulations about those seized as slaves, also no. 558, IIA, 14. On *sula* see note 14 above and on rescue Harrison, 1968, I.221.

29. Livy VII.12.2-3, III.15.6, VIII.37.7, IX.24.9, cf. XXIX.28.9 (describing Punic Africa); *Lex Francorum Chamavorum* XXXVII (*Monum. German. Hist.* V, 275).

30. Lintott, 1968, 11-14; Lintott, 1974, 228-34; on the etymology, Szemerényi, 1969, 182-91.

31. ML 86. 10; Dem. 43.57; Plato, *Laws* 865a; cf. Schapera, 1956, 124.

32. Cloud, 1971, with references and earlier bibliography.

33. Exodus 21.24-6; Deuteronomy 19.21; Diod. XII.17.4; Dem.24.140 (cf. Aesch., *Cho.* 306); FIRA I, p. 53, Tab. 8.2-3; MacCormack, 1973.

34. Aesch., *Septem.* 199; Soph., *Ant.* 36; Soph., *OC* 435; Eur., *Heraclid.* 60; *Ion.* 1112, 1222; *Orest.* 50, 614, 863; Deut. 17.5, 22.21; cf. Hipponax, fr. 37 West; Nicol. Dam., FGH 90, F51; Arist., *Ach.* 280; Arr., *Anab.* I.17.12.

35. Hdt. IX.5.2; V.38; Thuc. V.50.6; Diod. XIII.87.4-5; Pol. XXVII.1.5,

cf. 2.3; see further Thuc. VIII.75.1, 84.3; Xen., *Hell*. I.2.13; *Anab*. I.3.1, VI.6.7, 15; Pol. I.69.10.

36. Arr., *Anab*. IV.14.3; Curt. VI.11.38; Hdt. IX.120.4; Plut., *Mor*. 300a; Acts 14.5, 15.19 (cf. 7.58, 13.50); Plut., *Philop*. 21.9; Strabo V.2.3 (230).

37. Cic. 2. Verr. I.69-70, V.94; Arist., *Clouds* 1484; Herondas 2.63; cf. Curt. IV.8.9.

38. Arist., *Pl*. 130-97; cf. *Frogs* 553-78; *Knights* 786-835; Usener, 1900; Fraenkel, 1961; Lintott, 1968, 8; Gluckman, 1967, 87, 303.

39. Lipsius, 1905, 804; Harrison, 1968, II.85, 221.

40. IG V.2.357 (Schmitt, 567), 89; Schmitt, 558, IB 8; FIRA I, p. 26, XII Tab. I.1; Cic., *Clu*. 38.

41. Aeschin. 1.62; Lys. 23.9-11; Aesch., *Supp*. 609-14; cf. the documents cited in note 28, esp. SGDI 1938.

42. Arist., *Clouds* 35; Dem. 24.197, 38.7; Harrison, 1968, I.217, II.244; Lipsius, 1905, 725; Finley, 1952, 28. See also Syll.³ 364. 71, 742. 53; SGDI 4986, 4992; Schmitt, 558, IIB 14.

43. Willetts, *Law Code of Gortyn* I.56 – II.2; Lys. 12.98; Isoc. 14.48; Syll.³ 692A, 48; Westerman, *Upon Slavery in Ptolemaic Egypt*, 4, 84; Schmitt, 567, 94; Pol. XXXVIII.11.10.

44. FIRA I, p. 32, XII Tab. III; see e.g. Lintott, 1968, 26-7 with further references.

45. *Sic*. 133; Schmitt, 567. 94. The Berezan letter (Austin, 1977, no. 41) probably documents such a seizure c. 500 BC.

46. Cf. Gluckman, 1967, 207.

47. *Sic*. 183-271; *Ath. Pol*. 16.5.

48. Gluckman, 1967, 108; MacCormack, 1973.

49. Ar., fr. 586; Athen. 6.263e; Plut., *Mor*. 291e; Pollux, 3.8.3; Cartledge, 1979, 160.

50. Hdt. V.69; *Ath. Pol*. 21; Lacey, 1968, 84; Hignett, 1952, 61, 132.

51. ML 13, A7; GHI I.34 (ATPW 33, 87; Austin, 1977, no. 46).

52. IG IX².1.1.136; ibid. 3, A 11; Syll.³ 472.10; SGDI 5040. 11; Robert, 1969, I.204; Gawantka, 1975.

53. Plut., *Mor*. 295e; Hdt. VI.16.2; cf. ML 30, B18 (ATPW 63).

54. Gluckman, 1967, 36.

55. Hesiod *WD* 37, 341; Asheri, 1966, for evidence on land distribution. For arguments for and against the general inalienability of land, see Asheri, 1966, 16; Fine, 1951, 167, 198; Finley, 1968; Andrewes, 1971(1), 106; Lacey, 1968, 333.

2 POLITICAL CONFLICTS IN THE GROWING CITY-STATES

The word for civil strife or political revolution in the Greek world was *stasis*. It meant primarily 'standing' and thus 'a way' or 'place of standing', a posture or position. It may have come to mean 'civil strife' after being used to refer to a political faction, a position taken in politics. It has this latter meaning in Herodotus' account of the Athenian tyrant Peisistratus. However, we find it used already (over 150 years earlier) in the poems of Solon, Alcaeus and Theognis in the sense of civil strife (c. 600 BC).[1]

The period in which these three writers lived was generally characterised by oligarchic government, and the corresponding form of *stasis*, which we are about to investigate, is the quarrel among the leading aristocrats of a city — a type which is fundamental to the history of civil strife in the ancient world. Strife of a milder kind could simmer while still being contained by the existing oligarchic government; when more violent, it led to *coups d'état* by individuals (tyrannies) and conversely to struggles by other aristocrats to unseat the tyrants who had seized power. However, we have not only to examine the politics of the aristocracy, but their relation to the rest of the community. Aristocratic struggles and tyrannies were in fact to prepare the ground for constitutions more broadly based than the close oligarchies of the early Archaic age. We must therefore consider the extent to which citizens outside the ruling class participated in these struggles and how much the democracies and broad oligarchies that developed owed to the conscious efforts of those who were to benefit from them. Furthermore, apart from any participation by the lower classes in the political contests of the aristocracy, we find tensions arising from the fundamental inequality between rich and poor. The comparative rareness of genuine class conflicts, as far as we can tell from our evidence, is perhaps their most striking feature. Nevertheless the nature of the original socio-economic subjection of the poor and the extent of their emancipation are essential background to the strife that occurred. The picture that emerges is fragmentary and unevenly illuminated; many of the episodes, however romantic, seem of trivial importance in the long term. Yet in the end the central position of *stasis* in the evolution of politics becomes clear.

The first evidence we have of *stasis* in Archaic Greece is contained in the accounts of the establishment of tyrannies. The societies, in which these occurred, had already substituted for dynastic monarchy some kind of oligarchy, even if the old royal families were still members of it. How the change had happened is another matter. One need not assume that all the old kings had been unique holders of supreme authority in political, religious and military matters. Their change of status may have been the outcome of a gradual decline in authority *vis-à-vis* the other princes with similar functions. In so far as their position had involved great expenditure on entertainment and gifts for other nobles and their own clients, some may have been induced to withdraw voluntarily from formal primacy, when their resources were inadequate for their post, particularly in a period when wealth and living standards were generally increasing. The *Odyssey* shows us the kind of pressure, psychological and economic, that could be exerted by rival nobles, when the head of the royal house (as Telemachus was *de facto*) was weak.

However, the existence of the threat of *stasis* in the period before we have any direct evidence of it, is probably implicit in some Greek colonising expeditions. 'Another widespread device (sc. for countering the dangers of assassination by his kindred) is for the chief to send his near-relatives to take charge of outlying areas' (Schapera, 1956, on the Bantu). Similar statecraft was at work in early Greece, to judge from the legendary story of the despatch of the Minyai — a migrant and dis-affected tribe — from Sparta to Thera under Theras. He was uncle on his mother's side and guardian to the young sons of the late king Aristo-demos, while descended on his father's side from the pre-Dorian nobility. He was already restive because the boys were coming of age and his continued presence at Sparta was a menace to stability. The founder of the historical colony of Cyrene in the seventh century, Battos, was in one version of his story a Minyan, in another an illegitimate child of a union between a noble Theran and an exiled daughter of a Cretan king. Although not as powerful as Theras he may be another example of a dangerous member of the nobility. Later still, about 520 BC, the Spartans were clearly influenced by such a threat when they sent out Dorieus, the second son of the dead King Anaxandridas, on a colonising expedition first to Cyrene and then to the West.[2]

The First Tyrants

The oligarchies which became common in Greece by the seventh century were in theory less vulnerable to usurpations than the early monarchies,

in so far as there was safety in numbers. Nevertheless they often succumbed to *coups d'état* by a single man, the tyrant (*turannos*). The
word appears to have become current in Greece about 650 BC, to judge
from the appearance of its associated noun, *turannis* (tyranny) in the
poems of Archilochus. This is associated with Gyges, an upstart monarch
of Lydia, and seems to refer to power seized rather than inherited.[3]
Such power was probably more autocratic than that of the old kings
and it is easy to see why it was resented by noble members of oligarchies long before it became anathema to those who enjoyed a more
broadly based constitution. Thucydides associates the occurrence of
tyrannies with increasing power and riches in Greece, which meant that
cities had greater sources of revenue. He seems to be suggesting that this
wealth was a prize, and perhaps that the power of tyrants could only be
maintained by wealth, inasmuch as it required the payment of a force
of mercenaries to be a bodyguard and primitive kind of political police.
Mercenaries are attested from about 550 onwards as servants of Peisistratus of Athens, Phalaris of Agrigentum and Polycrates of Samos.[4]
However, our evidence on earlier tyrannies does not suggest that the re-
cruiting of soldiers through money was a decisive factor in their creation.

Probably the earliest tyrant, whose name we know, Pheidon of Argos,
is said by Aristotle to have taken power when he already had *basileia*,
'kingship' (by contrast to others who were previously in positions of
oligarchic privilege or demagogues). From what Aristotle has previously
said it seems most likely that he is treating Pheidon as 'a king who over-
stepped his traditional rights and aimed at a more despotic rule.' However, it is also possible that Pheidon seized autocratic power after being
an oligarchic official with the title of 'king'. This sort of thing happened
at one point at Miletus, when the *prytanis* (president) of the oligarchy
made himself into a tyrant. What little we know about Pheidon suggests
that he achieved military control over most of the Peloponnese (he is
supposed to have laid down standard weights and measures there and to
have taken upon himself the superintendence of the Olympic festival).
He is also plausibly associated by modern scholars with the victory of
Argos over Sparta at Hysiae, attributed to the year 669-668.[5]

Two other early tyrannies in mainland Greece were associated with
success in military office. In Sicyon, according to a papyrus fragment
— probably of the history of Ephorus, Orthagoras achieved promotion
within the regiment of frontier guards and, as their commander, won
a victory over the neighbouring city of Pellene. He was consequently
elected polemarch, minister of war, by the people, and it seems that this
office provided him with the basis for establishing a dynastic tyranny

which was to last 100 years (c. 650-550). He would have been one of those who seized a tyranny when holding a magistracy with full powers conferred by the people, a class of tyrants mentioned by Aristotle with the comment that in old times such men were elected for long periods of office.[6] In Corinth Cypselus was descended on his mother's side from the Bacchiadai, the clan who ruled the city as a narrow hereditary oligarchy, but was reared in exile or hiding, allegedly because of the prophesies of a Delphic oracle that he would promote revolution. When adult, he seems to have been accepted as a Bacchiad, but he also became a popular favourite through generosity to the people. As polemarch he curried favour by mitigating penalties he was due to impose, gathered a force of supporters (*hetairikon*) and seized power (about 640) by assassinating the current holder of supreme office among the Bacchiadai.[7]

Later still and better known is the example of the Athenian Peisistratus. Like Orthagoras, he gained fame in a war — that between Athens and Megara over Salamis and Nisaia — and on this basis asked the people to approve his use of a bodyguard to ensure his safety from his personal enemies. In fact he used this force to seize political supremacy. We do not know what magistracy or magistracies Peisistratus had been holding (he too may have been a polemarch), but his first seizure of power was founded on popularity, presumably with the men of the army in particular, and earlier tenure of an official military post.

Other tyrants are known, or can be plausibly assumed, to have shown distinction in war before they attained power. Pittacus, who was elected tyrant by the people at Mytilene, had apparently fought in single combat with Phrynon, an Athenian, over the territory of Sigeum in the Troad. Polycrates seized power in Samos by a military coup and used his tyranny (c. 530-520) to dominate the Cyclades and eastern Aegean with a navy and mercenary troops. Lygdamis, tyrant of Naxos, gave military aid to Peisistratus during the latter's third successful coup and, when tyrant, is said to have helped Polycrates to seize power.[8]

Both Polycrates and Peisistratus stabilised their power with external military aid. However, for the most part the prospective tyrant had to rely on natives of his own land in order to obtain power. We must now consider his relationship to these citizen soldiers and how far they were themselves a cause of tyranny.

The Tyrant and the Hoplite

Vase-painting, figurines and military artefacts themselves discovered by the archaeologist show that Greek infantry began to equip themselves in the fashion characteristic of the classical Greek 'hoplite' (heavily armed soldier) from a little before 700 BC onwards. A panoply from Argos, including a finely moulded breastplate, is dated in the late eighth century. The 'Corinthian' helmet and the *porpax* shield (with a central loop for the forearm and a grip inside the rim for the left hand) appear in the early seventh century, followed by greaves. The long thrusting spear, however, does not seem to have replaced a pair of lighter spears until much later, towards 600, and then perhaps only in mainland Greece. Nor is there clear evidence of hoplites fighting together in a phalanx before c. 650. The change of equipment was gradual and may be put down to individual experiment followed by technical progress and more widespread imitation.

However, more than a change of equipment was involved. A new style of fighting in close formation arose — different to that described by Homer and some of the early elegiac and iambic poets — to which the classical hoplite's equipment was particularly suited, since out of formation his right side was comparatively vulnerable because of the method by which he carried his shield and his heavy spear was inflexible in its use. Fighting in formation is first portrayed on an *aryballos* from Sicyon of c. 650; it also appears on other Protocorinthian *aryballoi* (including the Macmillan aryballos in the British Museum) and on the Chigi *oinochoe* dating from c. 640. However the men portrayed on this last vase have still a pair of light spears. It seems that the wholesale adoption of the heavy spear may have been a consequence of formation fighting rather than a cause of it. In Tyrtaeus' poetry of roughly the same period Spartan fighting methods against the Messenians are a mixture of standing in rank with spears (the classical hoplites' technique), individual combat, and the hurling of stones and javelins by mobile lightly armed men round the phalanx.[9]

This kind of warfare was developing in the period when Pheidon came to power. It is probable that Pheidon's military successes were brought about by heavily armed men, even if they had not fully adopted hoplite fighting in formation. The question arises, however, whether the technical military development had political consequences in that it created a political force which could and would overthrow existing monarchic or narrowly oligarchic constitutions. Aristotle believed that the oligarchies which succeeded primitive monarchies were based on the warriors, originally on the cavalry, later on the hoplites. This is clearly meant to be a neat theoretical model of development and deserves to be treated with caution for this reason; it may also be partly based on dubious evidence like the constitution of Drakon described in the *Constitution of the Athenians* – a historical fiction probably created by a late-fifth-century advocate of the hoplite franchise.[10] Nevertheless the view has some historical plausibility. Although the cities of Chalcis and Eretria had aristocracies who took their titles from being horse-breeders and riders respectively, by Archilochus' time the lords of Euboea were famed for their infantry fighting. Sparta by the mid-seventh century had a constitution in which an assembly of full Spartans, the 'equals', had recognised functions, and these 'equals' seem to have been the recipients of the 9,000 or 10,000 lots of land distributed to the victorious army after the conquest of Messenia. In the sixth century the hoplite class (it seems probable that the *zeugitai* had the minimum hoplite qualification) were given a specific status between the aristocracy and the poor in Solon's constitution. An early law of the Ozolian Locrians implies that if 200 new fighting men are brought into a settlement, they must be given some of the best land and thus a major position in the body politic.[11]

However, there are uncertainties about the relationship of hoplite warfare to tyranny, arising both from chronology and from the probable genesis of the hoplite army in the first place. The only state in which, to our knowledge, the ordinary infantry soldier was politically important by 650 was Sparta, which avoided tyranny completely. If we take Sparta's great constitutional reform as a concession which forestalled tyranny, this may have occurred in the aftermath of the first Messenian War which, on the usual dating of c. 730-710, was not fought in full hoplite armour or with hoplite tactics. Conversely, although vase-painting shows that there were hoplites in Attica in the first half of the seventh century, it was not until about 630 that a man tried to become tyrant and his *coup* was backed by only a fraction of the citizen body.

We do not know whether the Euboean aristocracy, who were masters of infantry fighting in Archilochus' time, yielded any measure of government to their social inferiors. Two Euboean tyrants probably belong to this period: one, Tunnondas, was elected and respected; the other, Antileon, was so unpopular that he was deposed and flayed.[12] However, we know next to nothing of their origin or achievement. In soldiering there may have been more continuity than revolution in Euboea. Archilochus talks of javelins and swords as well as spears, and the men renowned for prowess with these were the lords of Euboea. This suggests that at the time aristocrats fought in heavy armour as individual champions without any hoplite phalanx. They probably rode into battle accompanied by an attendant, a practice attested in archaic vase-painting.[13]

Although it is improbable that the mass of hoplites were politically significant by the time Pheidon came to power, Cypselus and other tyrants, who apparently gained power by holding military office and thus acquiring popular favour, are likely to have been backed by men who fought in a heavily armed phalanx. Thus hoplite power was at least an instrument of change. Moreover, in the long run the effective part of the citizen body of many cities was broadened not only in warfare but in politics, as Aristotle saw. However, it does not follow that the mass of the hoplites formed a coherent social and political group, still less that they had conscious political aims and put their weight behind tyrants to achieve this. Here we must face a fundamental problem about hoplite armies, which, unfortunately, can only be solved by guess-work. How far were these new-style armies simply a spontaneous development resulting from experimentation with heavy armour by individuals, and how far were they the result of a conscious policy by powerful and wealthy men, who encouraged and perhaps financed the operation?

To my mind, although in the initial development of hoplite equipment, individual experiment must have been of the greatest importance, the fact that the final equipment of hoplite armies (and their precursors such as we see on the Chigi vase) were adapted to disciplined fighting in a body, implies an overall policy. The creation of a hoplite army, as opposed to a number of hoplite soldiers, must have owed much to powerful magistrates or other dynasts in cities, who wanted a national or private army of the new kind. It is possible that such magnates supplied their dependants with arms, contrary to the common practice later, by which a man supplied his own. The Romans are said to have learnt to fight in heavy armour in a phalanx from the Etruscans, who are a classic example of an unequal society whose military organisation was based on an aristocracy surrounded by client dependants. A hoplite army, therefore need not imply a shift of power from the aristocracy and a trend to more broadly based government. It may have been that a man was not made a tyrant by a hoplite army, but that he became one with the intention of creating such an army and so gaining further support. Equally, the personal popularity of tyrants may have arisen through their leadership of hoplite armies created by the reforms of others. Thus the relationship between tyrant and army is unlikely to have been uniform throughout the Greek cities.

Even if we accept that the development of hoplite armies changed Greek society by promoting greater social coherence among those who fought in the phalanx (in my view it was certainly a contributory factor, but it is hard to judge its importance in isolation), there is no evidence that they provided political motivation or took the initiative in establishing tyranny. The tyrants probably justified themselves by claiming that they were providing an alternative to oligarchic corruption. Such is the implication of the first Delphic oracle about Cypselus in Herodotus. This would appeal to popular sentiment, but a tyrant did not need the hoplites to suggest such a programme. However, one should not underestimate the value of mere military support. Aristotle, when discussing why in the past popular leaders became tyrants, made two points: first, that it was generals, rather than orators, who became political leaders of any kind then (military service of course would have been the best way of getting to know, and be known by, a large number of people), and secondly that cities were small and the people lived on their land in the country as farmers. His implication seems to be that the people's champion had not got ever-present political support in the city to protect him against his powerful opponents — such as was possessed by a demagogue in fifth or fourth-century Athens. He therefore sought to maintain his position by force, eliminating any opposition. Even if his actual striking force, when he made the *coup*, was a small group of friends (*hetairikon*), as attested about Cypselus and Polycrates, he needed to ensure that the army would not be persuaded to act against him.[14]

A warning example was provided about 630 by the unsuccessful venture by the Athenian aristocrat Cylon, who, according to Thucydides, was noble and powerful (*dunatos*) and moreover married to the daughter of Theagenes, tyrant of Megara. Theagenes had seized power by misapplying a bodyguard granted him. He was regarded by Aristotle as a demagogic tyrant because he slaughtered the cattle of the rich, when these were grazing by a river. But his fall also was connected with an attack on rich creditors and insolence by the liberated *demos* against a Spartan embassy.[15] It is difficult to deduce Theagenes' political programme, if any, or his sources of political support from such evidence. He may have merely been an opportunist aristocrat, as Cylon appears to have been.

Cylon seized the Athenian acropolis, as Peisistratus was to do some 60 years later, with a force of friends and some men lent by Theagenes and with the moral backing of the Delphic oracle, but the Athenians rushed in from the countryside in full force in response to the alarm and besieged him there. The siege ended in the flight of Cylon himself and the slaughter of the insurgents in spite of their appeals to the gods as suppliants, and the Alkmeonid clan were held guilty of impiety in consequence.[16] There is no evidence that Cylon got or expected help from the Megarian army as a ....ole. Like Peisistratus later, he seems to have hoped that the seizure of the acropolis and the ensuing disturbance of normal city politics would encourage all the discontented citizens of Attica to join him. However, the bulk of the citizens of Attica including, we may safely infer, the majority of the hoplites, proved hostile or unresponsive.

On the other hand, if the majority of the hoplite class were favourable or even neutral in their attitude to a tyrant, this was sufficient. Their direct assistance was not necessarily required. Few men were needed in immature city-states to make a *coup*, to judge from the stories of Cypselus, Polycrates and Peisistratus' first seizure of power, and this conclusion is supported by the poems of Alcaeus. We even find testimony to this in an account of civil strife of a much later period in Rome. In the early fourth century M. Manlius Capitolinus was killed for aspiring to tyranny, and among the grounds alleged against him was the 'secession of the plebs into a private house, which also, as it happened, stood on the citadel'. Revolutions could be made by the number of people who could be contained in a house such as Manlius' on the Roman Capitol.

Class Conflict in the Age of the First Tyrants

In the last section I have tried to show the difficulty of treating the tyrant as the representative of the group interests of the hoplites. This is not to say that, while in power, he did not benefit the interests of the middling proprietors (I would apply this term to those who had on average an adequate surplus of produce over consumption every year to generate a small reserve of capital). The evidence of the economic activities of the early tyrants is not very revealing. Some can be associated with colonisation, which seems to have been directed at securing sources of food or raw materials or a route by which they could reach the homeland. We know of Peisistratus' interest in Sigeum and the Thracian Chersonese and that of Periander in Potidaea and the cities on the route to Italy and the Adriatic. Some money went into public works. Otherwise the best we learn about them is that they were moderate in taxation, as Peisistratus and Periander were, or (with sinister motives imputed) that they maintained full employment. If a tyrant possessed wealth already, as Peisistratus did by the time of his third successful *coup*, or acquired property from exiled opponents, much of it would have been needed to reward supporters and to pay for security forces. In so far as they were associated with the development of coinage, this may have been because of their need to pay mercenaries themselves and their desire to prevent others producing coin whose influence might be subversive.[17] It may be that important economic reforms have been suppressed by the loss of evidence, but I prefer to think that the tyrants' greatest assistance to the economy of their cities was to provide at least for a time a background of political stability. Such stability probably served the interests of the hoplite class better than any economic or social upheaval.

Two main forms of economic revolution came later to be associated with tyranny — the abolition of debts and the general redistribution of land. It should be noted that the second posed more of a threat to existing landholders of all kinds; only the first offered some advantage for members of the hoplite class. Neither of these changes is ascribed to any of the tyrants in Greece and Ionia in the Archaic Age.[18] However, abolition of debts did become a political issue in Attica before the occurrence of tyranny, leading instead to the appointment of a mediator from the aristocracy, Solon. The grievances of the Athenians in this period are important as evidence of incipient civil strife, which did not come immediately to fruition, and because they bear on the general problem of the relationship of the power-seeking politicians to the poor.

Agrarian conditions in Attica just before Solon's reforms are generally agreed to have been in outline as they are represented in the Aristotelian *Constitution of Athens* and Plutarch's *Life of Solon*. However, the precise interpretation of the tradition and the origin of the conditions that it describes are a matter of debate. We are told that the poor became enslaved to the rich and that they raised loans on the security of their bodies. Men were called *pelatai* (dependent labourers ?) and *hektemoroi* (sixth-parters), because this was the rent they paid for working the land. If they failed to pay the rent, they and their wives and children were liable to be taken into slavery. Solon, when discussing his reform of these conditions, talks about removing the *horoi* (markers) from the black land and making it free instead of its former slavery. He then adds that he recovered former citizens from foreign lands, to which they had gone either voluntarily in flight from their debts or because they had been sold, justly or unjustly, as slaves. Finally he tells of his liberation of those subject to unfair slavery in Attica itself.[19]

The general dependence of the poor on the rich is something to be expected in this period both in Attica and elsewhere, but the fate of those enslaved and sold was harsher than the normal lot of dependants, even if they had reached this condition because they owed payment or service for benefits already received. We have seen earlier (p. 27) that in

Greek law codes a debtor's person was frequently the ultimate security
for the payment of a sum of money, whether owed through debt or a
court judgement, although his property might also be taken in pledge or
occupied as a form of distraint. *Horoi* were later used either as simple
boundary stones or to publicise an encumbrance on the land, that is,
that it was being used as security for a financial obligation, arising from
a loan, a dowry or the administration of an orphan's property. It is
exceedingly difficult to understand their importance in this period
unless they were a sign that the land was in some way in pledge. They
can hardly have marked the extent of the expansion of the estates of
the rich, since Solon stated that he had removed them, yet he never
claimed, nor was he accused of, performing a redistribution of the land.
It seems best to conclude that land in Attica was generally alienable, as
it was in Hesiod's Boeotia, and thus could be seized as an alternative
or in addition to the debtor's person. The *horoi* mentioned by Solon
would have been placed in land not yet alienated, but pledged while
still being worked by a dependant farmer. His land could easily have
been regarded by Solon as already enslaved, since it was continuously
under the threat of seizure.[20]

What then was the crisis? Unlike some scholars, who have recently
treated this subject,[21] I believe that it arose from debt viewed as a legal
delict — that is, the failure to make stipulated repayment — not just
from the general dependence of the poor on the rich, since the most
striking feature of Solon's reform in this field was that Athens had
thereafter a more liberal debt law than other ancient states known to
us or indeed nineteenth-century Britain.

Poor peasants before the reform would have begun by contracting
obligations with the rich in the form of payment or services in return
for receiving help with the necessities of life. Their needs may well have
been supplied directly by the rich man, since coinage was not yet struck
in Attica and transactions in iron spits or weighed metal would have
been clumsy, if the poor man's primary need was food and seed for next
year's crop. We find this kind of transaction during the Hellenistic period
in Messenia, where the authorities resolved to distribute grain to those
in need, in the expectation of repayment in grain after the harvest.[22]

Even if the poor man entered into obligations which compelled him
to provide service rather than produce for his creditor, he was not yet
reduced to the standing of a chattel-slave, who could be bought and
sold. However, it is easy to see how he might be driven into greater and
greater dependence through his inability to meet his initial obligations
and at the same time have enough produce on which to survive. At some

point in this vicious spiral his land would have been taken in pledge to prevent him selling it to a third party and fleeing with the proceeds. He may also have bought time by placing his wife and children in slavery before himself.

Some debtors took what they could and escaped to another land, as Solon himself tells us. This was possible for owners of arable land, but easier for shepherds and goatherds who crossed frontiers in the course of their normal livelihood. There is a good example in documents from Hellenistic Egypt of goatherds defaulting on a payment they owed and decamping (they owed 216 six-month kids on the 144 she-goats they possessed).[23] Arable farmers, who failed to meet their obligations but did not flee the country, may have eventually lost their land through seizure by their creditors (it is not clear whether this required a formal lawsuit; later one was not needed when land had been specifically pledged in *hupothēkē* or *prasis epi lusei*, as in the agreements inscribed on fourth-century *horoi*). They may also have been turned into chattel-slaves, whether or not by due legal process, because of their undischarged obligations.

However, a creditor may have chosen not to foreclose but to continue to exploit a debtor's obligations to him. The status of *hektēmoros* was perhaps established by law for those who were shown before a judge to have defaulted; certainly the fixed rate of repayment suggests the sanction of public authority. By allowing the debtor to remain on his own land paying a sixth of his produce, the creditor got his services as a kind of serf, while possessing some security for his previous investment in the man through the value of his land. The very fact that the debtor remained a citizen and a landholder might have suited the creditor particularly well, as he had a dependant of potential political value. If rich men preferred the allegiance of theoretically free men to that of slaves, this has implications for the political divisions in Attica which did not result from the cleavage between rich and poor. Nevertheless, in spite of the palliative of hektemorage, the burden of debt on the poor seems to have become unsupportable by Solon's time. We do not know if there were particular causes of agrarian hardship in Attica or whether the appearance of tyrants improved conditions for the poor in other cities. We should not rule out the possibility that some cities continued to tolerate the same conditions which led to Solon's appointment at Athens.[24]

In 594-593 Solon liberated all those enslaved for debt, at home or abroad, that he could find, forbad for the future loans on the security of the body and cancelled outstanding debts secured on land (this last is implied by the removal of the *horoi*). However, distraint on land or other property and the seizure of pledges were bound to return, as they were the only resources left to the creditor to enforce payment. As I have noticed earlier, there is no sign of a redistribution of land to the landless. Solon himself implicitly denies this and so do our later sources. In consequence, it seems, the tendency of his reforms would have been to increase the amount of landless citizens, who worked as craftsmen or hired labourers for the landed. These would have been little, if any, better off financially than the previous hektemors, but they were secure in their liberty and more independent of the aristocracy. The word for hired labourers in Solon's time was *thētes* and it is perhaps no coincidence that this was the name given by Solon to the lowest class of citizens in his political structure, those who had only the right of voting in political or judicial assemblies. Thus one aim of Solon's reforms was probably that the poor should no longer be rigidly tied clients or serfs, bound by the threat of total enslavement, but mobile workers, who, if not independent from their employers, would have looser ties to them.[25]

Solon's poems are the earliest evidence of a class conflict between citizens in Greek history. They pick out the basic subjects of contention, land and debt, and also introduce a political terminology that later became a commonplace. On the one side is the *demos*, the common people; on the other 'those who held power and were awesome in their wealth', later labelled simply the *dunatoi* (powerful). Solon himself portrayed his work in moral terms. He restrained the wealthy and powerful from greed and insolence without humiliating them unfairly; at the same time he granted the *demos* adequate, but not excessive, rights, so that they would respond to the leadership of their betters but not be subject to brute compulsion. He deliberately avoided stirring up the people into a class struggle. This attitude seems to explain both his economic and political legislation. The poor were to be genuinely free and have a minimum political representation, both for their own good and to limit the ambitions of the *dunatoi*.[26]

Solon was later called the first *prostatēs tou dēmou*, champion of the people. At first sight this may seem an inexact title, resulting from rough and ready classification by a later Attic historian, but it can be given a precise sense. In later manumission inscriptions the passer-by who protects and rescues someone unjustly seized as a slave is termed *prostatēs* or *ho prostas* (the man who championed).[27] Solon was indeed a liberator from slavery by his social reforms, which in the long run may have influenced Athenian politics more than his legal and constitutional reforms. Much of the character of political strife outside Attica may be plausibly put down to the fact that they had had no Solon and the poor could come into total economic subservience to the rich.

Conflicts Among the Aristocracy

In the poetry of Solon which survives there are few clear indications of any other threatening conflict except the major one between the powerful and the people. However, Solon's remarks about the insatiable rivalry of the rich in their struggle for wealth may be taken as a hint that those who had power did not form a monolithic political bloc. Indeed, he prophesies that *stasis* will arise from the greed and plundering of the rich and then talks of the city being worn down in the societies dear to the unjust. It is the great men who are the ruin of a city, as surely as snow and hail come from cloud and thunder follows lightning.[28] As I have suggested above, the nature of Solon's social reforms implies that he was concerned with the way the surviving poor citizens had become bound to the wealthy and thus with the creation of factions in the citizen body by constraint rather than choice. We should have expected anyhow that a kinship group, especially if it was still based on one or a few neighbourhoods, had considerable political importance, just as it had social importance for the defence of the individual and his family against their enemies. The nobility would have exploited such groupings in its rivalries for office. If in addition hektemors or other debtors were exploited as clients, this would have created tensions with the ties they inherited through their families.

According to the *Constitution of the Athenians*, when four years had elapsed after Solon's archonship, conflict returned to Athens: no archon was elected, and there was a further year of anarchy after a similar interval. Political rivalries were so great that no orderly elections could be held. We may surmise that discontent among the poor members of the electorate contributed to the confusion (our source talks of cancellation of debts being once more mooted by one faction). However, it seems probable that the focus for this resentment was provided by a struggle between rival factions. If the aristocracy had been united, they should have been able to ensure the election of a titular head of state. After yet another four-year interval (c. 580) an archon held office for two years and two months, until he was driven out of office by force. This was in effect an abortive attempt at tyranny based on the holding of a constitutional office. Subsequent to this extraordinary archonship there were apparently for one year ten (instead of the usual

nine) archons — five *eupatridai* (nobles), three *agroikoi* (country dwel-
lers) and two *demiourgoi* (craftsmen or workers for the people). Our
source does not suggest, nor does it seem probable in this period, that
Solon's constitution was breached by the admission of men below the
rank of knight to the archonship. Nor in the years following is there any
evidence of the poorer citizens creating factions of their own. Therefore,
agroikoi and *demiourgoi* should be understood as the names of factions
led by men of substance, whatever their general composition. The
struggle was essentially between the more powerful members of society
for what they believed was their rightful place in Solon's new order and
had been made possible by Solon's opening of the archonship to a wider
section of society than the old nobility.[29]

Peisistratus

A different division of the citizens into factions is attested first by
Herodotus' account of Peisistratus' rise to tyranny. There are three
factions — *hoi ek tou pediou* (the men from the plain), the *paraloi* (men
by the sea) and the *hyperakrioi* (men of, or over, the heights), the last
so named by their leader Peisistratus. Plutarch suggests that these groups
existed before Solon's archonship, but Herodotus implies that the third
group was a recent creation about 560 BC. What is the meaning of these
terms? The existence of a powerful and wealthy commercial class, whose
fortunes were not invested in land, has been disproved as late as the
second and first century BC in Italy: it is hard to postulate it as early
as the sixth century in Attica. The *paralia* was a well-known regional
division in Attica, which basically embraced the south-east triangle of
Attica, and in the future political redistribution of citizens by Cleisthenes
was to include most of the coastline east of Athens. The *hyperakrioi* are
called *diakrioi* in the *Constitution of Athens*, perhaps the original Attic
term, and *diakria* was also a term for a geographical area. It thus appears
that in name at least these parties were regional, the men from the plain
being primarily those from the plains of Athens and Eleusis, those beside
the sea being from the south-east of Attica, and those of the heights
being from north-east Attica, perhaps including also Peisistratus' place
of origin at Brauron.[30]

According to the *Consitution of the Athenians* and Plutarch, Peisistratus was also supported by those who had been pauperised by debt
and those whose Attic parentage was suspect. I have suggested earlier
that at the time of his first *coup* he counted on tolerance from the less
wealthy proprietors, who were hoplites, because of his military exploits
at their head. Nor need we suppose that the other two groups were

rigidly regional in composition. For one thing, members of aristocratic clans had probably begun to take up residence in parts of Attica far from their ancestral homes.[31]

Although Peisistratus' support was based on more than ties of kinship and locality, his actions do not show that he had any particular reforms in mind or that he had planned to deal with the grievances of any specific group. His first *coup*, in 561, after the assembly had granted him a bodyguard and he had seized the acropolis, resulted, we are told, in a period of good administration. Perhaps it was simply this that his ex-soldiers expected from tyranny — a period of stability, and this was why they tolerated his *coup*, in contrast to the reaction against Cylon 70 years before. His first expulsion, after perhaps five years in power, is not clearly documented. The two faction leaders opposed to him may have only needed a few hundred men to overthrow him, if his direct support was confined to the club-bearers and some personal clients. His return followed quickly when his two opponents, Megakles and Lykourgos, quarrelled over the division of power they had seized themselves. The strange propaganda device used to bring Peisistratus back, in which a tall girl impersonated Pallas Athene, suggests that Peisistratus' previous rule had been accepted as legitimate. Although the reaction of the town of Athens was decisive, the people of the country demes to whom the news quickly spread were equally favourable.[32]

His second loss of office seems to betray a failure of nerve. He left as soon as he knew that Megakles, disgusted at Peisistratus' treatment of his new Alkmeonid wife, had reopened negotiations with Lykourgus. This implies that he himself did not have enough close supporters and clients, at least available in Athens, nor enough money. When he finally returned ten years later, he had remedied both these defects. His popularity in Attica may well have waned in the interval. But he had silver from the Strymon and other money from the Thebans and Lygdamis of Naxos. The latter also provided soldiers, and 1,000 Argive mercenaries came, led by Hegesistratos, his son by the Argive Timonassa. His own area of Marathon provided a secure base, to which supporters from Athens and country demes came. The Marathon area was regarded by those in the city as a law to itself, to judge from the fact that Peisistratus was ignored while collecting strength there. Possibly his aristocratic opponents were prepared for him to remain a local war-lord, as he had presumably done in the interval between his first two spells of tyranny. Only when he marched on Athens did he meet an opposing army. It is difficult to tell from Herodotus' account how far the army that opposed him had a genuine will to resist. If this existed, it certainly did not last

long. It is at least clear that few of the hoplites or other members of the
army were convinced opponents of his brand of tyranny.[33]

From this final *coup* Peisistratus and his sons secured a tyranny that
lasted about 33 years without a break. These were largely peaceful until
the last few years, when relations between Hippias and the Athenians
were embittered by the bungled plot of Harmodius and Aristogeiton, a
further assassination attempt by the Alkmeonidai and their guerrilla
warfare from Leipsydrion. There was no doubt *ad hoc* redistribution of
land in view of the availability of that of Peisistratus' enemies. In addition to providing loans for agriculture, the tyrant's capital which was
invested in public works would have contributed to employment. Otherwise, our sources state that these intelligent tyrants were conservative,
changing as little as possible, and moderate in their taxation demands.
This is similar to the tradition about other major tyrannies in this
period.[34] Some, like Periander and Thrasyboulos, are said to have been
harsh to their opponents and stand accused of personal immorality, but
we do not find ascribed to them on the whole works of political construction or revolution. The one major exception is the reconstruction
of the tribal system at Sicyon by Cleisthenes in order that the non-
Dorians, his own supporters, should have a privileged position. In
Athens there was a much more far-reaching reform on the same lines,
but this was carried out, not by the Peisistratidai, but by a *prostatēs tou
dēmou*, Cleisthenes, the grandson of the tyrant of Sicyon (p. 54).

In consequence, the ambitions of this and other tyrant-dynasties
seem to have been largely personal — to secure predominance for themselves and their families. Moreover, their ascents to power were not in
themselves documents of new social forces at work. What did operate
was a permanent feature of ancient Greek, Roman and indeed any form
of political life, the rivalry between those who had power. Only, in
this period such rivalry had a much freer rein because of the old social
system, in which kinship and shared locality created binding ties, and
because of the insecurity created by the comparative lack of authority
possessed by city government and its laws. Once in power tyrants in
some cities assisted economic development by creating stability, by
infusing their own money and on occasion by their interest in foreign
trade. Their contributions to political development seem, however, to be
mainly incidental and even unforeseen. Their achievement can best be
understood in the light of their exaggerated reputation later for *adikia*,
disregard of justice and propriety. They made a break in a political and
social tradition which sometimes was decisive in generating a new kind
of society.

Alcaeus

Two episodes illustrate most strikingly the personal element in the
creation and suppression of tyranny. The first is the in-fighting of the
aristocracy in Mytilene on Lesbos about 600 BC, recounted mainly in
the poems of Alcaeus and commentaries dependent on them. Earlier in
Mytilene's history, perhaps about 650 BC, a narrow oligarchy, the clan
of Penthilos (Penthilidai), had been killed by Megakles' faction because
of their brutality. Later, a member of this clan called Penthilos was
assassinated in revenge for an assault with a club. There seems to have
ensued a broader oligarchy elected by franchise, during which there
were frequent *coups d'état* by tyrants and counter-*coups* against them.
The tyrant Melanchros was overthrown about 610 BC by Pittacus with
the aid of Alcaeus' brothers. Then Alcaeus himself and Pittacus were
soldiers together in their city's struggle to annex Sigeum (c. 600), in
which Pittacus defeated Phrynon, the Athenian pankratiast, in single
combat. A second tyrant, Myrsilos, seized power, and Alcaeus and his
friends after an unsuccessful plot against him had to flee to Pyrrha,
another city on Lesbos. The struggle against Myrsilos is apparently represented by the image of the sailors caught in the storm in the famous
poem, 'I am bewildered by the *stasis* of the winds' (where *stasis* means
most naturally 'position' or 'direction' but also suggests 'strife').[35]

Myrsilos himself was expelled but returned. When he eventually died,
Alcaeus had brief cause for rejoicing. For in the meantime Myrsilos had
been joined by Pittacus, who had deserted his previous allegiance to
Alcaeus and his friends and married into the clan of Penthilos. About
590 Pittacus was elected *aisumnetes* (moderator), i.e. a constitutional
dictator, by the people as a whole with enthusiasm. Alcaeus was enraged
over what he believed was a breach of faith, and his group exchanged
oaths and again began to plot, this time against Pittacus. This ended
with him once more in exile, lamenting how he missed the *agora* and
the council chamber. His brother went to fight as a mercenary for the
Babylonian kingdom, while he himself probably became involved in a
war between the Lydian king Alyattes and Astyages of Media. He may
have even received money from Lydia in support of a plot to recover
his home city.[36]

Although Alcaeus longs for normal political life in the *agora* and the
council chamber, this is clearly no more than a desire to manage city
affairs on an equal footing with his aristocratic peers. Even the *demos*,
which, in his view, went astray when it elected Pittacus to be *aisumnetes*,
was probably unrepresentative of the entire community, but more like

the assembly of Colophon as depicted by the philosopher-poet Xenophanes.

> After learning useless luxuries from the Lydians, once they were free
> from hateful tyranny, they used to come into the *agora* in their
> purple-dyed cloaks, not more than about a thousand on the whole
> — arrogant men, preening themselves on their elegant hair-styles,
> drenched in cosmetics with recherché scents.

Alcaeus' motivation is not the pursuit of liberty and democracy for all;
it is personal and based on an aristocratic sense of honour. He and his
friends must live up to the reputation of their families. 'You must have
a reputation such as free men from good parents should have.'[37] The
chief skill of Alcaeus and his fellow aristocrats lies in war, and it is in
this way that they are accustomed to settle political conflicts. Nor is it
easy for the rest of the citizens to resist, since they lack social cohesion
and confidence in their still immature constitutional procedures.

The same sort of spirit that inspired Alcaeus can be found in those
who tried to overthrow Peisistratus' tyranny. Alcaeus' attitude to his
noble forefathers is reproduced in the drinking song (*skolion*) about the
Alkmeonidai's base at Leipsydrion. The fortress itself is there called a
betrayer of comrades for destroying good men and of good family
(*eupatridai*). In other songs we find loyalty to comrades stressed. A
hetairos (group or faction member) 'must be straight and not have
crooked thoughts'.[38] Even if the *skolia* were composed in the fifth
century, they show attitudes of the Athenian aristocracy which are
probably an inheritance from their ancestors.

The Tyrant-Slayers

When the assassination of Hipparchus took place in 514, the Alkmeonidai had probably already made their unsuccessful attempt to use Leipsydrion as a base for raids on Athens. The assassination attempt by
Cedon also may have preceded that of Harmodius and Aristogeiton.
Yet the genesis of their plot to overthrow the tyranny was a lover's
indignation — a fact which Thucydides was at pains to point out in a
special digression. He wished to explain the ingrained Athenian fear of
tyranny in his own time, which, he implied, derived from the efficiency
of the Peisistratids as much as their harshness, and to correct the false
impression that Harmodius and Aristogeiton had really slain the tyrant
and brought back liberty to Athens. This opinion probably was created
by drinking songs about Harmodius and the memorial statue group (the

original group was looted by the Persians in 480, but it was soon replaced by the work of Critios and Nesiotes, copies of which survive today). Moreover, there was public testimony to the importance of Harmodius' and Aristogeiton's deed in the award of free meals to their descendants.[39]

However, Thucydides, like Herodotus earlier, makes it clear that Hipparchus the victim of the plot was not a tyrant himself but a junior colleague to his brother Hippias. The occasion for the plot was the slight against the honour of Harmodius' family by Hipparchus, because he had been rejected as Harmodius' lover. Nevertheless, and here Thucydides is to some extent his own corrective, the plot was against both Hipparchus and Hippias. It was Hippias whom they were seeking to kill first, and they had chosen time and place, the procession of the Great Panathenaia, in the hope of rousing a general insurrection on a rare occasion when the citizens were under arms. Their major purpose failed, when in a panic over suspected discovery they ignored Hippias and killed Hipparchus in an angry and clumsy fashion. Although the unarmed by-standers within the gates of the city allowed Aristogeiton temporarily to escape arrest by the bodyguard, Hippias outside in the Ceramicus stripped the hoplites of their weapons before they realised what was up and disarmed those few in the know who had brought daggers as well.[40] Thus the effect of the plot was commensurate with its origin.

As Dover has pointed out, the origin of the plot probably worried Thucydides more than it did the average Athenian, who would have thought it an example of individuals striking a blow for freedom, love and honour. Yet Thucydides' account shows how superficial the assassination plot was as an attempt to overthrow tyranny. The assassins obviously met with some sympathy, but no one was prepared to spread the news of Hipparchus' and Harmodius' deaths to the hoplites before they were disarmed. Moreover, in view of the fact that Hippias himself, although on his guard, was still affable, before the plot was revealed, and prepared to meet the public face to face, there is little sign of a tide of popular feeling against the tyrants. Fear, one may say, was stronger than resentment, but it may be nearer the truth that the majority of Athenians felt that they had little in common with the aristocrats who had grievances against the Peisistratids.[41]

Cleisthenes and the Demos

As I have suggested earlier, where we have detailed evidence about tyranny, a certain disassociation appears between the rise and fall of tyrants and the remedy of the social and political grievances of the citizen bodies. Considering the struggles over tyranny and the struggles

of the weak for freedom and an adequate standard of living is like looking at two different registers of a piece of painted pottery. There is
often no direct connection between the two themes, although they are
recognisably part of the same creation. A tyrant like Peisistratus might
get support from those who had lost their property, but it was not a
critical contribution to his success nor does he seem to have been especially beholden to his poorest supporters, once firmly in power. If he
made loans to peasants, where other rich aristocrats would not, this was
not so much a favour as a transaction which assured him of further tied
dependants.

However, this does not mean that aristocrats thought of nothing but
grabbing power and had no plans for reform to benefit their cities. In
Athens, Solon is a great example of a reformer who prided himself on
curbing his own self-interest and that of his class, even though his over-
riding aim may be seen as the preservation of his class from the consequences of its own vices. Cleisthenes, the Alkmeonid, however, is even
more interesting, because of his involvement in the milieu of aristocratic
rivalry symbolised by the *skolia* and Alcaeus' poetry. First, he engaged
in a bitter struggle for supremacy in Athens by guerrilla warfare and
subversive intrigue against the Peisistratids. Later he was a sufficiently
serious and ruthless politician to go to the lengths of inducing Spartan
military aid to expel Hippias in 510. Once this had occurred, he found
himself contending with Isagoras, son of Teisandros, presumably of the
same family that has produced Hippokleides, the rival of his father
Megakles for the hand of Agariste, daughter of Cleisthenes tyrant of
Sicyon. Cleisthenes' reaction is described by Herodotus in a phrase
which seems a deliberate oxymoron: 'he introduced into his faction the
people [*ton demon prosetairizetai*] '.[42]

He acquired this general support by proposing a new tribal system as
a basis for Athenian politics, one which would tend to break up into
small units the influence of powerful families like his own and would
enable recent immigrants to Attica to be incorporated more easily into
the voting population. His success can be measured by the fact that when
the Spartan king Cleomenes declared Cleisthenes' family accursed and
he withdrew from Athens in consequence, Isagoras was unable to exploit
his absence, even when with Spartan military support he had expelled
700 other families who, like Cleisthenes, opposed the regime backed by
the Spartans. Isagoras met resistance from the existing council when he
tried to establish a new central oligarchy of 300; like Cylon he seized
the acropolis and like Cylon he was besieged there; his Spartan allies
were allowed to leave, but he and his faction were executed.[43] Thus,

Cleisthenes seems to merit the palm for being the first Athenian (and perhaps the first Greek) to win a civil war with a programme of political reform.

The Aegean and Ionia before the Persian Wars

We have already considered the parallel between the aristocratic rivalries of Lesbos and of Attica. In general in the Aegean Islands and Ionia there were similar bids for tyranny to those in mainland Greece. However, we also hear of popular revolution against the ruling class.

In Samos the *geomoroi* or landowners apparently took power after the murder of a monarch Demoteles. They were, however, overthrown by a faction commanded by generals who had distinguished themselves previously defending the Samian colony Perinthus in the Sea of Marmora against attack by Megara about 600 BC. According to the story, the generals did not use their own soldiers but 600 Megarian prisoners whom they brought back in specially weakened chains. These killed the *geomoroi* in their council chamber.[44] Thus, a narrow oligarchy like the Bacchiadai in Corinth and the Penthilidai in Mytilene was overthrown, but a tyranny was not immediately imposed. The result was probably the broadening of the governing class and the franchise in Samos.

In Miletus some time after the fall of the monarchy there were one or possibly two similar risings against the ruling landowners, collectively known as the *Ploutis* or Wealth, by the workers, *Cheiromacha* or *Gergithai*. This strife followed the fall of the faction of the tyrants Thoas and Damasenor. These had perhaps made the initial breach in the power of the landowners without wholeheartedly espousing the cause of the poor. We are told that the working people were for a time victorious and had the children of the wealthy exiles trodden to death by oxen on threshing floors. In return the rich burned everything they could get hold of belonging to the poor, including their children, and eventually prevailed in the war. Herodotus' story of a final settlement of Milesian strife through Parian arbitrators may refer to the end of this war, since it appears that the Parians placed in power a select group of landowners. If the tradition is true, this civil strife was more bitter than any other in a mainland Greek state during this period. A precise date is difficult to establish. But one can hardly imagine such a struggle occurring without Lydian or Persian intervention during the time when Miletus was the one Greek city on the mainland of Ionia which was an independent

ally of those powers. It seems most likely that it occurred before the
time of Thrasyboulos' tyranny (c. 600 BC). The latter is mainly renowned for his ruthlessness with the wealthy and powerful which is the
more understandable if he had gained power at a time when a victorious
plutocracy was rampant. Ironically, he may have gained his tyranny
through being the *prutanis* (president) in the newly formed oligarchy
after the civil wars.[45]

The revolution by the *demos* against the oligarchy of the Basilidai
at Erythrai probably occurred in the same period and followed a similar
pattern to that at Miletus. At Cnidos the *demos* took advantage of a
dispute over the oligarchic constitution to put their weight behind one
of the nobles in the same way that the indebted supported Peisistratus.
Although by 500 BC the conflict between rich and poor in mainland
Ionia had been temporarily quelled by the imposition of pro-Persian
tyrannies, it was a struggle of this kind on Naxos in the Cyclades between the *pacheis* ('fat' or 'rich') and the *demos* which led to Milesian
and Persian intervention and thus in the end to the Ionian revolt.[46]

Tyranny in Ionia

We have little information about how tyrants came to power in this
area, except when they were imposed by the Persians. What evidence
we have suggests that they were already members of the local aristocracy or plutocracy. Although Pittacus was elected tyrant by the mass
vote of an assembly, the plotting and counter-plotting in Alcaeus'
poems seem in general to have been manoeuvres of one small aristocratic political group to overthrow another. Whether the tyrants were
popular or not, the motive power for a political change came from
within the governing class.

Polycrates, according to a scornful remark attributed by Herodotus
to a Persian courtier, seized control of Samos with a force of 15 hoplites. This may well be an exaggeration, but suggests a plot by a group
like Alcaeus' in Lesbos and the indifference of the majority of the
Samian people. Polyaenus' later account describes a massacre by Polycrates, aided by his brothers and a small group of supporters, of some
Samian citizens who had laid down their arms during the festival of
Hera. The plotters then seized the citadel called Astypalaea and the
coup was completed by military aid from Lygdamis, tyrant of Naxos.
Although I do not find convincing the view that Polycrates had a father
of the same name who was tyrant before him (surely this is the sort of
story that Herodotus would have delighted to relate, if it had been in

circulation in his time?), it seems likely that his father, called Aiakes according to Herodotus, held high office in Samos, and the tradition that the poet Anacreon began his association with him by being his tutor as a young man may be thus far valid. The story of his rise to power rules out any inheritance of tyranny, but we may assume that he had been bred to expect a post like *prutanis* in Miletus or *aisumnetes*. There is another story in Polyaenus about a seizure of tyranny in Samos by one Syloson (if authentic, perhaps an earlier member of the family of Polycrates, one of whose brothers had this name). Syloson was thought, we are told, to be well disposed to the *demos* and seized the city with the aid of sailors, while the army he was in theory commanding was camped away from the city in the temple precinct of Hera. As told, this is not a very plausible story. If it has a basis in fact, Syloson does seem to have used a broader power base than Polycrates did later.[47]

The majority of Ionian tyrants known to us during this period were either imposed or given recognition by Darius from about 517 BC onwards when his armies were operating around the east and north of the Aegean. Syloson, Polycrates' brother, was imposed on Samos in place of Maiandrios, and he was soon succeeded by Aiakes, probably his son. The latter joined in Darius' Scythian expedition about 514. On the same expedition were a number of tyrants from the Hellespontine area, also Histiaeus of Miletus (later succeeded by his son-in-law and nephew Aristagoras), Laodamas of Phocaea, Strattis of Chios and Aristagoras of Cyme. Coes of Mytilene served as a general on that expedition and was subsequently appointed tyrant as a reward, while for his services as a counsellor Lykaretos, Maiandrios' brother, was given a tyranny in Lemnos — presumably he had stayed behind and collaborated when Syloson was imposed on Samos in place of Maiandrios.[48] Other tyrants known before the Ionian revolt are Oliatus of Mylasa, Histiaeus of Termera and Cadmos of Cos. The latter, according to Herodotus, voluntarily ceded the tyranny which he had inherited from his father Scythes, probably during the Ionian revolt. He then went to Sicily, where shortly after 494 he was appointed tyrant in Zancle (Messana) by the exiled Samians who had occupied it. Many of the other tyrants seem to have been replaced by the Persians after the revolt, in spite of Mardonius' policy of establishing 'democracies' — for example Aiakes, later succeeded in Samos by Theomestor, Strattis, Lygdamis of Halicarnassus and his daughter Artemisia, and the Carian tyrants.[49]

The Persian encouragement of tyrannies within the area dependent on them conformed to their own method of government, whereby orders came down personally from the great king to his senior subordinates, whose loyalty and good service was in turn a personal due to the monarch. However, the rule of a single man was probably less abhorrent in Ionia than it was in mainland Greece. Many Ionian tyrants may have obtained office by consent, like Pittacus in Lesbos, as an *aisumnetes* or *prutanis*. Nor would their rule have provided less freedom for those outside the aristocracy than the majority of the oligarchies established as an alternative.

We may understand better the acceptability of tyranny and the bitterness of class struggles, when they did occur, by trying to glimpse the socio-economic structure of Ionia at the time. Rostovtzeff in his study of the later Pergamene economy cited as the typical Asiatic landowner the master of the household in the parable of the husbandman, who planted a vineyard, placed a hedge around it, dug a wine press in it, built a tower, gave the land out to tenants and went into another district. Large estates or a multitude of smallholdings, owned by landlords who were often absentees, and farmed by men whose status verged on serfdom, were probably the dominant feature of the agrarian economy in Ionia during the Classical as well as the Hellenistic Eras. In Xenophon's descriptions of military operations in Asia Minor we find an estate owned by a Persian Asidates, where there were many cattle and slaves, with a *tursis* (fort) in the middle, in which the master lived with his own guards. Xenophon's allies in his attack on Asidates' estate, the descendants of Gongylos of Eretria and Procles, whose ancestor was the exiled King Demaratus of Sparta, seem to have been in possession of similar estates themselves, gifted by Xerxes for services rendered during his invasion of Greece and in its aftermath.[50]

Such estates were a standard form of royal reward. The practice is most precisely attested in documents from the Hellenistic Era. Antiochus I granted to Aristodikides Petra and a total of 3,500 plethra of land in addition to what he already possessed. Similarly, Antiochus II gave to his first queen Laodice the village of Pannou Kōmē and its appropriate land, including a fortified tower house (*baris*). Another enormous estate, including villages, is that which Mnesimachos sold to the temple of Artemis at Sardis. However, large landholdings like these were no new creation of the Persian and Hellenistic monarchs, as is shown by Herodotus' story of the Lydian Pythios, whose estate was at Celainai in Phrygia. He offered Xerxes for his campaign in Greece 2,000 talents of silver and 3,993,000 gold Darics, saying that he had sufficient to live on himself in his lands and slaves.[51]

The people we have been discussing were not members of independent city-states, but there is evidence in the *Ploutis* at Miletus for a similar class of landlords, even if their holdings were on a smaller scale. The story that Herodotus tells of the Parian arbitrators, invited to Miletus to settle civil strife, making a journey through the city's territory and placing its government in the hands of the few landowners whose property was well cultivated, is indicative of the sort of men who dominated politics there. It may also mean that the Parians chose those who had been able to get co-operation and hard work out of their tenants.

One consequence of such powerful landed proprietors within the territory of city-states would have been the accentuation of feuds between members of the oligarchies, because each could count on a host of dependants without appeal to any kind of political sentiment. In some communities the pre-eminent power of a few very rich men would have tended to produce a very narrow oligarchy, such as seems to have occurred at Miletus. On the other hand, the gulf between rich and poor and the lack of representation of the majority in politics would have entailed that, when the grievances of the poor became intolerable, their methods were violent.

The Ionian Revolt

Little resistance was offered to Cyrus' general, Harpagus, when he led a Persian army to the Aegean for the first time about 540 BC. Then, after roughly half a century of submission, we find a revolt against Persia. In view of my earlier argument that Persian rule was not inherently unacceptable to the ruling class in the cities, it is important to consider this first real challenge to Persian domination, even though this was more a multi-national war than a series of internal rebellions against established government.

Herodotus' account portrays it as a disaster brought about primarily by the personal ambitions of Aristagoras and Histiaeus of Miletus. This view is supported by his description of its origins, whose basic truth we are unable to contest through lack of alternative evidence and which in my view is in essence acceptable as far as it goes, although it does not tell the whole story. The immediate cause was a quarrel between Aristagoras and Megabates, the Persian commander, on their joint expedition to place a plutocratic oligarchy in power on Naxos. We need not follow Herodotus in believing that Megabates betrayed the arrival of the expedition to the Naxians, but it is clear that Aristagoras feared his Persian colleague's hostility and an adverse report from him to Susa. However, Herodotus' account, even when modified, does not explain the behaviour of the other leading men in Ionia nor that of the people in the cities as a whole.[52]

Aristagoras, we are told, had encouragement from his father-in-law Histiaeus, who was then at Susa, and his faction at Miletus agreed with him. The leading tyrants were secretly arrested, Aristagoras laid down his own tyranny and then began a general political movement for the removal of tyrants which implied revolt against Persia. There can be little doubt that in so doing he found favour with many of the common people in the Ionian cities. They were likely to follow the lead of the aristocrats anyhow, since many would have been their dependants; furthermore, some would have had good reason to hate their tyrant (Coes of Mytilene was stoned to death), and all would have had hopes of loot in a war with wealthy Persian overlords. It is not so easy to see why Aristagoras received such support from the leading men both in Miletus and elsewhere. However, it is significant that the core of the revolt was provided by Miletus and the three major offshore islands. Miletus had a special relationship with Persia by treaty, as she had before with Lydia, while the offshore islands seem to have maintained a degree of independence, in spite of the fact that, like Miletus, they were now subject to pro-Persian tyrants.

Herodotus states that the islanders surrendered themselves to Harpagus, but he had previously remarked that they were in no danger, since the Persians had no fleet with which to threaten them. Thucydides, on the other hand, says specifically that Cyrus subjugated the cities on the mainland, and Darius afterwards subjugated the islands also through a dominance established by the Phoenician navy. According to him the Ionians maintained control over their own sea in war against the Persians for a time during the reigns of Cyrus and Cambyses. In particular, Polycrates through sea power made the islands subject to him. In Herodotus, Polycrates' despatch of ships to help Cambyses' Egyptian expedition about 525 was his own idea, and this suits Thucydides' view of his general standing. Cambyses had also at least one Lesbian ship with him then. This means that the Lesbians then regarded themselves as Persian allies, but the relationship may have been a loose one *de iure* as well as *de facto* at this point.[53]

The tyrants of Miletus, Samos and Chios are mentioned among others as present on Darius' Scythian expedition, as well as Lesbian forces under their later tyrant Coes. We do not know the terms under which these tyrants were Persian allies, but they may have been as favourable as those governing Miletus' earlier relations with Persia. Both Syloson and Coes were benefactors of Darius and received their tyrannies for this reason (in Herodotus Darius addresses Coes as 'my Lesbian guest-friend'). In particular, the islands were probably not subject to tribute until after the Ionian revolt. Herodotus' account of the tribute paid to Darius at the beginning of his reign mentions that of the Ionians and Magnesians *in Asia*. By 'Ionians' and 'in Asia' he seems to mean those on the mainland by contrast with the islanders. He later adds that further tribute came in the course of time both from islands and parts of Europe as far as Thessaly. Furthermore, Herodotus makes a Persian refer to Samos under Polycrates' rule as 'an island lying near your district', i.e. that of the satrap of Sardis. This implies that the islands were not included originally in the system of satrapies.[54]

If this interpretation of the status of the islanders is correct, we can understand how the fears of Aristagoras for his own position may have spread to other previously pro-Persian aristocrats in Miletus and other favoured cities. In their view the failure at Naxos might have led to a more decisive Persian intervention. Histiaeus is supposed to have explained his support for the revolt by alleging that the Persian king planned to settle Ionians in Phoenicia and Phoenicians in Ionia. This was an extreme exaggeration of what many Ionians genuinely would have feared – a permanent Phoenician 'naval presence' in the Aegean. This was the more plausible, since it must have been becoming clear to the Ionian leaders that the ultimate aim of Persian policy was to occupy the Greek homeland and turn the Aegean into Persian waters. The Persians were already in Macedonia, and Athens herself had been unsuccessfully negotiating an alliance with Persia in order to forestall the return of Hippias. If the Persians succeeded in conquering Greece, the pro-Persian tyrants in Ionia were unlikely to keep any independence, since they would be no longer on the borders of the Persian empire nor would their naval aid be so indispensable to the Persians. I therefore suggest that the previously pro-Persian aristocrats in the more favoured cities foresaw an end to their conveniently anomalous position of privileged semi-independence and decided to gamble on complete liberty.

The revolt seems to have temporarily unified the Greeks of Ionia, but the discrediting of Aristagoras, the hardships of the war and Persian psychological pressure led to vital defections when the insurgents' navy, largely provided by the islanders and Miletus, had to face the Phoenicians. One suspects that a great many of those who manned the fleet had little enthusiasm for their local leaders (the Chians being the distinguished exception), and their rewards from the struggle after the sack of Sardis at the beginning of the revolt had been meagre. Thus, the first important attempt by the plutocrats of Ionia to espouse a popular cause ended in failure.

The Greeks in the West

The colonies planted by the Greeks in Magna Graecia and Sicily were often either joint foundations or supplemented later by colonists from a different city to that which founded the colony. For example, Zancle, later Messana, was a settlement of pirates from Italian Cumae, which was augmented by people from Chalcis (a joint founder of Cumae) and other Euboean cities; Gela was a joint Cretan and Rhodian foundation. The political mixture in their populaces and the frequent migrations were used in Thucydides' version of a speech by Alcibiades as proof of the perpetual disunity of the cities and the disloyalty of the citizens to the community as a whole. This was an exaggeration, as the Athenians found out, but these factors must have contributed to the likelihood of *stasis*.

Our knowledge of politics in these cities, not to mention revolution, is almost non-existent over a period of almost 200 years. We hear briefly of a tyrant backed by the people at Leontini, called Panaetius; another tyrant, Theron, appears at Selinous. There was *stasis* at Syracuse in the middle of the seventh century which led to a faction called the Myletidai joining with Zancle in founding Himera. This seems to have been a conflict among the aristocracy. Later, a *stasis* in Gela enabled Gelon's ancestor to seize an important hereditary priesthood.[55]

There is more information, if mainly from late sources, about the notorious Phalaris of Agrigentum, whose reign is placed about 550 BC. He was, according to Aristotle, from the privileged classes and is supposed to have exploited his position as contractor for the temple of Zeus on the acropolis of Agrigentum. He gathered slaves and captives ostensibly as workers, fortified the acropolis in the pretext of protecting it from theft and then used his labour force to seize control of the city at a time when the populace was outside. Subsequently during a gymnastic contest outside the city he took all the arms from the citizens' houses. Although there are some familiar features in this story in the seizure of the acropolis and the disarmament of the citizens, there is also sufficient originality to make the story plausible in outline. It seems likely that this was a *coup* by a man like Polycrates or Cylon, who came from the governing class and did not enjoy wide popular support.[56] Otherwise before about 525 it is probable that politics in the Greek cities of Italy and Sicily were dominated by landowning aristocracies. Herodotus tells us that the *gamoroi* (those who shared the land) were in power in Syracuse before 485, and it is likely that a similar group, who provided the cavalry, the city's main striking force, dominated Gela before the family of Cleandros and Hippokrates seized power.[57]

About 515 the Spartan prince Dorieus arrived in the West at the head of a colonising expedition. First, he joined Croton in the war against her neighbour Sybaris, which was begun by the latter and ended in its destruction. Subsequently, he went on to Sicily and, after failing to found a colony by Mount Eryx because of resistance from Segesta and the Carthaginians, he joined in civil strife in Selinous. He based himself on Minoa, a town dependent on Selinous, and helped to expel a tyrant, Pythagoras, but when he tried to become tyrant himself, he was assassinated.[58]

Meanwhile, the followers of the philosopher Pythagoras in Croton were in trouble after the city's victory — according to a late biography of the philosopher, which may be sound enough in outline, even though the chronology is vague and the details possibly fictitious. The disciples of the sect formed a narrow oligarchy of 300. Good birth and wealth were probably a necessary qualification for admission, but not in themselves sufficient. For a noble called Cylon, we are told, became embittered when excluded. He was supported by radical demagogues who exploited popular discontent over the refusal of the oligarchy to divide up the territory of Sybaris among the citizens of Croton. This agitation is associated in the biography with the expulsion of Pythagoras. Later, c. 500-490, a popular rising led to the seizure of the city from the oligarchy by a tyrant called Cleinias, who brought back anti-Pythagorean exiles, liberated slaves, and killed or expelled the cream of the aristocracy. He was overthrown by Anaxilas, tyrant of Rhegium, but apparently a series of tyrannies followed, which weakened Croton's power and wealth.

The old Sybaris was renowned for its luxury based on agricultural prosperity, but Croton in the sixth century may not have been far behind. The cities are exemplified by their athletic heroes. Philippos, son of Boutakides, and Phayllos from Croton are attested by Herodotus, while from Sybaris we have a recently discovered dedication by Cleombrotos, son of Dexilaos. Both Philippos and Phayllos were rich enough to provide their own triremes, and Cleombrotos probably had wealth on a similar scale if he had the resources to cross the sea to compete at Olympia or Delphi. Such riches would have helped to inspire the demands for land distribution and other forms of relief among the poor, while their owners would have been tempted to seize personal power, if disputes broke out among the governing oligarchies.[59]

Gelon

The tyranny, which was created at Gela c. 505-500 by Cleandros, son of Pantareus, seems to have been imposed on a somewhat reluctant oligarchy but not to have been radical or revolutionary like Cylon's at Croton. Cleandros was assassinated, but his brother Hippokrates succeeded him, and Gelon came to the fore as a man from the aristocracy and holder of a hereditary priesthood, who nevertheless deigned to join the tyrant's bodyguard and became the master of his horse. Hippokrates conquered most of central and eastern Sicily except Syracuse, but died while besieging the Sikel stronghold Hybla. Gelon then repressed a rebellion by the people of Gela against Hippokrates' children only to seize the tyranny himself. He added Syracuse to his empire in 485, by restoring to their homeland the Syracusan landowning aristocracy, who had been expelled by the *demos* and by a class called by Herodotus Kyllyrioi and said to have been the landowners' slaves. The latter were perhaps a subject race tied to the land. By *demos* Herodotus probably means the hoplite class as well as the free poor, and we must assume that at Syracuse, as in Attica, the great landowners were still balanced by a number with middling or small properties. Nevertheless, the slaves or serfs who worked the big estates were already significant politically, as in the struggles at Miletus.[60]

The Syracusan *demos* were forced to surrender to Gelon, but they cannot have been happy about the result. Gelon transported to Syracuse the people of Camarina wholesale, one half of the people of Gela and the wealthy from the small cities of Megara Hyblaea and Euboea (the *demos* from each of these cities were sold as slaves outside Sicily). His aims in this policy seem to have been simply to maintain his tyranny and to increase the power and glory of Syracuse, which he made his own capital, granting Gela to his brother Hieron. Gelon was deliberately prepared to build up the wealthy aristocracy in Syracuse, assuming that it would support him through fear of losing its property and thus provide a counter-weight to the already large amount of poorer free citizens who had created the revolution. He also kept the wealthy under his direct supervision by forcing them to make their homes in the city.

As for the Syracusan people, they were not only loaded with a heavier aristocracy but themselves mixed with an influx of outsiders, many of whom would have been dependants of Gelon himself. The wealth of the aristocracy was no doubt tapped to fill his treasury and finance his vast fleet and army, including 20,000 hoplites and 200 warships. In all it was a tricky balancing act, since he needed to hold the loyalty of his troops with adequate rewards and charismatic leadership, while satisfying the aristocracy by providing security from external and internal attack. In this way he became indispensable. The vast coin issues, which probably date from his assumption of power at Syracuse, are testimony to the finance required to maintain this system of protection.[61]

Aristodemus

Another striking example of tyranny occurred at Cumae. According to Dionysius of Halicarnassus, whose account probably derives from local Cumaean history, Aristodemus, surnamed 'the Soft', was an aristocrat who distinguished himself while serving with the Cumaean cavalry in 524-523 against the Etruscans, Umbrians and Daunians. Thus in his status he resembled Gelon. After the battle Aristodemus was supported by the common people in a claim for the highest award for gallantry, whereas the senate supported the cavalry commander (the Cumaeans at that time seem to have been ruled by an oligarchy of aristocratic cavalry). However, when through popular pressure Aristodemus was allowed to share the supreme military honours, he returned the favour by making himself a demagogue, attacking the corruption of the wealthy and helping the poor out of his own funds.

In 505-504 Etruscans under Arruns, son of Porsenna, attacked Aricia. During this critical war Aristodemus was sent by his government in response to an Arician appeal at the head of an army and navy allegedly composed of the poorest dregs of Cumaean society, whom the government wanted to see eliminated in company with Aristodemus. He was nevertheless victorious and, after gaining the devotion of his soldiers through his military success and the distribution of the booty he had gained, he attacked and massacred the aristocracy shortly after his return home. He then formed a bodyguard and got himself elected to a kind of dictatorship (a generalship with unrestricted powers), in theory in order to supervise a redistribution of land and cancellation of debts which was to provide the framework of a democratic constitution. In fact he used his office to deprive the citizens of their arms, killing more of his opponents in the process, and to build up an elaborate bodyguard, at least 2,000 strong, drawn from 'the filthiest citizens, the greatest blackguards among the slaves and the most savage barbarians', the latter probably Samnites or Lucanians. He was finally overthrown when the sons of the murdered aristocrats grew up. We do not know precisely when this occurred, but Roman tradition depicted him as still in power about 490.[62]

As the story appears in Dionysius of Halicarnassus, it is a tyrannical epic to end all epics, echoing the stories of Orthagoras, Cypselus and Peisistratus in its early stages and later those of Phalaris and Hippias. Nevertheless, the venomous presentation of the tyrant in Cumaean tradition suggests that he did temporarily destroy the power of the aristocracy. Cancellation of debts and redistribution of land appear more commonly as bogeys in the writings of philosophers and orators than in fact. Aristodemus may have gained his reputation by being one of the few people who successfully effected such measures. He is anyhow a fine example of a tyrant brought to power through the support of the citizens under arms, including both the hoplites and the poorer citizens who rowed the ships. Although we cannot infer that the citizens deliberately elevated him to power to carry out a political programme, he is also the best example we have of a tyrant who brought about a social revolution. Like Gelon, he may have directed his political reforms to securing his own tyranny, but their outcome would have been more far reaching, affecting the subsequent history of Cumae as a republic.

Thus on the evidence we possess in Croton, Cumae and Syracuse the struggle against the landowning aristocracy seems to have been more vigorous and the poor more conscious of political possibilities than in most other areas of the Greek world. However, they were matched by aristocracies who were equally determined, and at Syracuse the tyranny founded by Gelon developed means of repression as sophisticated as those found in the traditional monarchies of the Orient.

The Suppression of Revolution

Three states in antiquity had special reputations for the permanence of their constitutions and freedom from *stasis* and tyranny – Sparta, Carthage and Rome. Of Carthage's early political history we know next to nothing until 308, when we hear of an unsuccessful *coup d'état* by Bomilcar at the time of the invasion of Africa by the Syracusan tyrant Agathocles.[63] However, the extent to which Sparta and Rome were free from political strife and the reasons for this deserve study.

Sparta

According to Thucydides, Sparta suffered from *stasis* of unparalleled length in the period which followed its settlement by the Dorians, its current inhabitants, but nevertheless it was reformed at a very early date and was always free from tyranny. The point of reformation, to which Thucydides refers, is clearly the introduction of the constitution attributed to Lycurgus, with its associated system of land distribution among the full citizens of Sparta, the 'equals' (*homoioi*). It is not the place here to discuss in detail the perennial problem of the date of this reform and the nature of the constitution and social *mores* of classical Sparta. In brief, I believe that Spartan social *mores* were the product of the gradual historical development of very primitive features like the tribal men's house (the *sussition* or *phidition*) and the removal of young boys from their mothers at herding age. But the Spartan constitution, although perhaps the majority of its elements were in themselves primitive, was radically reconstructed at the time when a major allocation of land to the 'equals' took place. As to the date of this, I prefer the view that the great *rhētra* was enacted about 700 BC, in the time of Kings Theopompus and Polydorus, after the end of the first Messenian War. At this time Sparta had available sufficient territory for a redistribution to the citizens, who had constituted the core of her victorious army, and to their associated communities, the *perioikoi*.[64]

The first Messenian War lasted 19 years, according to the poet Tyrtaeus writing two generations later. The only specific evidence that we possess of social strains resulting from it are the story of the Partheniai, the maidens' sons, supposedly the illegitimate offspring of Spartan mothers, who were detected in a conspiracy and sent to found a colony at Tarentum in 708 BC, and Aristotle's report of agitation for land distribution. I do not see anything implausible in such a demand at this early date in a society which was in many respects tribal. A belief that the ordinary Spartans had a right to some territory as a gift from the kings has indeed a resemblance to attitudes in modern African tribes. The assignment of allotments and the creation of the 'equals' solved for a long time the problem of discontent among the full citizens of Sparta at the cost of creating a threat from the vastly increased population of serfs. The Spartans already possessed 'helots' in Laconia; they now added to these the recently independent Messenians who 'worn out like asses by great burdens, through cruel necessity bear to their masters a half of all the fruits the land bears'. Thus, the Messenians were considerably worse off than the Attic hektemors.[65]

The great *rhētra* itself and the clause that is said to have been a rider added subsequently are also evidence of specifically political unrest and the measures taken to quell it. The *rhētra* gave, perhaps for the first time in Greece, a fundamental importance to decisions of an assembly (this provision is contained in a corrupt line of text, which must nevertheless mean that power should fall to the *demos*, since the gist of it is reproduced in Tyrtaeus). Originally the Spartans were probably given considerable freedom to debate and propose motions, which was curbed by the rider allowing the kings and the elders to dissolve assemblies which were producing crooked motions. In practice in Classical Sparta the ordinary members of the assembly seem rarely to have taken the initiative in making proposals. It is possible that the rider followed a period of turbulence. Polydorus, a king who was colleague to Theopompus, the victor of the first Messenian War, was assassinated by a man from 'a not ignoble family'. At all events, any unrest was sufficiently blotted out from people's memory to be almost unknown to later historians. The official version was that the word of Apollo from Delphi produced constitutional change and that this in turn created *eunomia* — a 'reformed' society in every sense of the word.[66]

There were later threats of political schism in Sparta, usually arising from discontented members of the two royal families. Dorieus went to the West when Cleomenes was preferred to him as king; Cleomenes had two serious quarrels with Demaratus, the second of which led to Demaratus' deposition through intrigue and to his departure to Persia, and Cleomenes himself soon afterwards was exiled and then brought back to die at home, when allegedly plotting in Arcadia (c. 489 BC). Pausanias' private dealings with Persia, when he was regent, almost certainly led to further strains, especially when he had been brought back to Sparta but his guilt was not proven. After his defeat of Athens, probably in 403, Lysander was accused of plotting to make the kingship elective so that he himself, currently a popular hero, would be chosen king.[67] However, the bulk of the full citizens of Sparta were to prove submissive and loyal. The constitution was generally stable with the only danger coming from men who were for a long time in important executive posts.

More serious was the threat to Spartan society as a whole from the subjected helots. Originally, this took the form of nationalist insurrection in Messenia, though there was the possibility of support from within Laconia itself. In the time of the poet Tyrtaeus — about the middle of the seventh century — the Messenians made a great effort to liberate themselves. Little is known for sure about this revolt except that the Messenians were defeated, though Tyrtaeus' elegiac couplets, composed to encourage the Spartans, roughly date the revolt by reference to the first war and describe the methods of fighting. Later accounts seem to have either downdated this revolt or introduced a further revolt nearer the year 600. Among these was the epic of Rhianos, written in the Hellenistic Era, but the heroic exploits he attributes to the Messenian hero Aristomenes are chiefly evidence of the skill with which a national myth was created after Messenia's eventual liberation.

Plato apparently believed that there was a subsequent revolt in 490, which prevented Sparta aiding Athens at Marathon (a point unknown to Herodotus), and there is a Spartan dedication at Olympia, seen by Pausanias and still partly readable, which could have been made after that war and not the great revolt in 464. The great revolt followed an earthquake which disrupted life and government in Sparta. The helots seized their opportunity and induced two of the dependent communities in Laconia (*perioikoi*) to join them. They took Mount Ithome in Messenia as their base and survived siege there for nine years, the survivors eventually surrendering on condition that they be allowed to leave the country. These were settled at Naupactus by the Athenians (who at one time had been Sparta's allies in repressing them), and later some were sent back to Messenia to wage guerilla war against the Spartans during the Peloponnesian War.[68]

This was the last major revolt before Messenia was liberated from Spartan domination in 369. However, there were conspiracies, genuine or suspected. Thucydides mentions a secret massacre of 2,000 leading helots who had been falsely promised their freedom. This occurred before 424, perhaps in the early years of the Peloponnesian War. The Spartans were in the dilemma of needing the helots, as well as the members of dependent communities (*perioikoi*) to act as second-line soldiers. In the Persian War for every one Spartan there was one from a dependent city and seven helots. In the Peloponnesian War 700 helots went with Brasidas on his successful expedition against the Athenian allies in Thrace. Shortly after Agesilaus' succession to the throne, in 398, there was a plot to seize power in Sparta instigated by one Cinadon, who was not one of the 'equals' but nevertheless in a high executive position in the Spartan government. The conspirators were few, but he believed that his plans were in accord with the feelings of all the helots, *perioikoi* and two other groups, the *neodamodeis* and *hupomeiones* — the former of these may have been helots with limited citizen rights, of whom Cinadon himself was perhaps one. This conspiracy reflected the growing importance of these groups in Sparta. By the end of the Peloponnesian War the Spartans were not only employing their helots and *perioikoi* as rank and file but had given them posts of command.[69]

It is at first sight remarkable that the Spartans avoided succumbing to such conspiracies. An explanation may be found in the secrecy with which the government conducted its affairs, so that it was difficult for the helots to recognise that they had an opportunity, and the willingness of helots to inform, which enabled conspiracies to be stifled at their outset. A further contributory factor was probably the ban on the use of coined gold and silver since its introduction to Greece about 575. This would have made it difficult for the leader of a conspiracy to buy

off someone who had detected it or to corrupt members of the government charged with security. Thucydides remarked that on the whole
Spartan policy towards the Helots was primarily determined by their
need to be on their guard, and it was this habit of watchful suspicion
and the inability of individuals, even kings or regents like Cleomenes
and Pausanias, to keep their lives private which preserved Sparta from
revolution.

Early Rome

Sparta solved her agrarian problem by conquest and the exploitation of
non-citizens as serfs. Their privileged position and a rigid system of
social discipline ensured the loyalty of ordinary citizens to those in
government, while the extra problem raised by the serfs and other
dependants was handled by security precautions which made Sparta
the nearest Greek equivalent of a modern police-state. The Romans, by
contrast, although they could be equally ruthless, for example over the
threat of tyranny, proceeded more by compromise with the political
forces which threatened the ruling class in the city.

The main tradition that we possess about the Roman kingship is of
peaceful succession down to the time of the Etruscan kings. However,
the first of these, Tarquinius Priscus, is said to have been murdered by
the children of his predecessor, Ancus Martius. Similarly, his successor,
Servius Tullius, was assassinated as part of a *coup d'état* by a descendant
of Tarquinius Priscus, and this man, Tarquinius Superbus, was in turn
driven out of his kingdom 25 years later by an armed rising in the city
which spread to the army. Stripped of their romantic and anachronistic
colouring, the basic stories seem to go back to the earliest Roman annalists, who wrote from about 200 BC onwards, but even in outline
they are of uncertain value.[70]

Further light on the political unrest and confusion during the last
years of the kingship, when Rome was under Etruscan rule, is shed by
the evidence concerning Caelius Vibenna, Mastarna and Porsenna, which
to some extent conflicts with the standard Roman version. According
to an Etruscan tradition propagated by the Emperor Claudius, Vibenna
occupied the hill in Rome to which he gave his name, Caelius (Caeles),
apparently because it was given to him in return for military support.
To cede a hill as close to the centre of the city as this to a foreign commander looks like a decision made under some duress. Vibenna probably set himself up as a 'protector'. He was later defeated on a raid into
Etruria, but, according to the Etruscan tradition, his companion Mastarna returned to his old base in Rome and took over the kingship as

Servius Tullius. This version finds some support in paintings (dating from the early Hellenistic Era) on a wall of the 'Francois' tomb at Vulci, in which the brothers Aule and Cele Vipinas and Mastarna are fighting other warriors, amongst whom is a Tarquinius, Cneve Tarchunies Rumach, being killed by Marce Camitlnas. As for Porsenna, there was a similar story that he in fact seized the city after the fall of the second Tarquinius, before the Republic was established. Even the pro-Roman version of the story admitted that he used the Janiculum hill as a base from which to keep Rome under siege and that Rome could not extricate herself from this by military force. There is no reason necessarily to prefer the poorly preserved Etruscan to the Roman version of regal history, except that the former is almost entirely suppressed by the Roman annals and they cannot explain its origin, while the Roman tradition can be interpreted as a doctored version of a humiliating record of domination by foreign adventurers.[71]

Whatever interpretation is put on the relationships between Vibenna, Mastarna, the Tarquinii and Porsenna, Rome appears to have been subject to a series of Etruscan war-lords in the last years before the establishment of the Republic. These were perhaps given a constitutional title like Tiberie Velianas, a *zilath* or praetor for life, recently revealed to us on a Punic and Etruscan inscription of about 500 BC from Pyrgi. However, they probably broke the political tradition and weakened the grip of the aristocracy in the same way that the tyrants did in the Greek world. If Roman tradition is right in ascribing to Servius Tullius that reform of the registration and organisation of the citizens, which replaced the old *curiae*, dominated by the patrician *gentes*, with the tribes and centuries of the hoplite army, then Servius Tullius was the Roman Cleisthenes. Although the patron-client ties between the landed aristocrats and the plebeians remained of great importance, the dependants probably had henceforth more choice of patron and their standing in the community did not depend on kinship. It was appropriate that annalists later represented Tullius as the demagogic tyrant, the supporter of the lowest orders in society who won favour by distributing land.[72]

The hatred felt for the tyranny at Athens was based not just on the ultimate cruelties of Hippias but on the long-fostered resentment of rival aristocrats and the infringement of national pride caused by the association of tyranny with foreign domination by Sparta and Persia. Similar factors were probably present at Rome, and they would explain why, when the Republic was first established, there was such bitter hostility to *regnum*, far more than the alleged immorality of Sextus Tarquinius deserved to arouse. In the Roman Republic the word *rex* had the overtones of the Greek term *turannos*. It was tradition that *reges* were accursed and that anyone aspiring to a *regnum* should be killed out of hand (the enactment of this measure was ascribed to the founder of the Republic, Valerius Poplicola). The measure was especially applied to those alleged to be demagogic and thus to be seeking tyrannical power. Three men, Spurius Cassius, Spurius Maelius and M. Manlius Capitolinus were remembered for having been put down for this reason. They were all at the time popular heroes, Cassius and Manlius for distinguished military services, all three for assistance to the poor by offering land or relieving those oppressed by debt. In the main accounts that we possess, which are late, they were executed according to some constitutional form, but other traditions existed, almost certainly earlier, in which they were simply killed without legal formality. The swift extinction of such men was clearly thought to be a valuable example.

There is an inconsistency between this attitude to *reges* and the portrayal of the regal period in the surviving annals of early Rome, in which only the last king was bad, and he had redeeming features. Cicero had difficulty in explaining this in his survey of early Roman constitutional history. He at one point assumes that the expulsion of Tarquinius Superbus was the result of the natural antipathy to tyranny, according to Stoic principles, which was aroused when Tarquinius' insolence made him a tyrant rather than a king. However, he later thinks that the Romans overreacted against the kings and the family of Tarquinius. Indeed, earlier still in the work he treats the beginning of the Republic as an example of a people running wild in an egalitarian orgy of popular measures.[73]

However, if the kings played mainly a constructive part in the development of Roman institutions — and there is no good reason for disbelieving all the achievements at Rome credited to them — it is difficult to see why kingship was detested, unless we assume that there was more disruption in the late regal period than the annalists depict, and that the Etruscan kings were regarded by the aristocracy as the equivalent of Greek tyrants. The Roman annalists would have played down the disruption, firstly in order to minimise the fact that Rome was prey to foreign enemies, and secondly to assert the continuity between the lawful government created by their hero-founder Romulus with that of the Republic.

In the newly liberated Rome one source of unrest, as we have seen, was the suspicion of anyone thought to be aspiring to *regnum*. Another was the division between the *patres* and the *plebs*. When Rome seized its freedom at the time of Porsenna's defeat, the leaders of the patrician *gentes* provided the bulk of the new oligarchy who took over the government of the Republic. According to the annals, the tensions between the two orders came to a head over an issue which had divided rich and poor in the Greek world — debt.[74] Procedure before the first written law code is unlikely to have been milder than it was subsequently. As we have seen (p. 27), debtors might bind themselves voluntarily to a creditor in order to pay off a debt, or might be bound in consequence of failure to pay. The measures which the plebeians, according to the annals, used to protect themselves have also been discussed earlier (p. 23). *Provocatio*, the right to protection against arbitrary violence which was later sanctioned by law, in practice developed from the plebeians calling on their fellow citizens for physical support.

If we compare the social unrest in Rome about 490 with that, for example, in Attica a hundred years before, it appears that in Rome, which was at that time a smaller and more compact state, the common people were more capable of uniting to help one another. Two factors probably contributed to this. First, wealthy plebeians, who had not attained public office, were outside the governing class and thus available to offer leadership to the plebs; secondly, the patron-client ties of the patricians seem not to have extended over a great deal of the population.

However, more than the general unity of the plebeians must be postulated, if we are to explain the form of revolt which occurred. *Secessio*, the withdrawal from the city of a section of the population, was peculiar to Rome, though there it was repeated at least once. In the first secession (494-490 BC) the plebs did not attack the patricians but occupied under arms a strong-point near the city — reported variously as the Mons Sacer, north-east of Rome, or the Aventine to the south. This was a reaction not only to the perennial pressure of debt but also, according to Dionysius, to the senate's block on the distribution of conquered territory. The occasion was provided by the use of the military levy to repress sedition by subjecting the plebs to military discipline and leading them out of Rome.[75] The levy helps to explain the nature of the revolt, even if the patricians' motives were distorted by the annalists. It is exceedingly probable that the annalists were right to show the infant Republic threatened by continual border warfare. Because the Romans spent a great deal of their time under arms, the plebeians were able to develop co-ordinated resistance to the patricians, but equally they were reluctant to make an armed revolution, since neighbouring peoples would have been only too glad to exploit Roman civil war.

The division of Roman society was probably between the patricians and their clients on the one hand, and the plebs who were independent of the patricians on the other. Although we are told that the urban poor left the city to join the rebels, and the artisans and craftsmen, who were new immigrants and lacked social protection and constitutional recognition, would have had reason for discontent, it would be wrong to see them as the core of the revolt. For the rebellion was begun by a large section of the army when it had been led out of the city, including, one must presume, many of its hoplites, as at Cumae and Syracuse. Moreover, the base taken by the army is significant. The Aventine was certainly a *pagus* and so probably was the Mons Sacer. *Pagi* were centres of rural settlement, which acted as military strongholds. The fact that the rebels chose an existing rural military centre to be, as it were, their capital suggests that they were headed by those who worked the land.

The reaction of the patricians was compromise. Although the debt laws were not changed then, and it is difficult to find good evidence of land reform, the plebeian capability of mutual defence was augmented through patrician recognition of plebeian officials and spokesmen – the tribunes of the plebs. These were chosen exclusively by the plebs, and their performance was backed by an oath taken by the rebels to treat as *sacer* (accursed and doomed to die) anyone who physically violated their persons. This 'sacrosanctity' enabled the tribune to interpose his person, when individual plebeians were threatened, and eventually was exploited to block acts of government in general. The settlement did not stop conflict. Debt, land hunger and the demand for a written law code continued to produce agitation and rioting until the Twelve Tables were drawn up by a commission of law-givers about 450 BC. Shortly afterwards intermarriage between patricians and plebeians was allowed. More plebeians appeared in state magistracies, until they were guaranteed admission to the consulship, though this did not occur till the Republic was some 140 years old. Meanwhile plebeian institutions gradually became institutions of the state as a whole.

The method used by the Roman governing class for dealing with the unrest which threatened it from below was, for the ancient world, singular and remarkable. Essentially it consisted in recognising the right of the discontented plebeians to defend themselves (this was an important constituent of *libertas*, as it was understood in the Republic). Meanwhile the patricians were slow to concede material benefits and political privileges. They were helped in this policy by Rome's vulnerability to foreign enemies. In this period the dictum 'To create unity a foreign menace is the stoutest bond' was generally true. Another factor was the possession of loyal clients, whose support they did not have to buy through political concessions. However, it is difficult to tell if these

connections were any more strong and stable than those between aristocrat and dependant in Archaic Greek societies. Most important, the
patricians remained remarkably loyal to one another. Although they
were probably prepared to admit to the senate successful military leaders
among the plebeians who were too dangerous to be left outside, they
were slow to accept any innovation which might create rifts within their
own ranks. Moreover, any suspected tyrant was swiftly eliminated. If
we take the Roman aristocracy as an object-lesson in survival, they
showed that the two necessities were the restriction of internal quarrels
and the readiness to bow temporarily before a popular storm.

Herodotus and *Stasis*

The political conflicts which I have been considering cannot be neatly
circumscribed chronologically, although in mainland Greece they cor-
respond roughly with the 'Archaic Age'. However, they have certain
common characteristics. First, the societies in which they occurred did
not have a high political culture or a securely established constitution.
Secondly, political intervention from abroad was not common nor, when
it was made, did it have a decisive influence. Thirdly, the conflicts not
only usually sprang from aristocratic initiatives, but the aims pursued
were largely those of the aristocrats themselves, popular grievances
being mainly remedied incidentally. The chief exceptions to this last
generalisation were in the West, in Syracuse before Gelon, perhaps in
Croton and Cumae, and at Rome. Thus the majority of the conflicts
took place in societies where the community was still less important
than the aristocratic family and its clients.

However commonplace *stasis* became, it evoked a vigorous reaction
from moralists like Solon and Theognis, who set the tone for the treatment of *stasis* by subsequent writers. In Herodotus' fictitious debate
about the Persian constitution oligarchy is denounced for breeding
violent private feuds, because each man wants to be supreme and to
make his own policies prevail and that is the source of conflicts (*stasies*)
and bloodshed. The modern reader may find this a crude and exaggerated view, especially in so far as it implies that simple differences
over policy generate violence and are for that reason to be avoided.
Nevertheless, it is a view put forward by an intelligent Greek in the age
of Pericles and it surely reflects what was commonly believed.

It is to a great extent illustrated by Herodotus' treatment of events
at Athens. The 'men from the plain' and the 'men by the sea' were

engaged in *stasis* (*stasiazontes*) before Peisistratus' first *coup*, and Peisistratus raised a third *stasis*, i.e. competing faction, with the aim of obtaining a tyranny. Thus *stasis* quite clearly refers to a power struggle, though not necessarily a violent one: it is only Peisistratus who decides the issue by the open use of force. Later Herodotus says that in the aftermath of the expulsion of the Peisistratidai, Cleisthenes and Isagoras were engaged in *stasis* (*estasiasan*) about power, and this was the origin of Cleisthenes' bid for popular support by proposing the reform of the tribes. The struggle only became violent through Isagoras' appeal to Sparta. That every *stasis* leads to bloodshed is a typical orator's exaggeration and should be treated with caution where it appears in Herodotus. This is not necessarily the historian's view. On the other hand he does hold that the essence of *stasis* is conflict over power: the conflict over policy between Cleisthenes and Isagoras was merely a secondary development. This too was the view of Solon's enemies, who could not take his programme at its face value but only as the foundation of a tyranny.

This appreciation of politics had ample justification in the Archaic Age in Greece. Even when an aristocratic politician was not planning a *coup d'état*, his life would have been closely tied to the preservation of his honour and status (*timē*) *vis-à-vis* both his equals and his dependants. King Arcesilas III of Cyrene refused to accept the reduction of the kingship to religious functions, prescribed by a Mantinean law-giver, and took to *stasis* with the rest of the community over royal privileges (*timai* and *gerea*). Megakles reacted vigorously to the insult inherent in Peisistratus' treatment of his daughter; Alcaeus hated Pittacus because Pittacus had humiliated him by abandoning his friendship. Any defeat in a conflict over policy was also liable to create a loss of face and was resented for this reason.[76]

The consequence of this was that if one powerful aristocrat had a major political difference with another, he would be suspected of planning his opponent's overthrow, whatever his original intentions. In this situation he would be tempted to get his blow in first, and so the suspicions were self-fulfilling. Under Athenian democracy these tensions were to abate through the sovereignty of the assembly and the fact that any threat to established political influence was mediated and, as it were, refereed by the assembly. Nevertheless, the use of the law of ostracism shows the continuation of the conflicts of the Archaic Age in a constitutional form and, even if this was not the original intention behind the law, it was to act as a safety-valve by resolving such conflicts. In cities without such developed constitutions, the conditions of the Archaic Age seem to have persisted much longer, and this was to be drastically exploited by the great powers in their struggle for empire in Greece as a whole.

Notes

1. Hdt. I.59.3; Solon, fr. 4 West, line 19; Theognis 51, 781, 1081-2; Alcaeus, LGS 128, 26; cf. 148.1.

2. Schapera, 1956, 191; Hdt. IV. 146-8, 150.2, 154-5.1, V.42.2; cf. Justin XVIII.4; Sall., *Jug.* 78.1 for the founding of Carthage and Leptis Magna after political schisms in Tyre and Sidon.

3. Arch., fr. 19 West, cf. fr. 23.20, where 't[uran] nien' has been restored and Solon, fr. 33, 19 for *turannis*. The apparently neutral term, *monarchos*, is also used by Solon (fr. 9, 3) and Theognis (52) when criticising the growth of tyranny; cf. Hdt. V.92.B.2. Among recent studies of tyranny note Andrewes, 1956; Berve, 1967; Drews, 1972; Mossé, 1969.

4. Thuc. I.13.1; Hdt. I.61.4, I.64.1, III.39.3, III.45.3; Polyaen. V.1.1, cf. I.28.2 on Theron of Selinous.

5. Ar., *Pol.* 1310b; cf. 1305a; Hdt. VI.127.3 (apparently placing Pheidon c. 600 BC); Paus. II.24.8.

6. FGH 105, F2 = OP XI.1365; Diod. VIII.24; Ar., *Pol.* 1315b, cf. 1310b. For the date see Leahy, 1955-6 and 1959; *contra* White, 1958.

7. Hdt. V.92; Nicol. Dam., FGH 90, F57 (place of exile was Cleonai in the Argolid – 57.3, demagogue – 57.4; cf. Ar., *Pol.* 1310b).

8. Hdt. I.59; Plut. Solon 29-30; *Ath. Pol.* 13.4-14.2; Ar., *Rhet.* 1357b (Peisistratus modelled his *coup* on that of Theagenes in Megara); LGS 163 (Ar., *Pol.* 1285a); Diog. Laert. I.74; LGS 130; Hdt. III.39, III.45.3, cf. I.61.4; Polyaen. I.23.2.

9. Tyrt., fr. 11 West, 21ff.; Snodgrass, 1964, 84, 196; 1965; 1980, 99 with Figs. 11-16; Lorimer, 1947, Figs. 2, 3, 8, 9, 10.

10. Ar., *Pol.* 1289b, 1297b; *Ath. Pol.* 4. Cf. Wilamowitz, 1893, I.76; Fuks, 1953, 84.

11. Hdt. V.77.2; Ar., *Pol.* 1306a; Arch., fr. 3 West; Plut., *Solon* 18.1-2; ML 13 (= ATPW 33), A7ff.; p. 66 above on Sparta. For the connection between hoplite warfare and political change see Nilsson, 1929 and (most recently and judiciously) Salmon, 1977; denied by Drews, 1972. Cartledge, 1977, for the dependence of military reform on prior political initiatives.

12. Plut., *Solon* 14.7; Alcaeus, LGS 136 (cf. Ar., *Pol.* 1316a; Lloyd-Jones, 1975); also Ar., *Pol.* 1306a for Diagoras of Eretria, who overthrew the *hippeis* some time before 500 BC.

13. Helbig, 1904; Greenhalgh, 1973, 59, 84; Anderson, 1961, 146.

14. Hdt. V.92.B.2 (on which see Forrest, 1966, 111-12); Ar., *Pol.* 1305a; Nicol. Dam., FGH 90, F57.6; Hdt. III.120.3. Drews, 1972, rightly argues that the support of hoplites for the earliest tyrants was more important militarily than politically, but he goes too far when he suggests that all early tyrants were merely ambitious men backed by professional soldiers, usually recruited from abroad.

15. Ar., *Rhet.* 1357b; Ar., *Pol.* 1305a; Plut., *Mor.* 295d, 304e. Theognis 39-68 is best related to the subsequent period of democratic arrogance.

16. Thuc. I.126.5-7; Hdt. V.71 (passing over Theagenes' aid); *Ath. Pol.* 1; Plut., *Solon* 12.1-6.

17. Periander – Ar., fr. 611, 20; Ar., *Pol.* 1313b; Nicol. Dam. FGH 90, F57.7, 58, 59.1; Peisistratus – Hdt. V.94.1, VI.39ff.; Thuc. VI.54.5; Ar., *Pol.* 1313b;

Ath. Pol. 16.2-6. Peisistratus' loans to farmers are tendentiously treated as merely a means of getting the poor out of the city and politics (*Ath. Pol.* 16.3). Rather, Peisistratus would have gained dependants of some value, as well as increasing prosperity and revenues. The earliest Athenian coinage ('Wappenmunzen') should now be dated to Peisistratus' time and the earliest 'owls' to Hippias' reign (Kraay, 1976, 55, cf. 312 and Kraay, 1964, on the purpose of the early coin issues).

18. See Asheri, 1966, 108 and 1969, 98. Classic passages in ancient authors are Plato, *Rep.* 566a-e; Dion.Hal. VII.8.1.

19. Solon, fr. 36 West, cf. fr. 4.23-5; *Ath. Pol.* 2.2, 12.4; Plut. *Solon* 13.4-5; 15.6-7.

20. Solon, fr. 36.6; Hesiod, *WD* 37ff., 341. On *horoi* see Finley, 1952, esp. Ch. 1; Fine, 1951; Stinton, 1976. On the controversy over the alienability of land see above, Chapter 1, note 55. Different approaches to this problem based on a belief in the inalienability of private land may be found; e.g. in French, 1956 and 1964, and Woodhouse, 1938.

21. Andrewes, 1971, 114; Forrest, 1966, 147; Sealey, 1976, 110. Finley, 1965, retains the notion of debt, but with examples from the Near East (cf. Mendelsohn, 1949) argues that any sort of obligation through the prior receipt of benefits might be regarded as a debt and that service might have been the form of repayment preferred by the creditor at the outset. So far I agree, but it does not follow that every peasant's descent into slavery was immediate and inevitable. In particular, there is a difference between service to a creditor and chattel-slavery (as described in Solon, fr. 36). It is hard to suppose that peasants would accept chattel-slavery at the first pinch of poverty; it is more likely that they were forced into this state after failing to fulfil obligations of service which they had voluntarily accepted or inherited. As for hektemorage, if it was an institution recognised by law (cf. Forrest, 1966, 150), it is unlikely to have followed on every loan transaction: this would have been a threat to wealthy aristocrats in temporary financial difficulty.

22. Robert, 1969, I.426ff. It must be noted, however, that at Rome men placed themselves in voluntary bondage by a process involving weighed bronze, *per aes et libram* (Varro, *Ling. Lat.* VII.105).

23. Solon, fr. 36, 13-14; *P. Cairo Zeno* 59340; *P. Mich. Zeno* (Humanistic Ser. 24), 66, cf. 67; *Brit. Mus. Pap.* VII.2011. On shepherds see Robert, 1949.

24. For the desire of creditors to have dependants see French, 1956, 23; 1964, 14. French has argued that the problem of debt arose through the transition from a pastoral economy with a low population to an agricultural economy with a higher population. However, this transition had probably already begun about 200 years earlier. One may alternatively suggest that the cause of the crisis was social — the ambitions of a recently unified and highly competitive aristocracy in Attica, which used economic power to increase its landholdings and number of dependants.

25. Debt reform — *Ath. Pol.* 6.1, 12.4; Plut., *Solon* 15.2ff. Androtion (ap. Plut., FGH 324 F34) argued that there was only relief of interest, but this cannot make sense of the removal of the *horoi*. Lack of land redistribution — Solon, fr. 33 West, 13ff.; Plut., *Solon* 16.1, 22.1; *Ath. Pol.* 11.2, 12.3. Thetes — Plut., *Solon* 18.2; *Ath. Pol.* 7.3-4.

26. Terminology — fr. 5 West and see below, Chapter 3, pp. 92-5; Solon's views — fr. 4, 5, 6, 36, 37.

27. *Ath. Pol.* 28.2; cf. SGDI 1703.10, 1951, 2145.13, 2172.10; *Syll.* 841. 14ff., 843.

28. Solon, fr. 1. 71ff., 4.5-22; 9 West.

29. *Ath. Pol.* 13.2, cf. fr. 3 (alleged original division of people into *georgoi* (farmers) and *demiourgoi*), 7.3, 26.2 (limitation of archonship); Forrest, 1966,

166; Sealey, 1967, 30, 39.

30. Hdt. I.59.3; Plut., *Solon* 13.2; *Ath. Pol.* 13.4; Peisistratus' home – Plut., *Solon* 10.3. Hopper, 1961, provides the fullest survey of the three factions, but is too sceptical in rejecting the titles in Herodotus as an invention of his. Hopper's own scheme is no more convincing, viz. a conservative pro-Megarian aristocratic faction under Lykourgos ('the Plain'), an imperialist faction under Megakles ('the Coast') and a new faction backed by the very poor ('the Hill'). See now Traill, 1978, for evidence that *Diakris* was the name of the inland section of the Leontis tribe, probably between Parnes and the highlands running north from Pentelikon to the Boeotian border.

31. Poor – *Ath. Pol.* 13.5; Plut., *Solon* 29.1, 30.4. Movement of aristocrats – Hdt. VI.35.2, Plut., *Solon* 10.3; cf. Ferguson, 1938, on the scattering of the *genos* Salaminioi.

32. Hdt. I.59-60; Thuc. VI.54.5-6; *Ath. Pol.* 13.3-4. Possible allusions to this return on vases – Boardman, 1972; similar scene as propaganda on Polyneikes' shield, Aesch., *Septem* 644-8.

33. Hdt. I.61-4; *Ath. Pol.* 15, 17.4.

34. Thuc. VI.54.5-6; Hdt. I.59.5-6; *Ath. Pol.* 16. Cf. Ar., *Pol.* 1313b on the Orthagorids and Cypselids. Cf. note 17 above.

35. Ar., *Pol.* 1311b; Diog. Laert. I.74; Hdt. V.95; Strabo XIII.1.38 (599); LGS 123, 130, 148, 151, 184. Cf. Page, 1955.

36. Myrsilos and Pittacus – LGS 152, 117, 122, 163; Strabo XIII.2.3(617); Diog. Laert. I.81. *Aisumnetai* – cf. Ar., *Pol.* 1295a, fr. 524; Callimachus, fr. 102 Pfeiffer. Alcaeus – LGS 116, 127. 13ff., 128, 141, 165; OP XXIX.2506, fr. 98.

37. Xenophanes, DK 21.B3; LGS 118.11-13, cf. 107.12ff.

38. LGS 461, 462, 443, 446.

39. Thuc. VI.53.3-59; Hdt. V.55, 62.1-2; *Ath. Pol.* 18-19.3, 20.5 (LGS 460) – on Cedon. Popular tradition – *Parian Marble* (FGH 239) A.45; LGS 447-50. Statue group – Brunnsäker, 1955; Shefton, 1960. Free meals – Hill B.71; Dein. 1.101. See especially Forrest, 1969, on the chronology and Jacoby, 1949, 152-68 on the tradition.

40. Thuc. VI.56-8, esp. 56.2, 58.2. *Ath. Pol.* 18.4 attempts to correct Thucydides, alleging that the hoplites did not carry their weapons in the procession at this time, but neither this nor other discrepancies (e.g. the view that Hippias was on the Acropolis) are convincing.

41. Dover, HCT IV.322; Thuc. VI.57.2 on Hippias; Hdt. V.55ff., APF 12267 on lineage of tyrant-slayers (though Aristogeiton was less wealthy than Harmodius – Thuc. VI.54.2).

42. Hdt. V.62.2-63.1, 66.1-2; *Ath. Pol.* 19.3-4. Cf. Hdt. III.70.3 for *prosetairizetai*, VI.128.2 with ML 6a and APF 295 on Teisandros; Forrest, 1969, on variants in the tradition.

43. Hdt. V.72.1-4; *Ath. Pol.* 20.1-4.

44. Plut., *Mor.* 303e.

45. Plut., *Mor.* 298c; Athen. XII.524a; Hdt. V.28-9. On Thrasyboulos see Hdt. I.20, V.92.z; Ar., *Pol.* 1284a, 1311a, cf. 1305a. The standard view (Hiller, RE XV.1593-4) places the revolts of the Gergithes in the sixth century after the death of Thrasyboulos, then the Parian arbitration and a new oligarchy which gave way to Histiaeus' pro-Persian tyranny. In favour of the view expressed are its implications that Miletus was stable during the time of danger from Croesus and Cyrus, that Parian arbitration came during Archilochus' lifetime, when Paros was of some consequence, and that the two generations of bitter civil strife came before Thrasyboulos cut the aristocrats down to size.

46. Ar., *Pol.* 1305b; cf. Hippias of Erythrai (FGH 421 F1) for the earlier overthrow of the monarchy at Erythrai; *Pol.* 1306b for a similar revolution against an

oligarchy at Chios; Hdt. V.30 for Naxos.

47. Hdt. III.120.2; Polyaen. I.23.2; elder Polycrates – Suda, s.v. Ibykos; elder Syloson – Polyaen. VI.45; Anacreon – LGS 344. See in general Berve, 1967, I.107, II.589; for the theory of the elder Polycrates Barron, 1964, criticised by West, 1970; White, 1954, for an earlier start to the tyranny than the reign of Cambyses, i.e. 530 BC (Thuc. I.13.6).

48. Hdt. III.149, IV.138.2 (cf. ML 16), IV.97.2, 138.2, V.11, 27.2, 30.2; Berve, 1967, I.85, II.569.

49. Hdt. V.37.1, VII. 164 (cf. Thuc. VI.4.5-6). Democracy – Hdt. VI.43.3; later tyrannies – VI.25, VII.98-9, 195, VIII.132, IX.90; cf. Plut., Mor. 859c (Aristogenes of Miletus and Symmachos of Thasos).

50. Xen., Anab. II.1.3, VII.8.9ff.; Hell. III.1.6, 25, 4.15-16, Rostovtzeff, 1923, 372-5; Lewis, 1977, 53-4. Cf. on archaic Smyrna, Cook, 1958-9, 17ff. and on the fortified houses later attested at Teos, Hunt, 1947.

51. Hdt. VII.27-8; Welles, nos. 10-13, 18; W. Buckler and D. Robinson, Sardis VII. no. 1.

52. Origin – Hdt. V.30ff.; H's hostility, V.28, 97.3 – criticised by Plutarch (Mor. 861a ff.). Lang, 1968, details H's bias against Aristagoras and Histiaeus, but her own reconstruction tends to become arbitrary and discards too much in H.

53. Thuc. I.16; Hdt. I.143.1, 169.2, III.13.1, 44.1-2.

54. Tyrants – Hdt. IV.97, 137-8; tribute – III.90.1, 96.1, 120.3 (for the meaning of 'in Asia' see I.27.1, V.30.5; III.122.2 contrasts Ionia and the islands). Dareius himself in the inscription, 'Persepolis E', of c. 512-500 makes no clear reference to the islanders (R.M. Kent, Remains of Old Persian, 136).

55. Thuc. VI.4, 5, 17.2; Ar., Pol. 1303b, 1310b, 1316a; Polyaen. I.28.2; Hdt. VII.153; Diod. XIII.62.4.

56. Polyaen. V.1-4; Plut., Mor. 821e; Ar., Pol. 1310b; Suda, s.v. Phalaris; Berve I.129, II.593. For the folklore about his cruelty and the bull see Pindar, Pyth. I.95ff.; Diod. IX.18-19, XIII.90.4-5; Pol. XII.25.1ff. Schol. Pind., Ol. III.68 says that Phalaris was overthrown by Telemachos, Theron's great grandfather, but this is contradicted ibid. II.82.

57. Hdt. VII.155.2, 154.2; Ar., Pol. 1316a. A cavalryman is one of the types on fifth-century Gelan coins. On the class structure in Magna Graecia in this period see Dunbabin, 1948, 57, 111; Lepore, 1969.

58. Hdt. V.44-6, VI.21; Diod. X.23, XII.9.2ff., XI.90.3 (for the date).

59. Iamblichus, Vita Pyth. 255ff. (some contamination with later events); Diod. X.11.1; Dion. Hal., Ant. Rom. XX.7.1 (19.4); von Fritz, 1940. Luxury – Hdt. VI.127.1; Timaeus, FGH 566, F50 (Athen. 12.519-20); Diod. VIII.18-20; cavalry fighting – Ar., fr. 583; athletic heroes – Hdt. V.47; VIII.47, Guarducci, Rend. Acc. Lincei. Sc. Mor., 1965, 342ff.

60. Hdt. VII.154ff.; Berve, 1967, I.137, II.597. Serfs – cf. Ar., fr. 586; landowners – Pindar, Ol. VI, esp. 6.

61. Transportation – Hdt. VII.156.2-3; Thuc. VI.4.2. The coin issues in Gelon's lifetime remain vast, even if we accept the lower dating of the silver dekadrachms proposed by Kraay (1968, 17ff., cf. the criticisms of R. Williams, NC, 1972, 1 and Kraay's reply, ibid. 13). I cannot follow Berve (1967, I.143) in believing that Gelon was able to dispense with internal revenue from Syracuse. For Gelon's victory over the Carthaginians at Himera see Diod. XI.21ff.; ML 28; and on his successors, Diod. XI.38, 49, 51, 67; Ar., Pol. 1313b, 1315b.

62. Dion. Hal., Ant. Rom. 7.3-12; Plut., Mor. 261e-262d; Diod. VII.10; Livy II.14.5. On the historiography of Cumae see Alföldi, 1964, 56; Cornell, 1974, 206; Cozzoli, 1965. There is no literary evidence that Aristodemus used mercenaries and, according to Rutter, 1980, it is unlikely that Cumae began to issue coins until c. 475 BC.

63. Ar., *Pol.* 1272b, 1316b; Diod. XX.44.1-6. However, see Ar., *Pol.* 1307a; Justin XIX.2 for factional struggles within the aristocracy.

64. Thuc. I.18; social *mores* — Hdt. I.65.5; Ar., *Pol.* 1272a; Plut., *Lyc.* 12, 16.7ff.; date of *rhetra* (Plut., *Lyc.* 6) — Forrest, 1967, *contra* e.g. Toynbee, 1969, 221; Kiechle, 1963, 184.

65. Tyrtaeus, fr. 5, 6, 7 West; Ar., *Pol.* 1306b-7a; Plut., *Lyc.* 8; Strabo VI.3.2-3(278); ATPW 9 and 12. Cf. Gluckman, 1967, 36ff.

66. *Rhetra* — Tyrt., fr. 4; Plut., *Lyc.* 6.1-8 (translation and discussion in Forrest, 1968, 41ff.); later restrictions on assembly — Ar., *Pol.* 1273a; Polydorus — Paus. III.3.3.

67. Hdt. V.75.1, VI.61ff., 74; Thuc. I.128ff.; Diod. XIV.13.1-8, cf. Plut., *Lyc.* 24-6 (dating this less convincingly c. 395 BC).

68. Early helot revolts — Tyrt., fr. 5; Paus. IV.14.6-24.4; Plato, *Laws* 692d, 698d-e; ML 22; great revolt — Thuc. I.101.2ff., 103.1, IV.41.2-3 (cf. Reece, 1962, for the date); four revolts — Strabo VIII.4.10(362). Rhianos — FGH IIIa, 109ff. (no. 265); Wade-Gery, 1966; OP XXX 2522, XXXIX 2883. Status of helots — Cartledge, 1979, 160ff.

69. Thuc. IV.80.3-5; Hdt. IX.11.3, 28.2; Xen., *Hell.* III.3.4ff. (cf. V.2.24, 3.9; Thuc. VIII.6.4, 22.2; Cartledge, 1979, 178ff. on *perioikoi* and their relatively favoured standing).

70. Livy I.40, 47-8, 59-60; Dion. Hal., *Ant. Rom.* III.73, IV.38ff., 67ff.; Ogilvie, 1965, 226.

71. Mastarna — Vibenna, Tac., *Ann.* IV.65.1; *ILS* 212, Col.I.16ff.; Festus, 486-7L; Radke, RE 2.VII.2.2454ff.; Alföldi, 1965, 212ff. with plates 8-12; Cornell, 1975; Harris, 1971, 10ff. Porsenna — Tac., *Hist.* III.72; Livy II.11ff.; Dion. Hal. V.22, 27ff., 35.1; Alföldi, 1964, 72ff.; Ogilvie, 1976, 88ff.

72. Livy I.43, 46.1, 47.11; Dion. Hal. IV.16ff.; Festus 100L; Last, 1945, and on Pyrgi, Heurgon, 1966.

73. *Rex* and the three demagogues — Lintott, 1970; Cic., *Rep.* I.62.2, II.45-6, 52-3.

74. Reviews of patrician-plebeian problem in Momigliano, 1963; Ogilvie, 1976, 56ff.; see also Richard, 1978; Guarino, 1978.

75. Livy II.28-32; Dion. Hal. VI.33-47; Cic., *Rep.* II.58; Asc. 76-7C; Festus 424L. The standard term for revolt in Latin was *se(d)itio*, a synonym for *secessio*.

76. Hdt. III.82.3-4, cf. I.59.3, V.66.2, IV.162.2, I.61.2; LGS 127, 141. On Arkesilas cf. Mitchell, 1966.

3 IMPERIALISM AND THE CONFLICT OVER CONSTITUTIONS

For the violence discussed in Chapter 2 the term 'archaic' is appropriate, not only because of the conventional name of the period in which it occurred. Both the actions themselves and the ambitions which inspired them were usually small. Attempts to change by revolution the social system were comparatively rare – in the east apparently at Miletus and perhaps on Samos and Naxos, in the west at Syracuse, Croton, Cumae and Rome. Generally *stasis* was the business of the aristocracy and indeed one of their characteristic forms of behaviour.

Just as there is a considerable chronological overlap between this chapter and the last, so there persists a similarity in the type of phenomenon discussed. In the Classical Period of the city-state the centre of any *stasis* was for the most part a small group of powerful men at loggerheads with one or more other groups. However, these struggles within the governing class were complicated by a number of other factors. First, most cities by the middle of the fifth century BC had established constitutions and written law codes, often acquired after the fall of dynasties of tyrants. This affected the form which conflicts took, since those seeking power had to get control of the constitutional organs and, if necessary, manipulate the constitution itself in order to legitimise and secure their ascendancy. This had even been necessary for the Peisistratids in the sixth century because of the prior existence of Solon's laws.

Secondly, when constitutional regimes had become either broadly based oligarchies or democracies with thousands of enfranchised citizens, greater political consciousness arose among the common people, even if they had not been active in asserting their political rights earlier. In cities controlled by a narrow oligarchy or tyranny the use of hoplite armies and naval forces requiring the services of a large proportion of the citizen body would foster this awareness among the people, and it would be reinforced by contact with successful democratic states, in particular Athens.

Thirdly, foreign intervention became of paramount importance both in the stimulation of *stasis* and its resolution in favour of one or other faction. In the Archaic Age, as we have seen, many aspirants to tyranny – Cylon, Peisistratus and Polycrates, for example – received men and money from abroad. But this was usually a personal favour, whether the grant came from a community or individual, not an element in a long-term foreign policy, the exception being the tyrants supported by Persia. Moreover, those in power in Greek cities were frequently linked by intermarriage or guest-friendship and had a common interest in maintaining the *status quo*. Nevertheless, systematic foreign intervention in the internal politics of cities was begun by Sparta and Persia before 500.

Then, in the Classical Period, Sparta, Athens and later Thebes attempted to propagate their favoured type of constitutions. This may be understood in part as a convenient method of expansion abroad by the great powers. Cities were difficult to capture by siege through lack of technology, and difficult to dominate once captured. The common use of political subversion also seems to reflect the more thoroughgoing approach to inter-city war which characterised the fifth century and culminated in the Peloponnesian War. Warfare was no longer merely an extension of the cattle raid and the border confrontation. However, the ideological element cannot be denied. Both Athens and Sparta believed fervently in the excellence of their own political arrangements. Furthermore, the encouragement among neighbours of a government like one's own was, then as now, a defensive measure, rendering attacks on one's own constitution less likely. This led to a vicious spiral. The readiness of foreign powers to assist gave hope to would-be revolutionaries, while the prevalence of *stasis* and outside intervention made the mutual suspicions of cities more acute, so that the great powers intensified their efforts to maintain their own security by acquiring and exploiting subject-allies.[1]

In this chapter I will consider the exploitation of *stasis* by the major powers in Greece down to the end of the Peloponnesian War. The Spartans were the pace-makers, but their technique was originally limited to the direct application of military force, and they apparently found it difficult to work from inside a foreign city in co-operation with their own partisans. This may to some extent be explained by the negative motives of the Spartans: their foreign policy was primarily designed to cut down the danger to themselves from cities in opposition to them. The techniques of intervention practised by Athens were chiefly inspired by the need to hold the Delian League together under her leadership. The Athenians sought to ensure that their own friends were in power and gave them military backing, if there was a danger of the city's defection. However, from the middle of the fifth century this was associated with the encouragement of democracy, and in the years before the great Peloponnesian War this programme became deliberately contrasted with that of Sparta.

The Peloponnesian War provided the maximum opportunity for seducing cities from their existing allegiances by supporting factions and encouraging revolutions, where expedient, while conversely it created the greatest strains in the effort to retain existing allies. Some Spartans learnt how to encourage revolution and defection by diplomacy. The tenuousness of the ideological link between Athens and her allied democracies was exposed, though for a long time these tended 'to keep tight hold of nurse for fear of meeting something worse'. Ultimately, in face of strong Spartan military pressure Athens could not retain her allies' support and her pretensions received the *coup de grâce* when she herself succumbed to oligarchic revolution.

The First Steps

In the last two decades of the sixth century Darius had brought the Ionian islands into his sphere of influence (even if he did not exact tribute) by supporting local tyrants there, just as he supported kings elsewhere in his empire, e.g. Cyprus and Cilicia. After the Ionian Revolt Mardonius is said to have changed this policy and established *demokratiai* throughout Ionia, perhaps in truth broad oligarchies, although in fact many tyrants remained (p. 57). From that time onwards subjection by political manipulation became the rule among the Greek cities on and near the Asian seaboard. The Persian satraps after the expeditions against Greece rarely had the power to ensure their subjection by purely military means. Equally, Athens and Sparta often encouraged the resistance of the cities to Persia by regulating their constitutions.

However, political intervention by Greeks in foreign cities was not a lesson learnt from Persia alone. For Sparta had already begun to impose governments abroad in the sixth century. We have already considered the best-known example of this, the deposition of the Peisistratidai, from the Athenian point of view (p. 52). The Spartans undertook this on the instigation of a corrupt Delphic oracle. Later their king Cleomenes supported Isagoras when the latter was probably attempting to restore a constitution with a franchise limited to men who were Athenians by birth. In particular he planned to secure a dominating position in the constitution for Isagoras' own partisans, who were to form a council of 300. After this failed through popular resistance inspired by Cleisthenes' promised reforms and because Cleomenes' own force was inadequate, Cleomenes returned with an army from Sparta and her allies to establish Isagoras as tyrant, but he could not complete the operation because of the opposition of the Corinthians and Demaratus, his fellow king. Later still, he planned to restore Hippias, but this project was unanimously defeated in the assembly of the Peloponnesian League, the Corinthians once again leading the opposition.[2]

It is clear that Cleomenes, though no doubt opposed to the kind of democratic reforms proposed by Cleisthenes, was eager above all to get his own man or men in power at Athens, whatever form the constitution took. Why then remove the Peisistratidai, who were *xenoi* (guest-friends)? First, we should not underestimate the Spartan respect for Delphi. Their anger, when they discovered that the oracle had been corrupted, shows its importance for their decision.[3] It has also been argued that they were suspicious of the Peisistratidai as potential medisers. Certainly, the marriage of Hippias' daughter to the tyrant of Lampsacus, who was a friend of King Darius, provided the basis for Athenian contact with Persia. Yet, if this had been a decisive argument for Spartan action in 510, it is hard to see how Cleomenes could summon Hippias back from Sigeum on the Hellespont after about eight years of proximity to the Persians.[4] It seems more likely that the Spartans, stimulated by the Delphic Oracle, realised that the position of the Peisistratidai was becoming untenable after the assassination of Hipparchus and the guerilla warfare of the Alkmeonidai, and decided that they should be Athens' liberators: thus, they would be the guarantors of the new regime rather than the Alkmeonidai, represented by Cleisthenes, grandson of the anti-Dorian tyrant of Sicyon. Their subsequent bitterness, when they realised that they had been the tools of the Alkmeonidai, is understandable.

Two features of Cleomenes' relations with Athenian leaders lead us to a broader consideration of Spartan foreign policy — the Sicyonian connection of their opponent Cleisthenes, and the explanation that Herodotus attributes to the Corinthians for refusing to support the re-installation of Hippias as tyrant. Cleisthenes of Sicyon had tried to minimise the importance of the Dorian racial element in his city during a conflict with Argos, by giving humiliating names to the three Dorian tribes and renaming his own non-Dorian tribe the 'leaders of the people'. According to a papyrus fragment, the tyranny of a successor of his, called Aeschines, was among those overthrown by Cleomenes' father Anaxandridas and the ephor Chilon (probably between 570 and 530 BC). If we accept the tradition at least that the Spartans overthrew the Sicyonian tyranny, we know nothing about how and why. The fact that Cleisthenes' anti-Dorian reforms lasted 60 years — at least until c. 530 and more probably until c. 510 BC — may be explained by Sparta's reluctance to change anything which created hostility to Argos.[5]

According to the Corinthian speaker in Herodotus, Sparta had herself avoided tyranny and took the most formidable precautions against suffering it. It would have been a complete anomaly if Sparta guarded against this at home but imposed it on her allies. The speaker says nothing about Sparta eliminating tyranny overseas. However, Herodotus described earlier a Spartan naval expedition against Polycrates of Samos c. 525 BC. This account was criticised by Plutarch in his essay *On Herodotus' Malice* for failing to make clear that Sparta was traditionally *misoturannos*, a tyrant-hater. In support of his criticism Plutarch listed other tyrannies overthrown by Sparta — the Cypselids from Corinth and Ambracia, Lygdamis from Naxos (the friend of Peisistratus), the Peisistratids, Aeschines of Sicyon, Symmachos of Thasos, Aulis of Phocis, Aristogenes of Miletus, Aristomedes and Angelos deposed in Thessaly by King Leotychidas. The liberation of the Thessalians from the Aleuadai family probably occurred during Leotychidas' last expedition as king c. 478 BC before he was deposed for corruption. Symmachos, Aristogenes and perhaps Aulis seem also to have been pro-Persian tyrants expelled as a result of the Greek victories in 479. The others belong to the sixth century and show that Sparta's operations at Athens and Sicyon had other parallels.[6]

How should we interpret Spartan policy? In the first place it seems likely that before 500 BC the Spartans acted either in response to calls for help, such as that of Polycrates' opponents from Samos, or in consequence of existing resistance to tyranny, as at Athens. In modern terminology they were aiding 'wars of liberation'. Interesting in this context are their claims to represent the supposedly aboriginal non-Dorian peoples, as well as the Dorian. Cleomenes told the priestess on the Athenian acropolis, 'I am no Dorian, but an Achaean,' and the Spartans were eager to obtain the relics of pre-Dorian heroes,· Orestes at Tegea, and his son, Teisamenos, at Helike in Achaia. This policy may have been adopted to contrast Sparta with Dorian Argos; it also was better suited to leadership outside the Peloponnese.[7] However, to judge from their policy with Athens, their main aim was to extend their own foreign influence, and the expulsion of a tyrant was not an end in itself but an effective means to secure a government friendly to Sparta in other cities. As a result Corinth, Sicyon and probably Ambracia became members of the Spartan alliance. Certainly, there was ideological opposition to any movement towards tyranny within Sparta, but it is doubtful how far foreign tyrannies were regarded as threats to the Spartan constitution in this period. Although Theagenes of Megara and Lygdamis of Naxos assisted *coups d'état* in Athens and Samos, on the whole the tyrants in early Greece pursued what is now called a policy of non-involvement except with their immediate neighbours, as Thucydides noted. For her part, Sparta did not seem as suspicious of tyrannies before the Persian Wars as she was afterwards of democracies allied with Athens. When Maiandrios, Polycrates' successor expelled by Darius, came to Sparta for help, he was entertained for a time and not immediately sent away.[8] After the Persian invasion of Greece, however, Sparta took a harder line: pro-Persian tyrants were eliminated, evidently as a reprisal and because they could provide a base for a new Persian threat.

Sparta would have been happy to have become the protector of Athens before 500 BC and so bring the Isthmus of Corinth and the Saronic Gulf entirely under her influence. In fact, the promotion of a revolution brought uncomfortable results. The Athenian *demos* was most ungrateful. The Athenians had to fight for their liberty, not directly against a major Peloponnesian army, but against Boeotia, Chalcis and Aegina, and we find early evidence that they had learnt from Sparta to use political intervention as a weapon in inter-city relations. After defeating Chalcis, they settled 4,000 Athenian allotment-holders (*klerouchoi*) on land taken from the 'fat men', the aristocratic 'horsebreeders'. Thus, the power of the old Chalcidian aristocracy was broken, and the Athenians had the power to intervene decisively in Chalcidian affairs. Later, probably c. 489 after Marathon, they attempted to take reprisals on the Aeginetans for their seizure of a ship on a religious embassy and supported an exiled Aeginetan Nikodromos in a democratic *coup*. This failed, because their fleet did not arrive soon enough after Nikodromos' seizure of the old acropolis and the 'fat men' of Aegina were strong enough to suppress the *demos*, that is, in this context, the faction supporting Nikodromos and democratic institutions.[9] These Athenian actions were the first experiments which pointed the way to a more systematic and aggressive foreign policy after the Persian wars and the development of the Athenian navy.

Sparta, Argos and the Peloponnese

We learn more about the extent of Spartan intervention in other states from her relations with her enemy Argos and other cities in the Peloponnese which were nominally her allies in the first half of the fifth century. In 479 the Persian general Mardonios used as a soothsayer a distinguished citizen of Elis, Hegesistratos, who had been arrested and condemned to death by the Spartans as a kind of resistance leader. He had escaped from prison and imminent execution by cutting off his foot (which was held in stocks) and had taken refuge in Arcadia at Tegea, which was not at that time loyal to Sparta. This period of disloyalty probably began shortly after 490. At that time King Demaratus made Elis his first stop on his journey into self-imposed exile, while Cleomenes, who also fled Sparta after the discovery of his corrupt methods, was alleged to be plotting against his country in Arcadia and had to be brought back to Sparta. Deserters from Arcadia joined Xerxes after Thermopylae in 480, and the following year the allegiance of Mantinea and Elis was still half hearted. Their contingents arrived late at Plataea and on returning home they sent their generals into exile. These scraps of information indicate both Spartan readiness to intervene in her allies' domestic politics and the hostility this aroused.[10]

Sparta and Argos had contested supremacy in the eastern and central Peloponnese since the early seventh century. For a time this contest was resolved by formal battles over the borderland between them called Thyrea, whose result decided the current political ranking without entailing major loss of territory. This procedure was abandoned in about 494 when Cleomenes led a successful naval invasion of the Argolid and won a crushing victory at Sepeia, killing 6,000 Argives. He was subsequently accused by political opponents at home of missing an opportunity of capturing the town itself. The communities of the Argolid seem to have formed at that time a confederation under the leadership of Argos itself. Cleomenes' victory allowed Mycenai and Tiryns to secede, and they showed their gratitude to Sparta by providing contingents for the war against Persia in 480 and 479, while Argos was a pro-Persian non-belligerent.[11]

Apart from the acquisition of these allies in the Argolid, it is remarkable how little Sparta exploited her victory and the subsequent political confusion. According to Herodotus the slaves seized control of Argos until the next generation of Argives grew up. This report cannot be true as it stands. About five years later, the Aeginetans, at war with Athens after the failure of the democratic *coup d'état*, did not hesitate to summon Argive support on the basis of their old alliance. The Argives refused, but only on the grounds that in 494 Aeginetan ships had been empressed by Cleomenes to join in the landing in the Argolid. The oligarchic Aeginetan regime clearly did not think that it was dealing with a new and dangerous revolutionary government or summoning soldiers whose presence might stimulate political unrest. In fact 1,000 volunteers came from Argos to their aid, presumably hoplites. Some may have been dissatisfied with the new regime, but those who survived the war returned home. The account given by Aristotle and Plutarch of the aftermath of Sepeia is more plausible. The Argives admitted to citizenship *perioikoi* — most probably the serfs who farmed the land around, not members of neighbouring cities. These newly admitted citizens were no more favourable to Sparta than the kindred and friends of those killed at Sepeia. The city not only refused to assist the Greeks who resisted Persia under Spartan leadership, but apparently negotiated with Mardonius in the winter of 480-479 about preventing the Spartan army reaching the Isthmus.[12]

The political complexion of the new regime is likely to have been democratic in the sense that it would have been based on an assembly with generous qualifications for participation. Otherwise it would have been difficult to recruit new citizens after 494. The Olympic victories of a publicly owned horse and a publicly owned four-horse chariot from Argos in 480 and 472 respectively do not prove the existence of a democracy (in spite of the adjective *dēmosios*), but they do exclude a narrow oligarchy dominated by aristocrats who would enter for the Olympics as individuals. Another pointer is a decree with a democratic prescript conferring *proxenia* (the status of representative of the city in a foreign community) on a man from Oinos (who was in fact a *perioikos* dependent on Sparta), which can plausibly be ascribed to the first half of the fifth century on epigraphic grounds. Themistocles, intending that the regime should be a counter-balance to Sparta, showed it favour in the Amphiktyonic council. It was perhaps through sympathy with the political system there that he chose Argos as his first place of exile. Argos' official relations with the Athenian democracy were also apparently good, in so far as the Argives would not offer him protection from arrest about 470 BC.[13]

In the early 460s Argos supported the Tegeates in an unsuccessful battle against Sparta at Tegea, and at home campaigned against Mycenae with the support of Tegea and Cleonai — an operation which contributed at the same time to the weakening of Spartan influence and the unification of the Argolid. Subsequently the sons of those who fell at Sepeia, called the *epigonoi*, took back control of Argos, expelling the 'slaves'. Thus, there was not only a change of leadership but a purge of the citizen body. The expelled immigrant families took over Tiryns by force, but eventually Tiryns was subjected to Argos and so were three other towns in the Argolid. Only Cleonai retained some independence. The *epigonoi* pursued to a successful conclusion the policy of reuniting the Argolid planned by the regime that they had ousted. Nor did the internal struggle in Argos affect the constitution. More aristocrats may have now taken the lead in politics, having grown to maturity since Sepeia, but the government was probably, as before, based on a large assembly with ultimate sovereignty. According to Diodorus the Spartans failed to back Mycenae against Argos through the pressure of other wars and the famous earthquake about 465 BC which precipitated the great helot revolt. One of these wars was certainly that waged against the Arcadian peoples, except Mantinea, about the time of the revolt and decided by the Spartan victory at Dipaea. Although Argos failed to support the Arcadians here as at Tegea, the *epigonoi* were not surprisingly as hostile to Sparta as the immigrants and survivors of Sepeia. They negotiated with Persia and in 460-459 allied with Athens.[14]

Although Argos did not gain a great military victory over Sparta after Sepeia, she remained a threat, which Sparta failed to eliminate by war or diplomacy. Before 417 Sparta was unable to get the support of a faction inside the city itself. Instead she seems to have unintentionally strengthened the development of Argive democracy and inspired the democracy to unify the Argolid in a tighter form of subjection in order to gain security against her. In Elis about 460 a similar unification seems to have taken place, whose success was celebrated by the construction of the temple of Olympian Zeus, and it was perhaps at the same time that democratic institutions were instituted at Elis.[15] The story of Argos and the evidence we have of disaffection in other Spartan allies confirm what is implicit in Cleomenes' failure in Athens. The Spartans, although pathfinders in the pursuit of hegemony through the support of political movements in other states, were for a long time injudicious and ineffective, as soon as it was no longer a matter of fighting battles. It was only during the course of their major contest with Athens, the Peloponnesian War, that they came to pay as much attention to diplomacy as to brute force.

Thucydides and *Stasis*

The most important subjects for one studying the interrelation of civil strife and imperialism in the fifth century BC are the power politics of Athens and the efforts of the Spartan alliance to counter them in the Peloponnesian War. The central evidence for this study is the history of Thucydides. His stated aim was to help those who wished to examine the plain truth of the past and what was likely to be the same or similar in the future in accordance with the human condition. One of his chief examples of the constancy of the human condition was behaviour and sufferings in time of civil strife. After describing the *stasis* in 427 at Corcyra in its often grisly details, he noted the impression made on Greeks by its brutality and so began a digression on the general phenomenon of *stasis*. 'Such things,' he says, 'happen and always will, as long as human nature is the same, but will vary in their violence and form according to the changing circumstances that govern them.'

The strife at Corcyra is emphasised as the first significant occasion of *stasis* — presumably the first in the war, since Thucydides has reported important outbreaks before the war — and as a prelude to an epidemic of strife during the war. This was caused by the ability and readiness of factions to call in the aid of Athens or Sparta and the need of the great powers for allies in order to overcome each other. The excursus that follows thus anticipates conclusions from future items in the narrative. Some of the later occasions of *stasis* are treated in some detail, above all the oligarchic revolution in Athens and Samos in 411; others are simply mentioned in passing in a few lines. However, the excursus on the Corcyra episode cannot make up for the brevity of later narratives. It does not provide paradeigmatic descriptions of the way that *stasis* worked: instead it depicts the emotions and attitudes involved and especially the morality of *stasis*.[16] Thucydides argues that the differences in the violence which different occasions of *stasis* created depended on whether the cities were at peace or war. War was a brutal schoolmaster who made the emotions of the majority of people as harsh as the pressures to which they were subjected. Moreover, the deviousness of the plots and the viciousness of the reprisals escalated, as one city learnt from the strife in another.

He then discusses at length the change in moral vocabulary and judgement that, in his view, resulted from this. Through the discussion runs the theme of the *hetaireia*, the political group or faction, which was at the root of most plotting. The *hetaireia* became, according to Thucydides, the focus of loyalties and source of morality. Reckless daring was considered courage in the service of comrades (*andreia philetairos*); the cautious man was treated as the disrupter of the group (*hetaireia*). Kinship became a looser bond than group membership (*to hetairikon*). So faction not only corrupted existing morality, but generated a new priority of values. The groups' aim was domination, so that their members might monopolise political office and wealth. For this reason they came to disregard legal, religious and traditional moral sanctions, substituting the group solidarity which derived from being partners in illegality and a delight in their own cleverness. This was displayed in the first place in a cynical misuse of public political vocabulary as well as private. Leading statesmen in the cities on each side assumed specious slogans, professing as their ideals either political equality for the masses or the sound sense and discipline of rule by the best men. But the public resources which they pretended to be safeguarding were to be enjoyed as prizes by the victorious group. Secondly, after such cut-throat competition the exploitation of victory and reprisals were merciless. This, Thucydides believed, spelt the end to moderation, straight dealing in politics and even to first-rate political thinking, since the second-rate men were more ruthless in action, fearing that they might be outdone in argument and intrigue.

As a reflection on civil strife for all time, this passage wears exceedingly well. Much of the exposition of the methods of *hetaireiai* is not only relevant to the preceding Corcyra episode, but is echoed in Thucydides' interpretation of the oligarchic revolution in Athens and Samos of 411, where the *hetaireiai* were of prime importance both in the formation of its regime and its dissolution. It seems likely that these events and the subsequent political struggles at Athens in the last decade of the fifth century (of which no account by Thucydides survives) were his prime inspiration.[17]

Apart from this wholesale reduction of civil strife to its basest terms, Thucydides contributes a great deal in a less dramatic way to our understanding of the issues and the main contestants in civil strife. As we have seen, Solon described the two major social groups, between which he stood as mediator, as 'those who had power' and 'the people' (*demos*) (p. 46); Thucydides uses the same terminology, 'the powerful' (*dunatoi*) and 'the people'. The term *dunatoi* is sometimes used to designate the political group supporting an oligarchic government. Thucydides also talks of the 'most powerful men' (*dunatōtatoi*), perhaps having in mind the leading men among the *dunatoi* who would be the prime movers in an oligarchic faction or, not necessarily identical with these, the social and political élite.[18]

Should we equate *dunatoi* with oligarchs? This interpretation is too restrictive, if we take into account the passage in which Thucydides uses the term *dunatōtatoi* for the group who had obtained power through a democratic revolution, in which they had killed the 200 previous *dunatōtatoi*, and who were now being encouraged to restore an oligarchy. *Dunatoi* thus seems to mean basically the governing class, for example the men in democratic Chios who provided hostages to Athens, while *dunatōtatoi* means their *de facto* leaders, rather than the officials of a government.[19] The *dunatoi* would be wealthy men: Thucydides says that in 430 the *dunatoi* at Athens were angry with Pericles because they had lost their fine properties in the countryside with their buildings and expensive furnishings.

Such wealthy men would have provided the backbone to an oligarchy elsewhere. The pro-Peloponnesian group which made the *coup d'état* against the *demos*, which precipitated the *stasis* at Corcyra, clearly included wealthy men. The democratic leader Peithias chose five of the wealthiest among them as scapegoats in a court case; later, when the *demos* massacred its oligarchic opponents, unpaid creditors were among the victims. Nevertheless, Thucydides does not generally call the opponents of the *demos* 'the wealthy' (*plousioi*) or, like Herodotus, 'the fat men', presumably because he knew that some of the wealthy were with the *demos*.[20] As for the term 'the few' (*oligoi*), it is less common than *dunatoi* and does not denote a class as such, but is used for particular oligarchic revolutionary groups. 'The few' in the excursus on the Corcyra episode are those who actually summoned Spartan aid, like the pro-Peloponnesian founders of the oligarchic constitution at Argos and those who co-operated with Alcibiades in 412 at Chios. Thucydides also refers to pro-Spartan groups at Torone and Mende as 'few', but here he seems simply to be emphasising the size of the group involved in a plot.[21]

Demos means primarily the majority of people, including the poor, when opposed to *dunatoi*. Pericles claimed that the Athenian constitution was called *demokratia* because it was organised not for a few but for a greater number, but he had to qualify this by arguing that political leadership fell to those with *aretē*, that is, the best, noblest and ablest. The term *plēthos*, the mass of the people, is sometimes used as an alternative to *demos*, and here Thucydides seems to be stressing that it was the majority, not merely a faction calling itself democratic. *Demos* may mean specifically the common people, especially those with little part in decision-making. At Mytilene in 427 the *demos*, who had been taking no active part in the secession from Athens, were armed by the Spartan military adviser as a last resort and used their arms against the *dunatoi*. Similarly, the same year in Corcyra, after the democrat Peithias with 60 of his supporters had been murdered and other supporters had fled to Athens, the *demos* who were then attacked by the pro-Peloponnesian party were clearly the majority of ordinary citizens by contrast with their wealthy opponents who lived round the *agora*. The slaves were not counted among the *demos*. We are told that both factions at Corcyra tried to get the agricultural slaves to join them by promises of liberation, but in fact the majority joined the *demos*.[22]

On the other hand *demos* can designate the supporters of democracy, both common people and their leaders from the upper classes. Thus it means the democratic faction. The first example in Thucydides' work is probably the *demos* at Epidamnus who in 436 appealed to oligarchically ruled Corinth for help against their own *dunatoi*. The *demos* who expelled the newly established oligarchic government at Argos in 417 and renewed alliance with Athens, included friends of Alcibiades, whom the Argives later suspected of planning an attack on the *demos* at the time when Alcibiades was threatened with prosecution in Athens. At Samos in 412 there was a genuine democratic revolution of the *demos* against the *dunatōtatoi*, which led to the death or exile of 600 men and the perpetual loss of citizen rights by the class called landowners (*geomoroi*), but by the next year this regime in turn was dominated by a group of *dunatōtatoi* who were persuaded to attempt to establish an oligarchy. These are termed by Thucydides 'those who had in the past revolted against the *dunatoi* and were a *demos*'. They became a conspiracy of 300 and planned to attack the majority, i.e. the rest of the citizens, on the ground that these were a *demos*. Thus in the same chapter *demos* refers to two different kinds of partisans of democracy, a faction dominating ostensibly in the democratic interest and the bulk of the people who had been given a democratic constitution. One suspects that some of the new democrats had been members of the *dunatoi* before the first democratic revolution.[23]

By contrast, when describing the *stasis* at Megara in 424, Thucydides makes it plain that the move to surrender the city to Athens sprang only from a faction among the *demos*. The approaches to Athens were made by the *demos*'s political leaders (*prostatai tou demou*), and the long walls were betrayed by a small group of conspirators. When those who had negotiated with Athens tried to trick the rest of the Megarians into opening the gates, they had a number of people with them in the know, but they were insufficient to engineer the surrender to Athens. The *prostatai* were reluctant to declare themselves as pro-Athenian; the bulk of the *demos* remained uninvolved in the political struggle and indeed were eventually reconciled to the readmission to citizenship of the extreme oligarchs.[24]

Thucydides also offers in his narrative some clarification of, and perhaps a corrective to, his view that the political programmes put forward by the factions were mere slogans. Certainly, the first democratic revolution placed a new *hetaireia* in a dominating position at Samos in 412. However, it is a moot point whether the redistribution of the estates which had belonged to the 'landowners' merely profited the democratic leadership or was more general. If it was, then the revolution was in some sense genuinely democratic, creating a broader basis of wealth and power. We may compare the plan by the *demos* to redistribute land at Leontini. Moreover, revolution might also lead to a democracy which was strong enough to put down some of its own leaders, to judge from the history of Argos in 417-415.[25]

Thucydides does not draw any distinction between degrees of democracy. Democracy on the Athenian model is his base-line, and from this he calculates grades of oligarchy. So the result of the Megarian *stasis* is that 'they rendered the city an oligarchy in most respects'; the Spartans and the Argives 'put affairs in Sicyon more in the hands of a few'. Similar phraseology was employed by the advocates of oligarchic revolution at Athens, and those who later objected to the revolution talked about 'coming too much into the hands of a few'. No doubt this is the way that Athenians brought up under democracy thought. It does at least imply that distinctions between constitutions were considered important. Moreover, in 411 political programmes were put forward at Athens embodying different degrees of oligarchy. Indeed, Thucydides calls the constitution actually established after the counter-revolution a blend which was both in the power of the many and the few.[26] It is reasonable to suppose that men in other cities who undertook oligarchic revolutions were on occasion eager for a particular kind of constitution or a particular direction of policy, not merely to place themselves in authority. Nor can one treat the factions as isolated from the rest of the citizens. Although the germ of a revolution in either direction might be a small *hetaireia*, for example Peithias' group at Corcyra or the oligarchs at Mende and Torone, the total numbers involved even in an oligarchic takeover might run into hundreds. One should not necessarily think, therefore, that oligarchic revolutions were *coups* by small juntas with foreign military backing, although there were still instances of this, similar to the *coups* by tyrants in the Archaic Age.[27]

Finally, even when factions were self-interested and opportunist, they might still be patriotic. In the Peloponnesian War both democratic and oligarchic groups sought to transfer cities from one of the two opposing military camps to the other. Probably in every instance the faction involved sought to gain or preserve power for itself. Nevertheless, on some occasions at least they sought also the security or liberty of their own city. The Megarian democratic leaders, in spite of the raids of the exiled oligarchs from Pegai and the extreme economic pressure caused by Athenian raids and the restriction of trade, only resorted to collaboration with Athens because of the desperate plight their city was

in. If they had sought Athenian help at the moment of their expulsion
of the oligarchs, Megara might have easily fallen into Athens' grasp. On
the other hand, groups which supported the Spartan Brasidas in the
cities of Chalkidike and Thrace genuinely believed that he offered a
better future than membership of the Athenian Empire.[28]

Therefore if a reader should infer from Thucydides' general survey
of *stasis* that its history in the Peloponnesian War can be reduced to
some simple facts about moral corruption unendingly repeated, Thucydides himself provides the corrective. The vices and atrocities were
repetitive, but they did not exhaust the subject for Thucydides — any
more than the ill-conceived ambitions he stigmatised in Athenian politicians were enough to explain the history of the war.

Thucydides and the Athenian Empire

It was one of the fundamental points in Thucydides' account of *stasis*
that the leaders of a *demos* engaged in civil strife would call in Athenian
support, while the few called in the Spartans. This is attested at Corcyra,
Megara (though the democratic leaders had reservations), at Mende and
at Argos. In Thessaly, we are told, the *plethos* favoured Athens and, if
they had not been ruled by a *dunasteia*, that is a narrow oligarchy or
junta, Brasidas would never have got through to the North. When the
demos of Leontini were expelled in 422, it was to Athens that they
looked for aid. The ultimate refusal of the Mytilenean *demos* to support
continuing secession from Athens led to the surrender of the city, and
the fact is used in the speech of Diodotus at Athens as an argument
against wholesale reprisals on the population. According to Thucydides,
he argued that the *demos* in each city only seceded from Athens under
compulsion and was a fifth column on the Athenian side, when the
latter tried to bring the cities back into subjection.[29]

This division of loyalties was to be confused by the oligarchic revolution at Athens, and subsequently Athens' control of her empire was
never secure enough for it to be significant. The island of Thasos, which
was lost to Athens for four years after 411, is taken by Thucydides as
a paradigm of what happened in many other once subject cities. The
Athenian oligarchs believed that, if they encouraged oligarchic regimes
among their subject allies, these would remain loyal to the new regime
in Athens. In fact, once the democracies were overthrown and the
oligarchs were securely in power, the cities sought outright liberation,
knowing that they could count on Spartan support. The Athenian

general Phrynichos had apparently forecast this, when the proposals about oligarchic government were first mooted at Samos. Oligarchic government, he had argued, was no magnet to attract cities to Athens. The allies would not prefer subjection with the type of government they favoured, whether oligarchy or democracy, to freedom with whichever type of government circumstances might determine. In the context, since Phrynichos is arguing against the installation of oligarchy, this means in effect that the allies would prefer freedom even with democracy. According to Phrynichos, the allies believed that the so-called *kaloi k'agathoi*, the Athenian aristocracy, would cause just as much trouble to them in an oligarchy as the *demos* had previously, for they had provided leadership for the *demos* in their own interest and were its financiers. The allies were ready to take summary reprisals on Athenians, but any allied *demos* would check them and Athenians could call on its protection.[30]

How this situation had arisen, we are about to investigate. However, it is worth considering briefly first the implications of these passages, which recently have been the subject of controversy among scholars in a debate on the popularity of the Athenian Empire. The controversy, in my view, has been largely fostered by the difficulty of generalising about all the cities of the empire and the ambiguities of the notion of political popularity. However, at bottom there is a clear question: was the *demos* in an allied city prepared to back secession from Athens, if it meant loss of democratic government? On the evidence, as we shall see in detail, the answer to this is 'no', even when the *demos* was leaderless. Nor is Phrynichos' argument a serious obstacle. Phrynichos has the *dunatoi* particularly in mind, since he is trying to argue that giving them an oligarchy will not make them loyal. They are prepared to take a chance on independence because of their enmity to Athens: for the *demos* this motive was lacking.

Of course, for Phrynichos, Thucydides and the majority of Greeks of the period, it was axiomatic that freedom, *eleutheria*, was desirable. On the other hand, domination by a foreign power had become almost inevitable by the end of the fifth century for the cities of Ionia and the Aegean, though not yet in Thrace. Furthermore, in whatever circumstances Athenian democracy could be regarded as a liberator, it was welcome to any *demos*. In a revolutionary context, where oligarchs were aggressive and self-assertive, a *demos* might turn to Athens, even after a city had made a bid for independence. On the other hand, if a *demos* thought it could gain independence without losing democracy, it would not shed tears over losing Athenian overlordship.[31]

Stasis and the Athenian Empire

We have seen how Sparta, in developing an alliance of subject allies under her hegemony, had intervened with varying success in their internal struggles. What part had such intervention played in the development of the Athenian Empire? First, we must briefly recapitulate a well-known story.

The Athenian Empire arose out of the Delian League, which in turn sprang from the enlarged Spartan alliance created to fight Xerxes' expedition to Greece. The alliance was of autonomous states who had sworn to have the same friends and enemies — the normal formula later for full alliance (*summachia*). Policy was decided at meetings at Delos, but the organisation of the war effort was undertaken by Athens: the assessment of ship and money contributions was first carried out by Aristeides, and the money was handled by Athenian financial officials. The general programme was a war of reprisal against Persia. Soon Athenian leadership became harsh in face of desertion and the failure to provide basic contributions at the beginning of each year, their popularity waned and their own military contribution became greater relative to those of their allies, since the majority of these through dislike of active service came to contribute money instead of ships. Dislike of Athens caused outright secession from the alliance, and the military weakness of the seceding states led to their subjection by force and they became allies under duress. The first example of this was the island of Naxos c. 470 BC, the next was Thasos c. 465. Most other instances of subjection known to us from literature and inscriptions come from the period after 450.[32]

Two points arise from this. First, as long as assemblies continued to be held, any subjection of seceding allies must have been authorised or at least ratified by the assembly. The acquiescence of the allies might suggest that Athens had extended her political influence among the *dunatoi* and military leaders in many member-states, at least to the extent that there were some well-placed friends of the Athenians (*proxenoi* and *euergetai*) in every city.[33] Secondly, the occasion of military subjection could clearly have been used to put a pro-Athenian faction in power in a city; other military and diplomatic moves connected with the war against Persia might have provided similar opportunities.

There is little evidence about what happened to Naxos and Thasos. We know that land was assigned to Athenian *klerouchoi* in Naxos c. 450 BC. If this followed the pattern of settlement in Chalcis back in 507 (p. 87), it would have been on land confiscated from the wealthy, and thus we might associate it with an attempt to curtail the influence of the local *dunatoi*; 'the fat men' who had been influential in the democracy about 500 BC. The evidence about Thasos is even later. When the oligarchic revolution eventually came in 411, there had been a strong democratic government and an oligarchic faction was in exile. Moreover, regulations inscribed on stone shortly before or early in the Peloponnesian War show that the Thasians then had considerable control of trade, including permission to exact taxes and fines from traders and ship-masters. It is natural to interpret these powers as concessions by Athens to a regime that she wished to encourage.[34]

The next city, whose subjection is recorded, is Aegina. She fought with Athens, probably between 459 and 457, a war which was part of the more general hostilities between Athens and the Peloponnesians. (Aegina had a long-standing loyalty to Sparta, which she had honoured at the time of the helot revolt.) To what extent Athens encouraged a democratic faction during or after the war, as she had done c. 489 (p. 87), is difficult to tell. After the revolt Aegina contributed 30 talents to the league. A fragmentary inscription has a reference to guarding and a garrison, but this is not necessarily an Athenian garrison holding the Aeginetans down. It seems to me likely that Athens did install a democratic regime in 457 to which it allowed a considerable degree of freedom, exemplified by the coinage. The type was controlled and so a break with the past was made, but the popular coinage was allowed to circulate freely. In the long run, however, there was mutual distrust. The size of the tribute implies that many wealthy *dunatoi* continued to live and pay taxes in the island. They sought Spartan aid before the war, claiming infringement of their autonomy, and in consequence at its outset Athens evicted the inhabitants of the island *en masse*.[35]

In 458 the Athenians got control of affairs in Boeotia after the battle of Oenophyta. A democracy was set up in Thebes which was overthrown through bad government, according to Aristotle. Another source suggests that the aristocracy was favoured in Boeotia, and that this went on to enslave the *demos*. Perhaps the aristocracy was favoured in other cities in Boeotia, which were now made independent of Thebes. It appears that Athens hoped at this point to control affairs in Boeotia in the same way that Sparta aimed to do in Arcadia, by keeping the cities separate with a sympathetic government in each. How far this actually involved promoting democratic revolutions is not clear.[36]

On the other hand, epigraphic evidence shows plainly Athenian intervention in the internal politics of Erythrai on the Ionian seaboard c. 450 BC and the creation of a democracy there. A stone at Athens recorded a decree establishing at Erythrai a council selected by lot, like the Athenian council of 500. This was to be carried out by Athenian political supervisors and a garrison-commander who would remain there in subsequent years. The citizen bodies of both Erythrai and Athens are called *plēthos*, the majority or the mass of the people. There are also references to 'tyrants' and 'men who are in exile among the Persians'. It seems that a pro-Persian tyranny or oligarchic junta had attempted to seize the city and so Athens encouraged a thoroughly democratic constitution as a counter-measure.[37]

Events in Miletus in the same period seem to have followed a course in many respects similar. One inscription from Miletus shows a price being put on the heads of three men, then in exile, and their descendants. Another from Athens records regulations drawn up for Miletus, involving five commissioners from Athens, and there are to be garrison troops and ships. The constitution is still presided over by the old politico-religious officials, the *aisumnetes molpōn* and the *prosetairoi*, who seem to have been maintained for religious purposes throughout the Classical and Hellenistic Ages both under democracy and oligarchy. The oligarchic essay on the Athenian constitution has a tantalising reference to Miletus among the mistakes of Athenian democracy: normally the democracy had always chosen to side with the 'worse' men in civil strife: this was wrong but intelligent, as it supported those like itself: when it tried to choose the 'best' men as allies in Boeotia, these enslaved the *demos* there; when it chose the best men in Miletus, these had in a short while seceded and cut the *demos* to pieces.

By 440, Miletus probably had a democracy, since men conspiring to set up a democracy in Samos co-operated with a Milesian embassy to Athens. Confirmation may be found in a recently discovered Milesian sacred law with a democratic introductory formula, which is most plausibly dated to 437-436. Thus, there must have been two Athenian interventions before 440 BC. To judge from what happened when Miletus seceded from Athens in 412, the city was dominated by its aristocrats even under democracy. What appears in the epigraphic evidence is Athenian respect for existing Milesian institutions and thus the allowance made for the pride of the Milesian *dunatoi*. This pragmatic approach led to the initial support for an oligarchy, perhaps when the city's loyalty to the alliance had been threatened by a pro-Persian *coup*.[38]

In 446, after the lapse of a five-year truce between the Athenians and the Peloponnesians, Euboea revolted. It was swiftly recovered after the Peloponnesian army had been diverted from Attica; the Hestiaeans were evicted, their land was occupied by Athenians and more stringent regulations were made for the conduct of affairs here and in other cities. However, there is no evidence that the secession had involved *stasis*. The provisions made after the secession regarding Chalcis, on mutual oath-taking and other topics including hostages, are remarkable in that the Chalcidians are not called a *demos* or a *plēthos* at all, as in similar oaths exchanged with Erythrai and Samos. The Chalcidians were able to collect taxes for their own benefit and try non-capital court cases. But I suspect that the power of their legislative assembly may have been drastically curtailed, its functions being passed over to the Athenian assembly. If this interpretation is correct, Athens' policy here and probably elsewhere in Euboea (the arrangements for the Chalcis oaths followed and were modelled on the oaths with Eretria) was not to support democratic factions but to subject cities directly to the Athenian *demos*, as if they were outlying districts of Attica. This is intelligible in view of the strategic importance of Euboea, its economic value and the Athenian settlers there.[39]

After 445 Athens was at peace with Sparta and not campaigning actively against Persia. However, whether or not a treaty was in fact concluded with Persia in 449, the Persians were still able to exploit factions within Athens' allies and threaten the loyalty of the league. In 441 Samos had a war with Miletus over Priene, which up to that time had been a small independent city. Miletus lost and laid a complaint against Samos in conjunction with some Samians who wished to set up a democratic constitution. Accordingly in 440 Athens did establish a democracy, supporting this by a garrison, Athenian governors and the taking of hostages, as at Chalcis. However, some exiles got the support of the Persian satrap of Sardis. In collaboration with the *dunatōtatoi*, in this case the remnants of the oligarchic leadership left in positions of authority on Samos, they invaded the island with a mercenary force and defeated the mass of the population. They then recovered their hostages, handed over the Athenian governors and troops to the Persians and renewed the war with Miletus. This revolt inspired a secession by Byzantium in sympathy. The Peloponnesian League considered intervening on behalf of the Samian oligarchs, but decided against this after a speech by a Corinthian (perhaps because at this time they did not wish to appear to act in the Persian interest). The Athenians defeated the Samian fleet, and after an eight-month siege Samos capitulated.

In the settlement the Samians gave hostages, surrendered their fleet, took down their walls and promised to pay an indemnity. As for the constitution, Diodorus is our only explicit authority for the restoration of the democracy. This is anyhow probable in view of the danger posed by the *dunatoi*, and is perhaps confirmed by a fragmentary inscription containing the Athenian oath to the peace settlement: 'I shall act, speak and resolve as is good for the *demos* of the Samians.' The difficulty is that in 412 the *demos* required assistance from the Athenians to over-throw a faction of *dunatoi*, who were landowners. Whether we believe that a democracy was imposed or not, we must accept that the social structure of Samos was not greatly changed, probably because the Athenians wanted the surviving wealthy as guarantors of the formidable war indemnity of nearly 1,280 talents. I would accept the evidence pointing towards a democratic constitution, with a sovereign assembly and perhaps a council selected by lot, but I believe that, as in Miletus, it was led and dominated by rich men, who in different circumstances might be sympathetic to oligarchy.[40]

The Samian episode is the last evidence for Athenian intervention in civil strife among her allies before the Peloponnesian War. Athens is attested as having a reputation for being a supporter of democracy in other cities, and it is easy to see how she would have acquired this repu-tation in the years before the war. However, we must make some dis-tinctions and reservations. The Athenians did not necessarily seek to replace an oligarchy with a democracy at the first opportunity. Even when a democracy was installed, this did not necessarily entail the demise of the old governing class. Athens always had to ensure that she received the appropriate tribute and military support and so would be reluctant to disperse existing accumulations of capital (these enabled their owners to contract to collect local taxes or pay in advance to the state sums to be recovered later from the less fortunate).

The advantage to Athens of establishing a democracy in a city lay in the patronage of a new group of political leaders, if this could be achieved, and in the creation of a check on the powerful men with whom the Athenians had perforce to work, if the city was to be a valu-able ally. It was, therefore, a reasonable policy to leave the existing *dunatoi* alone (after the removal of the most intractable) but shackle them with an elaborate democratic constitution. So far idealism and pragmatism went hand in hand. However, the question remains, how much benefit the common people in allied cities derived from the democracies that Athens encouraged. Events in the Peloponnesian War showed that, although they were to varying degrees sensible of the pro-tection Athens afforded them, their contact with the Athenian *demos* was weak and their confidence shaky in a crisis. The Athenians certainly did not rely on the allies alone to control their own *dunatoi*: they also provided for the trial of important political offences and capital offences in general at Athens, and we are specifically told that this enabled informers to damage the wealthy aristocrats. One may infer that the Athenian *demos* did not treat the common people in democracies allied to it as partners: rather it was their 'big brother', whose dealings were largely with their *dunatoi* and who guided their affairs, as far as it thought necessary, by remote control. According to Plato's Seventh Letter, the Athenians preserved their empire for 70 years by acquiring friends in each of the cities. In practice these links were at least as important as the sharing of democracy.[41]

Stasis in the Peloponnesian War

It was Thucydides' view in his excursus on the events at Corcyra that *stasis* increased during the Peloponnesian War because Sparta and Athens were seeking to augment their alliances at each other's expense, and the competing factions, believing it best to get their blow in first, were only too eager to summon their aid. The detachment of Athenian allies was in fact, according to his account, part of the war programme put forward by the Corinthians at Sparta in late 432, after the Peloponnesian League had formally voted for war, the aim being to cut down Athens' financial resources, and this strategy was also advocated in the Mytilenean appeal for Spartan aid at the Olympic games of 428. It may be confidently accepted as part of the original war plans of the Peloponnesians; indeed, it was no new idea for Sparta, since as long before as 465 Sparta had considered helping Thasos. But it was a policy they were slow to execute.[42]

Spartan inactivity in this respect was the more remarkable, in that a secession was one of the immediate causes of the war and an attempted betrayal by a political faction began hostilities proper. When Potidaea left the Athenian alliance in 432 because of her Corinthian connection and the mutual suspicions this aroused, the siege tied down Athenian manpower and ships for three years and cost Athens 2,000 talents. At the end the Potidaeans negotiated their withdrawal into exile in other Chalcidic cities, where they became a threat to Athens later. However, Potidaea as a Corinthian colony with Corinthian visiting magistrates needed no special political manipulation to secede. It was not a good example of the exploitation of *stasis* as a war weapon.

The attempted betrayal of Plataea to the Thebans, which began the war, in one sense was not an episode of *stasis*, since there was no apparent political conflict beforehand. Yet the betrayal was by a group of Plataeans who sought political power for themselves through the elimination of their enemies and the attachment of the city to Thebes. This was the only political issue: the city was probably too small for there to be a significant constitutional conflict between oligarchy and democracy. The Plataean episode may at least be classified as belonging to a sub-group of *stasis* — a form rarely attested before this war, but common during it. A political faction, which would have had no chance of gaining power in peacetime even with aid from outside, might promise to betray a city to an enemy army in the hope of seizing power. Thucydides normally describes such acts simply as betrayal, *prodosia*, or remarks that men from inside the city were ready to surrender it.[43]

We owe the detailed description of the attempted betrayal of Plataea to Thucydides' good information about an event near Athens and also probably his desire to narrate in detail a typical event of this kind. The Thebans admitted by the traitors seized the Plataean *agora*. This was well planned to forestall resistance, as it prevented the inhabitants uniting and organising themselves. Aeneas, the fourth-century writer on sieges, recommended that all open spaces, including the *agora* and the theatre, should be either guarded by the defenders or, if useless, blocked up. In his view, it was highly dangerous if the conspirators seized control of the single open space in the city; not so serious, if there were two or three, since a conspiracy could not control them all. In fact, this Theban *coup* was a failure because the Plataeans communicated with one another by breaking through house walls and so built up a resistance. Nor did the main Theban force arrive soon enough to support its compatriots inside Plataea. The end of the episode was a foretaste of what was to come, since the Plataeans, after cutting off the Thebans in the city and capturing them, killed them in spite of having previously hinted to the Thebans that they could be ransomed.[44]

The attack on Plataea was the beginning of hostilities proper between Athens and the Spartan alliance. The Spartans kept their promise to the Potidaeans in 432 that they would invade Attica, but offered them no direct aid, nor did they straight away seek to make other cities secede. Although the invasions of Attica did not provoke Athens to risk a set battle, in 430 the plague led to an unsuccessful Athenian embassy seeking peace, and this may have led the Spartans to believe that they would win by traditional methods of warfare.

Mytilene

If Spartan official policy was hesitant, some Spartans thought differently and the Boeotians were not deterred by the Theban failure at Plataea. In 428 the government of the city of Mytilene began to force the rest of the population of the island of Lesbos (except the people of Methymna) to migrate into Mytilene and prepared to secede from the Athenian alliance. A few official friends (*proxenoi*) of Athens who were in political opposition could do no more than report the matter to Athens. Lesbos, like Chios, was still theoretically an autonomous ally, contributing ships. The constitution seems to have had an oligarchic bias, to judge from the exclusion of the *demos* from decision-making and the carrying of heavy armour, and this would explain why the supporters of Athens could not appeal to the citizen body. The oligarchy was not, however, especially narrow; those finally executed as ringleaders numbered a little over 1,000. Athens tried to dissuade the Mytileneans from their preparations but, when diplomacy failed, attacked forthwith. There followed an Athenian naval victory, further negotiations in which one of Athens' 'friends' became a representative of the independence movement, a Mytilenean embassy to Sparta and a final break with Athens. The Mytileneans were playing for time. They had sought Spartan aid for their revolt even before the war, but had been refused it. Nevertheless, they were in contact with individual Spartans and Boeotians, and one Spartan and one Theban were already on their way to Lesbos as advisers before the secession.

The Mytilenean ambassadors were referred to as an assembly of the Peloponnesian League at Olympia. Here, according to Thucydides, they argued that swift support from the league would lead to the defeat of Athens, since their example would be followed by others. The league at first prepared a land and sea attack on Attica, which proved abortive; then they planned to send a fleet to help Lesbos directly. The fleet did not sail until the next spring (427) and was slow on its voyage. Meanwhile the Spartan military adviser sent to Mytilene, in desperation through lack of food because of the Athenian siege, gave hoplite arms to the *demos* in order to make a sortie against the besiegers. Once armed, the people mutinied, demanding that the *dunatoi* should bring out their food stocks and distribute them and threatening that otherwise they would surrender the city. There were no food stocks and so the Lesbian leaders themselves negotiated a surrender with the Athenian commander.[45]

Thus the surrender of Mytilene came about through a popular revolt over bread. Clearly the Mytilenean leaders had not inspired confidence among the mass of their people. On the other hand, the leading pro-Athenians seem to have fled to Athens, the crews of ten ships were also there and little affection for Athens can be discerned among those who remained. The Athenians originally intended to execute all the males who were inside Mytilene on the ground of premeditated revolt and collaboration with the enemy. It took a second debate to make them change their mind. Although we find in Diodotus' speech emphasis on the contribution of the Mytilenean *demos* to the surrender and a general claim that the common people in the Athenian alliance were Athens' friends, the Athenian *demos* had evidently not developed strong ties of sympathy with that of Mytilene before the revolt. After the decision merely to execute the 1,000 judged most culpable, much of the land was assigned to cleruchs, and an autonomous state was set up in Mytilene, which was to prove more loyal to Athens. As for the Spartans, the operations of their fleet inspired no further revolt and tended to create enemies rather than friends.[46]

Corcyra

The Peloponnesians were, however, more successful the same year in creating trouble in Corcyra, one of Athens' non-tributary allies. Corcyra had a democratic constitution, though before the war the city had been prepared to aid the exiled *dunatoi* in Epidamnus. After the battle of Subota in 433, when Athenian aid to Corcyra thwarted a complete Corinthian victory, the Corinthians kept 250 of those they had captured as prisoners of war, the majority of whom formed the cream of the governing class in Corcyra. They looked after them well, intending that on their return home they should swing Corcyra over to the Peloponnesian side. They eventually released them (c. 429-428) under the pretext of an enormous ransom paid by the official friends of Corcyra at Corinth.

The returned prisoners canvassed support for their new allegiance and, at a meeting attended by embassies both from Athens and Corinth, they persuaded their assembly to vote for a strictly defensive alliance with Athens, such as had in fact been originally agreed in 433, and the maintenance of friendly relations with the Peloponnesian League. They then unsuccessfully indicted Peithias, the champion of the *demos*, for enslaving Corcyra to Athens, and he in revenge convicted five of the wealthiest among them for a technical violation of religious ground, which carried a heavy fine. Peithias was also suspected of planning to persuade the assembly to make a full alliance with Athens. Despairing of legal methods, the pro-Corinthians killed Peithias and some 60 other councillors and private citizens, no doubt those among the *dunatoi* who were Athenian supporters. A few of Peithias' group escaped onto the Athenian trireme which had brought their embassy.[47]

Once in power, the pro-Corinthians forced the assembly to declare neutrality and sent men to try to persuade the Athenians to accept the *fait accompli* (these were arrested on their arrival as rebels). After this they were persuaded by Spartan envoys, who arrived on a Corinthian warship, to attack the *demos*. We must conclude that, in spite of the *de facto* acceptance of the *coup* by the assembly, the pro-Corinthians did not trust the *demos*, and this attack was a preliminary to setting up a more oligarchic regime (the Spartans would have recommended this on principle). The initial attack of the oligarchs was successful, but the *demos* recovered and a full-scale civil war ensued, in which the *demos* got the support of the agricultural slaves while the oligarchs obtained 800 'volunteers', mercenary soldiers from the mainland.

Finally, on the fourth day after the initial attack by the oligarchs, the *demos*, who were defending the acropolis and the heights of the city, defeated and drove the oligarchic forces back to the *agora* and the eastern harbour, the area where the wealthy lived. The Corinthian warship then withdrew with the chief oligarchs aboard. The next day an Athenian squadron arrived and the oligarchs gave in. The terms were that a full alliance should be concluded with Athens and ten oligarchic ring-leaders, now conveniently on their way to Corinth, should be tried. These mild conditions could not in the event be observed. The ex-oligarchs became scared, when many of them were allotted to serve on seven Corcyrean ships which were being sent with Nikostratos' squadron as replacements for those left to garrison Corcyra. They occupied as suppliants the temple of Castor and Pollux; Nikostratos persuaded them out again; but the *demos* took up arms, removed the ex-oligarchs' arms from their houses and had to be prevented from killing those they met in the street. At least 400 more ex-oligarchs took fright at this and occupied a shrine, this time that of Hera, but they reached a compromise with the *demos*, by which they were removed to an offshore island.

There was even then some hope of a restoration of calm. But four or five days later the Peloponnesian fleet, which had miserably failed in the Aegean, attacked the island. The Corcyrean ships were forced to put to sea one by one as they were manned. Many men with Peloponnesian sympathies were aboard them: two ships deserted straight away and in others the crews fought one another. The Corcyrean fleet was thrown into complete confusion, losing 13 ships, and was only saved by the superior naval skill of the twelve from Athens. The Peloponnesians, however, did not effectively follow up their victory and the external security of Corcyra was assured by the approach of 60 Athenian ships, sent specifically to deal with the *stasis*. Before their arrival was announced, the Corcyrean *demos* had brought the 400 men back from the island and even persuaded some of the oligarchs to embark in the fleet. But once the *demos* knew that it was safe, with the aid of Messenians from Nikostratos' ships they instituted a massacre of all those who had been involved with the oligarchic movement. Most of the victims died without trial, many through acts of private vengeance or because they were unpaid creditors. Nevertheless, 500 men escaped to seize a fort which controlled Corcyrean territory on the mainland; they carried on guerrilla warfare against the democracy from there and later from Mt. Istone on the island.

After the Spartan defeat at Pylos, the Corcyreans were helped by an Athenian fleet to attack them. They surrendered on condition that they should be sent to Athens for trial, but the democratic leaders with the connivance of the Athenian generals contrived that the captives should break the truce by running away. They then imprisoned them and killed them, first by making them run the gauntlet and then by stoning or shooting the rest where they were. Thucydides' comment, that this was the end of the civil strife, seems to have been written before 411, since we learn of a very similar, though shorter, episode during the latter stages of the Peloponnesian War. The *dunatōtatoi* tried to make themselves an oligarchy in the Spartan interest; the *demos* summoned Conon, the Athenian general at Naupactus. Conon backed an attack on the oligarchs, in which some were killed and more than a thousand exiled, while the *demos* gave citizenship to slaves and foreigners to increase its fighting strength.[48]

The story of Corcyra in part bears out my earlier interpretation of Athens' relations with her allies, but it also introduces a further dimension. Athens' original alliance was with a democracy dominated by wealthy *dunatoi*, who were ready to help oligarchs in Epidamnus, ready to change allegiance when in Corinthian hands. Their property, attested by the ransom named for them, was probably based on landholdings not only on the island but in the mainland territory, which was later the oligarchs' base. The defensive alliance with Athens in 433 was not founded on ideology but was a way for them to escape defeat by the Peloponnesians. There were, however, over 60 leading Corcyreans who by 427 were supporters of Peithias, the champion of the common people, thus being committed to democracy and by the same token to Athens. The pro-Corinthians thought that eliminating these was sufficient to render Corcyra once again independent, as it had been before 433. The common people did little to protect their democratic leaders and seem to have acquiesced in the original *coup* until they were further provoked, while some of the democrats who fled to Athens after Peithias' murder were ready to co-operate with the embassy from the pro-Corinthians. As for the Athenians, in spite of having contracted a purely defensive alliance with Corcyra, they treated the islanders as subject allies and thus perhaps contributed to the failure of Peithias' faction to get broad-based support. Moreover, even after the civil war Nikostratos seems to have found it easier to deal with the defeated oligarchs than the new leaders of the *demos*.

Though many of the pro-Corinthians seem to have been satisfied with neutrality and the *status quo* at home, under the influence of the Spartan embassy they embarked on civil war to create an oligarchy. The oligarchic attack on the *demos* replaced what had been a struggle between two factions for competing programmes, with a class war, involving the whole population including slaves — something beyond the Athenian experience. Moreover, the 'few' were comparatively numerous. 250 came back from Corinth; over 400 went from the Heraion to the island opposite, and while they were there, other pro-Peloponnesians were embarked in the fleet — the dominant part of two ship-crews and smaller numbers in other ships. Even after the first massacre some 500 escaped. It would not be outrageous to assume that the total of the pro-Peloponnesian party exceeded the 1,000 attested at Mytilene and later at Argos.[49]

Civil strife probably shed more blood at Corcyra than anywhere else in the war, serving the Peloponnesian purpose by rendering Corcyrean armed forces practically useless to Athens. The annihilation of a major part of the original governing class, however, occurred as an unforeseen consequence of what was simply another move in the Peloponnesian campaign. It was not part of any democratic programme conceived by Athens for her empire.

Megara, Boeotia and Chalkidike

The Spartan reverse at Pylos and Sphacteria in 425 led to a new phase in the war, in which both sides concentrated on exploiting the internal weaknesses of the other. The Spartans were forced to abandon their policy of invading Attica, because the Athenians threatened to kill the 292 Spartan prisoners of war, should they do so. Moreover, the Athenians now had a serious threat to the stability of the Spartan homeland, envisaged by their General Demosthenes when he first went out with the fleet of Eurymedon and Sophocles in 425. Pylos was in a deserted corner of the land which had once been Messenia. After their victory the Athenians placed as a garrison there Messenians, drawn from those settled by them at Naupactus after the ten-year revolt. These raided the surrounding area, encouraged the helots to desert and join them, and posed the threat of a more general revolt. Thus, the Athenians probed Sparta's power where it was most vulnerable, in an area where her subjects had the strongest tradition of freedom-fighting.[50]

Inspired by their success, the Athenians pursued a more aggressive policy against the Peloponnesians. Among the operations mounted in 424 were two in support of democratic factions among members of the Peloponnesian League, a policy which had lapsed since the 450s. The first was against Megara. The Megarians had been under economic pressure since some time before the Peloponnesian War, when Athens on Pericles' motion banned the Megarians from the harbours of the Athenian Empire and the markets accessible by land in Attica, alleging the farming of sacred and disputed territory on the borders and the reception of runaway slaves. During the war itself the Megarians, who had a democratic constitution, had to cope with the threat of starvation, invasions by the Athenians twice a year and raids by a faction in exile based in Pegai on the Corinthian gulf. We are told that the latter had been driven out by the mass (*plēthos*) of the people after *stasis* and they were thus by then an oligarchic group, though they may have been originally one of those contesting for the leadership of the democracy. They still had supporters in the city to represent them when moves towards reconciliation were begun. The champions of the people (*prostatai tou demou*) realised that their leadership was in jeopardy: the people could not survive under present pressures, but the return of the exiles would threaten their own position. They therefore made approaches to Athens.

In consequence a small group of conspirators, enough to man a sculled long-boat, betrayed to an Athenian force the long walls between Megara and its eastern port Nisaea. A somewhat larger group joined the next day in urging the Megarians to open the city gates and go out to battle, in order to give the Athenians a chance to enter the city. The pro-Athenians were intended to be recognised by the invading army by having their bodies oiled. However, the plot was revealed by an accomplice to 'the other group', presumably the friends of the exiles. These managed to prevent the gates being opened without revealing that their reason for so doing was knowledge of the plot. The majority of the population was evidently ignorant of what was going on inside the city. There followed an uneasy period, during which the Athenians captured Nisaea and the Peloponnesian forces gathered, led by Brasidas. He wanted to get into Megara; the democrats were against this for obvious reasons, but so were the oligarchs' friends, who feared that this might provoke *stasis* and let the Athenians in. In fact there was no battle beyond a cavalry skirmish (the Athenians were outnumbered and satisfied with their earlier gains) and eventually the friends of the exiles were able to open their gates to Brasidas.

Considerable restraint was still shown inside Megara after the departure of both Brasidas and the main Athenian army. The pro-Athenian conspirators secretly escaped, while the rest of the Megarians negotiated with the friends of the exiles over conditions for their return. However, as soon as the exiles got back in office they had 100 men, either personal enemies or suspected pro-Athenians, condemned in a sort of lynch trial with open voting. They then set up an oligarchy which, Thucydides says, lasted a very long time, although it was founded by a very small group.[51]

The Megarian *stasis*, by contrast with that at Corcyra, was characterised by the small scale of activities. Both the exiles and the democratic leaders were small groups, each with a wider circle of friends who can hardly have numbered more than 100 (the number executed). The mass of the Megarians were apolitical and obviously not friendly to Athens. When the group of democratic politicians fled, there was no real alternative to the exiles and their supporters taking over. In other words they now formed the bulk of the *dunatoi*. The Athenians, for their part, treated the operation as a betrayal of a hostile city rather than a move to protect democracy and were satisfied with the strategic advantages gained.

In the same year Hippokrates, one of the Athenian generals who had negotiated with the Megarian democrats, had similar communications with men who wanted to set up democracies in the Boeotian cities now dominated by Thebes. A Theban exile initiated the plot: Siphai, a port in Thespiai's territory, and Chaironeia were to be betrayed to an Athenian force (exiles from Orchomenos, Peloponnesian mercenaries and some Phocians were also involved), while the main Boeotian army was distracted by an Athenian invasion. The plot came to nothing, first through a failure to synchronise the moves precisely, secondly because the Boeotians learned in advance of the move against Siphai and secured it before the main Athenian invasion. Thus, the Athenians failed to establish a domination by democracy, which they had attempted between 458 and 447.[52]

Meanwhile Sparta was forced to take more seriously the policy of persuading Athens' allies to secede, because she wished to distract Athens from attacking the Peloponnese and required bargaining-counters if she was to make a satisfactory peace. Sparta's campaign was directed at the cities in Thrace near the northern coast of the Aegean. Some of these

cities had been already in secession since the time of the revolt of Potidaea, as is shown not only by Thucydides but the records of Athenian
tribute (these were mainly cities a little distance from the coast and
Athenian naval power, though coastal Chalcidic towns were abandoned
and their inhabitants moved to Olynthus). An expedition was in preparation under Brasidas at the time that Athens attempted to seize
Megara. There had been appeals from the cities in Thrace and promises
of financial support. The Spartans sent out 700 helots in heavy armour
(they were eager for an excuse to remove them from their own homeland), and Brasidas recruited mercenaries from the Peloponnese. However, Brasidas' chief asset was to be his own moderation and fair dealing
with the cities he approached, the memory of which, we are told, stood
the Spartans in good stead later, when they came to promote general
revolt against Athens after her Sicilian defeat.[53]

The first Athenian ally he approached was Akanthos. A faction there
backed by the Chalcidians wanted him to be welcomed, but the *demos*
was hostile and only allowed him to address them through fear for their
vine harvest. According to Thucydides' version of his speech, Brasidas
denied that he had come to meddle in their internal affairs, either by
enslaving the majority to the few or the minority to the community as
a whole: his aim was to create freedom and autonomy. His persuasive
words and the threat to the harvest induced a majority in Akanthos to
secede, though they took the precaution of making him repeat by oath
that those he won over would be autonomous.

In the following winter the people of Argilos welcomed Brasidas and
immediately helped him to cross the river Strymon into the cultivated
land of Amphipolis. Inside Amphipolis there was at first a majority
against submission, who hoped for aid from the historian Thucydides
himself, then Athenian general at Thasos. Brasidas, however, quickly
made a moderate offer, allowing those who did not wish to help Sparta
to leave the city in five days, and the people of Amphipolis accepted.
Many of them were afraid for relatives outside the city in the power of
Brasidas outside the city. Thucydides kept for Athens the neighbouring
port of Eion, but Myrkinos, Galepsos and Oesyne followed Amphipolis'
example and many other cities made overtures to Brasidas. Thucydides,
in his role as historian, denounces this as an excess of optimism en-
gendered by misapprehension of the power still available to Athens. Yet
he shows that there was a widespread desire for independence from
Athens, if it did not involve subjection to Sparta. To what extent this
desire was found in all classes of the citizens is another matter. We may,
however, conclude that the people as a whole accepted secession when

it appears that a city seceded without delay.[54]

During the winter of 424-423 four of the cities on the Akte (Mt. Athos) peninsula of Chalcidice revolted. Further west in Torone, a few conspirators opened the city to Brasidas' troops. The surviving Athenian troops and the friends of Athens were forced to flee; the population were meanwhile reassured by a speech similar to that which Brasidas delivered at Akanthos. The following spring Skione on the Pallene peninsula came over with a great show of popular enthusiasm, publicly voting Brasidas a gold crown as saviour of Greece and individually giving him head-bands and treating him like a victorious athlete. This was perhaps the only major city in the area which changed sides with wholehearted unanimity.

After the armistice of 423 Mende also surrendered to Brasidas. This was in theory voluntary, but it resulted from the determination of a small faction, who had gone so far in plotting that discovery by the Athenians was inevitable and therefore forced the decision against the better judgement of the majority of the citizens. Later that summer, when the Athenians applied military pressure, political dissension arose and the *demos*, instead of going out to battle against the Athenians took up arms against the pro-Spartan party, the Peloponnesian garrison and their mercenaries. In consequence the city was recovered by Athens. This seems to have been a repetition of what happened at Mytilene. The Mendaians had no especial love for the Athenians: they fought them hard before *stasis* occurred, and there was no communication with the Athenians before they turned against their Spartan commander. The Mendaians quarrelled with the pro-Spartan faction because these had bulldozed them into secession when it was unnecessary and unsafe for the city. Independence was one thing, war and suffering was another.[55]

Brasidas' programme of subverting the Athenian alliance succeeded as far as it did, partly through sheer military force and partly because he did not try to stir up civil strife more than was necessary to secure the secession of a city from Athens. Brasidas disregarded Sparta's tradition of binding her allies to her by oligarchic governments in favour of good public relations and so became a patron of genuine autonomy. The cities where he had shown conspicuous diplomacy — Torone, Akanthos, Amphipolis — were especially hard to recover. However, Brasidas died defending Amphipolis in summer 422, and even before this his generosity had been impaired by Spartan appointment of governors to major cities. They did not remain long enough to infringe the liberty of these cities then, being withdrawn after the peace of 421, but they were a precedent for the later *harmostai*, the instruments of Spartan domination from 412 onwards.[56]

After the Peace of Nicias

In the period between the peace and the Athenian expedition to Sicily there occurred the oligarchic revolution at Argos, briefly mentioned above, and the democratic counter-revolution. In the winter of 418-417 after victory over Argos, Athens and their allies at Mantinea the Spartans marched towards Argos and sent an ambassador to propose peace terms. In spite of some opposition the Argive people yielded to this offer, persuaded by a pro-Spartan faction who had now come out into the open. These same men subsequently persuaded the Argives to drop their alliance with Athens, Argos, Elis and Mantinea and ally with Sparta. Later, 1,000 Spartans caused a revolution in Sicyon whereby its constitution became more oligarchic, and then returned to Argos to do the same there with the help of 1,000 Argive oligarchic partisans.

According to Diodorus, this revolution was led by the richest citizens with the greatest military reputation. The occasion chosen was apparently a procession of hoplites in armour. It is thus tempting to associate the 1,000 oligarchs with the picked regiment of 1,000 Argive soldiers at the battle of Mantinea. Many others were induced to support men of such distinction; the democratic leaders were killed and the constitution overthrown. But the regime did not last long. The *demos* gradually organised itself and took advantage of the Spartan preoccupation with their *gymnopaidia* games (mid-summer 417) to make a counter-attack on the oligarchs. Those who had been in power were either killed or exiled, and the Spartans could do nothing about it by subsequent invasion, although there was still a small group of pro-Spartans left in the city. Thus the Spartan attempt to follow up military victory with political infiltration failed, but it is noteworthy as the first example of Spartan political intervention in Argos known to us. This suggests that Brasidas' success had given the Spartans greater will to use such methods even before the disaster in Sicily damaged Athens' power. On the Argive side events in some respects foreshadowed what was to happen six years later at Athens. The oligarchs initially got considerable support from those of hoplite status. The *demos* was as resilient as that at Corcyra and perhaps better organised in that it achieved the counter-revolution without Athenian aid.[57]

During the Sicilian expedition the Athenians tried without success to make use of pro-Athenian factions. In Greece by this time their only effective means of subverting the Spartan alliance was the maintenance of the Messenian threat in Pylos. By contrast, Sparta after the Athenian defeat at Syracuse and her own development of sea power was in a far better position to stir up trouble in the Athenian alliance. Moreover, on their resumption of formal hostilities with Athens in 413, when the Athenians were approaching their crisis in Sicily, the Spartans had built a fort at Decelea in Attica. This did not in the event lead directly to political subversion in Athens, although the oligarchic government of the Four Hundred made two approaches to King Agis while he was there. However, it did produce a social and economic upheaval, since the Athenians lost all their herds and draught animals and 20,000 slaves.[58]

The story of the last part of the Peloponnesian War is the erosion of Athenian economic and financial resources on which her maritime power was based. Stimulation of secession and the encouragement of oligarchy made Spartan naval power more effective than perhaps its military prowess merited, aided by the discontent and ambition of the *dunatoi* in Athens and among her allies. Thucydides tells us that, when in the winter of 413-412 the Spartans turned their attention to the cities of the Athenian Empire, the majority of them in their rising tide of excitement did not think that Athens could last another year. First, the Euboeans approached Agis at Decelea for help in a revolt. Two Spartan commanders and a small force of enfranchised helots were organised for them, but one commander was reappointed as a harmost for Lesbos in response to an embassy from the island. Meanwhile, Chios and Erythrai appealed to the Spartan government at home, supported by a representative of the Persian satrap at Sardis, Tissaphernes. At the same time a Megarian and a Cyzicene exile arrived as ambassadors from Pharnabazos, the satrap at Daskyleion near the Sea of Marmora, proposing to detach Athenian allies in the Hellespontine area.

In the event, through lack of resources the Spartan alliance resolved to send a joint expedition, which was to go successively to Chios, Lesbos and the Hellespont. A harmost was appointed for each area. The harmosts had precedents in Salaithos, sent to Lesbos in 428, the governors who went to Thrace after Brasidas' successes, and Gylippos, the Spartan officer who had masterminded Syracusan resistance to Athens in 414-413. They were partly resistance-leaders and military organisers, partly political supervisors.

The forces for revolt within the cities themselves varied in strength. In Chios the business was managed by a small group of conspirators, who were obviously at the time in positions of power and able to direct public affairs, but were afraid of opposition from the majority of the population before the Peloponnesian arrival could give them backing.

They therefore actually sent seven ships to join the Athenian fleet in the spring of 412. Meanwhile the harbour barrier was removed for repairs and ladders were left about the harbour, ostensibly for the repair of leaking roofs on the shipyards, the nearby *stoa* and the fort. It was prearranged that a council should be in session when Alcibiades, the renegade Athenian, and Chalkideus, their Spartan organiser, sailed in without opposition. Thus, the secession was quickly arranged. However, a group remained who were ready to start a counter-revolution, when Athenian pressure was applied.[59]

Erythrai and Clazomenai quickly followed Chios' example, apparently without qualms in spite of the fact that Erythrai had a democratic constitution. However, the Athenians later easily reconquered Clazomenai and the faction that had caused the revolt had to flee. Thus, the instigators of the secession there were few and the majority had swum with the tide, as in the Chalkidic cities ten years earlier during Brasidas' operations. The population of Teos were at first induced by the presence of an Athenian fleet to remain loyal: they gave way to the land forces of Clazomenai and Erythrai when it departed. Teos had a wall protecting its mainland side and some of Tissaphernes' troops joined with the insurgents' army in pulling it down, once the city was occupied. Teos may have been grateful in the past for Athenian protection against the Persians. At any rate it soon returned to its allegiance to Athens.[60]

At Miletus initially the influence of Alcibiades was critical, since he was a personal friend of the political leaders. Although Miletus had been a democracy for some 30 years, it was dominated still by aristocratic families. When this constitution was overthrown with Spartan support in 405, 40 leaders of the democracy were killed at home and then 300 of the richest democrats in the *agora* (an echo of the sixth century democracy of Colophon described by Xenophanes). Nevertheless, 1,000 of the 'gentlefolk' (*chariestatoi*, Diodorus' equivalent for the 'best' or 'most powerful' men) escaped the revolution and took refuge with the Persian satrap. Such was the democracy that seceded in 412.

The Athenians seem to have suspected that the aristocracy at Samos would behave in a similar way. They encouraged a *coup d'état* against the existing regime by the *demos* – in this case a democratic faction which seems originally to have had general popular support. I argued earlier (p. 101) that the deposed regime was in form a democracy, as at Miletus, with a sovereign assembly and perhaps a council selected by lot, but dominated by those with the greater property qualifications. The object of the revolution was clearly to eliminate the leading *dunatoi* and redistribute their source of power. About 200 of the chief landowners (*geomoroi*) were killed, 400 exiled, and those who survived were cut off from all social and political ties with the rest of the population. The severity of these measures is striking. It is possible that the landowners had possessed estates in the mainland Anaia, which had been in the control of rebels since 428 at least, and had been collaborating with them. Their land and houses were reassigned, but it would appear from what followed that the new democratic leaders took the greatest share.[61]

The secession of Lesbos, promised to Agis the previous winter, was eventually undertaken with the aid of Chian warships and Peloponnesian troops. The forces of liberation won over Methymna and Mytilene, but they and their local supporters were defeated after the surprise arrival of an Athenian fleet. A Peloponnesian and Chian relief fleet persuaded other Lesbian cities — Pyrrha and Eresos — to secede, and landed a Spartan commander and a small force, but the commander was withdrawn when he made no further progress and this allowed the Athenians to resume control. It seems that the people of Lesbos remembered only too well their sufferings in 428-427, nor can we discount the influence of Athenian landlords assigned property after the previous revolt. The next summer exiles from Methymna, described by Thucydides as 'not the least powerful men', gathered together a force of some 300 partisan and mercenary hoplites and tried to seize Methymna. Beaten off by the Athenian garrison they made for Eresos as a second-best objective, which did in fact welcome them and seceded. However, this was the limit of their success.

By the winter of 412-411 the first wave of secession was over and with it the flood of confidence that the Athenian Empire would crack quickly. The island of Chios paid dearly for its revolt, because the Athenians landed a force on the island and devastated the countryside, establishing a strong-point not far from the city at Delphinion. In consequence the slaves, more numerous here than in any state except Sparta, deserted to the Athenians — a precise parallel to what was happening in Attica at the same time. Meanwhile, a conspiracy was mounted to bring the city back to allegiance to Athens and, although the Chians themselves were originally for less drastic measures, the Spartan military governor executed a group led by Tydeus, son of Ion, for 'Atticism', that is furthering Athens' interests. The rest of the city was by then being maintained as an oligarchy by force.[62]

The Peloponnesians, however, made further progress in the same winter by securing the revolt of the cities of Rhodes. The leading citizens (*dunatōtatoi*) invited a Peloponnesian fleet to sail over, and the frightened inhabitants of the island were persuaded to change their loyalty without bloodshed. It is tempting to detect here the influence of Dorieus the athlete, now commanding the ships of Italian Thurii in the Aegean. He and his family had been condemned to death and forced into exile from Rhodes and the Athenian Empire; he is attested to have been sent by the Spartans to suppress a counter-revolution there the next summer. Three years later, the regime made a synoecism, gathering the citizens into a new city at the north of the island called Rhodes. This certainly had an oligarchic constitution, which survived until it was overthrown in 395 by the Athenian Conon with the support of his Persian fleet.[63]

In the summer of 411 the Peloponnesians, assisted by the satrap Pharnabazos, detached Cyzicus, Abydos, Lampsacus and later Byzantium from Athens. Both Cyzicus and Lampsacus were quickly recovered. Byzantium had revolted from Athens spontaneously in 440, but on this occasion it only did so through the arrival of a Peloponnesian naval force, and it was later held by a Spartan harmost, Clearchos, and a garrison. After being besieged by the Athenians in 409-408, it was betrayed to them by five leading citizens, when Clearchos was temporarily absent.[64]

Further secessions ensued from the oligarchic revolution at Athens and the attempt to spread this revolution to other cities of the empire. What happened at Athens will be considered in the next chapter, but its effect on Athens' subject-allies provides a coda to the present discussion. When in the winter of 412-411 Alcibiades' original proposals for his own return and an oligarchic government were mooted, the implication was that the subject-allies would also be placed under oligarchies. This was one of the chief points seized upon by the Athenian general Phrynichos in his original objections to the plan (p. 97): it would neither bring back those who had revolted nor improve the allegiance of the loyal cities. They preferred freedom with the constitution they already possessed. The aristocrats were hostile to all Athenians and would be dangerous when in power, whereas the common people were the only counter-weight to these aristocrats and security for the Athenians.

When in the spring of 411 Peisandros and half of his commission of ten were sent home from Samos to set up the oligarchy at Athens, they were instructed to establish oligarchies also in the cities they visited on their voyage home, while the remaining five were detached and sent to do the same in different parts of the empire. Peisandros' group seem to have stopped at Andros, Tenos and Carystos — since they enlisted paramilitary supporters for the Athenian revolution from these places — also at Paros, but the oligarchy they set up there seceded. Eretria is another likely stopping-place, and they may have unwittingly contributed to the secession of Eretria later that summer. What followed was a bitter nationalist insurrection against the tight Athenian control imposed in 445. Dieitrephes, who had been appointed commander in Thrace, set up an oligarchy in Thasos, but the next month this group fortified the city and organised a secession. Thus Phrynichos was right, and the plans of the Athenian oligarchs achieved the opposite of what they intended. Thucydides surmises that the same was true in many other allied cities, which, when they received the 'discipline' of oligarchy and had no check on their policies, made for outright freedom.[65]

I have already discussed the problem of the attitude of the common people in the cities subject to Athens. I do not doubt that in some of them a majority of the citizens was eager for freedom through secession, if they thought it could be achieved without danger to themselves. This attitude was already in evidence at the time of Brasidas' expedition to Thrace and can be found in 412 in Euboea, at Erythrai and perhaps in Chios. However, during a full-scale war between Athens and Sparta, freedom was impossible without neutrality, and this could only be achieved by cities remote from the theatre of war. If a city seceded from Athens, it was liable to undergo not only an oligarchic government but one directed by a Spartan governor. This, aggravated by Athenian reprisals, nearly caused a counter-revolution on Chios and led eventually to the return of Byzantium to the Athenian side.

If we consider the events of 412-411, it appears from the evidence that we possess that the majority of citizens in Aegean, Ionian and Hellespontine cities were not involved in the decisions to secede. The revolts were arranged by small groups of influential people, and for the most part they took place under the threat of a Peloponnesian force. The chief revolts without coercion were those in Chios and at Miletus, and it can hardly be coincidence that there was, at least initially, more general enthusiasm for the move in these cities — shown in the Chian expedition to Clazomenai and Lesbos and the Milesian defence of their city by land (though they could only muster 800 hoplites). The political behaviour of the cities of the eastern Aegean suggests that they were still dominated by their wealthiest citizens, whatever their constitutions, as they had been before the Persian wars. The poor tended to follow the lead of the rich, especially when it was backed by military force, but hardship made them recalcitrant and in many cities a fresh military threat could persuade them to realign with Athens. This seems at first sight to imply that the common people there had no objection to the Athenian Empire. Maybe: but more significantly it implies that Athens had utterly failed to mobilise the feelings of the common people in the allied cities as a positive support for the empire. There were no popular uprisings against the Peloponnesian forces, only one in Samos against a faction Athens had herself helped to power.[66]

Events both before and during the war show that Athens tended to deal with the *dunatoi* in the allied cities, whether as oligarchs or democratic leaders. There are Alcibiades' friends in Miletos, the democratic faction which turned oligarchic in Samos and the various official friends (*proxenoi*) and benefactors attested in literature and on stones. The most detailed evidence we possess concerns Ion of Chios, the writer of drama and history, father of the Tydeus executed in 412 by the Spartans. He dined with Cimon at Athens as a young man and met the poet Sophocles at a dinner given by the Athenian *proxenos* at Chios in 440. Another important figure was Herakleides of Clazomenai, who helped Athens during the war and became an Athenian citizen and general. His nickname, 'the king', may reflect his membership of a family called 'kings' in his home town.[67]

The public role played by such men shows that their relationships were not exclusively with the Athenian aristocracy: they became, as it were, the *hetairoi* of the Athenian *demos*, and the *proxenos* inscriptions show how this was rewarded. Nor could any single group among the Athenian aristocracy necessarily claim an exclusive connection with them. However, their friendship with leading Athenians helps to explain Athens' astonishingly misconceived policy of establishing oligarchies in 411. The Athenian oligarchs thought that they could maintain good will between themselves and the governing classes of their allies, whatever the common people thought, by granting the local aristocracies the privileged position they were seeking. It was only when the oligarchic revolution was already taking place at Athens that representatives of the Samian *demos* formed a pact with the Athenian servicemen who were convinced democrats. This was to lead to a closer bond between Athens and Samos during the last years of the war than had ever before obtained between Athens and an allied city.

Notes

1. Ar., *Pol.* 1296a, 1307b; Thuc. I.19, 76.1, III.82.1, VI.11.7, VIII.47.6.
2. Hdt. V.62-93 (esp. 69-72); *Ath. Pol.* 20-2.2
3. Hdt. V.90.1, cf. 63.2. Forrest, 1969, 281, following Schweighäuser, argues that the text is wrong and that it was the Spartans, not the Athenians, who said that the Peisistratidai were their guest-friends. Nevertheless, this does

not discredit the story.

4. Thuc. VI.59.3; Hdt. V.91ff. For the belief that Spartan policy in Cleomenes' time was greatly influenced by opposition to Persia see e.g. Huxley, 1962, 73; Tomlinson, 1972, 92; *contra* Forrest, 1968, 84; Sealey, 1976, 196.

5. Hdt. V.68; *P. Ryl.* 18 (= FGH 105 Fl.), cf. Chapter 2, note 6.

6. Hdt. V.92.a; III.39.1, 44ff., VI.72; Plut., *Mor.* 859c.

7. Hdt. III.46, V.72,3, relics – I.67-8; Paus. VII.1.3; Leahy, 1955.

8. Thuc. I.17; Hdt. III.148, cf. V.49 on Aristagoras of Miletus.

9. Hdt. V.77-89, 91.2, VI.88-91.

10. Hdt. IX.37, VI.70.1, 74, VIII.26.1, IX.77; Andrewes, 1952; Wallace, 1954.

11. Hdt. I.82, VI.76-82 (cf. VII.148.2 for Argive dead); Mycenae and Tiryns – Hdt. VII.202, IX.28.4, ML 27, coils 6-7; stories of resistance within Argos – Paus. II.20.7-8, Socrates of Argos, FGH 310 F6.

12. Hdt. VI.83.1, 92, VII.148-50, IX.12; Ar., *Pol.* 1303a; Plut., *Mor.* 245f.; Willetts, 1959, on the meaning of the word *perioikoi*.

13. OP II, 222, lines 6, 31 (cf. Isoc. XVI.1); SEG XIII.239; Plut., *Them.* 20.3, 23.1; Thuc. I.135.3; Forrest, 1960.

14. Hdt. IX.35.2, VII.151; Diod. XI.65; Strabo VIII.6.11, 19 (372, 377); Paus. II.17.5, 25.7, V.23.3, VIII.27.1, X.10.4; *Syll.*[3] 28; Aesch., *Supp.* 600-24; Thuc. I.102.3; Andrewes, 1952; Forrest, 1960, though I have reservations about the latter's chronology.

15. Strabo VIII.3.2 (377); Diod. XI.54.1; Paus. V.10.2.

16. Thuc. III.82-3, esp. 82.1-2 with HCT II.372, cf. I.23.4. I take the excursus from 82.2 onwards to have been at least reworked in the light of the revolution at Athens. I do not believe 84 to be Thucydides' composition. Brief notices of *stasis* – IV.1.3 (Rhegium), V.4.3 (Leontini), V.5.1 (Messene), V.33 (Parrasia), VI.74 (Messene), 95 (Thespiai), VII.33.6 (Thurii), VII.46 (Agrigentum), VIII.44.1 (Rhodes).

17. Athens and Samos – VIII.47ff., 53ff., 63ff. Cf. VIII.89.2-3, which modifies III.82.8, suggesting that the greatest personal rivalries were among oligarchs. For *sophrosunē* (sound sense and discipline) as a catchword (III.82.8) see also VIII.53.3 and cf. 64.5 (ironical) and 48.6 (in my view a deliberate paradox). On loyalty to a *hetaireia* see Andoc. I.54ff. and below, pp. 127ff.

18. *Dunatoi* – I.24.5, 39.3, II.65.2, III.27.3, 47.3, IV.51, V.4.3, VIII.73.2. *Dunatōtatoi* – I.115.4-5, II.2.3, VIII.21*, 44.1, 47.2, 48.1*, 63.3*, 90.1 (* = preferred MS reading to *dunatoi*). Cf. VIII.100.3 – exiles not the least powerful (*adunatōtatoi*). By contrast Xenophon uses *beltistoi* ('the best men'). Diodorus has *dunatōtatoi* in XI.87.1, 4, XIII.48.3, 91.5, 93.3, 113.2, but also *chariestatoi* (XI.86.5, 87.4, 92.3, XIII.104.6), *epieikestatoi* (XIII.53.1) and *euporōtatoi* (XIII.93.2). Thucydidean terminology reappears in Arrian (I.17.3, 27.4) and Appian (*BC* I.7).

19. Contrast IV.51 and VIII.73.2 with II.2.3, VIII.21, 63.3. Cf. Ps. Xen., *Ath. Pol.* 1.3, where the *demos* allows the *dunatōtatoi archein* (those most capable of holding office) so to do.

20. II.65.2, III.70.4, 81.4. Cf. Xen., *Hipparch.* I.9-10 (cavalry to be *dunatoi* in wealth and physique). Fat men – Hdt. V.30.1 (Naxos), 77.2 (Chalkis), VI.91.1 (Aegina), VII.156.2 (Megarians in Sicily), cf. Arist., *Peace* 639.

21. III.74.2, V.82.2-3, VIII.9.3, 14.2, 38.3, cf. III.82.1, IV.86.4. Torone and Mende – IV.110.1, 123.2.

22. II.37.1 with HCT II.107ff. *Plēthos* – II.3.2, IV.104.4, 105.1, cf. I.115.5 – 'the greatest number'; VIII.73.3, 6 – 'the majority of the Samians'. Common people – III.27.2, 72.2, 73, 74.2, cf. IV.123.2, 130.4.

23. I.24.1, 25.1, V.82.2 (cf. VI.61.3), VIII.21, 63.3, 73.

24. IV.66.1, 3, 67.3, 68.4-6, 71.1, 73.4, 74.2.

25. VIII.21, V.4.2, V.82.2.

26. IV.76.2, 74.3, V.81.2, VIII.53.3, 89.2, 97.2. In the last passage one should perhaps understand *katastasa* with *xunkrasis* (cf. IV.74.3, V.81.2). See also Rhodes, 1972(2), 122f.

27. Small groups – III.70.6, IV.110.1, 123.2, cf. II.2.2, I.115.4-5; wider support – III.85.3 (cf. 70.1, 75.5); V.81.2, VIII.21, 73.2.

28. IV.66 (cf. II.31; Arist., *Acharn.* 729ff.), IV.81.2, 108.3.

29. III.82.1, 70ff., IV.66ff., 123.2, 130.4-6, V.76.2, 82.5, also IV.78.2, V.4.1-5, III.27.2, 47.1-3.

30. VIII.64.2-5, 48.5-6. On the latter passage see de Ste Croix, 1954, whose interpretation I accept in part; cf. HCT V.110ff. However, I take *'akritoi an . . . apothneskein'* to refer to leading Athenians like Phrynichos (the nominative marking a change of subject and denoting a group including the subject of the introductory verb).

31. Leaderless *demoi* – Corcyra (III.70), Mende (IV.130.4), Samos (VIII.73.4). Secession with democracy – Akanthos (IV.86.4; 88), Torone (IV.114.1-3). Cf. de Ste Croix, 1954; *contra* Bradeen, 1960; Quinn, 1964; de Romilly, 1966. Controversy summed up by Meiggs, 1972, 404ff.

32. Thuc. I.96.1-2, 97.1, 98.4-100; *Ath. Pol.* 23.5; Plut., *Arist.* 25.1 (cf. Thuc. I.44.1); Meiggs, 1972, 42ff.

33. Thuc. III.10.5, 11.4; Meiggs, 1972, 47f. *Proxenoi* – Arist., *Birds* 1021; Thuc. II.29.1, III.2.3; Hill B.33-5; ML 70, 80, 90, 91; GHI II.98, IG I².1034; ATPW 138.

34. Naxos – Plut., *Per.* 11.5; Diod. XI.88.3; Hdt. V.30.1; Meiggs, 1972, 121. Thasos – Pouilloux, 1954, I.121-34; Pleket, 1963; Meiggs, 1972, 85, 570-4.

35. War – Thuc. I.105.2-3, 108.4, II.27.1-2. Tribute and autonomy – Thuc. I.67.2, 144.2; Hill B.24 (cf. Lewis, 1954). Coinage-change dated by overstrikes – Robinson, *NC* 1961, 107; Kraay, *NC* 1969, 18. See also Meiggs, 1972, 182-4.

36. Thuc. I.108.2-3; Diod.XI.81-3; Pindar, *Isth.* 7.25ff.; Ar., *Pol.* 1302b; Ps. Xen., *Ath. Pol.* 3.11. Some time after 480 (Price and Waggoner, 1975, 53) and before the Herakles–Thebaios issues of the late fifth century there are separate coinages from Akraiphia, Coronea, Orchomenos, Tanagra and Haliartos; Tanagra also issued coins with 'B' for Boeotia instead of 'T' for Tanagra. However, it does not follow that all these should be precisely dated to 457-446 (Fowler, 1957).

37. ML 40, esp. lines 8, 13-14, 22, 25ff., 33; cf. Meiggs, 1972, 112; ATPW 71.

38. ML 43; Hill B.30 (ATPW 92), 115; Ps. Xen., *Ath. Pol.* 3,11; Thuc. I.115.2, VIII.17. Democratic formula – Herrman, 1970. Euthunos' archonship is either 426-425 or, if Diodorus has confused similar names, 450-449. For the later date see Mattingly, 1961, 174, 1966, 207; earlier date see e.g. Meiggs, 1972, 116, 562; Barron, 1962.

39. Thuc. I.114; ML 52; Hill B.52, 54; ATPW 102-3; Meiggs, 1972, 178, 565. Strategic importance – Thuc. II.14.1, VII.28.1.

40. Thuc. I.115-117, cf. I.40.5, 41.1, VIII.21; Plut., *Per.* 26-28; ML 56. 21 (ATPW 115), 72. 41; Nepos, *Timoth.* 1; Isoc. 15.111; Meiggs, 1972, 188-94; Will, 1969.

41. Democratic reputation – Thuc. III.47.2-3, IV.78.2-3; Ps. Xen., *Ath. Pol.* 1.14; Arist., *Acharn.* 642 (apparently ironical); jurisdiction – Meiggs, 1972, 220ff.; friends of Athens – Plato, *Ep.* VII, 332b-c; cf. note 33 above.

42. Thuc. I.122.1, III.13.5-6, cf. I.101.2. The effectiveness of this policy is not denied by Pericles in his pre-war speech (I.140-44).

43. Thuc. II.70.2-3, 79, II.2-6. *Prodosia* – Thuc. I.107.4, III.18.1, IV.7, 25.7, 49.1, 52.3, 89, 121.2, V.3.5, 33.1-3, 62.2, 64.1, 83.1-2, 116.3, VI.74.1, VII.48.2, VIII.60.1; Plut., *Alc.* 30 and Diod. XIII.66.4; Xen., *Hell.* I.3.20 and Diod.

XIII.76.5; cf. Losada, 1972.

44. Thuc. II.2.4, 3.3, 5.4-7. *Agora* – Aen. Pol. 1.9, 2.1, cf. Thuc. IV.113.2.

45. Thuc. III.2-18, 26-28; Peloponnesian advisers – 2.1, 3, 5.2, 13.1; *demos* – 27.2-3, cf. 3.4 for absence of ten ships serving with the Athenian fleet. Aristotle's statement (*Pol.* 1304a) that an Athenian *proxenos* began *stasis* there, after his sons were rejected as husbands, and stirred up Athenian hostility, seems to have little relevance to the story in Thucydides.

46. Thuc. III.27-8, 2.3, 3.4, 4.4, 36.1-3, 48.1-3, 50.1-2. Cleruchs – ATL D 22 (= SEG XIII.8); view of Spartans – Thuc. III.32.2.

47. Thuc. I.55.1, III.70 (the figure of 800 talents for the ransom is doubted in HCT II.359); Epidamnian *dunatoi* – I.24.6-7, 26, 29.5; treaty – I.44.1, but the Corcyreans acted in excess of this in 431 (II.25.1).

48. Thuc. III.71-81, 85, IV.46-48; cf. Diod. XIII.48.

49. Forts on the mainland annexed to Corcyra – III.85.2; attitudes – III.72.1, 75.1-4; numbers – I.55.1, III.75.5, 77.2, 85.2, cf. III.50.1, V.81.2 (difficult to assess the numbers of 'the many', especially as Corcyra used slaves among the rowers in her fleet, I.55.1).

50. Thuc. IV.37.5, 41.1-3, cf. I.103.1-3, IV.3.2-5.

51. Thuc. IV.66-74; Megarian decree – I.67.4, 139.1; Arist., *Acharn.* 515ff., 729ff.; *Peace* 606ff. with scholia; Plut., *Per.* 29-31; de Ste Croix, 1972, 225ff., in my view under-rating the effect of the decree on the Megarians. Cf. IG II^2.204; Dem.13.32 for later border disputes.

52. Thuc. IV.76, 89; cf. note 36 above for Theban domination now reflected in coinage.

53. Thuc. IV.70.1, 80-81, cf. I.56-58; ATL, list 23, col. II; HCT I.210f. for the extent of secession in 432.

54. Akanthos – Thuc. IV.84-88, Amphipolis – IV.103-08, Thucydides' comment – 108.3ff., cf. V.103, 111, VIII.24.5.

55. IV.109-116.2, 120-21, 123 (esp. 2), 130 (esp. 1, 4). Some seceding cities were later recovered by force (Torone – V.3.2, Galepsos – V.6.1, Skione – V.32.1).

56. V.7-10. Governors – IV.132.3, V.3.1-3, cf. VIII.5.1-2, 8.2, 28.5. *Harmostai* (VIII.5.2) is the official Spartan term for men whom Thucydides usually calls *archontes* (governors) – preferred by the pro-Spartan Xenophon. Cf. Diod. XIII.66.2; Schol. Pindar, *Ol.* VI.154 (where it is said that there were 20); Parke, 1930; Bockisch, 1965.

57. Thuc. V.76, 78, 80-84; Diod. XII.80.2-3; cf. Thuc. V.67.2; Aen. Pol. 17.2ff.; Paus. II.20.2; Plut., *Alc.* 15.3-4.

58. Sicily – Thuc. VI.52.1, 74.1, VII.48.2; Messenians – V.56.2-3, VI.105.2; cf. Diod. XIII.64.7 for loss of Pylos in 409-408; Decelea – Thuc. VII.19.1-2, 27-28; Lys. 20.33.

59. Thuc. VIII.2, 5-9, 14, cf. on Chios 24.4-6, 38.2-3; Aen. Pol. 11.3ff.; Quinn, 1969 (though I cannot believe with him that the council was in fact an oligarchic assembly); Meiggs, 1972, 358ff.

60. Thuc. VIII.14.2-3, 16, 20.2, 23.6, also 19.3-4 for secession of Ephesus, Lebedos and Hairai; Diod. XIII.71.1 and ML 88 for later allegiance of Clazomenians (including ex-rebels) to Athens.

61. Thuc. VIII.17 (cf. Diod. XIII.104.5-6; Plut., *Lys.* 19.2), VIII.21, 63.3 (cf. III.19.2, 32.2, IV.75.1, VIII.61.2).

62. Lesbos – Thuc. VIII.22-23, 32, 100.3, cf. III.50.2; SEG XIII.8; Chios – VIII.24, 38, 40; SGDI 5653; Meiggs, 1972, 13f., 362.

63. Thuc. VIII.44.1-2; Diod. XIII.38.5-6, 45.1, 75.1, XIV.79.6-7; *Hell. Oxy.* 15; Paus. VI.7.3-6; Androtion, FGH 324, F46.

64. Thuc. VIII.62, 80, 107; Xen., *Hell.* I.1.14-20, 1.35, 3.14ff.; Diod. XIII.66-67.

65. Thuc. VIII.64-65, 69.3; Diod. XIII.47.8; Eretria – Thuc. VIII.5.1-2, 95; ML 82 (ATPW 152); Thasos – Pouilloux, 1954, I.139; ML 83 (ATPW 153); *Hell. Oxy.* 7.4; Meiggs, 1972, 574ff.

66. Thuc. VIII.14.3, 22, 25.2ff., 73.4ff.

67. Ion, FGH 392, F13, F6; ML 70 (ATPW 138); Plato, *Ion* 541d; *Ath. Pol.* 41.3; cf. note 33 above and Meiggs, 1972, 13f.

4 DEMOCRACY AND OLIGARCHY IN ATHENS

From Cleisthenes to Ephialtes

In Chapter 3, largely thanks to Thucydides, we were able to view a panorama of the development of *stasis* in the fifth century. Such a view has its limitations: it is essentially external and distanced from its subject. There is only one city, where we can see the strife from inside, that is, from the point of view of the participants – Athens itself. Athens within ten years underwent two drastic revolutions from democracy to oligarchy and two corresponding counter-revolutions. The story has an enormous interest in itself, revealing the social and political tensions within Athens, as its empire weakened, and by contrast the remarkable resilience in the *demos* and the attachment to democratic institutions. These revolutions are also important for our analysis, because they reveal civil strife at its most sophisticated. Although the oligarchs of 411 were in many respects lineal descendants of the warring aristocrats of the Archaic Age, their motivation was more complex, as one would expect in men who had become previously adapted to pursuing their ambitions under democracy, and they operated with differing techniques since the task of revolution was much harder. Before we deal with the centrepiece of this chapter, we must trace the development of the politics of the Archaic Age into those of Classical Athens and see how the shape of conflict changed.

Cleisthenes' success in the civil war after the expulsion of the Peisistratidai enabled him to establish the basis for admission to and exercise of citizenship which he had advocated – the structure of the ten tribes with their constituent *trittyes* and *demoi*. This created a new social foundation for politics in the future, which would diminish the importance of the hereditary dependants of great families by its recognition of new citizens and disperse old factions into new political units. Apart from this, Cleisthenes created the institutional foundation for democracy in a revived sovereign assembly and an annual council selected by lot. Athens was soon sufficiently proud of her revolution to attempt to introduce it to her neighbour Aegina. Yet at the same time she felt threatened by the family of the deposed tyrant – not surprisingly in view of Cleomenes' attempt to restore Hippias. The direct descendants of Peisistratos were specifically listed on a monument, which recorded either their banishment for all time or perhaps their condemnation to death in their absence. As in the fifth-century decree from Miletus discussed earlier, at Athens anyone who should attempt a tyranny or support such an attempt was declared liable to be killed on sight without penalty.[1]

In the period after the battle of Marathon the Athenians also showed a more general suspicion of threats from powerful politicians through their use of ostracism. The invention of this device is attributed in the *Constitution of Athens* to Cleisthenes, although according to one text it was introduced shortly before it was first used in 487. The people had first to resolve to hold an ostracism; then at a further meeting without discussion they voted on potsherds (*ostraka*) whom they wished to leave Attica for ten years. These temporary exiles were allowed to retain the income from their property — a clear indication of the class of men against whom the measure was aimed. The first three victims were friends of the tyrants, we are told, including Hipparchos, son of Charmos, one of their relatives; then, after three years, the measure was turned against others whose power was uncomfortably great. It is not surprising that Athens feared the imposition of a tyranny in the decade after Hippias had been brought to Marathon by a Persian expedition. Indeed, it is arguable that the measure was directed on each occasion in this period at those who were suspected of being medisers and traitors. Hipparchos, son of Charmos, headed a list of *aliterioi kai prodotai* (accursed and traitors) on a bronze *stele*. Furthermore, we find on a number of early *ostraka* the words *aliterios* and *prodotes* and references to Median ancestry — associated with the names Callixenos, Aristeides, Menon and Xanthippos. Lack of hard evidence and the fear of blood-guilt would have precluded more direct action against these men according to the law against tyranny. The fear of Persian subversion must have continued at least until the withdrawal of Mardonius' army from Greece in 479. Athenian suspicions earlier that year were demonstrated when Lykides proposed that Xerxes' peace terms should be put to the Athenian assembly: he himself, his wife and children were stoned to death.[2]

However, the fear of a tyranny supported by the Persians was not the only factor behind the ostracisms, although it was the ostensible reason for them. Political rivalries between persons and groups were at work, exemplified by the famous deposit of 191 *ostraka* written in only 14 different hands and bearing Themistocles' name — probably prepared in advance but unused. These struggles continued after the failure of the Persian attacks and eventually did lead to Themistocles' ostracism (although he later joined the Persians when in exile, there was clearly no good evidence of such collaboration before he left Athens for Argos).

Unfortunately we have little evidence about this important period in Athenian politics, which was the prelude to a new political convulsion and the extension of Athenian democracy under Pericles. However, there can be little doubt about the nature of political alliances and conflicts. We have already seen how in the sixth century aristocrats formed groups of *hetairoi*, which were the material for the factional struggles in Lesbos and Attica. Although Cleisthenes went further in his political thinking to embrace the cause of the common people and so win a civil war, it was to be expected that the traditional aristocratic groups began to operate again, once the new democratic constitution was established. It appears from a number of authors, especially Plato and Xenophon, that a man was expected to help his personal friends and harm his enemies in politics. Moreover, an aristocrat, especially a politician of consequence, would surround himself with a *hetaireia* of close associates.[3]

Nevertheless, we should not assume that there was a single pattern of *hetaireia*, nor should we necessarily assimilate the followings of men like Themistocles or Cimon either to the upper-class drinking clubs attested at the time of the Peloponnesian War or to the groups of oligarchic conspirators that were formed during it. Certainly Cimon's friends (for example) met at *symposia* for entertainment, while the drinking clubs might be used to perform a political act, even if their members had no uniform political commitment. But these resemblances between groups do not imply a single type of association.

Initially, these associations were quite respectable, whether they were merely social gatherings of like-minded people or were used to coordinate their political and social strength. As we shall see, in spite of the suspicions raised by their involvement in the affair of the Herms in 415, they were still allowed to function without restriction and became the core of the oligarchic revolution in 411. After this they were to be viewed with more caution. The orator Hypereides tells us that the law regarding impeachment (*nomos eisangeltikos*) applied to any man who might gather a *hetairikon* to overthrow the democracy.[4]

About 460 BC, a new dimension was given to the rivalries between groups. Cimon, the general who had been regularly commanding the forces of the Delian confederacy, had great influence for this reason and increased it by largesse from the products of his family estates. This, we are told, led a certain Damonides to recommend to Pericles a policy of paying state officials and jurors from public funds: it was the only way that Pericles could outdo a richer man in captivating the voting public. However, Cimon's fall cannot be ascribed to Pericles' use of this strategy. His ostracism derived from a conflict with Ephialtes which had arisen over his own support for Sparta against the insurgent helots and Ephialtes' attack on the powers of the Areopagus, the aristocratic council of ex-archons.[5]

The Areopagus had acquired considerable *de facto* power at the time, allegedly through its conduct in the Persian wars, although one may suspect that this was not all. As a body, its explicit powers lay in the supervision of the constitution as a whole. It had come to supervise certain aspects of state administration and justice. A further possibility is that the Areopagus had deliberated on matters of state and passed on its collective opinions to the assembly through its leading members, as it did in the late fourth century. Ephialtes initiated prosecutions of individual members for their management of public affairs — Pericles' prosecution of Cimon may be numbered among them — and also introduced legislation. It is doubtful if any constitutional reforms could have immediately curbed the Areopagites' unofficial influence, but the prosecutions may have cowed them, and the weight carried by the council would have been diminished when in 457 it was opened to a lower property class and ceased to be an exclusive province of the aristocracy. Ephialtes' legislation itself can hardly have abolished the Areopagus' duty to watch over the constitution, as this was a feature of the democracy restored in 403 after the expulsion of the oligarchic faction of 'thirty tyrants'. More probably, Ephialtes and Archestratos deprived the Areopagus or individual ex-archons of supervisory functions in state administration and judicial functions, for example in handling the audits of retiring magistrates.[6]

However obscure the reforms are to us, they stirred up the greatest political conflict since the time of Cleisthenes. Ephialtes himself was murdered. Aristocratic resentment against the reforms was again manifested in 458. A Peloponnesian army, which was in Boeotia seeking a route home, was approached by Athenians who wished an end to the democracy and to the building of the Long Walls linking Athens to the Peiraeus (which would make Athens almost impregnable to land attack and Spartan pressure). This led to a fierce battle between the Peloponnesian and Athenian armies at Tanagra. The Spartans won but used their advantage merely to make a safe return home. Cimon had offered his help to Athens at this battle, but this was rejected as a trap. However, he begged his *hetairoi*, led by Euthippos, to fight bravely. Their valour and casualties, we are told, convinced the Athenians that they were not oligarchic revolutionaries, and Cimon himself was later recalled from exile on Pericles' proposal.[7]

Periclean Democracy and the Reaction

The closing of ranks against foreign enemies at Athens in the 450s in effect secured the permanence of Ephialtes' reforms and provided a base for Pericles' own programme of pay for public service. It also afforded a pretext for the removal of the treasury of the Delian League to Athens and thus facilitated the subsequent use of its funds for the building programme at Athens. However, after Cimon's death and the cessation of hostilities with Persia in 449, political conflict arose over the exploitation of this money between Pericles and Cimon's relative, Thucydides, son of Melesias. Plutarch regards this as a split between the aristocrats and the people as a whole which led to the aristocrats being called the few. Certainly, Thucydides tried to make the most of his supporters — presumably his group was based on Cimon's *hetairoi* — by making them sit in one part of the assembly. Yet their allegiance was primarily to him as a person: they were dispersed after his ostracism. Nor were such groups peculiar to oligarchs or representatives of the aristocracy. Pericles had his own group, who were perhaps also personal friends, like Damonides and Metiochos. A division between the many and the few had already made an appearance with the murder of Ephialtes and the invitation to the Spartans. The conduct of Thucydides may have reawakened suspicions, but his opposition was in the open, and his ostracism in 443 may be regarded as the normal fate of a powerful politician who was at the time not quite powerful enough.[8]

In the years of Pericles' ascendancy democracy was not in dispute. Criticisms of the behaviour and policy of Pericles and his friends seem to have come from those who had risen to political or military eminence after Ephialtes' reforms — Diopeithes, Drakontides and perhaps Glaukon. The atmosphere, however, changed during the Archidamian War — perhaps from the time of the plague and the attempted peace negotiations with Sparta in 430, certainly after Pericles' death. By then many Athenians would have had strong reasons for wanting peace. As the oligarchic essay, ascribed to Xenophon, on the constitution of Athens points out, it was the farmers and rich who were more vulnerable to the enemy when land was ravaged. For the author this meant that the major disadvantage of Athens' position, the fact that it was not an island, did not affect the common people. It must be admitted that this was an exaggeration: Thucydides states that both the common people and the rich suffered loss. Even so, not all farmers were eager for peace because of their losses, to judge from Aristophanes' *Acharnians*. However, the oligarchic sympathiser points out a further Athenian weakness, the possibility of revolution against the *demos*, since the insurgents could bring in enemy aid by land. Thus, we discover not only a possible source of bitterness between the classes during the war but also how suspicions might arise of a conspiracy against the democracy. This contrasts with the general theme of the essay, which sets out to illustrate, with some irony, the invulnerability of democracy through its efficiency in looking after itself: the final comment is that there are few with such a grudge that they would attack the democracy. If the essay was written c. 428-424, as has been argued with some plausibility, this reflects the continuing strength of the democratic constitution.[9]

Yet there is evidence of suspicion between rich and poor in Aristophanes' treatment of Cleon and his supporters in the *Knights* and *Wasps*, produced in 424 and 422, respectively. The character Bdelucleon complains, 'Everything for you is now tyrants and conspirators [*synomotai*].' He has aroused the wrath of the wasp jurymen for shutting up his father and preventing him joining them in court. They accuse him repeatedly of open tyranny, adding charges of conspiracy, consorting with the enemy (Brasidas), wearing woollen-fringed tunics and letting his beard grow. Bdelucleon alleges that the man who buys orphs for dinner rather than small anchovies gets the comment, 'This fellow seems to be giving a party in preparation for a tyranny.' Such remarks were a recent occurrence: Bdelucleon says that he has not heard the word tyranny in fifty years. Similar accusations are made by the Paphlagonian, Aristophanes' portrait of Cleon, in the *Knights*. When the chorus of knights attack Cleon, he calls them conspirators; then he threatens them and his rival, the Sausage-Seller, with denunciation before the Council of 500 for conspiracy, meetings by night, pledges exchanged with the Persians and intrigue with the Boeotians. He even carries out his threat, though to no avail.[10]

Such charges must have been part of Cleon's stock-in-trade. What, if anything, was their basis? The knights were young aristocrats, who appear in the play self-consciously patriotic and proud of their landing on the Peloponnesian coast near Corinth. As aristocrats they may have been embittered by Cleon's diligence in collecting taxes, and they had a particular grievance over a charge of desertion brought against them by Cleon, which they had countered by inspiring an accusation of him for embezzlement. Cleon, though of a wealthy family, is said by Plutarch to have distanced himself from his natural friends in order to enhance his ties with the common people. Yet he appears in the *Wasps* in an upper-class drinking party, and one may doubt whether he dispensed with the support of men of his own class in politics, even if like Pericles he tried to present himself as one whose interests were identical with those of the *demos*. So far these accusations of tyranny seem to be mere political abuse creating the public image of himself that Cleon desired. There was no serious rival to him as a demagogue at the time, no real counterpart to the Sausage-Seller. Nevertheless, he may have had genuine suspicions of some aristocrats and he certainly must have struck a chord among Athenians by employing such charges. When in 425 the assembly accepted Cleon's rhetorical offer to seize the Spartans marooned on the island of Sphacteria, there were men, called by Thucydides 'moderate' (*sōphrones*), who thought that they would benefit, whatever happened. Either they would be rid of Cleon — and this is what they expected — or they would be proved wrong and he would put the Spartans in their power. Thucydides seems to be describing men who accepted the democracy and were otherwise patriotic but would have liked to end the war on honourable terms, distrusting for this reason Cleon's leadership and his swift rejection of the Spartan offer of peace. It is easy to see how Cleon could have attacked such men as Spartan sympathisers and suggested that their only object was to preserve their own wealth and standing as fine gentlemen.[11]

Although Cleon played on suspicions of tyranny and oligarchy, there is no evidence for genuine conspiracy against the democracy at this stage. However, in addition to the usual overlapping political *hetaireiai* and social coteries among the aristocracy, there had probably already begun to grow the secret associations, formed among the wealthy *dunatoi* for their own advancement, that came to light some ten years later. When Peisandros was preparing the oligarchic revolution in the winter of 412-411 at Athens, he approached the *synomosiai*, conspiracies or sworn brotherhoods, 'which happened to exist already in the city for the purpose of law-suits and public offices', and urged them to unite to overthrow the democracy. Such groups had presumably pursued the interests of their own members exclusively before. The best example known of a member of such a group is the orator Antiphon. He did not speak in the assembly himself but advised those who spoke there or in the courts. Some of the speeches he wrote have survived as testimony to this. An Antiphon also appears as a member of an arrogant, rowdy, upper-class drinking party in Aristophanes' *Wasps*. We should not infer that every *symposion* like this was also a *synomosia*, but their memberships would have been drawn from similar social circles.

It was probably aristocratic in-groups like these who adopted the eccentricities in dress and grooming — letting their hair and beards grow and wearing Spartan clothes — that were associated with treachery to the democracy in Aristophanes' *Wasps*. Their characteristics overlapped those of the followers of Socrates (which some may have been but all were surely not), and these were lumped together by Aristophanes in the *Birds* of 414: 'Everyone used to be Spartan-mad, long-haired, fasting, filthy, Socratising and carrying little batons.' We also hear of a club to which the poet-turned-informer Cinesias belonged, which held dinners with secret rites and called themselves the damned, thus mocking the gods and the law of Athens.[12]

Athenian hostility to such eccentricities had a conspicuous target in Alcibiades, who was deliberately a law to himself in his luxurious living. Thucydides, explaining how his extravagance and need of new sources of wealth brought disaster to Athens, argues that this disregard of convention combined with flagrant ambition caused him to be resented and feared by the majority of people as an aspiring tyrant. Nevertheless, he was probably a general at least four times between 420 and 415. His private life became a serious impediment to his political career only in 415 on the eve of his departure with the great Athenian expedition to Sicily which he himself had advocated.

One night shortly before this armament departed, the majority of the stone herms, phallic embodiments of good luck found on many public and private sites throughout the city, were mutilated. The Athenian public took a serious view of this, regarding it as an ill omen for the expedition and the work of people conspiring to cause revolution and the overthrow of democracy. No evidence about the outrage was immediately forthcoming, but earlier acts of vandalism by drunken young men on other statues were denounced as were parodies of the mysteries. Alcibiades was accused of complicity in the latter, and this was seized on by his rivals for the leadership of the democracy. They made an outcry, alleging that he was deeply implicated in both the affair of the herms and the mysteries, and as proof dragged in all his past lawless behaviour. Two leading demagogues involved in the prosecution of the outrages were Cleonymos and Androkles, while two of the investigators, who fostered suspicions of an anti-democratic plot, were Peisandros and Charikles, later to be respectively the master-mind in the oligarchic revolution of 411 and a member of the junta of 30 tyrants in 404. The assembly decided that Alcibiades should sail, in spite of his offers to stand trial first. This was encouraged by his enemies who feared his popularity with the army and realised that he was unlikely to be convicted if it appeared that this would endanger the success of the expedition.[13]

Alcibiades' opponents seem to have had little genuine fear of him as a fomenter of revolution. Otherwise they would have been reluctant to see him leave at the head of this expedition. Nor can they have believed that he was responsible for the mutilation of the herms, which cast a shadow over the expedition which was his own pet project. They simply seized a chance to exploit a weakness in his public standing and that nervousness of the Athenians about oligarchy and tyranny, specifically attested by Thucydides in this context. They got the evidence they wanted about Alcibiades' participation in a mockery of the mysteries but also a much richer harvest.

There were four denunciations about parodies of the mysteries. The first, by the slave Andromachos, did not take place until after the expedition sailed and an investigating tribunal had been appointed. Further information was laid by a metic, Teukros, Agariste the wife of Alkmeonides, and a slave, Lydos. Both Andromachos and Agariste denounced Alcibiades and his friends and relatives, including Axiochos, Adeimantos and Archebiades. This testimony led to a formal prosecution of Alcibiades by Thessalos, son of Cimon. Teukros denounced a second group including Phaidros from the Socratic circle, while Lydos informed on his master Pherekles and some friends of his.

There is nothing in the denunciations or the lists of names to suggest that these groups were anything more than social gatherings seeking an unusual kind of entertainment. Alcibiades certainly had *hetairoi* in the sense of political friends, and those involved with him in the mock mysteries were probably also members of this group. Yet there is no reason to believe that these had oligarchic ambitions at this time. The same applies in general to the friends of Phaidros and Pherekles. However, Pherekles, Euphiletos, probably also Theodoros and Meletos were accused of both offences, and the informer Teukros knew those involved in both. Therefore, we cannot consider the mutilation and the parody to have been two entirely unrelated activities, even if it was cleverly exploited prejudice that caused them to be treated as part of a single plot.[14]

The first information about the mutilation of the herms was laid by Teukros. His list included Theodoros, Meletos, Pherekles and Euphiletos from among those implicated in the mock mysteries. Then Peisandros and Charikles, who were among the investigators, argued that the act must have required more than 18 men and had a wider purpose — that of overthrowing the democracy. This encouraged Diokleides to claim that he had seen on the night in question about 300 men coming down from Pericles' Odeion into the orchestra of the theatre of Dionysus (the implication was that they had been using the Odeion under the Acropolis as a secret meeting place). He gave 38 names including those of Andokides, his father Leogoras, eight other relatives of his and two sitting councillors. Among these were Eukrates, the brother of the general Nikias, and a Critias, who may have been later the head of the Thirty Tyrants. It was suggested that they should be tortured, and the two councillors first took refuge at the sacred hearth of the city and later escaped on horseback. At the same time there was an alarm and the whole city was called to arms, because a Boeotian force was on the frontier, perhaps hoping to exploit the confusion at Athens. Furthermore, then or a little later, a Spartan army arrived at the Isthmus and gave credibility to suspicions that an oligarchic plot was afoot and that Alcibiades was behind it.

Fearing the consequence for himself and his family, Andokides then laid information against a group led by Euphiletos and Meletos, of which he was a member, and in consequence Diokleides confessed that his accusation was trumped up. Andokides for the most part denounced those already accused by Teukros, adding only four names. However, he did reveal a little of what happened, while disassociating himself from voluntary complicity in the act. According to him, the mutilation was suggested by Euphiletos at a drinking party and opposed by himself. The project was carried out later, when Andokides had a broken collar-bone after a fall from a horse. So one herm apparently assigned to him remained untouched, that dedicated by the tribe Aigeis near his own house. However, he was urged by Euphiletos and Meletos not to inform on the group or it would be the worse for him. The aim of the vandalism against the herms was, we are told, to provide a mutual pledge among the members. It would have been thus an initiation test and also a bond through their shared guilt.[15]

The group seems therefore to have been not just a social club but a brotherhood for mutual assistance in lawsuits and elections, as described by Thucydides. Furthermore the mutilation was surely aimed at discrediting the Sicilian expedition. It is arguable that Andokides in his own defence has played down a serious attempt by an oligarchic conspiracy to damage a major policy adopted by the assembly. This *hetaireia* is a pointer to the general character of the brotherhoods later approached by Peisandros in 411.[16]

The major achievement of the herm-mutilators was one that they probably did not foresee. The scandal spread to the parodies of the mysteries (in which some of them had participated for reasons not political) and caused a split between Alcibiades and a large section of the *demos*, which had previously tolerated the licence of his private life because of his military ability. This alienation was fostered by men who at the time were rival demagogues, notably Androkles and Cleonymos. But it was probably regarded with favour by oligarchs, who would not have wished to see Alcibiades become another supreme demagogue like Pericles or Cleon.

The Revolution of 411

The apparently hopeless position of Athens after the failure of the Sicilian expedition needs no detailed recapitulation here. The Athenians were deprived of the use of land in Attica and of a land route to resources in Euboea by King Agis at Decelea; they were short of trained men, ships and money; most of their tribute-paying allies were planning revolt in co-operation with Sparta. The only immediate constitutional change was the appointment of an advisory board of ten *probouloi*, presumably as a check on the orators on the assembly who, in company with the seers and soothsayers, were blamed for the Sicilian expedition. Nor was there any attempt to negotiate a peace.

A year passed in which Athens' major allies in Ionia, apart from Samos and most of Lesbos, joined her enemies. Alcibiades was in the meantime prominent as an agent of revolt, especially through his contact with the aristocracies in the cities. Some time in winter 412-411 Alcibiades fled from the Peloponnesian camp to Tissaphernes in order to avoid execution for suspected treachery. He advised Tissaphernes to cut down the pay he provided for the Peloponnesian forces — a policy which suited the satrap's long-term interests and would earn Alcibiades himself credit with the Athenians. His influence with Tissaphernes was noted, and he sent letters to the leading men (*dunatōtatoi*) in the Athenian expedition on Samos, asking them to spread the word around the 'best men' (*beltistoi*), that is the upper class or *dunatoi* in general, that he wished to return to Athenian citizenship under an oligarchy and would offer an alliance with Tissaphernes as a bargaining counter. The majority of the leading Athenians and the wealthy trierarchs financing the fleet were in a mood to accept these proposals, as in their view they were suffering the greatest hardships and they saw in Persian aid the main hope of winning the war, which was still their object.

After a conference with Alcibiades on the mainland they formed a sworn brotherhood (*synōmosia*, also referred to as a *hetairikon*) and even announced their plan in general terms to the ordinary seamen. Only one of their party opposed Alcibiades' offer openly — Phrynichos. As we have seen, he did not believe that oligarchic government would help them to retain the empire, nor did he think that Persian aid would come. He correctly understood that Alcibiades was only concerned with his own recall to Athens, which required a change of regime. However, the oligarchic conference considering the proposals decided to send Peisandros at the head of an embassy to organise the execution of their programme at Athens.[17]

When Peisandros mooted his proposals in the Athenian assembly there was general opposition to the abandonment of democracy and Alcibiades' personal enemies protested against his return, supported by the priestly families of the Eleusinian cult. Peisandros argued that a Persian alliance was Athens' only hope of salvation and described the proposed constitutional changes in vague and soothing phrases: 'We will not achieve our aim without a more disciplined and responsible political framework, confining public office to a more limited circle of people and thinking of survival first rather than politics. For we will be able for sure to make adjustments of anything that is unsatisfactory later.' The assembly gave way and voted that Peisandros should return with a commission of ten to negotiate with Alcibiades and Tissaphernes. Meanwhile Phrynichos and Skironides were deprived of their posts as generals. So Peisandros got public support for his plan, but more important in the long run was the sinister and unofficial backing that he obtained from the *synomosiai*. We have already considered the growth of the secret associations, which Thucydides seems to have differentiated by this term from ordinary *hetaireiai* and which were exemplified in the group of Euphiletos. Previously, they had worked competitively for the interests of their own members in lawsuits and elections. Now they were urged by Peisandros to unite in a single organisation to overthrow the democracy.[18]

The negotiations with Tissaphernes failed. In Thucydides' view Tissaphernes feared an open break with the Peloponnesians, and he did not want to commit himself entirely to Athens. However, on their return to Samos in the early spring of 411 they and their fellow conspirators decided to continue on their own the oligarchic movement, simultaneously pursuing the war with finance from their own family fortunes. In harmony with the revolution planned at Athens they began to create oligarchies among Athens' remaining allies, perhaps in the hope that they could retain the allies' allegiance through their own personal links with the ruling groups. The previous summer the Athenians had helped to overthrow the ruling class of landowners on Samos. The conspirators now urged the new political elite in Samos to adopt oligarchic government, in spite of the fact that their previous revolution had been, in appearance at least, designed to ensure democracy. This policy was to be counter-productive on Samos and, as we have seen, encouraged rather than stifled secession elsewhere in the empire.

Peisandros and his five companions were, however, more successful on their return to Athens. The *hetairoi* of the oligarchic brotherhoods had prepared the ground, eliminating by assassination 'unsuitable' people who might impede the project, notably Androkles who with Peisandros had pressed the investigation against Alcibiades in 415. The murders may also have been intended to unite the conspirators through the common perpetration of crimes, as in the mutilation of the herms. One may compare the aim of the revolutionary Peter Verkhovensky in Dostoievsky's *The Devils*, when he arranges the murder of Shatov. Although the constitution was unchanged, the conspirators had come to take over control of the city. They had drawn up a programme for the abolition of pay for civilian officials and the limitation of political activity to a body of 5,000 — those who could most help the city with money or physical strength, that is probably a hoplite franchise. Thucydides brands this programme as spurious from the start, since the conspirators planned to take over the city themselves. In the meanwhile they had assumed the function of vetting what was on the agenda of the council and the assembly — presumably in conjunction with the existing *probouloi*, whose co-operation with the revolution is attested later. The speakers in the assembly were also members of the conspiracy, whose speeches had been discussed beforehand by the conspirators in caucus. Anyone who opposed them in the assembly died in some 'suitable' way. The effect was to cow the city. The conspiracy was considered greater and more formidable than it was in fact. The conspirators had the advantage of knowing who belonged to their group. The rest of the citizens were deterred by being unable to share their grievances with each other and so mount a policy of resistance. There was on a smaller scale in Athens the isolation that characterises a present-day metropolis. Moreover, one could not trust one's acquaintances, since many unexpected figures appeared as advocates of oligarchy.[19]

There were four main stages in the conspiracy: the preliminary work in Samos; the legitimising and publicising of the project at Athens during Peisandros' first visit; the creation of an underground movement and the elimination of opposition by violence; the constitutional *coup* itself. This last stage remains to be considered. The facts are a matter of some controversy, since at this point we have as source material not only the narrative of Thucydides but chapters from the *Constitution of Athens* and some passages from oratory of the period. To state my position briefly, I follow the view that while Chapter 29 of the *Constitution* may provide material which can supplement Thucydides' narrative, the two which follow are no more than draft constitutions, prepared as oligarchic publicity during the rule of the Four Hundred, but neither drawn up by an official commission appointed by an assembly of 5,000 nor ratified by this assembly. Indeed I follow the *Constitution* itself, when it states that the selection of this 5,000 was a pretence without practical effect. This statement endorses what is implicit in Thucydides' narrative — that the oligarchic council which seized power ruled without wider consultation, and that conflict and confusion over the creation of a broader assembly arose because it was a part of the oligarchic programme which the hard-line oligarchs did not want to realise, and thus it could be used as a weapon by their opponents. The following reconstruction of the oligarchic *coup* is based on these assumptions.[20]

When Peisandros and his five fellow ambassadors returned, an assembly was held at their instance. Pythodoros then proposed a decree that a commission, either of ten (Thucydides) or 30 including the existing *probouloi* (other sources), should be elected to redraw the constitution and to present proposals to a future assembly on a preappointed day. Cleitophon added a rider, that the commission should examine the 'ancestral constitution' of Cleisthenes, when he founded the democracy, on the ground that it was less *demotikos* (in the power of the people) and more like Solon's. There is no sign that this had any practical effect — indeed, such study would not have helped the oligarchs much — but it reveals the psychology of the assembly. Democracy was accepted then as Athens' 'ancestral constitution', but the current political norms were out of favour. So they wanted a democracy that was not ruled by the common people.[21]

After the lapse of some time, the next assembly was held at Colonos, a precinct of Poseidon over a mile outside the city walls. The commissioners simply proposed a ban on prosecution for illegal proposals to the assembly (*graphē paranomōn*), the major impediment to swift alterations of Athenian law in the fifth century. The declared aim was to allow any Athenian the freedom to propose anything, but they may have been unable to agree among themselves about a precise constitution. Then Peisandros advocated openly that the magistracies should be changed, that pay for office should be abolished, and that they should choose five presidents, who should in turn choose 100 men, each of whom should co-opt three more. The resulting body of 400 should take over the council chamber and have full discretionary powers to govern Athens. They should call an assembly of the Five Thousand, when they saw fit.

We find also in the *Constitution of Athens* proposals that the presidents of the council and nine archons were to be paid, that the Five Thousand should have powers to conclude international agreements with whom they wished, and that they should be selected by a commission of 100 registrars, ten chosen from each tribe. The first of these proposals may well be genuine, assuming that Thucydides left out a qualification to the main motion about pay. The second conflicts with the discretionary powers assigned to the Four Hundred in Thucydides' account and does not suit the oligarchic plan to keep power among the revolutionaries. On the last point the speech for Polystratos in the Lysias corpus casts some uncertain light. Polystratos was selected by his tribe as a candidate for some office, but it is not clear when and as what: he was perhaps already in office in some capacity, when the revolution occurred, since this is used as an argument that he was not an oligarch, when he became a councillor under the Four Hundred. He apparently was a registrar and, although the Athenians voted to put power in the hands of 5,000, in order to avoid animosities, he had registered 9,000 citizens. If Polystratos was elected registrar by an assembly, it must have been at the Colonos assembly, the last for some time. Equally, he may have been appointed by the Four Hundred. His claim that he enrolled 9,000 citizens need not imply any real achievement. More probably, he failed to cut down an original list (perhaps of cavalry and hoplites) provided him. The speech in fact suggests what we might have guessed otherwise, that the registration of 5,000 was an afterthought of the Four Hundred, not undertaken with any conviction.[22]

There was no opposition to Peisandros' proposal and the assembly approved it. In theory this decree was enough to effect the revolution. However, if there had been any sufficiently determined group in the democratic council, they might have held another assembly in another place and reversed Peisandros' motion. For the ultimate sovereignty of the assembly had not been overthrown; only the nature of the assembly had been changed and, since the Five Thousand had not yet been selected, an assembly convened in the democratic interest could have masqueraded as 5,000. For this reason it was essential for the conspirators to remove the democratic council of 500, which had the initiative in calling assemblies. They did this by force straight away after the Colonos meeting. The conspirators were told not to go to their usual military posts like the rest of the citizens but to stay apart and prevent others leaving their posts and interfering. Three hundred men from Andros, Tenos, Carystos, and the Athenian colony on Aegina, who had come to Athens under arms to help the oligarchs make their *coup*, were also assigned to this task. It may be that Pythophanes, a man honoured in an oligarchic decree on stone, was one of them. The Four Hundred themselves came each with a hidden dagger (the traditional weapon for political assassinations), and were supported by a group of 120 young men, whom they used when they needed physical force, probably those mentioned later as drawn from the cavalry. They told the democratic councillors to take their pay and go. And the councillors complied, solemnly receiving at the door the sum due to them for their remaining month of office, which the Four Hundred themselves had brought, probably from their own funds. The Four Hundred then took their seats in the council chamber, chose their committee of chairmen by lot and performed the prayers and sacrifices appropriate to the beginning of a year of office. Subsequently they made many alterations to the democratic system of administration without reference to any assembly and managed the city by force. Men 'suitable' for elimination were killed, others imprisoned or banished. They also tried without success to negotiate with the Spartan king Agis at Decelea. The regime was to last some four months.[23]

The Four Hundred evidently had doubts about the future reaction to their *coup* among those on Samos, especially the rowers in the fleet. They sent an embassy to reassure the expeditionary force that the oligarchy was for the good of the city, claiming that it was indeed a body of 5,000, not 400, and that 5,000 was more than usually met in an Athenian assembly. However, at almost the same time the oligarchs remaining on Samos had failed in a plot to establish the oligarchy among the Samians themselves. They had persuaded the 300-strong elite of the newly established democracy to change into an oligarchy. In order to cement the conspiracy, a group of Samians and Athenians, including General Charminos, assassinated the ostracised Athenian demagogue Hyperbolos, just as the conspirators in Athens killed Androkles. They were about to mount a *coup* against the Samian citizen body as a whole but were forestalled by the Samian democrats, who had learnt of the plot. These approached Athenians known to be hostile to oligarchy, including two generals, Leon and Diomedon, and Thrasyboulos and Thrasyllos, a trierarch and hoplite soldier. The Athenian democrats had to leave Samos on war service but arranged that a force, including the crew of the state-trireme Paralos, should stay behind to protect the Samian democracy, and so the *coup* of the 300 was frustrated. Reprisals were kept to a minimum, and under new leadership the democracy was stronger and more loyal to Athens than before.

The Athenians on Samos, not knowing yet of the revolution at

Athens, sent back Chaireas on the Paralos to tell their story. The Four Hundred detained the crew, but Chaireas got back to Samos with exaggerated stories of past atrocities against the democrats and their families and of threatened reprisals. His listeners were eager to stone the oligarchs but were restrained. Then Thrasyboulos and Thrasyllos made the whole army, oligarchs included, swear a great oath to maintain the democracy without political faction, to carry on the war against the Peloponnesians and to treat the Four Hundred as enemies with whom there should be no negotiation. The generals and trierarchs whose politics were suspect were then deposed and replaced, Thrasyboulos and Thrasyllos becoming generals. This may be regarded as the first major military revolt in ancient Greece, one in which the military set themselves up as the true embodiment of the state. It was also a revolt of the Athenian Empire, since through it Athens lost not only her major remaining ally but also the means of exacting tribute from other cities.[24]

The embassy from the Four Hundred did not dare for the moment to proceed to Samos but waited on Delos. Meanwhile, Thrasyboulos persuaded the expeditionary force to receive back Alcibiades, who they still hoped would provide Persian money. He did his best to encourage this belief by some magniloquent promises. But he also had to ensure that this new confidence did not lead the men on Samos to make war on the government at home. Their feelings were again embittered by the arrival of the oligarchic envoys. The envoys denied the atrocities and the suggestion that they were planning to surrender the city to Sparta, and made a promise either that all the Five Thousand would take part in government in turn or that everyone in turn would be members of the Five Thousand. They did not convince their audience and Alcibiades made a timely intervention to cool emotions. He himself put forward counter-proposals to the ambassadors. The sovereignty of the Five Thousand was acceptable, economy measures which would increase supplies to the army were admirable, but they must reinstate the democratic council, abolish the Four Hundred and above all refuse to surrender. If either of the two communities was defeated, the political schism would be necessarily perpetuated.[25]

When the embassy brought this message back from Alcibiades, the majority of those who had participated in the oligarchic conspiracy were already discontented and ready to abandon it, if they could do so without risk to themselves. The message gave them encouragement and a pretext for complaint. They found leaders from the inner circle of oligarchs, including Theramenes and Aristokrates. These voiced fears about both the attitude of Alcibiades and of the forces on Samos and

the mischief that those currently on an embassy to Sparta might do
without consulting the opinion of the majority. In fact three Athenian
ambassadors had been detained in Argos at the instance of the crew of
their Athenian trireme and then taken from there to Samos. The objec-
tors urged that extreme oligarchy should be avoided, the Five Thousand
should be established in reality and there should be greater equality
among the citizen body. According to Thucydides, the majority of the
important oligarchs who adopted this line did so through personal
jealousies and ambitions. They thought that the oligarchy would not
last, and Alcibiades' strong position in Samos induced them to follow
his policy in the hope of becoming the leading representatives of the
people in the new regime.[26]

In consequence those most committed to the oligarchy sent a new
embassy to Sparta, including Antiphon, with instructions to press for
any settlement with Sparta which was at all acceptable. They speeded
up work on a stronghold they were building on the Eetioneia promontory by the entrance to the Peiraeus. Not surprisingly, this stirred Theramenes' group to allege that they were preparing a reception point for a
Spartan sea-borne expedition. When the negotiations by the last embassy
to Sparta had failed and a fleet of 42 Spartan ships was in the neighbourhood on the way to Euboea, these charges became more insistent and,
as Thucydides admits, had a grain of truth in them. For by then Antiphon and his friends were prepared to betray Athens to Sparta, if they
could retain power on any conditions and so save their skins. Meanwhile
Phrynichos had been killed by Thrasyboulos of Calydon, with a number
of accomplices, and this assassination was said to have been the result
of a conspiracy. Theramenes and his friends were not blamed for it, but
they took heart from the failure of the Four Hundred to take reprisals.

The Peloponnesian fleet had raided Aegina and was anchored off
Epidauros. At this point after renewed charges by Theramenes that this
was part of a plot, Aristokrates and a force of hoplites employed building the new wall at Eetioneia arrested Alexikles, a general devoted to the
hetairoi, that is the confirmed oligarchs. They were supported by the
Peiraeus guard and other Athenians. The Four Hundred held an indig-
nant council meeting, threatening Theramenes' group, and in the end
Theramenes promised to help rescue Alexikles. Aristarchos, an associate
of Peisandros and Antiphon, led the force of 120 young knights (who
had overthrown the democratic council) down to the Peiraeus; the elder
citizens and a certain Thucydides of Pharsalos managed to prevent a
general attack. When he arrived, Theramenes made a show of anger;
Aristarchos was genuinely angry; the hoplites were truculent and un-

repentant. Theramenes agreed to their suggestion that the new wall should be demolished, and they promptly carried this out with the co-operation of many of the inhabitants: at the same time they released Alexikles. The hoplites got popular support for the demolition of the new wall by calling on anyone who wanted the Five Thousand instead of the Four Hundred. Thucydides explains that the term 'five thousand' was used because the hoplites still did not want to risk talk about demo-cracy, fearing that the Five Thousand secretly existed and they might unwittingly offend members of it. Thucydides adds that the Four Hundred, for their part, did not want the Five Thousand to exist, since such a large political body was in their eyes outright unvarnished demo-cracy, and they preferred to keep its existence concealed, in order to create a secret menace.[27]

The next day the hoplites met in the theatre at Munichia and after-wards marched up to the city, to take up a position at the Anakeion (below the northern slopes of the Acropolis). The Four Hundred per-suaded them to do nothing before a meeting which was to be held in the theatre of Dionysus on a prearranged day. They promised to publish the names of the Five Thousand and that the Four Hundred should be selected from them in whatever way the Five Thousand decided. This may have been the occasion for which the document in Chapter 30 of the *Constitution of Athens* was produced. In this document men over 30 among the Five Thousand were to be divided into four councils, one of which was to be selected by lot to rule in turn. The meeting in fact could not take place, because at the last minute the Peloponnesian fleet in the area sailed from Megara past Salamis and the people rushed to their ships. The Athenians smelt betrayal. The Spartan commander may have waited at Epidauros and Megara by prearrangement; by then he had turned his attention to his professed object, Euboea. The hastily launched Athenian fleet was subsequently defeated off Eretria, and all of Euboea except Oreus was taken from them.

The Athenians thus lost most of the ships remaining at the Peiraeus and their chief surviving source of economic support. They were more shaken and demoralised than ever before, and the Spartans missed a great opportunity of besieging Athens and bringing the war to an end. However, the Athenians set to man 20 ships and summon an assembly. In the first assembly held for some time at the normal democratic venue, the Pnyx, they brought the Four Hundred to an end and voted to put matters in the hands of the Five Thousand. Anyone who could provide his own arms was to be a member of this; no official, even a military one, was to receive pay. They placed a curse on anyone who should disobey. There were later assemblies to establish a commission of law-givers and to enact other requirements for the constitution. There followed in the ten remaining months of the archon-year 411-410 a form of government to which Thucydides gives especial praise, describing it as a blend, or *rapprochement*, leading to the power of both the few and the many, which was moderate and first rescued the city from its plight.[28]

The Four Hundred: An Analysis

The expulsion of the democratic council was a bloodless *coup*, but violence had prepared the ground and was a barely concealed threat on the day. Thus, the critical move which gave the Four Hundred power was neither a legal act itself nor the outcome of a peaceful and purely constitutional process, in spite of the extensive preparation of public opinion. It is for this reason that the documents in Chapters 30 and 31 of Aristotle's *Constitution* — the supposed final and provisional forms of oligarchic government — are both misleading, as they were originally intended to be, and on a clear view inept. As we have seen, in assigning an active role to the Five Thousand they conflict both with the *Constitution*'s own statement that this body was ineffective and with Thucydides' detailed evidence about the oligarchic government. What is more important is that they do not fit the historical context of the revolution. The Four Hundred wanted authoritarian power with as few trimmings and impediments as possible. Their preliminary politicking sought to secure the appearance of legitimacy, and they eventually achieved this through the approval of a single motion in an assembly where the attendance of their opponents was likely to have been thin. Peisandros' proposal to that assembly was designed to secure that approval. The pill of authoritarian rule was coated in what for the rich and the soldiers at least was sugar — the abolition of pay for civilian office. Apart from this it was as vague as possible. Once the oligarchs had obtained this *fiat*, it would have been folly for them to have reopened issues by discussion of detailed constitutions, whether at the Colonos assembly itself or at some other time before the overthrow of the Council. This might have created confusion or even opposition and was irrelevant to their actual plans. As Thucydides says, it was difficult to deprive of liberty a people used to being a ruling power. Even after the Colonos assembly things might have gone wrong. There was a limit to the effectiveness of propaganda: ultimately the threat of physical force had to be used to finish the job quickly. In the event it was to take only one assembly on the Pnyx to overthrow the arbitrary power that the Four Hundred seized on the basis of the vote at Colonos.

Draft constitutions were not needed until the Four Hundred were safely in power and questions were raised about the existence of the Five Thousand. However, I doubt if the documents in the *Constitution* were ever taken seriously by the Four Hundred's leadership. The long-term constitution depended on an exact register of the Five Thousand, was in general over-theoretical and above all eliminated the Four Hundred as a body. Even the short-term constitution was contingent on the previous existence and political activity of the Five Thousand. Until the Five Thousand were named and met, the drafts could never be more than window-dressing.[29]

The hard fact of the revolution was that the Athenians had to surrender their liberties to a narrow oligarchy. Many more than 400 helped to create this oligarchy. We may ask why. Some no doubt were deceived into thinking that it would be a broad oligarchy based on 5,000 and preferred this to full democracy. But the members of the sworn brotherhoods are unlikely to have had such illusions, and one wonders how much the supporters of the revolution thought or cared initially about the Five Thousand. The origin of the revolution was the hope of winning the war. This was used to justify the political sacrifices. Peisandros' reference to 'discipline' on his first winter visit to Athens would have found a response among those whose life at Athens was rigidly limited by the necessities of war and almost unceasing military duty. The demand to abolish pay for civilian office, which became current during Peisandros' absence, was also evidently a rallying cry for the soldiers, who themselves may have been short of pay. No doubt they hoped as soldiers to be members of the Five Thousand, but this may have been more an aspiration to status than political influence. The implication of the oligarchic programme for the average hoplite was that Athens would give up pretences and turn herself into a military camp like Sparta, in order to survive.

The wealthy upper class, on whose shoulders lay the burden of maintaining the triremes and paying personal taxes to finance the war, had a special interest in the revolution. At home the involvement of members of the cavalry, like Polystratos, is significant. One hundred and twenty young knights acted as SS men for the Four Hundred. In Samos, we are told, the trierarchs and the political leaders had been inclined to oligarchy before Alcibiades' first message arrived. They no doubt hoped for relief from some of their burdens through Persian subventions, but more generally they held that, since they were making the greatest sacrifices, they should determine policy. Indeed, when the hope of Persian aid failed, they resolved to make voluntary contributions from their private fortunes to pay for the war and the continuation of the oligarchic movement.[30] They did not contemplate an early peace treaty: indeed, it was the war which for them made oligarchy desirable.

In this respect they contrast with an important group among the Four Hundred in Athens. Soon after the Four Hundred seized power, they sent an exploratory embassy to King Agis, hoping that oligarchic government would be the key to a peace with Sparta. He at first thought that there would be civil war in Athens and, with the aid of reinforcements from the Peloponnese, tried to get control of the Long Walls. However, the Athenians remained loyal to the Four Hundred and Agis' army suffered casualties. When he therefore gave encouragement to a second Athenian embassy, the Athenians sent Laispodias, Aristophon and Melesias to Sparta, but they were seized by the crew on the voyage and taken eventually to Samos. Later, after the pressure from Samos to democratise their regime, when the majority of those who were involved in establishing the oligarchy were discontented, the most intransigent oligarchs sent a third embassy, headed by Antiphon and Phrynichos, with instructions to settle with Sparta on any tolerable terms.

This was unsuccessful but, as has become already plain, aroused the gravest suspicions. Its protagonists were believed to be planning to receive a Spartan force on the Eetioneia promontory. According to Thucydides, the group's primary aim was to maintain the Athenian Empire under their oligarchy; failing that, they wanted an independent Athens, retaining its ships and walls, under their oligarchy; if this was impossible, rather than be the first in line for execution by a returned democracy, they preferred to invite the enemy in and to surrender the walls and ships by treaty, in order to retain control of the city and so save their lives. To be fair to them, they do not seem initially to have desired to betray Athens' interests, but they thought a little naively that Sparta would tolerate an Athens which was still powerful, provided that it was oligarchically ruled. They may well have had some sympathy for the Spartan political and social system. Nevertheless, they only contemplated becoming Spartan quislings in a desperate effort to survive: they did not want to subject themselves and the rest of the Athenians to Sparta through any political principle. In this respect they differ little from those who became members of the Thirty Tyrants after the war.[31] The supporters of oligarchy on Samos, however, did not have the same motives for seeking peace. Although they were on the defensive in their war with the Peloponnesians, they were achieving some successes and were not suffering a steady and inexorable economic attrition, like the Athenians at home. As for those temperamentally inclined to oligarchic government, the expeditionary force was inevitably managed on authoritarian lines. What happened in effect in 411 was the disassociation of this force from the civil government at home, and in many respects this must have satisfied those who wanted to win the war untrammelled by the Athenian assembly.

This brings us to a fundamental question about the oligarchic movement: how far were the supporters of the Four Hundred ideological partisans of oligarchy, as opposed to pragmatists who wanted limitation of democracy in order to win victory? To begin with, it is evident that some people considered limited participation in government and a limited franchise desirable things in themselves. A constitution based on the Five Thousand was introduced to replace the Four Hundred; in 403 after the re-establishment of democracy Phormisios proposed the limitation of full citizenship to landholders; in the apologia assigned to him by Xenophon, Theramenes defends hoplite democracy. We cannot attribute belief in a limited franchise to the protagonists in the Four Hundred, since they thought the use of the Five Thousand pure democracy and only used the phrase to cajole and baffle their opponents. Yet theirs too was a political doctrine — an opposition on principle to anything that smelled of democracy. As for the oligarchic drafts in Aristotle's *Constitution*, although they tell us little about what happened, they show that men were prepared to theorise not only about rule by the Five Thousand but also about a narrow oligarchy. I find it reasonable to suppose that, even when democracy was most successful at Athens, there were men who still saw oligarchy as an unattainable ideal, although some of these, like the author of the oligarchic essay on the constitution, may have wrily conceded that on its own premisses democracy worked very well.[32]

Men with a theoretical preference for oligarchy might or might not seek to attain eminence in the democracy. Antiphon of Rhamnous is described by Thucydides as the chief brain behind the oligarchic plot. He did not speak in the assembly or involve himself in lawsuits except under compulsion; he was unpopular through his reputation for cleverness, but his intelligent advice was of tremendous help to anyone speaking whether in an assembly or law court.[33]

Antiphon no doubt was involved with one or more of the sworn brotherhoods which worked for their members' success in attaining high office and fighting lawsuits. Other members of these groups, we

may infer, took the opposite view and did not shun the courting of popular favour. We should not be too easily misled by the gibes of Aristophanes and the evidence of Andokides into believing that the majority
of the aristocrats were alienated from the democracy, cultivating eccen-
tric behaviour and disregarding conventions. Aristocratic values were not
irreconcilable with democracy, even that of Pericles and Cleon. If an
aristocrat thought he was born for high office, he stood a good chance
of achieving this through allotment to the boards of treasurers reserved
for the wealthy; otherwise he could test his standing by candidature for
one of the elective offices — military posts from general downwards,
special commissions and embassies, and the secretaryship of the council,
if he became a member of it. There is nothing more gratifying to the ego
than the sense of being the people's choice for a post. It would have given
aristocrats greater confidence and authority than any office acquired
through intrigue within an oligarchy. On the other hand, as Thucydides
points out, if they failed in a democratic election, they could bear the
result better, since it was not the judgement of their peers. Under an
oligarchy such a rejection was an insult. Thus, even those with a theoretical attachment to oligarchy may have found profit for themselves
in democratic politics.[34]

When the democracy showed signs of fallibility, it was another matter.
The plague in 430 and subsequent years was a shock, which stimulated
doubts, though these were mitigated for a time by Athenian military
success in the first part of the Peloponnesian War. After the Sicilian
expedition, with the prospect of economic ruin in Attica to be crowned
by a humiliating political subjection to Sparta, many of those who had
pursued office under the democracy would have become irritated with
what they saw as the irresponsibility of the assembly, especially when
it blamed the advocates of the expedition and forgot that the decision
was its own. The wealthy were burdened with a greater share in financing the war, now that money was difficult to obtain from the allies;
their estates in Attica were devastated, and those in the empire lost or
under threat. It was not hard for them to be persuaded that their survival demanded a change to oligarchic government. Once the proposal
had been voiced by Peisandros at Athens, people would have hastened
to join the conspiracy, for fear of being out of favour, when it had succeeded.

People were dismayed at the most unlikely figures who appeared on
the oligarchic side. We know some oligarchs by name who had been
men of importance under the democracy. Peisandros and Phrynichos
were both labelled demagogues in a speech in Lysias: the former had

been influential in the investigations of 415 and may have had some subordinate military post on Samos; Phrynichos, apparently a man from a poor family, was a member of the elected board of generals in 412-411. Another general, Charminos, was a supporter of oligarchy, though he remained on Samos. A third, Onomakles, is probably the later associate of Antiphon on the embassy to Sparta. Another oligarchic ambassador, Laispodias, had been general in 414-413. His colleague on that journey, Melesias, may be the elder son of Pericles' rival, Thucydides, or perhaps the treasurer of Athene in 415-414. Callaischros, who is associated by Lysias with Peisandros, was perhaps the treasurer of Athene in 412-411 (probably not the father of the notorious Critias, but a relative), while the defector from the revolution, Aristokrates, son of Skellias, was general in 422-421 and took the oath to the peace of Nicias. In the early stages of the revolution at Athens the conspirators counted on the co-operation of the advisory board of *probouloi* – elderly men, probably chosen for their good record in public affairs. One of these, Hagnon, was specifically accused by Lysias of co-operation with the Four Hundred, and his son Theramenes was a leading conspirator before leading the movement towards a more broadly based constitution. Another was Sophocles, whom in my view we must presume to be the octagenarian writer of tragedy, in his time a general during the subjugation of Samos.[35] Their previous offices show that all these men had experienced power, and so it would be naive to think them devoid of personal ambition when they joined the oligarchy. However, one can hardly regard them all as examples of frustrated ambition for whom oligarchy seemed to provide the only opportunity of exercising their talents. In this respect they differed from Antiphon, whose engineering of the revolution was the culmination of his career.

The speech for Polystratos tells us about a person in a lower stratum of the conspiracy, many of whose characteristics are likely to be typical. Polystratos was a man with grown-up children, who had held some elected post, probably military, and was one of the political officials at Oropos when it was captured by the Boeotians in the late winter of 411. The family was evidently prosperous, since the children served in the cavalry. They had a farm in the country which was devastated during the war, but it is clear in spite of the speaker's protestations that they had not lost all their capital. The son pleads that, while Phrynichos was a poor shepherd boy, his father was being educated in the city; when Phrynichos grew up to make a living from prosecutions in the city, his father was respectably farming. Polystratos had presumably a town house also with some land attached. As far as we can judge, he seems to exemplify the upper-class military man, who thought that his class should direct strategy as it was paying for the war, and who wanted a more authoritarian regime so that the state might come under military discipline. He was out to protect his own interests, but could be hardly accused of sacrificing the interests of the city, as he understood them, to his own. On the other hand, one may suspect that there were also many opportunists at this level of the conspiracy like Eratosthenes and Iatrokles. They seem to have abandoned their military service in the Hellespont, where Eratosthenes was a trierarch, in order to join the revolution.[36]

How far then should the revolution be attributed to personal ambitions and rivalries? Some passages in ancient authors stress such motives. The most general argument is in a defence speech written by Lysias against a charge of association with the later 'Thirty Tyrants'. The speaker is claiming that he has no reason to be hostile to the common people because of his past career under both oligarchy and democracy. 'You must reason in the first place', he says, 'that no man is oligarchic or democratic by nature (*phusei*), but desires to establish whatever constitution is in his interest.' What the democracy now needs is satisfied customers. To substantiate this point he adduces the changes of attitude of the protagonists of different constitutions. Peisandros, Phrynichos and their fellow demagogues established the oligarchy to avoid punishment for their past political errors; many of the Four Hundred joined with the men from the Peiraeus in the re-establishment of democracy in 403, while some of those who overthrew the Four Hundred became members of the Thirty. This last statement is borne out by the careers of Theramenes and also Critias, who proposed the trial of the dead Phrynichos after the counter-revolution in 411. As for the one-time members of the Four Hundred who supported the restoration of democracy in 403, there is nothing inherently improbable in men like Polystratos having opposed a puppet government of Sparta; furthermore, to judge from the accusation of Philon, a number of opportunists tried to profit from the movement in 403. The speaker draws the conclusion that political differences between individuals do not arise over the constitution but over their own personal interests. He goes on to plead that he himself had done nothing to put himself at a disadvantage under democracy or at an advantage under oligarchy: thus he could not be an enemy of the *demos*.

This argument has an interesting pedigree. As far as we can judge from the surviving papyrus fragments, in the speech he delivered in his own defence after the fall of the Four Hundred Antiphon claimed that he had no reason to desire a change in the established government, since he was in no personal or political trouble and his business as a speech-writer was best suited by democratic government: he surely knew where his own best interests lay. This speech was admired by Thucydides, even though it was of no avail. Lysias too must have known it and perhaps drew from it the argument that no man was democratic or oligarchic by nature. At all events, Antiphon's speech is a warning that we should not accept the Lysias argument uncritically. Certainly, people did not acquire political ideologies by birth at Athens, but their political aims were not circumscribed by the narrow range of interests that the speakers discuss. The examples used in the Lysias speech are at first sight more impressive. Later history showed that Theramenes and Critias were ready to go to considerable lengths to keep themselves in power, and it is not difficult to argue that in the long run their careers were dominated by personal ambitions and rivalries. On the other hand, there is no evidence that Peisandros was in danger from the democratic system in 411, while Phrynichos, who initially opposed the revolution, because he doubted whether it would preserve the empire, and suspected Alcibiades, judged the oligarchic programme on its political merits.[37]

Thucydides in Book VIII does not attribute the original revolution to personal factors but only the leadership of the counter-revolution. In the first place he makes it clear that for the majority of those, who had some part in the oligarchy, it had turned sour. He seems to be refer-ring to those who were not even members of the Four Hundred and certainly not in office. So this general disappointment was not over failure to gain personal power, which the majority of oligarchic sup-porters cannot have expected. However, the leaders of the counter-revolution, drawn from those really in the oligarchy and in office, such as Theramenes and Aristokrates, were for the most part motivated by personal ambition. They did not like being in the second rank, and they hoped to exploit Alcibiades' strong position on Samos (which they welcomed, rather than feared) and the instability of the oligarchy in Athens in order to become champions of the common people (*prostatai tou demou*). This explanation is introduced as a contrast to their public programme of moderating the oligarchy and genuinely creating the Five Thousand. Thucydides thus means that for the majority of its leading advocates the moderate oligarchic programme was a facade: whatever their original attitude to the oligarchic revolution had been, they wanted to abandon it, and, since they believed a swing back to democracy had started, they decided to put themselves at its head. I see no reason to contest this explanation as far as it goes, though it has some important

consequences for our view of the blended constitution of the Five Thous-
and which followed. But it does not say anything about the reasons why
Theramenes, Aristokrates and their like supported the Four Hundred
originally. We may suspect that for some of them Peisandros' arguments
about economy, discipline and the need to secure Alcibiades' return
were decisive. Others may have wanted to try oligarchic government
for its own sake. Doubtless, men with political ambitions such as Theramenes wanted a leading role in the oligarchy: they would not have pursued such a form of government otherwise. However, we cannot argue,
at least on the basis of this Thucydidean passage, that their initial support for the Four Hundred involved no sympathy for oligarchy as such
but sprang merely from a personal lust for power. As for Thucydides'
more general characterisation of democratic and oligarchic *hetairoi* as
men who strove ruthlessly for their own power in spite of specious
slogans, this is surely based in part on his interpretation of events at
Athens. However, we must not press too far a passage which is striving
to give a general appreciation of politics — especially one which is based
on a contrast with Thucydides' ideal, the detached unbiased statesman,
a type which was to become the stock-in-trade of Greek political philosophy from Plato onwards.[38]

The question whether the Four Hundred were driven by private
ambition or political beliefs is a good debating point, but it is to a large
extent unreal in that it seeks to separate motives which in practice are
interconnected. Those in politics tend anyhow to identify the best interest of the state with their own, while an illogical amalgam of political
beliefs frequently appears to the observer to derive from *ad hoc* con-
siderations of expediency rather than principle. We cannot necessarily
expect to find a pure ideological oligarch among the Four Hundred.
Antiphon comes nearest to satisfying our search, in spite or rather because of his own self-exculpation. One may argue that, since he did
master-mind the oligarchic movement, although he had no personal
motive for running away from democracy, he must have believed in the
form of government itself. More generally, it must be firmly asserted that
the personal ambitions and jealousies of politicians do not make them
any the less oligarchs. The very fact that the argument from self-interest
was used by oligarchs to prove they were not, illustrates its dangers.

The Five Thousand and the Return to Democracy

The Four Hundred were overthrown in late summer 411 after two

months of the Attic archon-year; the democracy was fully restored before the last month of that year had elapsed. The direct evidence for
the nature of the intermediate regime is minimal because of the end of
Thucydides' writings, and this deficiency has given scope for scholarly
controversy. In his notice of the creation of the regime, which is followed
by Aristotle's *Constitution*, Thucydides talks of a critical assembly,
which voted that they should hand over affairs to the Five Thousand,
that all those who provided themselves with hoplite arms should be
members of this body and there should be no pay for any official post.
It is to be noted that Thucydides does not associate these proposals with
Theramenes, but merely with the agitation which led to the crisis.[39]

The assembly could have claimed that they were simply developing
a previous proposal of the oligarchic movement, enunciated before
Peisandros' return from Samos and much discussed under the Four
Hundred: indeed, this is an obvious explanation of why it was so easily
accepted by previous supporters of the Four Hundred. It could also be
argued that they were restoring democracy. The Four Hundred had
been against the implementation of the Five Thousand, because they
thought it would be outright democracy; the hoplites, who demolished
the wall on Eetioneia, apparently regarded themselves as restorers of
democracy and sought support on that principle from the proletariat,
although they talked openly of the Five Thousand. Men like Theramenes had urged the establishment of the Five Thousand, because they
wanted to be champions of the common people (*prostatai tou demou*).

Thus the new regime seemed all things to all men. What was it in
fact? Government by the Five Thousand would not have changed its
meaning for the majority of people between the period before the Four
Hundred were established and the time when that body was overthrown
(one cannot, however, expect such consistency in the propaganda statements of the Four Hundred, who did not want it and at most conceded
that it should be the body which chose from among its own members
the Four Hundred). It has been suggested that in late summer 411 there
was a return to democracy with public office limited to those of hoplite
status and some restrictions on the assembly. I find this view difficult to
accept, since the limitation of public office to men of hoplite status was
to some extent part of the earlier democracy. At best one could argue
that the difference between the intermediate regime and the democracy
lay in membership of the council being limited to men of hoplite status.
But was this what was being canvassed during the preliminaries to the
revolution? It was not the council *per se* that supporters of the oligarchy
criticised, but tne irresponsibility of the assembly. Alcibiades on Samos

visualised the rule of the Five Thousand mediated by the restoration of
the democratic council. It is true that, when Antiphon was tried under
the intermediate regime for his political crimes, he talks of trial by the
demos, but this would be a natural way to describe the *dikasterion* that
tried him, and of course the regime by Antiphon's standards was a
democracy. Thucydides distinguished the Five Thousand from the
earlier and later democracy by saying that it was a compromise both
in the power of the few and the many. If we regard the 'few' as the
dunatoi who had seized power and the 'many' as the generality of
people who had opposed them, then a constitution based on a hoplite
franchise fits this description.[40]

Given that the assembly under this regime was restricted to hoplites,
the council must have been likewise, and there would have been the
normal qualifications for the magistracies and the official posts. The
council probably acquired some new discretionary powers, to judge from
the fact that it made special arrangements for the trial of Antiphon and
his colleagues without reference to the people. It may even have been
elected rather than chosen by lot. These new political arrangements
must be understood in the light of the circumstances of their creation.
They were an attempt to secure unity at a time when a direct attack on
the city was to be expected. As such they would have been acceptable
in the short run to those who sought eventually to return to full democracy.

Antiphon, Archeptolemos and Onomakles were charged with treachery for their part in the last embassy to Sparta and the first two were
condemned to death. Phrynichos was already dead: so his murderers
were released from prison and rewarded with citizenship or lesser benefits. Phrynichos' bones were later tried for treason and after condemnation banished from Attica, this procedure being proposed by Critias,
the later member of the Thirty. Subsequently, Aristarchos, who had
apparently returned from Oenoe, and Alexikles were condemned for
speaking in defence of the dead Phrynichos. Peisandros too must have
been condemned to death, since his property was confiscated and one
farm was given later as a reward to Apollodoros, a murderer of Phrynichos. In my view the dialogue between Peisandros and Sophocles recounted by Aristotle implies that Peisandros was put on trial and called
Sophocles as defence witness. Sophocles admitted that he and the other
members of the advisory board (*probouloi*) had set up the Four Hundred, even though they disapproved of it, but Sophocles added that
there was no better course available.

Lowlier members of the Four Hundred were also accused, like Polystratos. In another speech for a man accused of oligarchic sympathies we find a general complaint about the persistence of such reprisals long after the fall of the Four Hundred. Epigenes, Demophanes and Cleisthenes are singled out as the chief accusers and charged with corruption and persuading the people to condemn men to death without trial. In 405 Aristophanes used the second parabasis of the *Frogs* to address the audience with a plea for an amnesty to be granted those who had been banished or had lost citizen privileges through alleged involvement with the Four Hundred. The antagonism to oligarchs manifested in the trials would have made it the more difficult for those, who believed in the Five Thousand as a good constitution in itself, to oppose the movement to restore full democracy. After the return of full democracy in 410, that is, with the assembly open to all free men and the council selected by lot, the decree of Demophantos provided that anyone who overthrew the democracy in the future or held office under an oligarchy should be killed on the spot.[41]

The Athenians avoided civil war both in the revolution and counterrevolution. However, there remained a deep fund of resentment after 411 against oligarchs, and this must have been complicated by personal feuds, as the successful prosecutions multiplied. Class bitterness against the wealthy, attested in the early plays of Aristophanes, probably intensified in Athens' dire economic straits. One major issue which did create divisions among politicians and the people was the attitude to be taken to Sparta. After Sparta's defeat at Cyzicus in 410 the Athenians rejected a Spartan offer of peace, conditional on the maintenance of the territorial *status quo* and the removal of garrisons in each other's territory (like Decelea). According to Diodorus, the *epieikestatoi* (most respectable men) supported it, but Cleophon was against it. It is evident that men with landed property in Attica would have been glad to see the Spartans leave on any honourable terms. However, since this peace would have involved abandoning control of the Black Sea trade route and much of the empire, it would not have suited those with land and business interests overseas, nor those who lived on imported grain, especially the poor. It is doubtful whether Alcibiades' current supporters would have favoured a settlement of this kind.[42]

The Last Years of the War

Alcibiades eventually celebrated a hero's return to his home city in 407. According to Xenophon, the common people were at the time ready to forgive him everything, as a man who had been unjustly plotted against by his political enemies and not the sort who required a revolution to acquire primacy in the state. He himself was so afraid of personal enemies that he hesitated before landing and then went up to the city with a bodyguard of partisans who were ready to prevent anyone seizing him (seizure as part of formal arrest may have been feared). After being elected as supreme commander with full powers, he was deposed from his command because of the defeat at Notion. No doubt his enemies were glad to see this happen, but there is no sign that the people as a whole wished to take any action against him on political grounds, once they believed his military usefulness was over.[43]

The most notorious manifestation of bitterness towards their leaders by the Athenian people occurred after Alcibiades' dismissal and the subsequent costly victory at Arginousai. In 406 the Athenians had assembled a force of 150 ships in order to relieve 40 ships under Conon, which were cut off by the Spartans in Mytilene. Of these 110 were manned by Athenians, drawn from all the propertied classes, including the cavalry, and supplemented by slaves. The victory cost them 25 ships and all their crews except a few men. The Athenians split their forces after the victory, assigning to Theramenes and Thrasyboulos, who were in charge of triremes, and other officers the task of rescuing the survivors by the wrecks. The remaining ships were to sail against the Spartan force blockading Mytilene. A gale and storm intervened and neither task was accomplished. We are told that the Athenian soldiers were against putting out to sea again.

When Thrasyboulos and Theramenes' force returned to Athens with the news, the people, in spite of their joy at the victory, were angry over the failure to rescue the survivors. According to Diodorus, the generals suspected the two trierarchs of creating the agitation and sent home letters, asserting that the death of these sailors was the fault of the trierarchs. This move rebounded and made Theramenes and Thrasyboulos their enemies. Moreover, an earlier letter of the generals, which was to be read out by Theramenes in the assembly, had apparently blamed nothing but the storm. The assembly voted to depose all the generals who survived the battle, except Conon. Two wisely did not return to Athens, but the rest were imprisoned. In the assembly the generals were attacked by a number of speakers including Theramenes, but they called the coxswains and other crew members to bear witness to the difficulties caused by the storm. One of them, Lysias, had himself been rescued by clinging to the hull of his sunk ship. The discussion was adjourned and in the interval the *Apatouria*, an autumn festival of the *phratriai*, took place. This allowed many relatives of the dead to publicise their grief, which was exploited by Theramenes' friends: they organised people in black with shaved heads to come to the next assembly. The use of mourning as a political demonstration is rarely attested in Greece, but it was a feature of Roman political life, where it might become a stimulus to violence rather than a mere protest.[44]

At the next assembly Callixenos moved on behalf of the council that the generals should be decided guilty or not guilty of a capital offence by a single vote of the assembly. He was charged with making an illegal proposal by Alcibiades' nephew Euryptolemos and others, but they abandoned their opposition in face of the hostile assembly and the threat that they too should be included in that vote. Some of the presiding tribe were reluctant to put the motion to the vote, but they were cowed with the exception of Socrates. A motion by Euryptolemos that the generals should be tried under existing procedure for wronging the *demos* was barred from being considered first, and the council's motion was carried. Eight generals were then condemned to death, two in their absence.

It is at first sight tempting to see in this a backlash by crypto-oligarchs against the democracy. Many of the men executed were protagonists of democratic government. Thrasyllos and Diomedon had been pioneers of the counter-revolution on Samos in 411; Pericles was the son of the great Pericles; Aristokrates was probably the son of Skellias, who after being a taxiarch under the Four Hundred had been prominent in its overthrow; Erasinides had proposed rewards for Phrynichos' assassins in 409. On the other hand, Theramenes and Thrasyboulos, who contributed to the attack on the generals, had co-operated politically with Aristokrates and Thrasyllos respectively in 411, and Thrasyboulos was to survive to lead the democratic counter-revolution in 403. Nor is it likely that the prosecution was an act of revenge by Alcibiades' friends. Both Thrasyboulos and Theramenes had a political connection with Alcibiades. The former had been the chief advocate of his return after the counter-revolution on Samos; the latter had secured his reconciliation with the Five Thousand. Again, the name of the accuser, Callixenos, was held by Alkmeonidai early in the fifth century. Yet Alcibiades' cousin and close friend, Euryptolemos son of Peisianax, led the attempt to defend the generals. According to Xenophon, he claimed that he was moved by his kinship to Pericles and his friendship with Diomedon. If the condemnation of the generals was really being engineered by Alcibiades' friends, he should have been able to do more to prevent it in private.[45]

The most striking features of the episode are that Theramenes and Thrasyboulos escaped involvement and that Theramenes' friends encouraged public demonstrations of indignation in a matter which might have become dangerous for the man himself. I can only conclude that Theramenes and Thrasyboulos had been induced on their return home to make a deal with one or more of the orators who planned to attack the generals: if they supported the attack on the generals with all the means in their power, they would be ignored themselves.

However, what happened can only be understood against the background of public bitterness, verging on hysteria, by the time of the critical assembly. The losses must have affected many households not usually involved in the war at sea. In particular, many members of eminent wealthy families would have died, if even cavalrymen served in the fleet. Much of the agitation and passion may have stemmed, not from the plebeian families of the oarsmen, but from aristocrats and their *hetairoi*. Thus, the generals' trial does not seem to be an example of class bitterness, but rather an occasion when ex-oligarchs, democratic leaders and the *demos* pooled their resentments and combined against six scapegoats.

The Second Fall of the Democracy

In the summer of 405 the Athenians lost the battle of Aigospotamoi in the Hellespont and with it most of their 180-ship fleet. There was initially considerable determination to carry on the fight — through fear of the reprisals likely to be taken by the Peloponnesian alliance for Athenian brutality — not only among Athenians, but their chief surviving allies, the Samians. The latter prepared themselves for a siege after a massacre of some of the leading citizens, presumably because they were suspected of an oligarchic *coup*. We possess the text of a remarkable Athenian decree passed in the summer of 405. The Samians were to become Athenian citizens in any respects they might wish, while retaining their autonomy, and they were to be involved in any Athenian decision-making about peace and war.[46]

Meanwhile, there were once again preparations for oligarchy in Athens. When Athens came under siege through the arrival of the Spartan fleet, the *hetairoi* (presumably political associations such as had been exploited by Peisandros in 411) established among themselves five overseers (ephors) whose job was to build up and manage a conspiracy against the democracy. Lysias' enemy Eratosthenes was among them, also Critias, who had returned from exile in Thessaly after the recent general restoration of full citizen rights. The conspiracy functioned in a similar way to the conspiracy of 411 in its early stages. Leaders were appointed in each tribe to organise the votes of the members of the conspiracy in elections and assembly meetings. We are not told what their chief aims were but we may assume that they hoped to induce an early settlement with Sparta, which would spare their own lives and financial interests, and furthermore to be the group which Sparta would back in any regime she imposed as part of the settlement terms.[47]

When Athens' food supply ran low in late 405, the Athenians tried to negotiate a peace, which would allow them to retain their walls including those of the Peiraeus (presumably also some sort of a fleet), but this was summarily rejected by the ephors at Sparta. The Spartans proposed instead that ten stades of the Long Walls joining Athens to the Peiraeus should be destroyed. This offer was rejected by the assembly, the demagogue Cleophon taking the lead. At this point evidently the oligarchic *hetairoi* had little influence. However, Theramenes offered to go to Lysander on Samos in order to find out why the Spartans wanted to demolish the walls: was it to be a guarantee of Athenian good behaviour or a prelude to enslavement?

Theramenes then spent three months with Lysander, waiting for utter starvation to change the mood of the Athenian assembly, according to Xenophon. How far he was working in collusion with the oligarchic *hetairoi* at this point is not clear: Lysias does not accuse him of this until after his return. This period in Theramenes' generally ambivalent and controversial career was the subject of especially fierce argument, as is shown not only by Lysias, but by a recently published papyrus fragment of either a history or a political pamphlet. In this Theramenes is accused (in similar terms to those used by Lysias) of being more sincere with the enemy than his countrymen, and he replies that, if the Athenians had been open about the terms they would accept, the Spartans would have simply piled further conditions on top of these.[48]

After three months Theramenes returned to Athens and said that the matter had to be settled at Sparta by the ephors. He was therefore sent there at the head of a commission of ten with authority to negotiate. Perhaps before this assembly, Cleophon had been eliminated mainly through the efforts of the oligarchs. Two of them, Satyros and Chremon, had him arrested by the council of Five Hundred because of his criticisms of it, and he was subsequently condemned by a court which included members of that council. The oligarchs' motive was no doubt, as Lysias alleges, to remove the greatest obstacle in Athens to accepting Spartan terms. Two oligarchic councillors led the attack, but they persuaded the rest of that theoretically democratic body to co-operate. According to Lysias, many ex-members of that council served later on the council created by the Thirty, and this suggests a distinct change of political allegiance. On the other hand, the Areopagus was originally exceedingly suspicious of Theramenes' negotiations.[49]

The terms which Theramenes brought back from Sparta in the early spring of 404 involved the demolition of both the Long Walls and the Peiraeus defences and the reduction of the Athenian navy to twelve ships. According to Xenophon, the terms were announced in the assembly and accepted the day after Theramenes' return. However, during the delay before Lysander arrived, there was opposition from some of the generals and taxiarchs including Strombichides, Dionysodoros, Nikias, Nikomenes and probably Eukrates, brother of the Nikias killed in Sicily. A certain Theokritos gave evidence to the council of Five Hundred that there was a conspiracy to block any settlement with Sparta, apparently not naming those involved. But the council sent a group of its members to the Peiraeus to arrest his friend Agoratos. Nikias, Nikomenes and others went bail for Agoratos and they all took refuge at the altar at Munichia. The council then came down in a body to Munichia and Agoratos voluntarily gave evidence not only in the council but also in a hastily improvised assembly in the theatre there. In it he denounced his own sureties and other military officials and private citizens. These were imprisoned and remained there until after Lysander sailed into the Peiraeus on the conclusion of peace and the Thirty were established.

The Athenian public as a whole did not want to resist further and were ready to agree to the terms Theramenes brought. Xenophon states this explicitly, and it is implied by the acceptance in the assembly at Munichia of the council's arrest of the alleged conspirators. However, concerted opposition to Theramenes' terms was being prepared by the generals and taxiarchs, as Lysias concedes, though it is not clear what methods they were intending. Lysias alleges that Dionysodoros and his friends were cunningly framed by Agoratos, but it seems more likely that he was a minor member of their political group who panicked under pressure. The argument is plainly inconsistent in alleging that Agoratos had nothing to do with the generals and taxiarchs and then describing the efforts his sureties made to remove him from the city. There is a great contrast with 411. Then the oligarchs had to secure power by deceit and force; on this occasion they could rely on the normal organs of Athenian democracy, and their opponents became the conspirators. Ironically, the council of Five Hundred, whose elimination was critical for the oligarchs in 411, was in 404 their willing instrument.[50]

The Thirty

On Lysander's arrival in the Peiraeus the Athenian navy was surrendered and the walls pulled down. When the city had been demilitarised, the assembly appointed a commission of 30 to write down Athens' ancestral laws and to administer the city as an oligarchy. The assembly was supervised by the Spartans. The proposal in the name of Drakontides was advocated by Theramenes himself and he had a rough reception. Lysander threatened the assembly that he would treat opposition as a breach of the peace, and with an ironical, even if unconscious, echo of Peisandros' argument in 411, said that it would not be a matter of their constitution but their survival, if they did not support Theramenes. After the proposal was approved, the Thirty were elected: the Athenians were instructed to choose ten pre-selected by Theramenes and ten Spartan nominees, adding ten from the body of the assembly.[51]

Among those chosen were Theramenes and Drakontides; Critias and Eratosthenes, leaders of the new oligarchic conspiracy; Aristoteles, once a member of the Four Hundred and until recently an exile, who had been used as an agent by Lysander; Onomakles, another member of the Four Hundred and ex-associate of Antiphon; Melobios, a promoter of the Four Hundred; and Charikles, a man who had helped Peisandros in the days when they were both apparently democrats. Others probably had a background of office or demagogy under the democracy — Diokles as the proposer of the decree honouring the assassins of Phrynichos; Anaitios as *hellenotamias* in 410-409; Cleomedes as general in 417-416.[52]

Aristotle argues that there was a moderate party, led by Theramenes, who supported the ancestral constitution at this time, and this view is presented at length with some obvious historical distortions by Diodorus. It is hard to see how the exculpation of Theramenes squares with the facts. None of the men cited by Aristotle as supporters of the moderate line in fact joined the Thirty who were to redraft 'the ancestral laws', in spite of the fact that Theramenes had ten of his supporters on it. Of the men in question, Anytos, Archinos, Cleitophon and Phormisios, the two first might be regarded as moderates in the later restored democracy, and the latter two are actually associated with proposals in 411 and 403 regarding ancestral laws and a moderate constitution. If Lysias' account of the critical assembly at which the Thirty were voted into power is correct as to fact (granted that its presentation is hostile to Theramenes), such moderate political leaders were invisible at this time, while Theramenes himself urged submission to Lysander. Indeed, according to

Lysias' account of Theramenes' trial under the Thirty, Theramenes in his apologia claimed credit for the negotiations which led to the return of the exiles and for the establishment of the Thirty. The names associated with the moderate movement do not add credibility to the story (they were obvious choices for a falsifier), and the tradition in Aristotle is clearly a variant of that in Diodorus, which alleges that Lysander only arrived in Athens when summoned by the extreme oligarchs to settle a dispute between them and the supporters of the ancestral constitution led by Theramenes. This, like the Michigan papyrus, attests the efforts made in the fourth century to rehabilitate Theramenes' reputation after his death, but nothing more.[53]

The Thirty were theoretically commissioned to draw up a constitution in detail according to the 'ancestral laws' but, just as the Four Hundred never chose the Five Thousand, so they kept on putting off their appointed task. Instead they arbitrarily established a council and selected magistrates from among their own supporters. One of their first acts was to try Strombichides, Dionysodoros and their supporters for the alleged plot to prevent the settlement with Sparta. The assembly in the theatre at Munichia had voted that this should take place in a public law court of 2,000 men; instead they were brought before the new council, over which the Thirty presided, and were condemned in an open ballot. Probably about the same time, Eukrates, brother to Nikias, was killed apparently after refusing an offer to join the regime. Xenophon and Diodorus both neglect these deaths and argue that the Thirty began by executing those who made a living by prosecutions and harassed the aristocracy. This must have been in fact the next stage in the bloodshed. Subsequently the regime became preoccupied with its own security — with reason, since they were not carrying out their assigned function — and sent Aeschines and Aristoteles to Sparta, where they obtained from Lysander military support in the shape of Callibios, a harmost, and a Spartan garrison.[54]

With this protection the Thirty proceeded to arrest and execute men of substance not members of the regime, because they were possible leaders of resistance, because of personal feuds and in order to obtain money. Among the victims were Autolykos, Nikeratos son of Nikias, a certain Antiphon who was rich enough to provide two triremes during the war and another rich man, Leon of Salamis. When the arrests began to provoke concerted protests, they selected a body of 3,000 as theoretical partners in the regime and stripped the rest of the citizens of their arms. We know that Socrates and a certain Meletos were among the group of five sent to arrest Leon, but Socrates refused to obey his order. It seems to me likely that they received the order as members of the Three Thousand.

By now greed and private enmity were the prime motives for the judicial terror, and it was logical to include in it metics, who were of little political significance but rich. We have a vivid picture of what happened from Lysias' account of his personal experiences in the speech against Eratosthenes. Ten metics were to be arrested at first, of whom two were to be poor — so that the Thirty might claim that they were not just out for money. Lysias and Polemarchos had inherited from their father Cephalos a prosperous shield-making business. Lysias was seized by Peison while holding a dinner party and tried to bribe him. Peison accepted over 300 talents and would have let his prisoner go but Lysias was taken over by other representatives of the Thirty. He was being temporarily detained in a friend's house, when he managed to escape out the back (three doors being fortunately unlocked), and he made his way to a ship captain's house and thence by boat to Megara. Before he left, he learnt that his brother had been arrested and made to drink hemlock before discovering the charge on which he had been held. The Thirty seized the brothers' three houses with their contents, including their money and their workshop with its 120 slaves and the stock of 700 shields, thus securing not only finance but valuable military equipment, which may have been a special reason for the selection of Lysias and Polemarchos.[55]

Theramenes and Critias had been political allies when the regime began. Although Theramenes had argued that the regime required broader support, and this was one of the reasons for the establishment of the militia of 3,000, he was dissatisfied with this, since it did not give a constitutional foundation to the government and left it physically weaker than those whom it was trying to govern. He also objected to their executing without provocation men who had been eminent under the democracy and the wealthy metics. In consequence other members of the Thirty organised a meeting of the council and ordered the toughest of the young men to attend with daggers under their armpits. This group resembles the 120 young thugs used by the Four Hundred. At this meeting Critias indicted Theramenes for treachery. According to Xenophon, he argued that in spite of being the founder of the oligarchic movement, Theramenes was about to perform one of his notorious changes of side, now that it had become unpopular. He appealed to the Spartan constitution in which, he said, every ephor was bound to stand by the collective decisions of his board. In reply Theramenes did not deny responsibility for the oligarchy or his previous changes of position, but argued that he had acted for the best and declared his support for an oligarchy based on the cavalry and hoplites. He convinced the council, but Critias and his toughs intervened and exploited a new law, according to which anyone not on the register of 3,000 could be killed without trial by the Thirty. He accordingly removed Theramenes from this list and the Thirty condemned him. Although Theramenes took refuge at the altar, the eleven prison officials were summoned and dragged him off to execution.[56]

The event was elevated to a high point in the narrative of Xenophon and also probably in other historians. It seems in fact to have been merely a preliminary to the establishment of the oligarchy on a stronger but much more ruthless basis. For the Thirty then banned all those outside the register from the town of Athens and drove them from their landholdings in order that they themselves might have property. The fugitives were in turn expelled from the Peiraeus and fled over the frontier to Megara and Thebes. This action may be viewed as an attempt to put into practice some oligarchic theory: the Thirty were perhaps trying to establish an oligarchy on the Spartan or Cretan model in which a ruling caste had total political dominance over the other citizens and possessed all or the best of the land, while the poor either lived in remote areas or became serfs. In support of this one may point to Critias' professed love of Sparta and the influence of the Spartan harmost and garrison.

On the other hand a more mundane explanation can be provided. It was a desperate reaction first to the problem of security and secondly to the economic problems of the Athenian upper class. Now that it was clear that the Thirty planned permanent oligarchy, they had to maintain their regime in face of a large majority of hostile citizens, most of whom had lost by the revolution. Moreover, Athens even after the war was a populous state, cut down by famine but swelled by the citizens sent home by Lysander. The Spartan garrison provided a useful gendarmerie to deal with isolated attacks on the oligarchy, but the example of Cleomenes in 508 showed that it would have been useless against a large-scale rising without a major Spartan force at its back. The regime had to be broadened, as both Critias and Theramenes saw in their own ways. Hence the 3,000 hoplite citizens. These had not been chosen purely on grounds of wealth: rather they were those, it seems, whom the Thirty believed could be bound securely to the regime. But could they be relied on to support the Thirty, unless they were given sufficient material rewards to match their higher citizen status? Even if they were loyal, were they adequate when scattered among a citizen body several times their number, many of whom had themselves been hoplite soldiers? The Thirty's solution was a sort of *apartheid*. The few had to live in an area where they could be relatively many.

There were perquisites too. The expulsions enabled the regime to satisfy the greed which no doubt had grown with consuming the property of men like Lysias. Owing to the depredations caused by the war in Attica and the desertion of slaves, landed families would have found it hard to maintain anything like their previous standard of living. This is devastatingly portrayed by Xenophon in one of his 'Memories of Socrates'. Socrates meets Aristarchos at a time (after Thrasyboulos' march from Phyle) when there is *stasis* in the city and all Aristarchos' female relations have collected in his house in the Peiraeus. His land, however, is in enemy hands and he cannot feed them all. Socrates points out by contrast a number of men who have households of skilled slaves who earn them money, and urges Aristarchos to make the free members of his family work for their keep. Aristarchos, we are told, turned them into wool-workers. It is not surprising that the Thirty and their supporters were jealous of those who remained rich through commerce and manufacture, especially the metics. Their final programme allowed men like Lysias' client, the owner of the olive stump, to keep for themselves the land close to Athens which was fertile and would have suffered least in the war.[57]

Thrasyboulos and the Democratic Counter-revolution

The movement to overthrow the Thirty began after the beginning of winter in 404, when Thrasyboulos left Thebes with about 70 men to cross the Athenian border and occupy Phyle. This is dated after the creation of the Three Thousand and the mass expulsions by Xenophon, but before these events by Aristotle. The latter also places the arrival of the Spartan harmost and his 700 men after Theramenes' trial and the expulsions. This account is favourable to the Thirty in suggesting that the most extreme measures were a reaction to Thrasyboulos, whereas Xenophon and Diodorus argue that they simply sprang from greed and the Thirty's problems in retaining power. Apart from the greater credibility of the fuller narrative of Xenophon, there are two particular reasons for preferring the version here common to him and Diodorus. First, the success of the mass expulsions and the creation of the new citizen body is easier to understand if Spartan military backing was available. Secondly, we need to explain the Boeotian support for

Thrasyboulos. Diodorus notes the Spartan decree which allowed the Thirty to remove by force Athenian fugitives from any state in Greece and ordained a penalty of five talents for those who disregarded it. This shocked Sparta's allies, and both Argos and Thebes in fact contravened it, the Thebans passing the law which penalised those who did not give physical aid to a fugitive threatened with arrest. The Spartan decree and their allies' reaction should fall in the period of the mass expulsions. Thrasyboulos' return to Attica now falls into place as a move encouraged by Thebes in further defiance of Sparta. Apart from resentment of Spartan highhandedness, the Thebans would have had practical grounds for their policy: it was not in their interest to be swamped by refugees.[58]

The counter-revolution was also made possible by the sheer bulk of Athenians alienated by the regime, who were either over the frontier or in the Peiraeus. The immediate attempt by the Thirty to dislodge Thrasyboulos failed owing to the determination of the defenders and a panic in a snowstorm. A subsequent force made up of the Spartan garrison and two tribal squadrons of Athenian cavalry was defeated by Thrasyboulos with a group which had now grown from 70 to 700. The Thirty seized Eleusis as a refuge, executing 300 of its inhabitants, and Thrasyboulos' numbers grew still further. He had 1,000 men when, in early summer 403, he decided to move to the Peiraeus. This was already a centre for fugitives from the Thirty and provided a bigger base with access to the sea. The Thirty immediately attacked. Against their forces — the 700 Spartan garrison troops, the 3,000 hoplites on the register and the cavalry — Thrasyboulos could only raise about a fifth their number of hoplites, but he had plenty of light-armed troops from the Peiraeus itself. With these he defeated the forces of the Thirty on the road leading up from the *agora* to the temples of Artemis and Bendis. In the battle two of the Thirty, Critias and Hippomachos, died and with them Charmides son of Glaukon, Critias' cousin and the uncle of Plato.[59]

An offer of reconciliation was made by Cleokritos, the Eleusinian herald, on behalf of the democrats. No response was made, but in consequence the Thirty were deposed from power in the city by the 3,000 warriors they had themselves registered as citizens, and the majority of them retired to Eleusis. However, in their place those in the city chose a new commission of ten, and two of the Thirty reappeared in this group, Pheidon and Lysias' enemy Eratosthenes. Another leading figure was Epichares who had been a councillor under the Thirty. Lysias argues that these supposed opponents of Critias and Charikles' faction were even more dangerous when they got into power. Certainly, they and the democrats in the Peiraeus had skirmishes and the latter even tried to storm the city. The city faction sent ambassadors to Sparta asking for help, just as the Thirty did from Eleusis. There they were lent 100 talents to hire mercenaries, and Lysander offered himself as their harmost for land operations and the co-operation of his brother Libys, the Spartan admiral, by sea.

Later, King Pausanias led a regular expedition of the Peloponnesian League into Attica (the Corinthians and Boeotians refused to join). He did not wish to see Lysander master of Athens and, although initially he demanded that the men from the Peiraeus should disperse and he became involved in a battle in the plain north of the town, he sent secret messages advising them of the peace terms they should offer him and the ephors. He also approached those in the city, and the commission of ten there was overthrown and replaced by a group who had been previously in favour of a reconciliation. After representatives of the city and the Peiraeus had visited Sparta, an agreement was reached. Both groups were to be at peace with one another and remain in the Spartan alliance. Only the Thirty and their ten-man executive in the Peiraeus were excluded from this arrangement. Anyone from the city, who was afraid to remain when the citizen body was reunited, could retire to join them at Eleusis. Thus in Boedromion (c. September of 403) the Peiraeus men marched back into the city and sacrificed to Athena.[60]

After the return, accusations for murder were allowed against those who had personally used violence. Otherwise, there was an amnesty for past political behaviour, except for members of the Thirty, their executive in the Peiraeus, their prison commissioners and the first commission of ten in the city. One stumbling block in the reconciliation was the status of the men on whose support Thrasyboulos originally depended, many of whom were slaves or foreigners. After Thrasyboulos had entered the Peiraeus he had offered the latter the privilege of *isoteleia*, that is, having the same public duties as citizens. He now tried to secure citizenship for all those who had returned from the Peiraeus, but this was blocked by Archinos through a charge that the proposal was illegal. Two years later non-citizens, who had contributed to the restoration of democracy, were given some reward, probably either citizenship or *isoteleia*. The fragments of the stone displaying this decree and a list of those rewarded provide a fascinating list of rural and city trades and show the broad social backing for the counter-revolution. This confirms the view expressed in the speech ascribed to Thrasyboulos by Xenophon, that this was essentially a victory of the 'have-nots' over the 'haves'.[61]

The successful return of the democracy was first due to the courage of Thrasyboulos and his originally small and motley force. Later the general support mobilised from the artisans and shopkeepers in the Peiraeus is remarkable, since on our evidence such men rarely took up arms to fight for their own freedom in this period. The *stasis* at Corcyra provides the closest parallel. Pressures from outside eventually balanced themselves. We must set against the Spartan desire to protect the regime which they had created, the hostility of Corinth and Thebes, who aided the democrats, and the jealousy felt towards Lysander in Sparta itself. Above all, however, the counter-revolution was provoked by the sheer brutality of the Thirty which itself was in part a response to their insecurity. The Thirty could not hope to establish an absolutist government over a state as populous and prosperous as Athens without a considerable army which could also serve as a political police. The forces sent by Sparta were inadequate for the purpose, nor until the loan made by Sparta after the capture of the Peiraeus was there finance for the hire of mercenaries. The Thirty had to recruit support from Athenians, and they did so by increasing the conflicts inside Athenian society and by blatantly robbing rich and poor. Yet it was no use: when it came to defending their greed, the Thirty could not cope with a force of about 600 hoplites backed by light-armed troops. Oligarchy could be imposed on Athens either by overwhelming military force or by consent and the appearance of legitimacy. The Thirty, perhaps deterred by the precedent of 411, did not attempt the second course and they had not the strength to achieve the first.

The Philosophical Background to the Oligarchic Movement

When Socrates was accused of wronging his city, his association with Critias was considered an important item of proof of his guilt. The famous case is the best evidence of the connection made by the Athenian people between sophistic learning and oligarchic sentiments. No discussion of the oligarchic movement, therefore, can ignore the possible contribution made to it by the political and ethical ideas current in the late fifth century — in particular those views which identified the right and just with the interest of the stronger man or group, whether this was based on an objective description of the way the world behaved or an enthusiastic belief in the glory of might.

It should be said at the beginning that the oligarchic movement in Athens can be explained, as I have tried to do earlier, without any philosophical background. Moreover, the revolutions in many other Greek

cities were not created by men on whom the influence of sophistic train-
ing is attested. However, one cannot say *a priori* in history what the sufficient conditions of any event are: an apparent surplus of causes may be
valuable. The sophistic movement was strong in Athens. What is more,
one leading oligarch, Critias, can be seen by his own writings to have been
influenced by its philosophy, while another, Antiphon of Rhamnous,
was a teacher of rhetoric and is probably to be identified with the sophist
who, among other philosophical topics, treated of the contradictions
inherent in everyday notions of right and wrong. A third, Andron son
of Androtion, who prosecuted his former leader Antiphon after the fall
of the Four Hundred, is named by Plato in the *Gorgias* as one of a group
of students of philosophy with whom Callikles associated.[62]

Justice and violence had been portrayed as opposing forces from the
time of Hesiod, although, as we have seen, many acts of violence, even
when there had been little or no provocation, were not regarded as viola-
tions of justice. Among the guarantors of justice in Greek religion Zeus
was pre-eminent. Yet Zeus had, according to traditional mythology,
both committed acts of violence himself and sanctioned them for others.
This is highlighted in a poem of Pindar, written before sophistic doc-
trines were widely known in Greece and by a man who professed a
belief in the sovereignty of the Olympian gods. Lines from it were used
by Plato in the *Gorgias* as part of Callikles' initial argument; a recently
discovered papyrus has provided a fuller text of the poem. This showed
how Pindar had used the story of Herakles and the horses of Diomedes
to prove the proposition that *nomos*, king of all gods and men, (that is,
custom or conventional belief) justifies the greatest violence. The theft
of the horses, although apparently unjust, was approved by Zeus.[63]

Later in the fifth century there were various forms in which the
theme of the subordination of right to might was presented, sometimes
separated by little more than a nuance. In Thucydides' history speakers
claim it to be an accepted fact of life that the powerful extend their
power and the weak give way: justice therefore can only arise from a
balance of power. In my view we should trust the historian sufficiently
to conclude that this belief was held and enunciated by politicians during the war — whether or not it was Thucydides' view is another matter
— but it was not necessarily regarded by the speakers as relevant to events
within a city like Athens, since the context of the speeches is inter-city
relations. In this field power is still today the final arbiter of justice. In
the Greek world of the fifth century BC, moreover, the violence of war
was taken to be an inevitable feature of life and the ultimate test of
greatness.

The inferior status of justice to force within a given society is argued by philosophical opponents of Socrates in Platonic dialogues. Thrasymachos in the *Republic* defines the just as the advantage of the superior: laws are framed to suit the governing body so that they may enjoy more than their fair share of benefits. Although the reasoning behind his view seems empirical, as in Thucydides, and to derive from a cynical acceptance of the way of the world, Thrasymachos treats his definition of justice as an ideal: it is what the true governor or ruling class would choose in its own interest. Justice is thus for the superior man a means to an end, that he himself may be more unjust.

A different approach, closer to that of the speakers in Thucydides, is taken by Callikles in the *Gorgias*. In his view it is natural to be unjust and to seek to have more than the many (that is, the common people): the unnatural thing is to suffer injustice. It is the law of nature for the superior to dominate and have more than the inferior. Callikles quotes the passage of Pindar discussed earlier in order to support his view. Justice by contrast is only comprehensible as a means for the majority of weak and inferior people to protect themselves against the strong. Thus, while Thrasymachos accepts law and social organisation as a natural form of self-expression by the superior, undertaken in order to minimise the likelihood of him suffering injustice himself while allowing him the greatest freedom to perform it, Callikles rejects society as a prison for the strong created by his inferiors.

What is the relevance of these arguments to the oligarchic movements? That of Thrasymachos is on the face of it merely a cynical piece of *realpolitik*, in itself no more subversive than the Thucydidean view of justice in international relations was or is today. Thrasymachos' portrayal of the rule of the superior applies equally well to a monarch, oligarchy or democracy, without appearing to advocate any one of these forms of government. It is, however, particularly trenchant as a picture of the way Athenian democracy worked — the mass of people, once in power, organising affairs specifically for their own benefit. As such, in outline, it resembles closely the theme of the oligarchic essay on the Athenian constitution. In the latter it is argued, first that it is just that the poor and common people should have more than the wealthy and well-bred, because it is they who row the warships and create power, secondly that it is just that the common people organise the city so that they remain in control and reap the benefits of the power that they have acquired. Therefore, the oligarchic attitudes which should follow from Thrasymachos' view of justice are respectful detestation of democracy, as long as it is successful, but a conviction that it should be overthrown, once it has failed.[64]

Callikles' argument is essentially opposed to any ordered government except a tyranny or narrow oligarchy, in which the superior men do as they please. Such men, it is implied, should exploit both laws and other people for their own benefit and should not be sorry if their society collapses. Plato associated Callikles with a known oligarch, Andron son of Androtion. Moreover, Callikles' view of law is close to that implicit in a speech from a satyr-play written by Critias himself, the *Sisyphos*. In this Sisyphos describes the origin of law and fear of the gods. Men first wish to repress disorder and crime and so make the law king. Then they are forced to find a way to deter themselves from secret offences, and so a clever man invents the gods in heaven and their vengeance. In its context this passage was spoken by a man normally held to be bad, presumably a sort of anti-hero in the play. It obliquely presents the view that law, society and morality are constraints invented to shackle those who would otherwise do what they wanted. This belief jars somewhat with Critias' admiration for Spartan discipline, but on the limited evidence of the fragments it seems that what Critias admired was the Spartan mode of personal behaviour, which he held to be beautiful and desirable in itself, producing health and happiness.

The relativity of justice is discussed by Antiphon in a papyrus fragment of his work *On Truth*. The right approach to justice is said to lie in a man's obeying the law in front of witnesses, but the requirements of nature when he is alone. For the requirements of law (*nomos*) are the product of contract, while the requirements of nature (*phusis*) are the product of natural growth. No penalty or disgrace results from the unobserved disobedience of the first, but a man who disregards the second is harmed in truth and not according to mere opinion. It is pleasure rather than pain that helps nature. Thus, those who want to suffer harm before resisting, those who are kind to parents who have ill-treated them, those who allow others to denounce them but do not themselves denounce, all are acting contrary to nature. There would be some sense in these actions, if the law did provide aid, but it does not prevent the original injury nor does it put the injured party in a more favourable position than the injurer.

In another fragment Antiphon exposes a contradiction in two features of the conventional interpretation of justice which he attacks as contrary to nature in the first passage. These are the beliefs that it is just not to wrong any person, when one has not been wronged by him first, and that it is just to give true testimony. Such testimony may lead to the conviction of a man who has done you no wrong in the first place and may also cause him to take reprisals against you. Thus, so-called justice leads to injustice both in this situation and when men act as jurors, judges and arbitrators.[65]

These original sophistic texts are much more comprehensive and subtle than the arguments ascribed to Socrates' opponents by Plato. The precept of following the dictates of nature rather than law, except where one may suffer by being found out, is a less absolutist version of that advocated by Callikles and implied by Critias in the *Sisyphos*. However, unlike Callikles, Antiphon is not only concerned with superior people but all those who suffer from following the prescriptions of the law and the conventional interpretation of justice. He will not even allow that the law is a protection for the weak, and the logic of his argument perhaps leads in the end towards the view of Thrasymachos that the law is there for the exploitation of those who slavishly obey it. If one presses the argument to an ethical conclusion, it must be that a man should prefer self-sufficiency and the liberty to choose his own associates to existing society, unless he is above the law.

The bulk of the ancient evidence suggests that this Antiphon is identical with Antiphon of Rhamnous, the speech-writer and oligarchic politician. There seems no great difference in style between the philosophical papyrus fragments and the main fragment of Antiphon's speech in his own defence. The social egalitarianism in the sophist's attitude to rich and poor, Greek and barbarian, does not mean that he preferred Athenian democracy, where great families had great influence and there was as much chauvinistic contempt for barbarians as in other Greek states, to the rule of a narrow oligarchy.

Membership of a narrow oligarchic junta or the possession of a tyranny that was above the law would avoid the objections that Antiphon makes to conventional justice. More important, perhaps, is a characteristic which Antiphon's opinions have in common with those of Callikles, Critias and Thrasymachos, the purely pragmatic attitude to existing societies, according to which these only deserve respect in so far as they compel respect. This is the most significant feature of these theories from the historical point of view. Yet this is a commonplace attitude of no great philosophical profundity, which may have been equally characteristic of a man of action like Phrynichos, a political tactician like Theramenes, or a rank and file member of the oligarchy like Polystratos. Sophistic learning merely helped oligarchs to formulate their existing political convictions.

There is a further feature of the views of Callikles, Critias and Antiphon which may help us to understand the psychology of the thinkers

— the admiration for the primitive. These men regarded the existing complexities of Athenian society as contrary to nature, and for the most part looked back to the days before organised society developed, where men freely pursued their own desires, as a kind of utopia for those who had superior abilities. They did not believe in a collectivist or organic state. However, their assessment of man's position before law had developed was extraordinarily naive. They failed to understand the constraints which limited the actions of superior men in that period, those which we have considered in Chapter 1. Even then men were not free to use their power as they liked, but were opposed by collective action and themselves found it preferable to act according to certain understood rules, which restricted the scope of brute force. If men were blind to this in the late fifth century, this may reflect a general inability of the Athenian oligarchs to understand that they could not shed the chains of existing society as easily as they thought.

Violence and the Law Code

What I have just said may appear to conflict with one of the themes in Chapter 1, where I showed the extent to which force still had a role to play in settling disputes within mature Greek societies such as that of Athens. Was there not enough scope in these for man to exploit his own superiority and pursue the dictates of nature as Antiphon, Critias and Callikles recommended? We have seen how private force was necessary for self-defence and, although not generally prescribed in Athens for ensuring the appearance of an opponent in court, as it was in Rome, it was regularly permitted as a mode of executing debts or court judgements. Perhaps the most striking are the occasions when a man with legal backing invaded the home of his opponent to seize property. If self-help in the seizure of property or moveables was resisted in a procedure known as *exagōgē*, this compelled the man trying to execute a judgement to resort to a 'suit arising from ejection', *dikē exoulēs* – an action either for legal immunity to carry out self-help or financial compensation or both, with a fine being paid to the state by the convicted man in any case as a component of the penalty. Apart from this, in a state which had not the means to police such matters, bands of young men had plenty of opportunity for violence in the streets, which was not necessarily random but directed at redressing alleged wrongs or taking vengeance on private enemies. Conon and his sons assaulted Ariston in the Ceramicos in consequence of a previous quarrel when they were on guard-duty at Eleutherai; the speaker of Lysias III was attacked by Simon because he had taken over his boyfriend.[66]

On the other hand, there was a range of legal remedies against improper violence. Apart from murder, there were suits for *trauma* (wounding or grievous bodily harm), *aikeia* (personal affront or assault) and *hubris* (outrage) — the last of these terms covered a great variety of insulting acts, not necessarily involving physical violence; there were in addition suits for verbal abuse (*kakēgoria*). Certain features of these actions are not only interesting in themselves but have important implications 'for the Athenian attitude to violence and their democratic constitution. First, it was not necessary to have suffered any permanent physical harm to bring a suit for assault (*aikeia*) or *hubris*. Indeed, it is argued that one of the reasons for the existence of these charges is that the man worsted in a fight should not resort to a weapon like a stone and so cause serious harm to his opponent. In a case of *aikeia* what was critical was not the amount of hurt suffered by either side but who started the fight. By contrast, such an action, where the only permanent injury had been to a person's dignity and standing, was not available in Rome until the *actio iniuriarum* was introduced by Sulla in the last century BC.[67] Secondly, the *graphē hubreōs*, the action for *hubris*, carried no compensation for the man injured: it was a criminal action open to any Athenian citizen with the penalty being paid to the state. Thus, outrage and insult was regarded as disruptive to the community as a whole. It is remarkable that this action could even be brought over an outrage to a slave. Aeschines' explanation is that the lawgiver wished to check in every possible way the man who was inclined to commit violent outrages because he was a danger to democracy. Thirdly, although one of the aims of the legislators was probably, as the orators argue, to prevent an exchange of kicks and punches becoming something more lethal, the notion of dignity, in Greek terminology *timē*, was at the root of the legislation. 'If there had been no outrage [*hubris*] in what was done, I would never have come to court,' runs Isocrates' speech against Lochites. 'As it is, I am not here to prosecute him because of the injury I also suffered from his blows, but because of the affront and dishonour [*atimia* — loss of *timē*], which should be a particular cause of indignation to free men and for which they should receive the greatest recompense.' Similarly, in the discussion of *hubris* in Aristotle's *Rhetoric*, the essence of the notion is that the agent brings pleasure to himself through the sense of superiority which arises from harming other people, while inflicting disgrace and dishonour on the victims.[68]

The Athenian law code thus tried to provide a peaceful substitute,

dependent on the vote of a democratic jury, for the violence which
might result from a man's sense of his own worth and his resentment at
being belittled. These feelings had been of course especially characteristic of the aristocracy, and one might be tempted to see in this legislation an attempt to cut down the sort of feuding, which in its most
developed form had led to tyrannies and the assassination of tyrants in
the Archaic Age. Yet even a brief reflection about the terms of the law
and its likely use makes clear that it was not particularly designed for
the benefit of aristocrats. *Dunatoi* were likely to come off on even
terms, if not victorious, in physical contests because of the strength
of their entourages, nor would their reputation among their peers be
necessarily improved by the vote of a democratic jury. Isocrates argued
that the law of *hubris* was a remedy against the dishonour any free man
would resent, and this is surely its key feature. The laws regarding *hubris*,
aikeia and *kakēgoria* in fact treated the members of the Athenian *demos*
as aristocrats by enabling them to protect their *timē* as free men. It is
arguable that much of the motive power in Athenian democracy came
from the fact that it was the rule of a people who were conscious that
they were superior collectively and individually. These laws were the
fitting protection of such *amour-propre*.

A certain amount of private violence was endemic in Athenian society, either encouraged by the law itself, because the city had not the
resources to enforce all its judgements and decrees, or permitted to
flourish by the absence of an executive charged with maintaining the
peace. Yet there were legal remedies, which were regarded by the Athenians as a deterrent and, to judge from the small sample of court cases
known to us, frequently invoked. I have no doubt that without these
laws Athenian society would have been much more violent. Furthermore, it was not far-fetched when Isocrates compared an offender
against the law of *hubris* to the oligarchs under the Thirty. For both
had offended against the social foundations of democracy. Private
violence was on the whole considered a danger to personal liberty in
Athens, whereas in Rome it was for long held to be not only compat-
ible with liberty but liberty's ally and guarantor.

This was one reason why what was in many ways a tough society,
where wealth and physical strength might win contests which morally
they did not deserve to do, was still far too restrictive for men like Antiphon and Critias. Not only the laws against private violence but Athenian
law in general was a net in which powerful men might be enmeshed by
informers and reduced to the level of any other citizen. When the Thirty
took to executing those who had made a profession of prosecution under

the democracy, superficially they appeared to be performing a public service by ridding the state of those who tried to advance themselves by exploiting the failings of their fellows, but we may suspect that this justification concealed a resentment against the general working of Athenian law as a check on individual self-assertion and a guarantee of the liberty of the ordinary citizen.

Athenian Politics after the Revolutions

The Athenians were swift to create a new constitution, in which the assembly was to be dominant. They were not, however, over-generous to the people of dubious citizen status who contributed to the over-throw of the Thirty. This may be put down to traditional exclusiveness: more precisely it may be regarded as the price Thrasyboulos and his supporters had to pay for their reconciliation with those who remained in the city. However, the reconciliation was still subject to strain. Fiercer class prejudice seems to have been roused during 404 and 403 than in the earlier struggles between democrats and oligarchs. The Four Hundred had merely tried to eliminate inconvenient leading democrats, and defectors from the oligarchs had helped to bring back democracy. In the expeditionary force on Samos no insuperable gulf had been created between the hoplites and the rowers in the fleet. By contrast, the Thirty had killed not only democratic leaders but men of lesser rank. Furthermore, they had enlisted the support of the comparatively wealthy by redistributing property at the expense of the poor and cutting off the poor from their roots in the neighbourhood of the city. It was not surprising that there was bitterness against the cavalry, their most conspicuous supporters — manifest for example in Theozotides' decree and in the speeches by Lysias for Mantitheos and against Evandros.[69]

At least ten speeches in the main corpus of Lysias concern at some point behaviour during the revolutionary period. To these we may add the speech for Eryximachos, surviving in a papyrus fragment, and perhaps the speech for Phanias, quoted by Athenaeus. Isocrates' speeches against Euthunos and Callimachos concern actions under the Thirty and the city administration in 404-403, while the speech against Lochites, alleging assault (*hubris*), argues that the defendant, although too young to have participated in the oligarchy, is of the type brought to light by that regime.[70] In some cases charges of oligarchic activity were legitimate under the terms of the amnesty because of an act of personal violence or the defendant's membership of one of the oligarchic governing bodies, as in Lysias' accusation of Eratosthenes. Moreover, behaviour under the earlier oligarchy was not covered by the amnesty.

Andokides was accused in 399 of entering sacred places although he had confessed to impiety – a charge deriving from his involvement in the Herm scandal of 415. It was an obvious weapon for a political opponent to grasp. But its particular value was that it labelled him as an oligarch, in spite of the fact that he had been imprisoned by the Four Hundred when he attempted to return from exile. Earlier in 399, association with Critias and Alcibiades had been one of the proofs that Socrates' accuser had adduced to show that he had corrupted young men, and in Aeschines' view this was the main ground for his condemnation. One argument employed to advocate toughness with oligarchs is significant and reflects on the hostility to Andokides and Socrates as impious men. In the conclusion of the speech against Lochites, Isocrates states that such men do not respect the established laws, but they do treat as laws the decisions of the law courts. Men like Antiphon had in the past exploited the courts to the advantage of themselves and their friends. Protagoras' claim to make the weaker argument the stronger had been ascribed to Socrates by Aristophanes in the *Clouds*. What could be more satisfying for the *demos* than to defeat oligarchs educated by the sophists on what they believed to be their own ground?[71]

There was also hostility to the rich. Isocrates in the speech against Lochites deliberately exploits it, and its importance can be inferred from many speeches in the corpus of Lysias, quite apart from allegations of complicity in the oligarchic revolutions. The nephew of Nikias, when speaking against a proposal to confiscate the estate of his father, warns against the danger of *stasis* arising out of the proposals for confiscation of property. These, he alleges, enrich the accusers rather than the state, and leave some private property undisturbed while allowing the rest to be the victim of the greed of individual citizens. Elsewhere Lysias alleges that the Council welcomed denunciations in years of poor income. Such prosecutions would have been expected in the fifth century and are not in themselves proof of a surge of class hostility. Moreover, we must allow in all cases against wealthy men that the prosecution may stem not so much from the struggle between the traditionally rich and their traditional inferiors but from that between those presently rich and those whose wealth had been lost through the devastation of their estates and the confiscation of property. Nevertheless, the envy of the rich that was expected in a jury may have reinforced anti-oligarchic sentiments.[72]

The rich also had to pay for Athens' rearmament and military enterprises and, according to Isocrates, this led to their alienation from the rest of the community. Some resentment would have been natural but, although riches were indeed a cause of harassment rather than respect, one may doubt whether they were more burdensome than real poverty, as Isocrates implies. Moreover, the position of the wealthy was basically protected as a cornerstone of the restored democracy, since in the oath taken by the 6,000 jurors every year the clause abjuring any vote for tyranny or oligarchy, or support for the overthrow of democracy, was immediately followed by one abjuring obedience to any proposal for the abolition of debt or the redistribution of land.[73]

We can document how the grievances of the wealthy over the burdens imposed by the state first arose from Athens' military activity overseas. In 396, when an Athenian tried to damage the Spartan hegemony in Ionia by sailing to join Conon, the Athenian admiral of the Persian fleet, there was a conflict of policy arising from a conflict of interest. According to the *Oxyrhynchus Hellenica*, the *gnorimoi* and *charientes* (the nobles and men of quality) were against offending the Spartans and hazarding the survival of the city: in particular a group led by Thrasyboulos, Anytos and Aisymos, all participants in the rebellion against the Thirty, urged that the city should disclaim responsibility for the voyage of the Athenian trireme to Conon. Respectable men (*epieikeis*), that is the men of property, were content with the present state of affairs anyhow, while the masses, that is the common people, were persuaded to follow this advice. This is confirmed by Aristophanes in his *Women in the Assembly*, produced in 391: the poor approve of launching a fleet, but the wealthy and the farmers disagree.

The argument was thus not simply between rich and poor, but between those who had some land to live on and the city poor, who in the past had been provided with employment by the empire and the economic activity that went with it. In fact the politicians, who are said to have advocated caution in 396, seem only to have advised it for tactical reasons. Thrasyboulos himself was later an opponent of peace with Sparta and the leader of an important expedition which sought to reestablish something of Athens' old maritime empire. Whatever the attitude of the wealthy and the farm-owners, Athens in spite of setbacks became committed to a reconstruction of her fifth century naval league on a smaller scale, and this policy seems to have remained unchallenged in principle until the Social War in 357-355. A few years later Demosthenes in the *Third Olynthiac* still argued for a return to the principles of the fifth century, when Athenian citizens earned their welfare at home by fighting to gain wealth overseas.[74]

Isocrates complained in 355 that the Athenians were suspicious of advocates of peace, on the ground that they were supporters of oligarchy, but it is difficult to find confirmation for this from other evidence from this period. There is certainly no suspicion of an oligarchic *coup* at Athens during the first half of the fourth century; which is remarkable, inasmuch as the rest of Greece was plagued by revolution and counter-revolution during that period. One explanation is that after 378 Sparta was not powerful enough to back revolution in Athens and no such move could have occurred without external support. With the rising power of Philip II of Macedon, foreign support for a revolution became the more credible. Yet it is striking how little the charge of oligarchy figures in the political controversies of the period following the Social War. Demosthenes in the *Second Philippic* of 344-343 BC discourses on the occasions when Philip has overthrown other constitutions, but he does not suggest that this will happen at Athens. In his speech *On the Chersonese* of 342-341 he argues that Philip is hostile to Athens because of her democracy, which constitutes a political force opposed to the tyrannies Philip favoured, but his assumption here is that there is no threat to the democracy except from outside.

The first suggestion that Athens may be subverted from inside occurs after the Athenian humiliation on the battlefield of Chaeronea in 338 BC. A year or two later Hypereides indicted Philippides for illegally proposing honorific crowns for the presidents, on the ground that they had illegally proposed honours for Macedonians. He alleges that Philippides and his friends had once been friends of Sparta and flatterers of the enemies of the *demos*: they had forgotten that the Thirty had been overthrown. However, this is all innuendo and somewhat stale; there is little evidence in what remains of the speech of oligarchic activity by Philippides' group, only of support for Macedon.[75]

More interesting is the recently discovered law against tyranny, which was passed in 337-336. In this Eukrates proposed that any man who killed an incipient tyrant or his supporter or a destroyer of the democracy should be free from guilt. This clause, deriving from the decree of Demophantos of 410 BC, encouraged citizens not to await a court case but to proceed directly by force against enemies of the constitution. A further clause forbad the councillors of the Areopagus to sit in council after the democracy had fallen and threatened them with loss of citizen rights if they did. It would have been natural if in the aftermath of Chaeronea the Athenians feared some attempt at a tyranny on the analogy of the *coups* by oligarchs after great military disasters in the fifth century. Yet this decree was slow to appear, and meanwhile the Macedonians had not been openly trying to overthrow Athenian democracy.

On the contrary, the treaty creating the new league of Corinth in 338-337, by which Philip was established as a leader of the united Greek cities, specifically forbad subversion of all existing constitutions.[76]

It is, therefore, legitimate to suspect that the cause of the decree lay in internal Athenian politics. The reference to the Areopagus is clearly tendentious, seeking to bring some current activity of this body into disrepute. Whether the decree was aimed at supporters of friendship with Macedon, like Demades or (to a lesser extent) Phokion, or opponents of theirs, like Demosthenes, Lykourgos and Hypereides, it does not seem to anticipate either betrayal to a foreign power or an attempt to manipulate the assembly. The impression given by the decree is that the shadow cast by the events of 411 and 404 was long, but that there was still only a shadow, not a replica in being. For this to occur, Athens had to suffer a further disastrous military defeat and subjection to Macedon.

Notes

1. Hdt. V.69, 91-3, VI.88-91; *Ath. Pol.* 22.1-2; Ar., *Pol.* 1275b. Measures against tyranny – Thuc. VI.55.1; *Ath. Pol.* 16.10 (cf. ML 43; also Dem. 9.44, 23.62 for the original meaning of *atimos*, misunderstood in *Ath. Pol.*). I take the anti-tyranny decree not to have been in force in Peisistratus' time, as *Ath. Pol.* suggests. On Cleisthenes see Lévêque, 1964, 13ff.; Lewis, 1963, 26ff.; Rhodes, 1972 (1), 208ff.

2. *Ath. Pol.* 22, 43.5; Androtion, FGH 324, F6; Plut., *Arist.* 7.5-7; Philochorus, FGH 328, F30; cf. Hdt. IX.5. Ostraka evidence in ML 21 (ATPW 41); Thomsen, 1972, 69ff.; interesting late Byzantine text in Keaney, 1972; Lungo, 1980. See Dover, 1963, on Androtion; Stanton, 1970, on origins; Schreiner, 1976 on medisers; Thomsen and Lungo for summaries of interpretations to date.

3. Thuc. I.135.3; Plut., *Them.* 22.4-5; *Arist.* 2; Xen., *Mem.* II.6.5, 9.1, II.7.9; Plato, *Meno* 71e; *Rep.* I.332a, II.365d; *Ep.* VII.325c-d. Discussion and further references in Connor, 1971; Calhoun, 1913.

4. Plut., *Cim.* 9 (cf. Plato, *Theaet.* 173d); Hyp. 4.7-8. While *hetaireia* was a neutral word, *hetairikon* in classical authors seems always to refer to a group engaged in conspiracy or revolution.

5. Theopompus, FGH 115, F89; Plut., *Per.* 9; *Cim.* 14-17; *Ath. Pol.* 27.3-4; cf. APF 9688 XIII.

6. Ar., *Pol.* 1274a; *Ath. Pol.* 4.4, 8.4, 23.5, 25-6, 35.2; Philochorus, F64b; Plut., *Sol.* 19; *Cim.* 14-15; *Phoc.* 16.4; Dem. 18.132-4; Dein. I.14; Rhodes, 1972(1), 201; Sealey, 1967, 42.

7. Ant. 5.68; *Ath. Pol.* 25.4; Diod. XI.77.6; Plut., *Per.* 10.7-8; *Cim.* 17.4-8; Thuc. I.107.4-6; Theopompus, F88.

8. Plut., *Per.* 11.1-3, 12.1-2, 14.1-3, 16.1 (Pericles' *hetairoi* were called Peisistratidai by comic dramatists); *Mor.* 811e. For a sceptical view of the tradition about Thucydides son of Melesias, see Andrewes, 1978.

9. Plut., *Per.* 31-2 (cf. Arist., *Wasps* 380, 438; ML 56. 30, 61. 70; Androtion, F38; APF 4551); Thuc. II.59.2, 65.2; ps. Xen., *Ath. Pol.* 1.14-15; Arist., *Acharn.* 178ff.; Forrest, 1970 with references to earlier studies.

10. *Wasps* 488, cf. 417, 463-76, 483, 489-94; 953 (the dog Labes accused of stealing and conspiracy); *Knights* 452, 475-9, 626-9.

11. *Knights* 565-610; *Acharn.* 6-8; *Wasps* 1220ff.; Thuc. III.26.3, IV.21-2, 28.5, cf. II.63.2, III.40.4; Theopompus, F93, 94; Plut., *Mor.* 806f-7a; APF 8674; Connor, 1971, 91, 128ff.

12. *Synomosia* – Thuc. VIII.54.4, cf. 65.2, 92.4 (where called *hetairoi*); Antiphon – VIII.68.1; cf. *Wasps* 1269-70, 1301; eccentrics – *Wasps* 474-5; *Birds* 1281-3, Athen. XII.551d-e = Lys. fr. 23.53.

13. Thuc. VI.15.3-4, 27-28; Plut., *Alc.* 16.1-2, 20; And. 1.11ff., 27, 36, 101; cf. Thuc. VIII.49, 65.2; Xen., *Hell.* II.3.2. On the story that follows see HCT IV, 264ff.; Macdowell, 1962, 167ff.; Hatzfeld, 1940, 158ff.

14. Thuc. VI.53.3; And. I.12-18; Plut., *Alc.* 19.1-2, 22.3; ML 79 (ATPW 147), A12, B53, 93, 112, 116; cf. B89; And. I.35. Investigators (*zetetai*) – And. I.36; Thuc. VI.29.3, 53.2.

15. And. I.34-53, 61-7; Thuc. VI.60-1; Plut., *Alc.* 20.5-21.5.

16. I assume that Andokides' picture of Euphiletos' group is basically true (cf. Hatzfeld, 1940, 181; *contra* Plutarch), though he does not tell the whole story. See also Aurenche, 1974, who has a useful collection of material, but is too schematic and too ready to assume that every group was oligarchic. On Andokides' family see APF 828, V-VI. Blood ties were important in *hetaireiai*, but not necessarily the chief factor.

17. Thuc. VIII.1.1-4, 6.3, 17.2, 45-49. *Probouloi* – Arist., *Lys.* 387; Lys. 12.65; Ar., *Rhet.* 1419b. On Peisandros' career under the democracy see Eupolis, fr. 31; Arist. fr. 81; *Peace* 395; *Birds* 1556; *Lys.* 490; Plato Com. fr. 95ff. (*Peisandros*).

18. Thuc. VIII.53-4. The *Kērukes* of Eleusis would have been represented by the Callias, son of Hipponikos, whose sister Hipparete had been married to Alcibiades (Plut., *Alc.* 8.3; cf. APF 7826 VIII. 600 VIII).

19. Thuc. VIII.56, 63.3-66 (cf. 21, 73 on Samos). The words 'suitable' and 'unsuitable' (*epitedeios* and *anepitedeios*) seem to have been current oligarchic jargon – 63.4, 65.2, 66.2, 70.2. Hoplite franchise – 65.3, cf. 97.1; *Ath. Pol.* 29.5.

20. Thuc. VIII.67.3, 70.1, 89.2, 92.11, 93.2, *Ath. Pol.* 32.3. My view is essentially that of Meyer (1899, II.406ff.), followed *inter alios* by Hignett, 1952, 258ff. and 356ff. and recently by Andrewes, 1976, and HCT V, 184-256. For contrary views see e.g. Wilamowitz, 1893, I, 99ff., II, 113ff. and most recently Flach, 1977, which I discuss in Appendix I.

21. Thuc. VIII.67.1; *Ath. Pol.* 29.1-3; Androtion, F43; Philochorus, F130. Pythodorus was probably the man who accused and exiled Protagoras (Diog. Laert. 9.54), later one of the Four Hundred. On the 'ancestral constitution' see Thrasymachos, DK 78, B1; Isoc. 7.15-16 (Cleitophon is linked with Thrasymachos in Plato, *Cleit.* 406a; *Rep.* I.328b); Fuks, 1953, for whom it is a concrete political programme; Finley, 1971, who takes it to be an ambiguous and tendentious propaganda phrase.

22. Thuc. VIII.67.2-3, cf. 66.1, 70.1; *Ath. Pol.* 29.4-5; ML 80 (for five presidents); registration – Lys. 20.2, 13-14, 22; cf. Rhodes, 1972(2), 117.

23. Thuc. VIII.69-70, cf. 64.1, 92.6, VI.57.1 and Plato, *Gorg.* 469d for daggers; *Ath. Pol.* 32.1, 33.1 with HCT V, 234ff. on chronology.

24. Thuc. VIII.72-6; Hyperbolos – APF 13910; Connor, 1971, 79ff.; Samos – IG I^2.101 (Lewis, 1954, 20). The fleet planned to collect tribute for itself (VIII.76.4).

25. VIII.72.1, 77, 81-2, 86. I take 82.2 and 86.4ff. to be duplicate references to the same occasion. The uncertainty about the Five Thousand depends on a problem of translation (cf. Rhodes, 1972(2), 119; HCT V, 285). I prefer the first alternative, but the phrase may have been deliberately ambiguous when first spoken, so as to suggest the second (more democratic) possibility.

26. VIII.89; on ambassadors – 86.1, 90.1. In 89.1 I understand 'the majority of those who had participated . . .' to include those who thought themselves members of the Five Thousand, while 'those truly in the oligarchy and in office' are members of the Four Hundred. In 89.2 there is no contradiction between *hos ephasan* and *spoude panu*. They had genuine fears of the forces on Samos which they openly expressed, though they did not voice their own plans.

27. VIII.90-2; cf. ps. Plut., *Mor.* 833b-e on the embassy (other members were Archeptolemos and Onomakles); Lys. 13.71; ML 85 (ATPW 155) on Phrynichos' death; HCT V, 302-11.

28. VIII.93-97; cf. *Ath. Pol.* 30.2-3, 33, on Euboea Diod. XIII.47.3-6; ML 82.

29. VIII.67.3, 68.4, 69.2-4, 97.1; *Ath. Pol.* 30.2-6, 31.2.

30. Pay – VIII.53.3, 65.3; cf. 48.3; Sealey, 1967, 126f. (in my view pressed a little too far). Cavalry – VIII.69.4, 92.6. Wealthy – VIII.47.2, 48.1, 63.4, 65.3; cf. Xen., *Symp.* 4.30-1.

31. VIII.70.2, 71.3, 86.9, 89.1, 90-1; ps. Plut., *Mor.* 833b-4b. Spartan sympathies – Arist., *Wasps* 474-6; *Birds* 1281-3; Critias DK B6-9; Plato, *Prot.* 342a-c.

32. Thuc. VIII.97.1-2; *Ath. Pol.* 30-1, 33; Lys. 34, hypoth. 1-4; Xen., *Hell.* II.3.48; ps. Xen., *Ath. Pol.* 1.1-2, 3.8-9.

33. VIII.68.1; cf. the praise of Themistocles in I.138.3. I take Thucydides' comments on the ability of the men behind the conspiracy as the tribute of one politician to others of a different persuasion in the same field.

34. VIII.54.4, 66.5, 89.3 – where *hos ouk apo ton homoion elassoumenos* means 'on the ground that he was not being worsted by men of his own class'.

35. VIII.66.5; Phrynichos, Peisandros – Lys. 25.9, 20.11; And. 1.27, 36, 43; Charminos – Thuc. VIII.30.1, 41-2, 73.3; Onomakles – VIII.25.1, 30.2, ps. Plut., *Mor.* 833e; Laispodias – Thuc. VI.105.2, VIII.86.9; Melesias – APF 7268 IIIA or 9816; Callaischros – Lys. 12.66; APF 8792 VI C; Aristocrates – APF 1904; HCT V, 294f.; Hagnon – Lys. 12.65; APF 7234; Sophocles – Ar., *Rhet.* 1419a; also Aristoteles (Xen., *Hell.* II.3.46) – Thuc. III.105.3; HCT II, 417, V, 302.

36. Polystratos – Lys. 20.2, 6, 11-12, 24-8, 33; cf. Thuc. VIII.60.1. Eratosthenes – Lys. 12.42, 62-6.

37. Lys. 25.7-12; Critias – Lyc. *Leocr.* 113; Philon – Lys. 31.8-9, 17-18; Antiphon – Nicole, 1907, Col. I-III (Maidment, *Attic Orators* I, 294); Thuc. VIII.68.2; Ar., *Eth. Eud.* 1232b; Phrynichos – Thuc. VIII.48.4-7, 50.1, 54.3, 68.3, 90.1-2, 92.2.

38. Thuc. VIII.89.2-4 (more crudely in Lys. 12.66), cf. III.82.8, II.65.8-11.

39. *Ath. Pol.* 33; And. 1.96; ML 84; Thuc. VIII.97.1-2; reforms ascribed to Theramenes – Diod. XIII.38.2.

40. The Five Thousand – Thuc. VIII.65.3, 67.3, 72.1, 86.3, 6, 89.2, 92.11, 93.2, 97.1. There is a close similarity between the proposals in VIII.65.3 and 97.1. One must, however, distinguish these from propaganda statements intended to mystify. I take Lys. 30.8 to refer to the register under this regime. Antiphon – Nicole, 1907, col. III (cf. ps. Plut., *Mor.* 833e). For discussion see de Ste Croix, 1956; Sealey, 1967, 111ff.; Rhodes, 1972(2); HCT V, 323ff.

41. Council – ps. Plut., *Mor.* 833e-34b; And. 1.96; Rhodes, 1972(1), 185-90; 1972(2), 117; Hignett, 1952, 372. Dangers to the Five Thousand – Thuc. VIII.96.3-4, 98.1-3. Trials – ps. Plut., *Mor.* 833e-34b; Lyc. Leocr. 112-21; Xen., *Hell.* I.7.28, *Mem.* II.9.4-8; Lys. 7.4, 20.14, 22, 25.25-6, cf. 18.9; Ar., *Rhet.* 1375b, 1400b, 1419a; Arist., *Frogs* 687-92, 709.

42. Peace offer – Diod. XIII.52-3; Philochorus F139a-b, cf. Andrewes, 1953. For the two-obol dole, introduced by Cleophon, *Ath. Pol.* 28.3; ML 84. 23; IG I².304B; financial crisis of 407-406 – Philochorus F141; IG I².255. 328ff. ATPW 164.

43. Xen., *Hell.* I.4.10-5.15; Diod. XIII.68-71; Plut., *Alc.* 33-5; *Hell. Oxy.* 4.
44. Xen., *Hell.* I.6.16-7.8, 7.32; Diod. XIII.77-9, 97-101 (esp. 100.2-3). Re-valuation of Diodorus — Andrewes, 1974. Mourning — cf. Lintott, 1968, 16.
45. Xen., *Hell.* I.7.9-34; Diod. XIII.101; *Ath. Pol.* 34.1. Procedure — Rhodes, 1972(1), 62, 148, 182; political background — Hatzfeld, 1940, 325ff. (though I do not see a plot by A.'s friends). Thrasyllos, Diomedon — Thuc. VIII.73.4; Pericles — Plut., *Per.* 37.5-6; cf. ML 84. 8; Callixenos — APF 9688 VI-VII; Euryptolemos — ibid., VIII; Aristocrates — APF 1904; Erasinides — ML 85. 5.
46. Xen., *Hell.* II.1.28-30, 2.3-10; ML 94 (ATPW 166).
47. Lys. 12.43-4, cf. 55; Thuc. VIII.54.4, 66.1. Restoration to citizenship — Xen., *Hell.* II.2.11; Lys. 12.47; And. 1.78-9 (applying even to members of the Four Hundred, provided that they had not been condemned as murderers or tyrants nor had fled into exile to escape trial). See Appendix I on the controversy over chronology.
48. Xen., *Hell.* II.2.11-16; Lys. 13.8, 17. Cf. the Theramenes papyrus (P. Mich. inv. 5982; Youtie-Merkelbach, 1968), lines 39ff. Lysias (12.68, 13.9) alleges that Theramenes promised that there would be no need to take down the walls or surrender the ships, but this is clearly tendentious. The papyrus (cf. Henrichs, 1968; Andrewes, 1970) seems to be an answer to these allegations.
49. Cleophon — Xen., *Hell.* II.2.17, 3.2, 54; Lys. 30.10-12, 13.12 — he probably died in an attempt to break out of prison (Xen. I.7.35). Council — Lys. 13.20; Areopagus — Lys. 12.69.
50. Xen., *Hell.* II.2.20-2; Plut., *Lys.* 14; Lys. 13.13-35. Other democratic con-spirators — Menestratos (Lys. 13.55); Aristophanes of Cholleidai (13.58); Calliades (30.14).
51. Xen., *Hell.* II.2.23, 3.2-3, 11; Plut., *Lys.* 15 (date of surrender — Munichion 16); Lys. 12.71-6; *Ath. Pol.* 34.3. Both Lys. and *Ath. Pol.* suggest that a form of constitution was outlined in the assembly, as at Colonos in 411, but the details seem to have been left to the discretion of the Thirty. See also Appendix I. Echo of Peisandros — Lys. 74; Thuc. VIII.53.3.
52. Xen., *Hell.* II.3.2. Cf. Lys. 12.43; Xen. II.2.18, 3.46; Thuc. VIII.30.2; ps. Plut., *Mor.* 833e; *Ath. Pol.* 29.1; And. I.36; Thuc. VII.20, 26; Isoc. 16.42; ML 85. 14, 84.20; APF 9238.
53. *Ath. Pol.* 34.3; Diod. XIV.3; Lys. 12.77; cf. on the four 'moderates' — *Hell. Oxy.* 6.2; *Ath. Pol.* 40.2, 29.3; Lys. 34 and note 21 above. Papyrus — see note 48 above and on the Theramenes myth, Harding, 1974.
54. Xen., *Hell.* II.3.2, 11-14; *Ath. Pol.* 35; Diod. XIV.4; Lys. 12.73, 13.35-8, 74, 18.4, 25.19, 30.14. See Appendix I.
55. Xen., *Hell.* II.3.14, 21, 39-41; *Ath. Pol.* 35.4; Diod. XIV.5.5-7; Lys. 12.6-19, 18.6; Plato, *Apol.* 32c-d; And. 1.94; cf. Isoc. 21.12-15. Xenophon implies that Leon's arrest preceded the trials of the metics and of Theramenes himself. Diodorus characteristically places these trials *after* the death of Theramenes.
56. Xen., *Hell.* II.3.15-56 (esp. 15-19); Diod. XIV.4.5-5.4 (chronologically misplaced and unconvincingly embellished). Young thugs — Xen., *Hell.* II.323; Thuc. VIII.69.4, 92.6.
57. Xen., *Hell.* II.4.1; Lys. 12.95-7. Leading citizens not enrolled in the Three Thousand were put on a black-list, 'Lysander's list' — Isoc. 18.16, 21.2. Spartan sympathies — Xen. II.3.34; Critias, DK B6-9. Wealthy and property — Xen., *Mem.* II.7.1-12, *Symp.* 4.30-1; Lys. 7.9; cf. Isoc. 18.23.
58. Xen., *Hell.* II.4.2, *Ath. Pol.* 37.1-2; Diod. XIV.6, 32.1; *Hell. Oxy.* 17.1. Motivation — Xen. II.3.17-18, 21, 4.1; Diod. XIV.4.3-4, 5.5-7.
59. Xen. II.4.1-19; Diod. XIV.32.2-4, 33.1-2; Lys. 12.52. Date of Peiraeus battle — Xen. II.4.21 (brutality of the Thirty for eight months); epitaph for Critias and his followers erected by comrades, recalling how they quelled the

insolence of the *demos* − Schol. Aeschin. I.39; Charmides − APF 8792 IX.

60. Xen. II.4.20-39; Lys. 12.53-61; Diod. XIV.33.5-6; *Ath. Pol.* 38.3-4; And. 1.95; Plut., *Mor.* 349e. Rhinon was another member of the Ten in the city; Patrokles remained as *archon basileus* and Lysimachos as cavalry commander (Isoc. 18.5-7; Xen. II.4.8, 26).

61. Amnesty − *Ath. Pol.* 39.5-6; Xen. II.4.38, 43; And. 1.90-1; Lys. 13.88-90; cf. Isoc. 18.2-3 on Archinos' law reinforcing the amnesty and *Ath. Pol.* 40.2. Rewards − Xen. II.4.25; *Ath. Pol.* 40.2; Aeschin. III.187; GHI II, 100 (cf. Hereward, 1952, though I cannot agree with her chronology); have-nots − Xen. II.4.40-2.

62. Socrates, Critias − Xen., *Mem.* I.1.1, 2.12ff.; Aeschin. I.173; Antiphon − Morrison, 1961; Andron − Plato, *Gorg.* 487c; Plut., *Mor.* 833e; Harpokration, s.v. Andron. Aristoteles, the member of both the Four Hundred and the Thirty (Xen., *Hell.* II.2.18, 3.2, 13, 46) appears in a philosophical discussion in Plato, *Parm.* 127d.

63. Hesiod, WD 212ff. (contrast *Theog.* 510ff.); OP XXVI.2450; Plato, *Gorg.* 484b = Pindar, fr. 152 Bowra; Guthrie, 1971, 131ff.

64. Thuc. I.76, V.89, 97, 105.2, cf. II.41-2 on war; Plato, *Rep.* I.338c-e, 340d-41b, 343b-44c; *Gorg.* 483aff.; ps. Xen., *Ath. Pol.* 1.2-9. The historical Thrasymachos' views are not plain from the main surviving fragment, DK B1 (on the ancestral constitution).

65. Plato, *Gorg.* 487c; Critias, DK B25, cf. B6-9; Antiphon, DK B44 A-B = OP XI.1364, XV.1797; Guthrie, 1971, 107ff.; Morrison, 1961.

66. Dem. 21.79, 47.38, 62, 54.3ff., 14ff., 20ff.; Lys. 3.6ff. (contrast Demosthenes' own caution about violence, 21.81). See Harrison, 1968, I, 217-20, 311-14, and on Scythians, Oehler, RE 2.III.692-3 (they are conspicuously unmentioned in speeches about private violence).

67. Comparisons between actions − Isoc. 20.2-3; Dem. 21.32, 35, 54.1, 17-19; non-physical *hubris* − Dem. 45.4; avoidance of grievous harm − 54.18; Isoc. 20.7-9; *aikeia* − Dem. 47.40, 47. Contrast Lintott, 1968, 125f.

68. Dem. 21.45; ps. Xen., *Ath. Pol.* 1.10; Aeschin. I.15-17; Isoc. 20.5-6; Ar., *Rhet.* 1378b (cf. Dem. 21.23); Harrison, 1968, I, 168, 172, II, 75-6.

69. P. Hibeh, 14, 65ff.; Lys. 16.3, 26.10.

70. Lys. 7; 10; 12; 13; 18; 25; 26; 30; 31; 32; P. Ryl. III.103ff.; Athen. XII.551e; Isoc. 21; 18; 20.4, 10-11.

71. And. 1.71, cf. 2.13-15; Xen., *Mem.* I.2.12ff.; Aeschin. I.173; Isoc. 20.22; Ar., *Rhet.* 1402a; Arist., *Clouds* 98, 112ff., 882ff.

72. Wealthy attacked − Lys. 7; 21; 22; 25.30, 26.23, 30.27, 31.18. Confiscations − Lys. 18.16-20, 30.22. Cf. Hyp. 4.32-7 for the situation over 50 years later. New poor − Lys. 7.6, 32, 20.33, 30.22, 31.18; Isoc. 21.12ff.

73. Isoc. 8.128, 5.159-60, 7.31-5, 51-2. The last speech advocates respect for wealth, strict interpretation of the law on debt, repression of professional accusers and limitation of capital levies. Cf. Dem. 24.149.

74. *Hell. Oxy.* 6.1-7.2; Lys. 13.81-2; Arist., *Eccles.* 197-8; Dem. 3.30ff.; Mossé, 1962, 287ff.; 1973, 12ff., 21ff.; Seager, 1967. Thrasyboulos − Arist., *Eccles.* 356; Xen., *Hell.* IV.8.25ff.; GHI II, 114; Lys. 28.4ff.; Diod. XIV.94, 99.

75. Isoc. 8.51-2; Dem. 6.20-5; 8.40-1; Hyp. 2.1, 8, 10 (cf. Diod. XVI.92.1-2). On the treaties made by Athens which provide for reciprocal assistance against revolution see Chapter 8 with notes 15-16. *Pace* Mossé, 1973, 31, one cannot deduce that there was a threat of *stasis* in Athens from them: the relevant clauses may be explained by the unquestionable threats to the stability of Athens' new allies.

76. Meritt, 1952, 355, no. 5 = Pouilloux, 1960, no. 32, esp. lines 7ff.; cf. And. 1.96-8; Lyc., *Leocr.* 125-7 (which ignores Eukrates' decree a few years later) and contrast Hyp. 4.7-8 on impeachment. League of Corinth − GHI II.177, 12ff.; ps. Dem. 17.10. See Ostwald, 1955; Sealey, 1967, 183ff.

5 SYRACUSE – DEMOCRACY AND TYRANNY

The Struggles of Democracy

Syracuse in the fifth century was a city which could be justly matched
with Athens. She withstood the greatest overseas expedition that Athens
ever mounted, although her population was perhaps about half that of
Athens and she possessed no equivalent of the tribute of the Delian
league to finance her. After the expulsion of the family of Gelon (c. 465)
a democracy was established, which survived the Athenian attack and
was subsequently reformed so that it should be more in the interest of
the masses. It succumbed in 405 to a combination of internal divisions,
Carthaginian military pressure and the ruthless ambition of one man,
Dionysius I. His tyranny lasted 38 years, uncontested except in its
formative stages. The rule of his son was challenged by other powerful
men and their wars led to political chaos and a decline in manpower
and wealth. The city was repopulated and the constitution reformed by
Timoleon but, although the economy was to remain strong, the constitution survived only 20 years before a new tyrant, Agathocles, seized
power.

Democracy thus originally lasted some 60 years, roughly the equivalent of the period between Cleisthenes' reforms and the peak of Pericles'
ascendancy in Athens, and it seems wrong to regard it *a priori* as an
exotic plant which could not be expected to survive on Sicilian soil.
The reasons for its demise are therefore of great interest, especially as
Syracuse provides a contrast with Athens, whose democracy overcame
two oligarchic interludes at about the same time. Dionysius too deserves
the special attention accorded him by historians of antiquity. He was
for them a paradigm of the evil and misery that was held to be insepar-
able from tyranny by Plato and later philosophers, and this was elabor-
ated in the anecdotes that grew up about him and his son. He was also
held to be a prime example of a tyrant who rose to power through
demagogy (the type selected as the essential form of tyranny in Plato's
Republic). In fact he was more remarkable than this. Among Aristotle's
list of demagogue tyrants – Theagenes of Megara, Peisistratus, Cypselus,
Panaetius of Leontini and Dionysius, only Dionysius overthrew a truly
democratic constitution by rabble-rousing and attacks on the rich.
Agathocles was later to imitate Dionysius' methods (too late to be
included in Aristotle's account), but we do not know the exact nature

185

of the constitution that he overthrew, and it is hard to find another example. Thus, in the field of action Dionysius' achievement was almost unparalleled, and in the realm of ideas he was the foundation of Plato's portrait of tyranny.[1]

Unfortunately we have no equivalent in our information on Sicily to Thucydides' account of the events of 411. Our main authority for political strife in Syracuse is Diodorus the Sicilian, a historian of the first century BC, the value of whose history varies from period to period according to the sources he was following. His account of Syracusan politics in the fifth century and the early part of Dionysius' reign goes back, probably via the third century historian Timaeus, to Philistus, who was an associate of Dionysius himself. Thus, we may be fairly confident over basic facts, though the motivation of Dionysius himself and the attitude of others to him may have been distorted through the partisanship of Philistus or, conversely, through Timaeus' prejudice against tyranny.[2]

We must first, however, consider Syracusan democracy and the revolution which created it. Gelon had been succeeded by his brother Hieron, but before the latter's death the external bulwarks of their tyranny had been weakened. Their ally Theron, tyrant of Agrigentum, died about 472 BC and his son Thrasydaios took over the city in addition to Himera, which he had been assigned during his father's lifetime. A quarrel with Syracuse followed and a pre-emptive strike by Hieron led to a fierce but indecisive battle. However, Thrasydaios' power was sufficiently damaged to allow the Agrigentines to expel him, and Himera too became free. According to a story in Timaeus about the philosopher Empedokles, an oligarchic faction of 1,000 men were in power at Agrigentum for three years but subsequently the body politic was broadened at Empedokles' instigation. Empedokles was also depicted as vigilant against a restoration of tyranny.[3]

Hieron died shortly after 468, and his successor Thrasyboulos was alleged to have been more brutal than his predecessors. In view of the drastic measures taken by Gelon and Hieron in their time (p. 64) this conventional portrait should be viewed with some suspicion. However, it is clear that Thrasyboulos did make enemies of certain powerful men, many ordinary citizens and probably some of his own mercenary soldiers, with the result that after ten months there was a revolt against him. Aristotle says that Thrasyboulos was acting as a guardian for Gelon's son (his own nephew) and indulging him in order to keep power for himself. His own family then banded together against him, in the hope that they could preserve the tyranny at the expense of Thrasyboulos himself, but their associates developed the revolt into a true revolution.

Thrasyboulos tried to resist by collecting his most devoted supporters, including the men settled by Hieron at Catane (Aitna) and a number of mercenaries, to the number of 15,000. With these he held on to the Island (Ortygia) and Achradina, the part of the city adjoining it on the mainland – a strategy employed frequently by later tyrants – but after being besieged and defeated by land and sea, he withdrew by agreement to Locri. The Syracusans were helped by contingents from Agrigentum, Selinous and Gela. If the latter had not escaped from tyranny before, it also became free with the overthrow of Thrasyboulos and so did the other cities which had been under Syracuse's control.[4]

The revolution gave an outlet to all the tensions and problems that had accumulated through the tyrants' repression and political engineering. There were peoples displaced from their native lands who wished to return to them, new citizens in Aitna and Syracuse worried about retaining tenure of their land, mercenaries who had no longer a focus of loyalty, and still the antagonism remained between rich and poor, which had provided Gelon with his opportunity some 20 years earlier. The strength of the revolt seems to have come from the countryside, which was no doubt dominated by the landowners installed by Gelon. Underneath them there may have been still some middling proprietors and free peasants, but much of the rural population would have been closely tied to the landowners, even though we hear no more of the class of serfs who had helped to precipitate the crisis in 485 (p. 64).

The first action of the assembly in newly liberated Syracuse was to set up a statue to Zeus the Liberator and create an appropriate cult (we know that this divinity was also introduced at Himera about 470). Office in the new constitution was to be confined to 'old citizens'. Thus, immigrants during the tyranny and those from serf families were placed in an inferior category; so in particular were the mercenaries of the tyrants. According to Aristotle, an exception was made for those mercenaries who had fought with the liberators and similarly for foreigners who had joined in the revolution (some of these may have been men of Syracusan family driven out by the tyrants). Nevertheless, Gelon had made more than 10,000 mercenaries Syracusan citizens and over 7,000 of these were still in the city, obviously discontented with their lot. If accounts of their numbers are true, it is hard to see how a motion expelling them from citizenship was passed by an assembly of the adult males in Syracuse, and this suggests that originally a broad oligarchy based on the revolutionary forces seized power. In any case the mercenaries followed Thrasyboulos' example and seized the Island and Achradina, where they too were besieged.

After some time (two years in Diodorus' account) the mercenaries were defeated in a battle in which a group of patriots called 'The Elect' (*Eklektoi*) fought especially valiantly and were awarded a silver mina each. Subsequently, the Syracusans attacked the settlers placed by Hieron in Catane, joining forces with Douketios, a leader of the native Sikels, who had risen to power with the collapse of the domination of the Syracusan tyrants abroad. About the same time many men exiled under the tyrannies were restored to Gela, Agrigentum and Himera, while those who owed their citizenship to the tyrants were expelled. Finally, after a congress the Greek cities of Sicily made a general agreement to allow exiles to return home and to place the cities in the power of the original citizens. This was apparently followed by a reallotment of land to the newly constituted citizen bodies.[5]

The new registration of citizens and the allocation of land led to further strife, especially in Syracuse. According to Diodorus this was because many people were casually assigned citizenship without justification. A man called Tyndarides recruited many of the poor as a bodyguard and was condemned to death on this account on the ground that he was aiming at a tyranny (the story resembles those of the suspected tyrants, Sp. Maelius and M. Manlius Capitolinus at Rome). Tyndarides' supporters tried to rescue him as he was being led to the prison, but the *chariestatoi* (the 'gentlefolk') rallied against them and killed both Tyndarides and his group.

This was apparently the first of a series of similar threats to the constitution which led the Syracusans to introduce their equivalent of Athenian ostracism, 'petalism', in which the citizens were required to write the name of the most powerful man, most capable of seizing a tyranny, on olive leaves (the man who received most votes went into exile for only five years). The institution did not last long, we are told, because the *chariestatoi* were deterred from politics and instead pursued private wealth, while in their place there sprang up many demagogic agitators. However, it would have been illogical to place a vote on potential tyrants in the hands of the poor, who were the chief supporters of tyranny. Either we must assume a severely restricted franchise, or petalism was designed to further the factional interests of those who believed they had popular support rather than to suppress tyranny on principle. Nor is it easy to see how it came to be abolished unless the *chariestatoi* retained their primacy in the state. Nevertheless, the essential features of Diodorus' account are in part confirmed by Aristotle. The latter mentions first the strife that followed the new enrolment of citizens, including foreigners and ex-mercenaries, and secondly that the Syracusans overthrew several tyrannies 'at the time when they had good government' – he was presumably referring to the period when they had a *politeia* (moderately democratic constitution) rather than the full democracy that followed the Athenian expedition.[6]

The causes of instability were no doubt basically economic. Men like Tyndarides could maintain great wealth, which could be used to acquire social and political dependants from among the poor like Roman *clientes*. The connection with petalism (which, even if it rests on an original inference by an historian like Philistus, is highly plausible) indicates how seriously the threat was taken: the aristocracy would not have forged a weapon against themselves, except to avoid a greater evil. Yet there was on our evidence no external menace (from Carthage, for example) comparable to the Persian threat to Athens.

Further precision about the poor who supported Tyndarides and men like him is desirable but difficult to achieve. These men were citizens and therefore free men; nor had they been diehard partisans of the tyrants. Aristotle seems to regard the admission of men from other cities and ex-mercenaries as a cause of the trouble, but such men would not have been necessarily short of money and a living. We can, however, assume with confidence confusion over land-assignment since, through the changes in population under the tyranny and the allocations to new arrivals and returned exiles, many people would have had rival claims to the same pieces of land, and these would have to be surrendered in full by one party or subdivided. According to Cicero, the fall of the Sicilian tyrants led to the beginnings of forensic oratory because of the revival of private lawsuits, and it is easy to see how these arose.[7]

The nature of the constitution which was established for the new citizen body is not discussed explicitly by Diodorus at this point. Our main evidence comes from Thucydides' account of Syracuse in the Peloponnesian War and the inferences that can be drawn from the later reform of the constitution achieved by Diokles in 412. For Aristotle this change was from *politeia* to democracy. In Diodorus the major elements were the drafting of a new law code and the introduction of selection by lot for office. This implies that the previous constitution had oligarchic as well as democratic features, was based on the principle of elected magistrates and continued to use a pre-existing law code, perhaps drawn up before Gelon's time.

We know from Thucydides that the army was originally commanded in 415 by 15 elected generals, who in that year were reduced to three and given greater discretion. Prior to this, the board had been required to consult the assembly over most matters, as the generals did at Athens. Policy was decided in the assembly which was open to 'the many', the citizens as a whole. On one occasion we know that it was presided over by one or more generals, and perhaps, as at Rome, it was under the supervision of whichever magistrate convened it. Property qualifications were necessary for the holding of financial magistracies, as at Athens, but there is no evidence for any other restriction on holding office except *de facto*, in so far as it was the better off and the better educated who were likely to get elected. Furthermore, it is highly unlikely that there was pay for attendance at the assembly or a jury court. Thus before 412 Syracuse's constitution resembled that established by Cleisthenes at Athens; after 412 it came closer to that developed by Ephialtes and Pericles. The poor had their part in government even before 412, if they wished to use it to remedy their grievances. The course of Syracusan history suggests, however, that socially and economically they had difficulty in emancipating themselves.[8]

The Syracusans about 453 made naval expeditions against Etruria which seem to have been attempts to provide capital in the form of money or slaves not only for the aristocratic leaders but for the population at large. This seems clear from the condemnation of the first commander for bribery and the substitution of one who prudently returned with a mass of prisoners and other forms of profit. They also tried to restrict the expansion of the Sikel leader, Douketios, who had forced most of the Sikel communities into a confederation with a capital at Palike (Menai) about 40 miles from Syracuse. In his policies Sicilian nationalism was combined with the propagation of urban settlement on the Hellenic model. He was trying to establish himself in Agrigentine territory when his garrison was overcome and he decided to place himself and his empire in Syracusan hands. The Syracusan assembly sent Douketios to Corinth with finance for his retirement (c. 450). However, his return (to found a new city at Kale Akte on the north coast of the island) precipitated a war between Syracuse and Agrigentum in which many people of Sicily joined; Agrigentum was defeated, and a further campaign against the Sikel city of Trinakria (c. 440) left Syracuse with the hegemony of most of non-Punic Sicily.[9]

The great Athenian expedition of 415 was to precipitate further political changes in Syracuse and was an important background cause for the revolution which destroyed the democracy. What can we deduce about the nature of Syracusan society before that expedition and how was it affected by it? As at Athens at the time of Cimon's supremacy, foreign wars and the acquisition of tribute-paying subjects contributed to Syracuse's public prosperity and may have alleviated the economic difficulties of some of the poorer citizens at home, although Syracusan operations were not on such a large scale as those of Athens. Apart from the formidable aristocratic cavalry, Syracuse was able to call on a considerable force of citizen hoplites (certainly not inferior in numbers to the 5,100 fielded by the Athenians at the battle by the Anapus) and were able to man over 60 ships from their free poor. The contribution made by all sections of the free population to Syracusan power was reflected in their conduct in politics. The *demos* was active: Phayllos was banished for receiving bribes from the Etruscans; the decision to send Douketios to Corinth was ultimately a popular decision although the initiative came from the *chariestatoi*. Throughout the Athenian attack on Sicily the Syracusan assembly was consulted (a contrast with Pericles' methods at the beginning of the Peloponnesian War): even after the appointment of three generals with full powers, the assembly not only met to depose one board and replace it with another, but were also consulted when a change of strategy was mooted, that the Syracusans should take the offensive by sea.[10]

On the other hand the Syracusan strength in cavalry (1,000 fought against the Athenians when they first landed) reflects the continued importance of wealthy landowners, who probably tended to monopolise high office. We have already noticed the controlling hand of the *chariestatoi* in the early years of the democracy. Thucydides does not specifically mention the Syracusan aristocracy as a political force, yet hints of their influence emerge. For example, in 422 the *dunatoi* in Leontini called in Syracusan aid when threatened with a redivision of the land by their *demos*, and the Syracusans responded. The Leontine aristocracy were allowed to move their homes to Syracuse, while the *demos* were broken up as a community by being driven out of their city and were reduced to waging guerilla warfare from two strongholds in the countryside.[11] There was no question here of co-operating with an aristocracy in a subject city as a matter of administrative convenience — a frequent characteristic of Athenian policy — since Leontini was in effect being incorporated into Syracuse. The positive support for the *dunatoi* of Leontini contrasts with the negative attitude to the city as a whole and suggests that personal ties and guest-friendships between the two aristocracies were decisive here. This, therefore, is an occasion on which the Syracusan *dunatoi* were able to control policy.

Thucydides' account of a debate which took place on the arrival of the news of the Athenian expedition is also important evidence, though

difficult to interpret. Athenagoras is shown answering Hermokrates, a
man of good family and of political influence in Syracuse for at least
ten years, who has just advocated an immediate naval expedition to
confront the Athenians before they reach Sicily. He accuses unspecified
people, obviously including Hermokrates, of rumour-mongering in order
to exploit the ensuing panic as a pretext for seizing authoritarian power
in the city. He professes himself a defender of the city against faction,
tyranny and oligarchic *dunasteiai* and goes on to compare oligarchy
unfavourably with democracy. In particular he casts aspersions on the
younger men, alleging that they want high office before the legitimate
age and other improper privileges. In the event Hermokrates' proposal
is not accepted, but preliminary military preparations are undertaken.

Athenagoras' speech is a clever demagogic brew, using in equal parts
apparently sober reasoning and totally unsupported innuendo. It recalls
Nikias' attack on Alcibiades and the younger men of Athens for their
devotion to enterprises perilous for their city in the pursuit of their
own self-interest. Thucydides states as a fact that the majority of Syracusans did not believe the initial reports of the Athenian invasion; it is
also clear from later history that Hermokrates had many enemies. Thus,
there is no difficulty in accepting that Athenagoras combined an attack
on Hermokrates' policy with aspersions on his motives. The speech also
implies that suspicions of young aristocrats already existed, and this
again seems highly plausible, given the inequalities of wealth and the
past history of Syracuse.[12]

What then should we make of the parallel that Thucydides himself
insinuates between Hermokrates and Alcibiades, Athenagoras and
Nikias, by his highlighting of similar arguments in the debates at Syracuse and Athens? In my view we should trust Thucydides and follow
the hints that he has left us. Hermokrates should then be regarded as
a brilliant but maverick aristocrat who had both the ability and the
ambition to become a demagogue himself but was for this reason envied
and suspected by his rivals. Their task was made easier by the somewhat
uncomfortable relationship between the *demos* and the *dunatoi* as a
whole. As for Hermokrates' enemies, Athenagoras and his like, there is
no reason to think that they were poor. Athenagoras is careful in his
speech not to stir up hostility against the rich as such: they have their
respected place in the democracy. It is tempting to see in him the sort
of man with whom Nikias was in communication during the siege (the
negotiations began at the time of Hermokrates' deposition from office)
and through whom he was well aware of Syracuse's financial exhaustion.
These were men of some eminence, to judge from the story that after

the Athenian defeat they encouraged the execution of Nikias in order that he might not reveal under questioning their dealings with him. It would not have been surprising if some wealthy men, like certain oligarchs at Athens, wanted an end to the war, if their fortunes could thereby be preserved.[13]

Syracuse's victory over Athens was a splendid vindication for those aristocrats like Hermokrates who wished to maintain Syracuse's domination in Greek Sicily at all costs. Hermokrates' own influence with the assembly at this time is shown by their acceptance of his proposal that they should aid the Peloponnesians against Athens in the East and his appointment in 412 to this command. The other demagogue who clearly profited from the victory was Diokles, a later opponent of Hermokrates. Diodorus represents him in an otherwise not very plausible debate on the fate of the Athenian prisoners as demanding the death penalty for the generals. He is also credited with introducing the reform of the law code and the constitution, which entailed the selection of civil officials by lot and was regarded by Aristotle as a change from a mixed constitution to democracy. Aristotle attributed this to the increase in power and reputation of the common people resulting from the victory, and his judgement here seems sound, whatever the value of the other examples he gives.[14]

It was in the end a 'people's war', in which the poorer citizens, both the crews of the Syracusan fleet and those who were specially equipped with hoplite armour to serve by land, made a great contribution. The war would have made them more conscious of their political importance: indeed it may have brought those who had worked in the countryside into the city in greater numbers than before. Meanwhile those among the Syracusan *dunatoi* who had been lukewarm about the war would have been discredited, while the demagogues whose reputation was untarnished had a fine opportunity to secure their position.

It is difficult to point to any social and economic factors associated with the change in constitution. The countryside had not been seriously devastated, though it may have suffered temporary neglect when a soldier's family had failed to maintain adequately a peasant holding during the siege. There was a plethora of cheap slaves arising from the prisoners-of-war who were sold or had earlier been privately made captive, and a fair amount of booty besides. In the short term there may have been a post-war boom in manufacture and trade, but little change in agriculture. Over a longer period the amount of slaves available may have cut down the work available for free tenants and hired labour. Whereas the political position of the poor became stronger, this does not seem to have been matched by their social and economic conditions.[15]

Hermokrates and Dionysius

Hermokrates, in command of a fleet of 21 Syracusan ships and two from Selinous, shared the mixed fortunes of the Peloponnesians in the Aegean. He was a hard-working and inspiring leader, on good terms with his officers and conspicuous for his attempts to get good pay for his men. However, he and his colleagues were not merely dismissed by the Syracusans but condemned to exile in their absence, apparently victims of a plot by an opposing faction. The fleet, however, was not recalled. Hermokrates' opponents would have been happy to keep the fleet away, because of its goodwill towards him. We are told of his close relations with his trierarchs, steersmen and marines: indeed the majority of the trierarchs swore that they would get his banishment repealed when they returned.[16]

Meanwhile, Carthaginian forces once again were sent to Sicily after an appeal from Segesta, which again had a border dispute with Selinous. The Punic general Hannibal was eager to restore his nation's power in western Sicily and the military reputation of his own family. In 409 he captured Selinous and then, perhaps the following year, Himera. Syracuse had a war with the Chalkidic cities to bring to a settlement and was too late to help Selinous. She sent a relief force under Diokles and a fleet to Himera, but in spite of some Greek successes Diokles was diverted from his mission by his fear of a Punic attack on Syracuse and he advised the evacuation of Himera.

In 408-407 Hermokrates returned to Sicily and used his money to acquire five triremes and about 2,000 men. He still had friends inside Syracuse and tried to obtain his recall. We are told that Diokles led the opposition to this. In consequence Hermokrates based himself on the ruins of Selinous and took up the struggle against Carthage on his own account, partly no doubt to get booty in order to maintain his army, partly to improve his standing in the eyes of the Syracusans. In 407 he made a dramatic gesture by sending back to Syracuse the bones of those who had died defending Himera. This was intended to bring Diokles into odium for abandoning Himera too easily and failing to recover the dead. So far it succeeded: the bones were buried and Diokles driven into exile. However, the Syracusans still did not recall Hermokrates for fear that he might become a tyrant. He then confirmed these suspicions by assembling a force of 3,000 men for a *coup d'état*. Some of his troops arrived late, which allowed his opponents to mass in the *agora*. There he and most of his followers were killed; the majority of the survivors were condemned to banishment, but some of the wounded were announced to be dead by their kinsmen and were thus retained in the city. Among these was Dionysius, a man said to have been of undistinguished family and trained as a scribe.[17]

If Hermokrates had returned to Syracuse peacefully, his quarrel with his old opponents might well have induced him to seek special powers and protection in order to survive, and this would have been the beginning of *stasis*, if not tyranny. His original exile was certainly unjust; those who subsequently opposed his recall had probably disreputable reasons of their own for keeping him out. Nevertheless, the fear of tyranny had an objective validity and Diodorus is probably right in believing that this was decisive with the assembly. On the other hand his memory lived on after his death and there were a number of ex-soldiers and sailors in the population who would have retained their loyalty and been ready to support a man who appeared to be his successor. For such a man the moral was obvious: the fortunes of a demagogue, however well intentioned, were insecure; authoritarian power was preferable, if it could be secured by consent.

A further expedition descended on Sicily in 406 under Hannibal's relative, Hamilcar. In spite of an early Syracusan naval victory the Carthaginians successfully transported their army and laid siege to Agrigentum. Daphnaios led an army of Syracusans and their allies to relieve the siege and won a victory by the river Himera. However, the Agrigentines in the city were prevented by their commanders from attacking the retreating Carthaginians and, when the relief force eventually reached the city, they held an assembly which stoned to death four of their generals on account of this failure. For a time the Agrigentines and their allies held the upper hand, besieging the Punic camp and cutting off its food supplies. But after Hamilcar in desperation had used his fleet to seize a Syracusan grain convoy, fortunes were reversed: starvation threatened the overcrowded city instead, and it was decided to evacuate it shortly before the winter solstice of 406-405.

Many of those who fled from Agrigentum arrived via Gela at Syracuse (they were soon to be assigned land at Leontini), and they bitterly attacked the Syracusan generals for betraying their city. At the same time other Sicilians took refuge in Syracuse and complained that the policy of the current leaders there would bring about the downfall of Greek Sicily as a whole. When an assembly was held at Syracuse, none of the current magistrates dared to speak, and the way was open for Dionysius to urge the people to lynch the generals for treachery without the delay of due legal process. The presiding magistrates imposed a fine on him for provoking a riot, but Philistus, the historian to whose account most later histories must have been largely indebted, paid the fine and exhorted Dionysius to go on the whole day with his speech if he wished, promising that he would pay any further fines. Dionysius resumed his harangue, claiming that the generals had been bribed to betray Agrigentum and widening the charges to include the other wealthy leading citizens, who he declared were friends of oligarchy; he recommended that in future they should choose as generals not the most powerful men (*dunatōtatoi*) but those who were best disposed to the *demos*.[18]

As a result of this speech the assembly deposed the board of generals and elected a new one, including Dionysius himself. The other newly elected generals were apparently members of the governing class. Dionysius set about discrediting his colleagues by refusing to co-operate with them on the ground that they were in communication with the Carthaginians. He procured a political following for himself by securing from the assembly the recall of exiles, many of whom would have been old associates of his and friends of Hermokrates.

When Gela appealed for help against Carthage, it was Dionysius who was sent there at the head of a small force (probably in the early months of 405). There he again supported the *demos* against the wealthy, condemning many of them to death and seizing their property in order to pay the mercenaries there and double the salary of his own troops. The people of Gela awarded him honours for their liberation and sent copies of these decrees back to Syracuse. Shortly before the Carthaginians were expected to attack Gela he returned to Syracuse. Here he alleged that the Punic commander Himilco, when sending him a herald about prisoners of war, had requested him not to interfere in Carthaginian plans with regard to Syracuse, since the majority of his colleagues had already been persuaded not to be obstructive. As a result of these charges of treachery the assembly elected him general without colleagues and with full discretion in policy (*strategos autokrator*) – Gelon was cited as a precedent – and he responded by proposing double pay for all soldiers. Afterwards some Syracusans regretted the assembly's decision as the first step towards a tyranny, and Dionysius decided that he had reached a point of no return. He ordered the army to assemble at Leontini, where already many of the fugitives from the captured Sicilian towns had gathered. After arriving the evening before the rest of the army, he raised an outcry during the night, pretending that an attempt had been made on his life. The next day he persuaded an unofficial military assembly (he had assumed that those who did not support him would not obey the summons to go to Leontini) to vote him 600 guards to be chosen by himself. Thus, he imitated in a more elaborate way

Peisistratus' device at Athens in 561.[19]

The bodyguard in fact grew to over 1,000 men, chosen from the poorest and toughest of the citizens and armed at great expense by Dionysius himself. Further support came from mercenaries, the exiles in Syracusan territory and the Syracusans who had returned from banishment. He set up house in the dockyard area on the Island for additional security, a site easy to defend and surrounded by the naval proletariat, many of whom had been devoted to Hermokrates. A further link with the past and evidence of the backing of some noble families was his own marriage to Hermokrates' daughter and the marriage of his sister Theste to Polyxenos, Hermokrates' brother-in-law. We only hear of two major opponents eliminated at this time: Daphnaios was the unsuccessful commander at Agrigentum in 406, probably an opponent of Hermokrates, while Demarchos may have been the son of Epikydes, one of the three generals sent out in 410 to the Aegean to replace Hermokrates and his colleagues.[20]

In the early summer Dionysius returned to Gela, which was already under siege, its countryside and that of neighbouring Camarina ravaged by the invaders. An elaborate three-pronged attack on the Carthaginian camp failed and within a few days Dionysius, after a council of war with his friends, evacuated both Gela and Camarina (it seems that the Geloans were in principle prepared to leave, when the Greek attack failed). However, the calamities of Gela and Camarina aroused great indignation in the Syracusan army. They were, it is true, only repetitions of what had happened at Selinous, Himera and Agrigentum, but Gela was even closer to Syracuse and Dionysius had seized power with the claim that the previous disasters had only happened through treachery. Furthermore in the last battle Dionysius and his mercenaries (whose appointed task had been to make an attack on the Punic camp through the centre of the city) had failed to make contact with the enemy at all. Dionysius' opponents thought that this was the moment to unseat him. The regular Syracusan cavalry tried to ambush the tyrant on his journey back to Syracuse, but desisted because of the force of mercenaries with him. Instead they returned to Syracuse, entered the dockyard, looted the house of Dionysius and beat his wife.

When Dionysius learnt this, he picked out the most reliable men in his bodyguard, 600 infantry and 100 cavalry, and after a 50-mile dash arrived at the Achradina gate about midnight. He had the gate burnt down; his mercenaries surrounded and shot down a few of the leading cavalrymen they met near the *agora*; then he went round the city, picking off the small groups who sallied out against him, and visited the

homes of all his political opponents, whom he either killed or drove
into exile. The majority of the cavalry in fact escaped to the city of
Aitna.[21]

The Carthaginians tried to besiege Syracuse, but an epidemic forced
them to abandon this and make peace with Syracuse in 405. In this
they confirmed their territorial gains during the war; their only concession was that Dionysius was recognised as overlord of Syracuse. He
for his part built himself a stronghold on the Island, cutting it off on
the mainland side of the causeway link by a massive wall and con-
structing a citadel as his final refuge: the shipyards by the smaller
northern harbour were within the area enclosed. He also undertook a
redivision of land and houses: the best went to his friends and to various
officials; the rest were given not only to citizens but to foreigners and
liberated slaves (the so-called 'new citizens'). Only 'friends' and his
mercenaries were allowed to live on the Island.

Inevitably, this redistribution increased resentment among the old
citizens who were equated with the new and may have lost valuable
property thereby. Men also regretted the chances missed earlier. So,
when once again Dionysius led out the Syracusans under arms to attack
the Sikel town of Herbita (404-403), groups of soldiers began to discuss
their failure to overthrow the tyrant. An officer of Dionysius tried to
check a soldier talking in this way, first with a reprimand and then by
raising his fist, and this provoked an outright mutiny. The officer was
killed; the cry of liberty was raised and a message was sent to the exiled
cavalry in Aitna asking for support. Dionysius got back to Syracuse but
was besieged there and a fleet came from Messana and Rhegium to
attack the Island itself.[22]

Dionysius lulled the suspicions of the besiegers by asking for permission to leave the Island with his friends, and wrote to Campanian mercenaries offering them any money they wanted if they came to his aid.
Meanwhile the Syracusans let the cavalry go back to Aitna, while the
majority of the infantry returned to their homes in the countryside in
the expectation that all was over. The Campanians, however, made a
forced march with minimum equipment and broke through the besiegers to join Dionysius; 300 more mercenaries came in by sea. This
change of fortunes caused a division of opinion among the besiegers:
some wished to abandon the city altogether, others to see the siege
through. At this point Dionysius took the offensive and defeated them
in the New City on the edge of the Epipolai plateau. Over 7,000 fled to
Aitna. Dionysius then offered the exiles an amnesty if they would return. A few accepted through fear for the families they had left behind,

but the majority remained, only to be defeated and expelled by a sub-sequent expedition.[23]

In the same period Dionysius suppressed another rising led by a Corinthian Nikoteles, using the Spartan ambassador Aristos as a kind of *agent provocateur* (Aristos pretended that his mission was to restore liberty to Syracuse, when in reality it was to secure the tyrant as a Spartan client). Finally Dionysius abandoned any pretence of being an emergency leader of the citizen body by stripping them of their arms and leaving them no resource against his mercenaries. Nikoteles' was the last act of open revolt against his tyranny. The only subsequent threat of this kind occurred in 396 during the great war against Carthage, when Syracuse itself was under siege. Then members of Dionysius' navy and army became discontented with his leadership in his absence and suggested that he was dispensable, but the talk came to nothing.[24]

The Causes of Dionysius' Success

The immediate causes of the re-establishment of tyranny in Syracuse are easy to find. Dionysius' own ruthless and scheming ambition was one. The demoralisation at Syracuse arising from Punic victories was another obvious factor. There is no reason to suppose that those who had lived under the Syracusan democracy, whether rich or poor, desired a tyranny for its own sake. The appeal of the name of Gelon lay in its associations with Carthaginian humiliation. Before the crisis of 406 a majority of the Syracusans had been reluctant to recall Hermokrates for fear that a tyranny might arise. Nevertheless, as at Athens, democracy commanded respect from politicians and public so long as it delivered the goods: military failure brought the constitution into question. Furthermore, even if they did not officially have votes, the presence of an increasing number of foreign refugees in Syracusan territory created additional pressure from below on the magistrates and eventually swelled the faction of Dionysius. However, these are not in themselves sufficient explanations.

I have argued earlier that some of the wealthy *dunatoi* lost their influence in Syracuse during the Athenian attack and this made Diokles' reforms possible. Dionysius' allegations in 405 that the rich had olig-archic ambitions suggest that they were recovering the lost ground. The death of Hermokrates and the exile of Diokles would have been welcome to the politicians eclipsed at the end of the war. Should we believe, then, that there was an oligarchic conspiracy among the rich, and that

Syracuse before Dionysius' appointment was like Athens in early 411?
To begin with, Dionysius' charges in the assembly need have been no
better founded than the insinuations allegedly made by Athenagoras in
415. There was no attempt to impose oligarchic government in Syracuse
in 414, when the Athenian siege was at its tightest; there is no evidence
that it was contemplated in 405. Indeed, it is significant that Dionysius,
as an aspirant to tyranny, chose to exploit the support of the poor in
the assembly rather than become a protagonist of the rich as Gelon had
done. His own sympathies may have lain more on the side of the poor,
but events showed that he was primarily concerned with political tactics. Granted that there was no oligarchic conspiracy as at Athens in
411, had the rich formed a single dominant faction? We can only argue
from silence here, but the lack of concerted resistance by the rich to
Dionysius is striking. Even the attempted counter-*coup* by the cavalry
seems to have been an ill-co-ordinated and hastily planned enterprise.
Initially Dionysius found it only necessary to kill Daphnaios and Demarchos – presumably the men he feared as potential leaders of a reaction.
This would have been quite inadequate if the majority of the wealthy
were banded together against him. We must conclude then that the
rich operated politically either as individuals or in comparatively small
groups.

The major political development in the years after the Athenian
expedition was probably the disintegration of the political followings
of Hermokrates and Diokles, their own mutual rivalries having been
exacerbated by other politicians who wished to see them both eliminated. The outcome was not only a general splintering of political power,
but a vacant place in popular esteem, which Dionysius was to occupy.

Apart from this, the social and economic cleavage between rich and
poor may have been more important than political differences as such
– over the form of democracy and the choice between an aggressive or
defensive foreign policy. We have little idea of the relative prosperity of
the various social classes in Syracuse at the time. However, striking inequalities in other Greek cities are shown, first by the glowing account
of Agrigentum's prosperity before the Punic attack in 406 (deriving
from Timaeus) and secondly by the struggle between rich and poor at
Gela, in which Dionysius intervened. In Syracuse there was a large free
proletariat (the strength of the Syracusan fleet, which was manned by
free citizens, is testimony to this). Another significant group was the
middling and small-scale farmers who served as infantrymen in the
army. Once Dionysius had seized power these social groups were unwilling or at least reluctant to unite with the rich against him.

Dionysius trusted the navy sufficiently to make his home in the dockyards. The sailors did not support the cavalry revolt of 405: indeed their failure to prevent the raid on Dionysius' house was thought surprising (perhaps the fleet had not yet returned from Gela). Nor did they participate in the military rising of 404-403. The insurgents then required naval aid from Messana and Rhegium, while Dionysius himself still had ships available in the dockyards he controlled. As for the citizen infantry, they played no part in the revolt of 405. We have a picture of the leading cavalrymen cut down alone in the *agora*, near which they, like the oligarchs of Corcyra, may have had their homes. In the later mutiny the infantry took the leading role, calling in the exiled cavalry to help and releasing them before the issue was finally decided. There was greater co-operation here, but the premature departure of the cavalry may have arisen from their own impatience and reluctance to see the revolt through. The old division subsisted. Thus, even if we do not take seriously the charges of oligarchy voiced by Dionysius in 406, there is no reason to doubt the existence of a massive resentment of the rich by the poor which Dionysius could turn to his own advantage.[25]

Yet we must not underestimate Dionysius' contribution to his own success, and the logic behind his political strategy deserves further examination, especially in view of the contrast it provides with that of Gelon, who had exploited the conflict between rich and poor in the interest of the rich. Granted that Dionysius did not come from one of the leading political families, he was acceptable to wealthy men like Philistus, Hipparinos and the family of his old commander Hermokrates.[26] His demand for the trial of Daphnaios and his colleagues after their failure at Agrigentum had precendents in the early years of Syracusan democracy – the banishment of Phayllus for bribery after the Etruscan expedition and the execution of Bolkon after his defeat by Douketios – and more recently in the deposition of fifteen generals in the winter of 415 in favour of Hermokrates, Herakleides and Sikanos.[27] However, it was exceptional in that it was combined with a wholesale attack on the governing class. Dionysius might have chosen to form a new oligarchic group with the object of building a tyranny thereon; instead, he made as many enemies among the rich as he could.

This approach implies a recent revival in the apparent influence of the rich which could be used as a bogy. On the other hand, it only made sense if the assembly was still fundamentally its own master. It could be persuaded to cast off demagogues like Hermokrates and Diokles, but this was not out of docility in the hands of the governing class as a whole but through divided loyalties and the desire of the common people to assert their own sovereignty. The attitude of the men who rowed the triremes may have been especially important here. As at Athens, they probably attended the assembly in greater numbers and more regularly than poor farmers. They had been chiefly responsible for the victory over Athens; indeed, Aristotle compares the *demos* at Syracuse in 413 with the naval proletariat (*nautikos ochlos*) at Athens. They were still self-confident enough to oppose any oligarchic *coup* (as the Athenian navy had in 411) and would have been suspicious of any collaboration by their new champion and watchdog, Dionysius, with the men whom he was supposed to be keeping in check. This was one reason why Dionysius could not have followed Gelon's policy, even if he had wanted to.

Another consideration was Dionysius' shortage of close political allies. He apparently had no sympathetic colleagues among the new board of generals elected in early 405. But he made an asset out of this by his allegations of corruption, and his advertisement of himself as the one true patriot kept his hold on the assembly. The suggestion that the Carthaginians had opened negotiations with his colleagues was not implausible, given the precedents during the Athenian siege, and may have had more ground than our sources admit. Whether Syracuse was already finding it difficult to pay its own soldiers, as he alleged, we do not know. He may have been right in claiming that the wealthy had been slow to make the necessary contributions. Furthermore, the other generals had done little towards preparing the Syracusans for the Carthaginian attack.[28]

Once Dionysius was chosen supreme commander, he realised that he had got as much from the assembly as he could hope for, nor could he satisfy all the expectations he had aroused. From then on legality was of minimal importance. He rebuilt his army round a core of loyal troops who were his bodyguard (theoretically voted him by the informal and irregular assembly at Leontini): he must have made good his promise of double pay for the existing citizen soldiers, the mercenaries and the new recruits. The regime he established was a total military dictatorship. This is not to say that there was no consent by the ruled. The tyrant would have been popular among those to whom he assigned land and urban property and among the craftsmen whose workshops supplied his arsenals; he retained the support of the naval proletariat, at least until 396. However, he founded his position on his popularity among his own troops, of whom many owed their position to him directly as newly enrolled citizens and others were mercenaries (including *perioikoi* and helots from Sparta). In the last resort he had a fortress, which the ordinary Syracusan could not enter.[29]

The constitution was not changed; it was overridden, whenever necessary. Although assemblies were held from time to time, there is no sign of the formal political machinery which had provided the chief means of bringing together the various social groups in the past. Dionysius succeeded in dividing and ruling. All this would have been impossible without money. His wealthy friends and the proceeds of the revolution at Gela gave him a start; the confiscation and redivision of the estates of the rich after the withdrawal of the cavalry to Aitna would have allowed him to build up the finances of himself and his friends for later military expenditure. Further, a wide range of financial exactions were attributed to him including capital levies (*eisphorai*), the seizure of temple treasures and the appropriation of the income of orphans until they were adult. For the rest, wars against Carthage and the operations in Italy and the Adriatic were undertaken *inter alia* with a view to the booty and tribute that they might provide. The reign was to be sustained by military adventures. In this respect, it was unlike those of the tyrants of the Archaic Age, unlike too the reigns of Gelon and Hieron, since they mainly used their power in self-defence once it was established. However, the systematic deployment of military power, manifest in the technology that Dionysius developed, the professional troops, the fortifications and the stronghold on the Island, placed his tyranny in a class by itself and made it exceedingly difficult to topple.[30]

Dynastic Struggles in Syracuse after Dionysius

Dionysius' tyranny, like that of most other Greek tyrants, was not a safe inheritance for his family. After his death in 367 his son was to rule somewhat uneasily over his empire for ten years, but afterwards rebellion and war, both civil and foreign, kept Syracuse's affairs in turmoil until 343. During this period many of the Syracusans were fighting for liberation from tyranny, but events were dominated by powerful individuals, almost all connected with the tyrant's family. Dionysius' rule, in spite of being nominally based on popular support, in effect narrowed the body politic to a small oligarchy of 'friends', whom he customarily consulted on policy.[31]

Before we consider the struggles of the new governing group brought to power by the tyranny, they should be set against their background, the social composition of Dionysius' Syracuse. This bore some resemblance to that of the preceding democracy in spite of Dionysius' population-surgery. From 398 onwards a considerable contingent of Syracusans, both cavalry and infantry, were rearmed, and these presumably had an appropriate amount of land to support them as a result of the redivision of property. Some of these would have been slaves liberated at the beginning of the tyranny, new citizens as they were called. The crews of the triremes were originally drawn from the free poor under the democracy, and we have seen how this group were supporters of Dionysius both during and after his *coup d'état*. At the time when he augmented his fleet before the war of reprisal on Carthage (c. 398), he added 200 triremes to the existing 110, manning half of these with citizen crews, including the officers, half with men hired from abroad. Some hulls must have formed a reserve — certainly he took no more than 200 ships to Motya and, when 100 ships had been lost, 60 replacements had to be manned with liberated slaves. Thus, some 20,000 free poor would have been employed in the navy. Though these sailors fought loyally for Syracuse, they were once involved in a near-mutiny against Dionysius' leadership in 396, when Syracuse came under siege. Later both the citizen-soldiers and the navy based at Syracuse were to make a great contribution to the overthrow of Dionysius II. However grateful the people may have been to Dionysius for the grants of citizenship and land about 400 BC, their political and social aspirations after Dionysius' death do not seem to have been very different from those they had before his rise to power.[32]

There was still an aristocracy but different in composition and importance. In 405, after the leading members of the cavalry had been killed during their revolt, the rest took refuge in Aitna; only a few of them returned in 404-403. So maybe about 1,000 representatives of the wealthiest Syracusan families departed. They were replaced: Dionysius took over 3,000 cavalry to Motya, of which we may assume some 1,000 at least were Syracusans. But apart from military service such men seem to have had few opportunities to distinguish themselves and gain the public eye. Indeed, we know of few magistracies remaining which they could hold. One cavalryman, Theodoros, is portrayed by Diodorus haranguing the mutineers in 396, but he is exceptional, perhaps even an historian's invention. So the class which had probably provided most of the Syracusan leaders under the democracy was politically sterilised.[33]

Who then were the men in power in Syracuse during Dionysius' reign? The friends of Dionysius whom we know by name came from his own family and its connections. Dionysius' own brothers Leptines and Thearidas both served under him as admirals; Thearidas was also ambassador to the Olympic games of 388, while Leptines died at Cronion as a subordinate commander to Dionysius on land. They were both associated with Dionysius in the honorific decree passed by the Athenians in 393. Another admiral, Polyxenos, was the brother of Hermokrates' wife, thus uncle to Dionysius' first wife, and also the husband of Dionysius' sister Theste. His association with Dionysius may go back to the days when Hermokrates was trying to secure his return to Syracuse.[34]

Perhaps the most important of the early friends was Philistus, who backed Dionysius in the assembly which led to his first election as general. Although not immediately brought into Dionysius' family he was later to marry a daughter of Leptines without consulting Dionysius, a move which led to his banishment. The third important family to support Dionysius was that of Hipparinos. According to Aristotle Hipparinos himself backed Dionysius' revolution in the hope of restoring his family fortunes. We hear little else of him. However, his daughter Aristomache was one of the pair of wives married by Dionysius in 397, and his son Dion was highly favoured: he was given the hand of Arete, the tyrant's daughter and his own niece, on the death of Thearidas; he was admiral at the end of Dionysius' reign, and he had been sent on embassies to Carthage. Dion's brother Megakles, who assisted in the *coup* against Dionysius II, does not figure in earlier history except for his participation in the council of Dionysius' friends in 405. One friend may have been outside the family circle – Heloris, who first appears as an adviser in this same council. One tradition maintained that he was Dionysius' adoptive father.[35]

Factions and rivalries did not come into the open until the death of Dionysius. However, the banishments of leading men are significant. We do not know the background to those of Heloris and Polyxenos. Leptines was dismissed from his naval command in 389 after promoting a reconciliation between Thurii and the Lucanians which did not suit the tyrant's plans. Some three years later both he and Philistus went into exile at Thurii after Philistus' marriage to his daughter. He himself returned, only to die at Cronion, but Philistus remained in exile. They may have been suspected by Dionysius of building up a faction which might take over the tyranny from his own children.[36]

It would not have been easy for Dionysius to find among his Syracusan friends protectors for the children of his Locrian wife Doris. By contrast, Aristomache's children could count on the backing of Dion. It was perhaps in order to redress this inequality that the younger Dionysius was married to Sophrosyne, Dion's niece and later sister-in-law, and it seems that Dion was expected to lend his support to Dionysius II's succession rather than further the cause of his own nephews, Hipparinos and Nysaios. There was a story that Dion tried on their behalf to approach Dionysius I on his deathbed but was foiled by the doctors. In fact, he seems to have done nothing to press their claims but emerged as the younger Dionysius' principal adviser at the beginning of his reign.[37]

In 367 Dionysius the younger was the obvious successor by reason of primogeniture (Hipparinos and Nysaios may have been as much as ten years younger than him), while Dion's enormous influence, which sprang both from his political reputation and his central position in the ruling family, provoked jealousies and suspicions. Dionysius II probably shared these. Dion's very acquiescence in the subordinate position of himself and his blood relatives may have worried him, and Dion had important allies in Theodotes and Herakleides (the latter had command of Dionysius II's mercenary cavalry). Moreover, Dionysius II had an immediate problem in an impending war with Carthage. These seem to have been the reasons for the recall of Philistus as a counter-balance and alternative adviser, perhaps in 366.[38]

About the same time Dionysius and Dion by common consent summoned Plato back to Syracuse (he had acquired a reputation there through a previous visit in 387). Plato found the court full of factional intrigue with suggestions that Dion was aiming at power for himself. Three months later Dionysius got possession of a letter from Dion to Punic envoys urging them to ensure that they only discussed peace terms with Dionysius in his own presence, since he would help them to a lasting agreement. The letter was taken as treachery, but Dion was treated leniently. He was merely sent away on a visit to Greece well supplied with money, expensive utensils and slaves. His brother Megakles probably accompanied him.[39]

The phenomenon of a young monarch shedding an inherited adviser is not uncommon; the only remarkable feature was the painless way this was achieved. Subsequent history suggests that from his own point of view Dionysius was remiss. Yet the whole issue is clouded in our sources by the later story of the liberation of Syracuse, which, wittingly or unwittingly, Dion began, and by the interpretation put on events both by the Platonic tradition, concerned with defending Plato's reputation, and by later Sicilian historians hostile to Dionysius' tyranny, like Timonides, Athanis and Timaeus. The point of view of Timaeus seems to have been that Dion was a man wronged by the tyranny, who became an opponent of it and was thus to be commended, in contrast to Philistus, who remained loyal to it in spite of being wronged. How Timaeus dealt with Dion's own period of rule is hard to surmise. Perhaps he took the view that, unlike Timoleon, Dion was not given time to carry out his reforms; he certainly contributed to the portrait of

Dion as a man who refused to curry favour with the common people and suffered thereby.[40]

I take the Platonic epistles referring to Sicily to be either edited versions of Plato's own correspondence or fourth-century productions by his own pupils intended to answer questions raised by Plato's involvement with the family of Dionysius. They justify Plato's behaviour on a number of counts: first, his acceptance of the tyrants' patronage; secondly his severance of friendship with Dionysius II; thirdly his practical association with Dion at the time that Dion was preparing his *coup*; fourthly his association with Dion's policy and aspirations for Sicily. It is argued that Plato was primarily concerned with the education of Dionysius into becoming a better man by casting aside luxury and flattery and thus into becoming a better ruler. He had been from the beginning devoted to Dion but did not on that account neglect his duties to Dionysius. The *coup d'état* by Dion was the only way that Dionysius' own morality could be corrected, but Plato was unwilling personally to be an accomplice in it. Plato did share Dion's plans for Sicily, which were the refounding of Greek cities, and the creation of a just society in Syracuse without the characteristic vices of tyranny, oligarchy and democracy.[41]

There are traces of a less enthusiastic and apologetic interpretation of Dion in the brief biography of Cornelius Nepos. However, the best corrective is to let the facts speak for themselves. On his arrival in Greece Dion based himself in Athens, lodging in town with Callippos and spending some time in a country estate he had bought. He was friendly with members of Plato's Academy, especially Speusippos. Dion visited other Greek cities, where he moved in the best circles, in particular Sparta, which was still calling on Syracusan aid in her conflict with Thebes. Dionysius II sent them a fleet of twelve ships under Timokrates in about 365, probably shortly after Dion's arrival in Greece and before Syracuse's renewed war with Carthage. It is quite clear from the honorific decrees which are said to have been made in Dion's honour that he was acting as Dionysius' ambassador. Plato meanwhile had also returned to Athens.[42]

In 362-361, however, Plato was persuaded to come to Syracuse without Dion on a Syracusan trireme sent for the purpose. Dionysius wanted neither Dion himself to come home, nor the proceeds of his property in Syracuse to be transferred to him in Greece; no doubt he feared that it would be used, as it was in fact, to purchase military support. Meanwhile he considered selling the property, keeping half for Dion's son Hipparinos and sending the rest to Dion. The following winter, relations became more uneasy. Part of the trouble may have been the investigation of public opinion by Speusippos and his friends, who, we are told, eventually induced the people of Syracuse to speak freely of their wish to be liberated. Dionysius decided to sell up all Dion's property without waiting for his reply to the proposal made in the summer. There was a mutiny over pay by mercenaries who charged the walls of the acropolis on the Island, which drove Dionysius to pay more both to them and the 'peltasts' of his own guard. Herakleides, the commander of the Syracusan cavalry and a friend of Plato and Dion, was accused of fomenting the mutiny. He fled, and in spite of Plato's protests was hunted by Dionysius' peltasts until he took refuge in Punic territory. In consequence Plato persuaded his Tarentine friends to send him a ship with which to leave Syracuse.[43]

The impression given by Plato's letters is that even after his final return to Athens he was trying to maintain good relations with Dionysius. However, Dion, who met Plato at the Olympic games of 360, was enraged at what had happened, regarding himself as now in effect an exile. Dionysius kept in contact with Plato but, after inquiring from him about Dion's likely reaction, he made Arete leave her marriage with her uncle Dion and marry Timokrates, the man who had been admiral in 365. It is not clear whether this was before or after news of Dion's preparations for war, but in any case it provided another deadly insult. By now Dion had embarked on military preparations with the co-operation of members of the Academy – including Speusippos and perhaps Xenokrates. Little support, however, was forthcoming from Sicilian opponents of the tyranny – only 25 or 30 out of over 1,000 exiles. We cannot tell whether this was because they thought Dion's cause was disreputable, as a member of the tyrant's own family, or merely unlikely to succeed. Prominent among the exiles who joined was Herakleides, who had escaped from western Sicily and was placed by Dion in charge of the triremes and merchant ships which were to follow the initial attack.[44]

Dion's expedition set off from its assembly-point at Zacynthus immediately after the eclipse of the moon in the summer of 357 (9 August by the Julian calendar). It consisted of two merchant ships carrying a little less than 800 veteran mercenaries, together with 2,000 spare shields and a supply of offensive weapons, escorted by two 30-oared galleys and a light craft. Dionysius was preparing to cut off any attack before it reached Syracuse, using his bases in Italy, but Dion's apparently contemptible force surprised his defences by sailing directly across the Ionian Sea and eventually making a landfall at Heraclea Minoa in what was then Punic Sicily. There – perhaps not by chance as our sources suggest – Dion met an old friend in command of the Punic garrison and obtained from him wagons for the conveyance of the armour to Syracuse. He reached Syracuse two days after arriving at Heraclea Minoa. On the way he was joined by cavalry from Agrigentum and Gela and a force from Camarina. Furthermore, the Syracusans in the countryside were stirred to rebellion on his approach.[45]

Dionysius was still in Italy. Although the Island acropolis remained guarded by its own force, Timokrates, Arete's new husband, had no resources to defend the rest of Syracuse, since its garrison of mercenaries from Leontini and Catane had been persuaded to return home by a false pronouncement of Dion's that he would attack their cities first. So Dion was able to enter mainland Syracuse without a battle. However, he took the opportunity to hold an assembly outside the gates, where he proclaimed his intention of liberating Greek Sicily and had himself and his brother Megakles elected as generals with full powers to accomplish this. In fact their appointment resembled that of Dionysius I in the crisis of 406. There followed celebrations, attacks on the tyrant's informers and the creation of a council of 20 (ten of whom were companions of Dion's) as subordinate officials.[46]

A week later Dionysius returned to the Island from near Caulonia, after summoning Philistus and his fleet from the Adriatic. He failed to persuade the Syracusans to accept a relaxation of tribute and diminution of compulsory military service in return for a renewal of their allegiance; Dion demanded simply that Dionysius should abandon his tyranny on condition that he should retain certain rights (presumably to property in Sicily). Dionysius is said to have sent back letters from other members of their family and one from himself recalling their past co-operation and offering Dion a share in the tyranny, with the threat of reprisals on his kin if he did not agree. This was intended to arouse suspicions of Dion among his followers and in the long run may have succeeded. Dion rejected these terms, and the siege continued with part of the Syracusan navy joining the insurgents and contributing to the blockade of the Island.

Herakleides arrived with 20 triremes and 1,500 soldiers (much smaller numbers in Plutarch), perhaps in early 356, and he was later elected admiral. He is portrayed in Plutarch as a persuasive but irresponsible demagogue, who began to cut the ground of popular support from under Dion's feet, but a different picture is outlined in Nepos suggesting sympathies with the aristocracy. Moreover, Plutarch fails to point out that Herakleides was an old friend of Dion's at Syracuse, and his appointment to command the reinforcements shows the trust that Dion placed in him.[47]

At all events Herakleides' fleet defeated 60 triremes under Philistus, who was himself captured and executed, his body being humiliated. Dionysius then offered to return to Italy on condition that he retained the so-called Gyas, an estate stretching from the sea into the hinterland, presumably the personal property of the tyrants. When this was refused by the assembly against Dion's advice, he escaped himself but left his elder son Apollokrates in charge of the Island citadel. Subsequently, about midsummer 356 the division among the liberators deepened and Herakleides put himself forward as Dion's opponent. A certain Hippon proposed a redivision of land in the assembly. At the same time the payment of Dion's mercenaries seemed an unnecessary burden to the city and it was proposed that their wages should be stopped but they should be offered instead Syracusan citizenship (and perhaps *ipso facto* a share in the land division). The assembly also decided to depose Dion himself and create a new board of 25 generals. Dion's stern unbending character had already given him a reputation as an autocrat; his mercenaries had an unfortunate but unquestionable similarity to Dionysius' bodyguard, and wc can understand why people did not want to pay for a force that might oppress them. Dion for his part had not anticipated the drive to self-determination and a social revolution which he had set in motion.[48]

Dion's mercenaries reacted violently to these proposals and fighting had almost broken out between them and the Syracusans when Dion led them off to Leontini, sacrificing his position in Syracuse in order to retain their allegiance. The Syracusans no doubt feared that he might exploit the mercenary soldiers of the tyrant settled there, and after a pursuit they brought Dion's forces to battle but were defeated. Meanwhile at Syracuse the siege took a new turn when the starving garrison of the Island was relieved by Dionysius' admiral Nympsius. The Syracusans won a battle against his fleet before his supplies were fully landed, but Nympsius more than retrieved this through a night attack by land during the Syracusan celebrations. After murderous fighting that night and the following day Nympsius took possession of the *agora*, and his troops ranged the residential quarters of the city, looting where they could but meeting resistance in the streets and alleys from knots of Syracusans. At this point successive embassies were sent to recall Dion and his mercenaries (according to Plutarch and Diodorus it was Dion they wanted, but his veteran soldiers were surely his greatest asset). These envoys seem to have requested Dion's return on any conditions he chose, and spurred by the emergency he reached the city in a day and drove Nympsius' men once more back onto the Island.[49]

Dion was reappointed general with full powers. According to Plutarch, most of his political opponents among the insurgents now fled, but Dion was reconciled with Herakleides and Theodotes, and the former retained his naval command. The previous proposal for the redistribution of land was rescinded, not surprisingly, since it was hardly in Dion's own interest nor would it have suited the cavalrymen who were then his strongest supporters. As for the siege, the cross-wall was rebuilt, and naval warfare was intensified in 356-355 to ensure that no further reinforcements reached the Island. It was probably during 355 that Apollokrates surrendered the citadel and was allowed to depart with five triremes in the company of his mother Doris and his sisters. Dion was now master of Syracuse and reunited with his own family, including Aristomache, the widow of Dionysius I, his own wife Arete and his son. Family loyalty was evident when he forestalled an attempt to cast out Dionysius' body from its tomb. He held on to his own autocratic position, maintained some at least of his mercenaries and used the Island citadel now as his own base. Meanwhile, he deferred any constitutional reforms until he had summoned advisers from Corinth, the mother-city of Syracuse. It was said that he was impressed by Corinthian oligarchy and that, because he shared Plato's hostility to pure democracy, he planned a constitution on the Spartan or Cretan model. Yet, whatever plans he professed, there is no evidence that he foresaw any constitution, which did not allocate a major position to himself. Indeed, it was alleged that he wanted a monarchy like that of a Spartan king.[50]

According to Plutarch, Herakleides criticised Dion in assemblies on account of this tendency towards oligarchy, and he is generally portrayed as a demagogue and antagonist of the wealthy cavalrymen. However, Cornelius Nepos argues that Herakleides was also popular among the wealthy, who disliked Dion confiscating property to raise ready money to pay his mercenaries. In his view Herakleides held his command of the fleet by the agreement of the aristocratic cavalry. Certainly, he had been a cavalry commander under Dionysius II and had no doubt learnt to further the interests of the Syracusan as well as the mercenary soldiers. It is also said that he was in communication with Sparta, and it may be that Gaisulos, the Spartan envoy in the West, had recommended that Sparta should back him. In short he was a serious rival to Dion as a leader of Syracuse with a breadth of popularity that recalls Hermokrates, and we can see why Dion dropped hints about the undesirability of divided command.

Dion's eventual reaction to Herakleides' criticisms was to have him assassinated (354-353). The murder and Dion's seizure of the property of other opponents aroused fears among his friends and led to his own death. His Athenian friend Callippos persuaded the Zacynthian mercenaries, now Dion's bodyguard, to carry out the deed, and it took place in a room where a number of Dion's friends were present but did nothing to help him. Moreover, Callippos himself was able to seize power as his successor, and it would seem that a number of Dion's associates were prepared to co-operate with the change of leadership. It was alleged that Callippos was rewarded by Dion's enemies, but the attitude of Dion's friends made enemies redundant.[51]

As for the Syracusans themselves, some supporters of Dion actually tried to lynch those who they thought were his murderers. According to Nepos, Dion's death changed popular attitudes towards him, and many who had called him tyrant before now called him liberator and co-operated in a splendid funeral. Yet, although there was little public participation in Dion's overthrow, there was also little effective public opposition to the change in regime. The murder was something of a domestic crime. Dion had put a distance between himself and the populace, and this contributed to the ease of his suppression.

Dion's ultimate plans for Syracuse must remain obscure. There is no suggestion that he was willing to abdicate. Perhaps his admiration for Sparta was, like that of the Athenian oligarch Critias, more related to her disciplined and authoritarian social order than the technicalities of her constitution. Instead, he may have been aiming for a constitutional monarchy, such as it was Plato's ambition to create, when he visited the courts of Dionysius I and his son – one where the vices inherent in one man's rule were mitigated by law, wisely chosen subordinates and the avoidance of tyrannical expropriations of property. However, his achievement fell short even of this, and it is admitted in Plato's seventh letter that many Syracusans thought that he was seeking to be the third Dionysius.[52] At all events, the central position of Dion's mercenaries in the episode is testimony to the fact that liberation in Syracuse had lost its way. They had been essential to the military defeat of Dionysius, but Dion's retention of this force for his own security made him unpopular through its financial consequences and at the same time provided a useful tool of tyrannical government for whoever could seize it.

What of the Syracusans' part in these events? If ultimately they were unable to control their own destiny, this was not through want of trying. Dion recruited on his first march to Syracuse several thousand men from the countryside as infantry, and his Syracusan cavalry made an important contribution to his later military strength. Many of those who rallied to him would have already served as soldiers under Dionysius and his son (the latter's promise to the insurgents of a reduction in military service is significant). Moreover, even before Herakleides' arrival, the insurgents' fleet put pressure on the intake of supplies to the Island. After Herakleides came, the Syracusans were able to raise a combined fleet of about 60 ships to defeat Philistus' force (of which some 40 would have been their own). Plutarch seems right to stress the political importance of the naval crews, particularly in the dispute among the besiegers which led to the withdrawal of Dion and his mercenaries to Leontini. As earlier during Syracuse's war with Athens, it reflected their military success, especially when compared with the inadequacies of the citizen land forces.[53]

All these groups had a common cause in expelling Dionysius and his representatives, but in other respects their interests would have diverged. We must accept that the wealthy wished to preserve their existing property rights, as Nepos asserts, whereas the poorer citizens backed the proposal for the redistribution of land.[54] Nevertheless, Plutarch's attempt to show this conflict of interests reflected in faction among the insurgents is unconvincing. Herakleides was not so much factious as adept at conciliating all sections of the Syracusan people. If anything, he represented the view that Syracuse should achieve liberation by self-help rather than mercenaries. The Syracusan cavalrymen would have supported him, not only because of their fears of Dion's confiscations, but because he would have allowed them to regain their political influence.

If we ask why Syracuse did not become a democracy dominated by the wealthy as it did after the expulsion of Thrasyboulos in 465, although Dion's own ability and ambition contributed to this, the military factor was paramount. The creation of the Island citadel as a base by Dionysius I made the elimination of any tyrant a long and costly business. Moreover, professional mercenary soldiers were difficult to defeat without enlisting mercenaries on one's own side. On the other hand, although Syracusan political institutions revived remarkably well after their long subjection, there was a lack of men with both political and military experience and with authority, who could compete with Dion for the leadership. Finally, the grievances of those with little or no land were still there to divide the participants in the revolution, once the tyrant had been expelled.

Timoleon

Callippos ruled for 13 months. He had a honeymoon of popularity and wrote to Athens about his achievement. Then he tried to expand Syracuse's power abroad, capturing Catane and Rhegium. However, Hipparinos, son of Dionysius I and Aristomache, attacked Syracuse; Callippos was driven out; Dion's family were liberated from prison, and the old power of the tyranny was restored (352-351). In Syracuse Hipparinos ruled for two years (the period to which Plato's eighth letter seems to belong) and was succeeded by his brother Nysaios, the Syracusan people being apparently exhausted and quiescent. His reign was brought to an end in 346 when Dionysius returned from Locri, where he had become increasingly unpopular.[55]

The original impulse among the population of Syracuse to liberate themselves from tyranny had by 346 become almost exhausted. Deaths in civil war and the flight of men opposed to the tyrannies depopulated the city, the quarters on the mainland becoming especially deserted. The land by the outer fortifications became a hunting ground; the Syracusan *agora*, it was said, grew deep grass and pastured horses; other towns in the countryside were abandoned in favour of walled fortresses, whose inhabitants were reluctant to descend from them. Depopulation and economic decline were not confined to Syracusan territory, but spread through all the Greek sector of Sicily because of the inter-city fighting that arose through the collapse of Syracusan power, and the number of *coups* by minor dynasts in the cities. In Syracuse the exhaustion of the common people was already evident in 355. They played little part in the downfall of Dion and Callippos, as far as we can tell. Although the second tyranny of Dionysius II was much weaker than the first (he had in the meantime lost control at Locri to a revolutionary government), it was difficult to gather adequate military power to expel him. However, some of the aristocracy survived amid the general poverty. The bigger estates were no doubt still productive: indeed, the owners may have withdrawn from Syracuse into their country estates and based themselves in fortified houses there. These chose to call in Hiketas, the tyrant of Leontini and old associate of Dion. An appeal was also made to Corinth, according to Plutarch, not only from Syracuse but from other Greek Sicilians, requiring aid both against their tyrants and a threatened Punic invasion. This was openly backed by Hiketas, although in fact he was planning to rely on Punic support in his attack on Syracuse.[56]

The Corinthians responded in 344 by sending Timoleon, a Corinthian noble of over middle age, whose reputation for good or ill rested mainly on his having engineered the assassination of his own brother Timophanes, when the latter had seized a tyranny at Corinth 20 years earlier.

His force was originally smaller than Dion's. Although he was given ten triremes by Corinth and her allies, he could only hire 700 mercenaries as infantry, and these were the curse-ridden remnants of the force employed by the Phocians during the so-called Sacred War (after they had seized the sanctuary at Delphi). His mission was to be outstandingly fortunate and become in histories a romantic success story, which for Timaeus rivalled that of Alexander the Great.[57] It was made difficult at the outset by Punic reluctance to allow a Greek force to enter the island and by the problem of Timoleon's relations with Hiketas, with whom in theory he was supposed to be co-operating. Having eluded the Carthaginians at Rhegium and landed in Sicily, he broke with Hiketas and secured supporters and bases of his own at Tauromenion, Adranon and Catane. His major stroke was diplomatic, in that he persuaded Dionysius II to surrender the Island fortress of Syracuse to him in return for a guaranteed safe-conduct to Corinth. In spite of being besieged not only by Hiketas, who had already got control of mainland Syracuse, but by the Punic fleet, he maintained his hold there and made further gains in northern Sicily. In consequence the Carthaginians, perhaps fearing that they would be trapped, retired, and Hiketas himself fled from the city when confronted with superior force. Thus, in 343 a tyranny was once again expelled from Syracuse, not by its own citizens this time but by outside military force — a liberation rather than a revolution.[58]

Timoleon's great victory over the Carthaginians at the River Crimisos (341?) and his other military achievements in Sicily lie outside the scope of this work. Let it suffice to say that by the time of his death in 337 a peace treaty had been concluded with Carthage according to which the majority of Greek cities on the island were outside the Punic Empire (*epikrateia*) and those still inside it were guaranteed internal autonomy. Moreover, most of the local tyrants had been overthrown and their cities brought under Syracusan supervision. So Syracusan foreign policy was now similar to what it had been under the democracy 100 years before.[59]

Another major aspect of Timoleon's success was his reconstruction of Syracusan society. Although our knowledge of this is inadequate, we can gain a glimpse from our sources of the effect his campaign had on the life of the Syracusan people. First of all, Timoleon set the tone of his liberation of Syracuse by demolishing the Island citadel. He then repopulated the city and Greek Sicily as a whole both with exiled citizens and new settlers, distributing the land among them — the land was apparently free, but houses were sold, the previous owners being given the first refusal. The total of settlers is alternatively given as 55,000 or

70,000, of which the bulk came from Italy. Thus, the *demos* in Syracuse and many other cities was physically re-created.[60]

The exact nature of Timoleon's constitutional reforms is a disputed point. On the one hand, his regime was termed *demokratia*; assembly meetings were important both for political decisions and public trials; moreover, it was implicit in Timoleon's proclamations that all new or returned citizens at Syracuse would have both a share in the land and full political rights. Diodorus gives two different accounts of the constitution. We are first told that Timoleon established democratic laws and laid down precisely the law about private disputes and all such things, paying the greatest attention to equality; also that he created the annual office of highest honour — that of celebrant (*amphipolos*) of Olympian Zeus. In a later section, following the account of the battle of the Crimisos, Timoleon is said to have revised the existing laws of Syracuse, drawn up by Diokles, leaving unamended those concerned with private disputes and inheritances, but revising the provisions about public matters in accordance with his own purpose. These are surely alternative accounts of the same process. Timoleon could not have first legislated about Syracusan private law himself and later left the code of private law drawn up by Diokles unchanged. According to the second passage the basis of Timoleon's whole legislation was that of Diokles, that is the democratic constitution and law code in force when Dionysius I seized power, whose political provisions had been in limbo for some 60 years. It is therefore probable that Timoleon's amendments rendered this more like the original democracy of 465-413, with magistracies assigned by election, not by lot, and perhaps property qualifications for all offices.[61]

In Timoleon's own time the assembly apparently deferred to his advice, but he gave it its head in political trials. The most drastic of these led to the execution of the women of the families of Hiketas and his supporters — presumably on the principle, already found in Athens, that the whole breed of a tyrant should be eliminated.[62] Our only other knowledge of the workings of the constitution comes from the sketch provided by Diodorus of the career of Agathocles before he seized his tyranny. From this it appears that by about 330 power in the democracy had fallen into the hand of a faction (*dunasteia*) of wealthy men. Agathokles' brother Antandros was elected general and he himself was elected chiliarch (a subordinate military post), but government was controlled by two supreme generals, Herakleides and Sostratos. Their faction formed an oligarchy of 600, on good terms with Carthage, with whom Agathokles quarrelled. Diodorus refers to 'the *synedrion* (con-

gress) of the 600 which had ruled the city in the time of the oligarchy'
and describes the 600 at the time of Agathokles' *coup* as past members
of an oligarchy, currently a *hetaireia*. It is clear from the texts that they
were an aristocratic political group, not an official body constituted by
Timoleon.

The 600 did not have a monopoly of wealth and power. Agathokles
himself, for example, had acquired a considerable property. Furthermore, we hear of other political groups (*hetaireiai*) apart from the 600
themselves. Nevertheless, there were no politicians who had such standing with the *demos* that they could dominate the faction-fighting among
the governing class before Agathokles seized power. There was, moreover, a section of the population deep in poverty and disillusioned with
politics, some of whom became personally attached to Agathokles and
provided part of the manpower for his *coup d'état*, the rest being soldiers recruited from inland cities subject to Syracuse. One of Agathokles'
first acts when he was created general with full powers in 317 was to
promise a redistribution of land and remission of debts. This was not
such a common act by tyrants as some ancient writers suggest, and it
probably was a response to genuine distress.[63]

Our view of Timoleon's liberated Syracuse must be overshadowed by
the fact that it was soon, if temporarily, subject to an oligarchic faction
and after a quarter of a century once more was ruled by one man. The
new aristocracy, many of whose fortunes may have been created under
Dionysius I, seem to have been more eager for power than any upper
class since Gelon became tyrant. The precedent of violent revolutions
leading both to and from tyranny must have encouraged a political
defensiveness among those with most to lose. On the other hand, the
suspicions of the upper class among the poor, which had assisted Dionysius I to power in 405, persisted in spite of their common subjection to
tyranny and the united front made by all classes against Dionysius II:
indeed, they were probably exacerbated by disappointment in the outcome of Dion's liberation, even though this was not the fault of the
Syracusan aristocracy. How many proletarian families in Timoleon's
Syracuse had lived through the tyrannies there cannot be estimated, but
neither the survivors nor the poor exiles who returned would have felt
great attachment to the new magnates. They had not even the bond of
shared military success. Timoleon's restoration of democracy was not
necessarily too little – a full return to Diokles' constitution might have
been dangerous before the new Syracusan society had time to cohere –
but it came too late.

Notes

1. Plato, *Rep.* VIII.564d-7a; anecdotal tradition – Stroheker, 1958, 18ff.; demagogues – Ar., *Pol.* 1305a, 1310b.

2. Stroheker, 1958, 14ff.; Lauritano, 1957; Jacoby, FGH IIIb, no. 556 (Philistus), no. 566 (Timaeus).

3. Diod. XI.38.7, 48.3-50, 53; Pindar, *Ol.* XII.1 (Himera); Berve, 1967, I, 132ff., II, 595ff.; Diog. Laert. VIII.66, 64 = Timaeus, FGH 566, F2, F134.

4. Ar., *Pol.* 1312b, 1315b, cf. 1303a-b; Diod. XI.67-8; Schol. Pind. *Ol.* I; Berve, 1967, I, 152ff.; II, 607ff. OP IV.665a = FGH 577, F1 (on fighting near Gela) seems to refer either to this war or fighting against Douketios.

5. Diod. XI.72-3, 76; Ar., *Pol.* 1303b; Pindar, *Ol.* XII.1. Numbers of mercenaries – Diod. 72.3, cf. 67.7 on the total of Thrasyboulos' forces.

6. Diod. XI.86-7; Ar., *Pol.* 1303b, 1312b.

7. Cic., *Brutus*, 46. Cf. the procedures attested at Mytilene and Tegea in the fourth century when Alexander ordered the return of exiles (GHI II, 201-2).

8. Ar., *Pol.* 1304a (cf. 1279b, 1293b on the meaning of *politeia*); Diod. XIII.34.6. Generals – Thuc. VI.40.2, 72.4-73.1; assembly and property qualifications – VI.39.1, 41, cf. 32.3ff., 72-3, VII.21; also *Pol.* 1294b for Aristotle's prescription for a *politeia* – election, not selection by lot, but no property qualification.

9. Diod. XI.88-92, XII.8, 26.3, 29.2-3. For the Etruscan expedition to Sicily under Velthur Spurinna – M. Torelli, *Elogia Tarquiniensia*, fr. 1. On Douketios and Syracuse see Adamesteanu, 1963; Rizzo, 1970.

10. Armed forces – Thuc. VI.43, 67, VII.7.1, 38.1 (no mention of slave-rowers in e.g. VII.21.2 and 5); cf. Diod. XII.30.1. Politics – Diod. XI.88.5, 92.3-4; Thuc. VI.32.3-4, 72-3, 103.4, VII.2.1, 21.1.

11. Thuc. VI.67.2, V.4.2-4 (cf. Diod. XII.54.7, alleging that all Leontines were made citizens of Syracuse).

12. Thuc. VI.36.1-2, 38.1-2, 5, 40-1, cf. 12.2-13.1, 35.1.

13. VI.39.1, 103.3-4, VII.48.2, 5-6, 49.1, 86.4.

14. VIII.26.1, 29.2; Diod. XIII.19.4, 20-33 (the account of the debate is vitiated by Gylippos' demanding the death penalty contrary to the clear statement of Thuc. VII.86.2-3). Reform – XIII.33.2, 34.6, 35, cf. 91.3 (juries); Ar., *Pol.* 1304a.

15. Thuc. VI.72.4 (hoplites), VII.85.3 (private captives), 87.3 (public selling of prisoners, not Athenian, Italian or Sikeliot); cf. Lys. 20.24-5. According to recent numismatic studies there is no sign of a flood of coinage resulting from booty. The issue of gold and the famous dekadrachms (including the 'athla' issues) of Kimon and Euainetos have been downdated to the early years of Dionysius I. See Jenkins, 1966, 27ff.; Kraay, 1978, 220ff.; Boehringer, 1979; S. Jameson, NC, 1969, xiv.

16. Thuc. VIII.26.1, 29.2, 35.1, 45.3, 85.2-3; Xen., *Hell.* I.1.27-31; Diod. XIII.63.1-2. Chronology of H's dismissal – HCT V, 281ff.

17. Diod. XIII.43, 54-63, 75; on Dionysius – XIII.96.4, XIV.66.5; Dem. 20.161; Berve, 1967, I, 221ff.; II, 635ff.; Stroheker, 1958, 32ff.

18. Diod. XIII.80-1, 85-91; Ar., *Pol.* 1305a (D. attacked Daphnaios and the rich). Cf. ML 92 for negotiations between Athens and Carthage in 406.

19. Diod. XIII.92-95; Gelon as precedent – 94.5; cf. Plut., *Dion* 5.8-10. Polyaenus' statement (V.2.2) that D. had been secretary to the previous board of generals is not convincing; he would have been tarred with the same brush as they, nor would he have acquired a military reputation.

20. Diod. XIII.96; exiles and mercenaries – 91.1-2, 92.7, 95.3; dockyard –

112.4; Daphnaios — 86.4, 88.1; Demarchos — Thuc. VIII.85.3; Xen., *Hell.* I.1.29.

21. Diod. XIII.109-13; on the topography and strategy of the battle of Gela — Adamesteanu, 1956.

22. XIII.114 (cf. the summary of XIII for the epidemic; XIV.8.5, 41.1, 3 for the zone of Punic domination (*epikrateia*), reflected in the cessation of coinage at Agrigentum, Gela, Camarina, Selinous and Segesta, in the last two cities permanent); XIV.7.2-8.3.

23. XIV.8.4-9.8, 14.2, cf. XX.78.3; Plut., *Dion* 35.6 (= Timaeus F115; Philistus F59) for the advice offered Dionysius by Megakles, according to Philistus, or by Philistus himself, according to Timaeus.

24. Diod. XIV.10.2-4, cf. 70.3 (where the Spartan is called Aretes), 64-9.

25. Agrigentum — Diod. XIII.81.4-84 (Timaeus F26) — wealth said to have derived from agricultural exports to Carthage; Gela — Diod. XIII.93.2; fleet — note 10 above; XIII.96.2, 112.4, XIV.7.3, 8.2, 9.1, 42-3; infantry and cavalry — XIII.113.2, XIV.7.7, 9.1.

26. XIII.91.4, 96.3; Ar., *Pol.* 1306a, Plut., *Dion* 21.7 (Polyxenos was brother-in-law both to Hermokrates and Dionysius).

27. Diod. XIII.91.3, cf. XI.88.4-5, 91.2; Thuc. VI.72-3, 103.4.

28. *Nautikos ochlos* — Ar., *Pol.* 1304a; corruption charges — Diod. XIII.92.2, 94.1-3; cf. Thuc. VI.103.3-4, VII.48.2, 5-6, 49.1, 86.4; lack of pay — Diod. XIII.94.1.

29. XIII.95.1-3, XIV.7, 41-4, 64.3-4 (cf. note 25 above).

30. Assemblies — XIV.45.2, 64.6, XV.79.5; large estate owned by Dionysius II — Plut., *Dion* 37.2; finance — Polyaen. V.2.19; Ar., *Pol.* 1259a, 1313b; Stroheker, 1958, 161ff.; proceeds of war — Diod. XIV.106.3, 75.1, 4, XV.15.4, XV.14.3ff.; technology — XIV.41-3. Note also the police spies (Plut., *Dion* 28.1; *Mor.* 523a; Ar., *Pol.* 1313b) modelled on those used by Hieron.

31. Friends — Diod. XIII.111.1, XIV.8.4, 18.6, cf. XV.6-7 for philosophers and literary men.

32. Syracusan soldiers — XIV.44.2, 64.4, contrast 10.4; new citizens — 7.4, 78.3; crews — 42.5, 43.4, 47.7, 49.1 (after c. 200 ships had sailed to Motya, no seaworthy ships left to resist Himilco's raid on Syracuse), 58.1 (liberated slaves), 64.3ff. (near-mutiny), cf. 75.2 for D.'s fear of public opinion.

33. XIII.113.3, XIV.9.7, 47.7, 64.5. It seems likely that D.'s Syracuse could support as many cavalry as the preceding democracy (cf. Thuc. VI.67.2). On the other hand, it seems unlikely that Syracuse and her Sicilian allies could raise much more than 2,000 (the number maintained by Gelon — Hdt. VII.158.4).

34. Leptines and Thearidas — Diod. XIV.48.4, 53.5, 59.7ff., 72.1, 102.2-3, 103.2-3, 109.2, XV.17.1; GHI II, 108; Polyxenos — XIII.96.3, XIV.8.5, 62-3; Xen., *Hell.* V.1.26, Plut., *Dion* 21.7.

35. Philistus — Diod. XIII.91.4, XIV.8.5; Plut., *Dion* 11.6; Hipparinos and Dion — Ar., *Pol.* 1306a; Plato, *Ep.* VIII.353b; Diod. XIV.44.4-45.1, XVI.6.1-3; Plut., *Dion* 3.3, 5.8, 6.1, 7.2; Megakles — Diod. XX.78.3, cf. XVI.6.4; Heloris — XIV.8.5, 87.1, 103.5.

36. Heloris — see note 35; Polyxenos — Plut., *Dion* 21.7; Leptines — Diod. XIV.102.2-3, XV.7.3-4, 17.1; Plut., *Dion* 11.6; *Tim.* 15.10; Plut., *Mor.* 338b for the story that L. was deliberately exposed to his death in battle; Philistus — Diod. XV.7.3-4; Plut., *Mor.* 605c; Stroheker, 1958, 227.

37. Diod. XVI.6.2; Plut., *Dion* 6, 10-11; Nepos, *Dion* 2.4-5. On Dion see Berve, 1956; 1967, I, 261ff., II, 657ff.

38. Plut., *Dion* 3.6 (delay before Aristomache became pregnant), 11.4, 12.1; Theodotes and Herakleides — Plato, *Ep.* III.318b-c, VII.348b ff.; cf. Plut., *Dion* 12.1, 32.3; Nepos 5.1; Carthage — Diod. XVI.5.1; Plut. 14.4ff. = Timaeus F113;

Philistus – Plut. 11.4; Nepos 3.2.

39. Plato, *Ep.* VII, 329b-c, cf. 326bff.; Plut., *Dion* 4-5, 11.1-3, 13-14; Timaeus F113; Nepos 4.1-2; Diod. XVI.6.4. The mild and honorific treatment of Dion is stressed in Nepos and Plutarch (15.2ff.), although P. was following sources hostile to Dionysius.

40. Timonides, FGH 561, F1 = Plut. 31.3; Athanas (or Athanis), FGH 562, F1; cf. Diod. XV.94.4 (he began his work at the end of Philistus' history and Dionysius I's reign); Timaeus F113, 115, 154; cf. Plut. 32ff.

41. See especially *Ep.* III.315b, 319a-b, VII.326d, 327a, 332e-3b, 334c, 335c, 336b, 350b, 351a-b, cf. VIII.355dff. for P.'s proposal of a constitutional monarchy. Recent attacks on their authenticity in representing what P. thought – Edelstein, 1966; Gulley, 1972 (with counter-arguments).

42. Academy – Plato, *Ep.* VII.333e; Plut. 54.1; *contra* Athen. XI.508e; Diog. Laert. III.46. Other activities – Plut. 17.7-8; Xen. *Hell.* VII.4.12; cf. Cic., *Att.* XV.10, where the corn commission given Brutus and Cassius in 44 BC is compared to Dion's embassy. Plato – *Ep.* III.317a, VII.329dff., 338a-b, Plut. 16.5-6.

43. *Ep.* III.317bff., VII.339aff., 345cff.; Plut. 18-20, 22.2-4; Nepos 5.1; Pythagoreans – *Ep.* VII.339d-e, XII; Plut. 18.5.

44. *Ep.* XIII; Olympics – VII.350b-c, II.310c-d; remarriage – *Ep.* XIII.362e; Plut. 21.1; Nepos 4.3; preparations – Plut. 22, 35.5 (Timonides F2); Diod. XVI.10.5, cf. 6.5; Diog. Laert. IV.11 for Xenokrates' earlier stay in Sicily.

45. Diod. XVI.6.5, 9.2-10.1; Nepos, 5.3-4; Plut. 22-7.

46. Mercenaries – Plut. 27.2; cf. Diod. XIV.68.3, 78.2-3; Dion's entry – Diod. XVI.10.3-11.2; Plut. 26.3-29.6. Diodorus describes an assembly before the entry into Syracuse; Plutarch only afterwards.

47. Diod. XVI.11.3-13, 16.2 (cf. 6.5); Plut. 29.7-34; Nepos 6.3-5; Plato, *Ep.* III.318c. Plutarch's story of the agitation by Sosis against Dion (34) may be substantially true, but the connection with Herakleides is inadequately attested.

48. Diod. XVI.16.3-17.3; Nepos 5.6; Plut. 35.3-38.4, cf. 32.5, 52.5.

49. Plut. 38.5-46; Diod. XVI.17.4-20.4. In Plutarch there are two embassies to Dion, both involving men from the cavalry, the second with a personal appeal from Herakleides.

50. Diod. XVI.20.5-6; Plut., *Dion* 47-51, 53.1-4; *Tim.* 41.3.

51. Herakleides' background – Plut., *Dion* 53.1, 5, cf. 33.4-5, 47.3, 48.7-9, 53.5; Nepos 5.1, 6.3-4, 7.2; connection with Sparta – Plato, *Ep.* IV.321b; Plut. 49.5ff.; see Orth, 1979. Dion's murder – Plut. 54-7, cf. 28.3; Diod. XVI.31.7; Nepos 6.5-9; on the importance of the mercenaries, Christian, 1975.

52. Funeral – Nepos 10.1-3; earlier heroic honours – Diod. XVI.20.6 (his sister and wife, the latter pregnant, were nevertheless imprisoned – Plut. 57.5, 58.8). Ambitions – Plut. 53.4, Plato, *Ep.* VII.326b-d, 332a-b, 334, 351a-c, contrast 333b and Nepos 7.3 for the popular Syracusan view of Dion.

53. Infantry – Plut. 27.1, Diod. XVI.10.1; cavalry – Plut. 42.2; reduction of service – Plut. 30.1; cf. Diod. XIV.7.4, 44.2. Some may have still had arms at home *pace* Diod. XVI.10.1; Dion only provided shields, 2,000 or 5,000 (Plut. 25.2; Diod. XVI.10.3) – not enough for all his forces. Naval forces – Plut. 35.2, 48.5-7, cf. 41-2; Diod. XVI.13.3, 16.3, 18.4-5 for their successes.

54. Nepos 7.1-2; Plut. 37.5-6, 48.6; cf. Diod. XIX.9.5 for Agathokles' promise in 317 BC.

55. Plut., *Dion* 58.1-7; *Tim.* 1.1-5; Diod. XVI.31.7, 36.5, cf. 45.9, 68.1; Justin XXI.3.9-10.

56. Depopulation and forts – Diod. XVI.69.4, 83.1; Plut., *Tim.* 22.4-6. Appeal to Hiketas – Plut., *Tim.* 1.6-2.4, 9.1-4; Diod. XVI.67.1, 68.1-3.

57. Diod. XVI.66.1; Plut., *Tim.* 7ff. (cf. 3-6 on T.'s background); Nepos, *Tim.* 1.3-6; men – Diod. says 700, Plut. 11.5 says 1,000 at Tauromenion; curse – Plut.

30.7. On Timoleon's career see Westlake, 1952; Sordi, 1961; Talbert, 1974.

58. Diod. XVI.68.4-11, 69.4-6, 70; Plut., *Tim.* 9-21; Theopompos F341 = Polyb. XII.4a.2; Nepos, *Tim.* 2.2. I follow Plutarch, according to whom Timoleon landed forces on the Island before the siege by the Carthaginians and Hiketas was lifted; Diodorus places Dionysius' surrender to Timoleon after the other armies had gone. T. may have got his mercenaries onto the Island under the pretence of helping D. and D.'s departure occurred later during the siege (cf. Westlake, 1952, 24ff.; Talbert, 1974, 48).

59. Diod. XVI.77.4-81 (Crimisos), 82.3-4 (treaty and tyrants); Plut. 25-9 (Crimisos), 34.2-4 (treaty), 24, 30-4 (tyrants); Nepos 2.3-4.

60. Nepos 3.3; Plut. 22.1-3, 23.1-7, including Athanis F2 — 10,000 settlers from Asia, Aegean and Greece, 60,000 from Italy; Diod. XVI.82.3-5 — 5,000 + 50,000. For the archaeological evidence of the revival of Greek cities see Talbert, 1974, 146-60, 219ff.; the whole issue of *Kokalos* IV, 1958.

61. Diod. XVI.70.5-6 (343 BC), 82.5-6; cf. Plut. 22.3 for rebuilding of law courts; Cic., *Verr.* II.126 for priesthood of Zeus. Cf. Talbert, 1974, 130ff., who, however, inclines to believe that Timoleon's arrangements were oligarchic and does not see the problem in believing that the Diodorus passages are correct accounts of two different acts of legislation.

62. Plut. 32-3, 38.5ff. Cf. Westlake, 1952, 11f; Talbert, 1974, 87.

63. Diod. XIX.3-9, esp. 4.3, 5.6, 6.3-4, 9.1 for the 600; 3.2 for A.'s property; 5.6 for other *hetaireiai*; 6.1-4, 9.5 on poor. Cf. Talbert, 1974, 140-2.

6 GREECE AND THE AEGEAN IN THE FOURTH CENTURY BC

In the last two chapters I have been examining in detail the political struggles of the two most powerful and populous cities of the classical Greek world. However, one cannot neglect the fortunes of the other city-states in the period before their world was transformed by the rise of Macedonian power. My treatment of these will be comparatively summary for two reasons. First, each main theme will be found to be a reprise of a subject of earlier chapters. Secondly, although we have a great deal of information about the incidence of *stasis* in the fourth century, most of the items are brief and devoted to the narration of action. This usually makes it difficult to detect what, if any, social forces were at work and what the motives of the participants were. However, most of the chief features of the earlier periods of Spartan and Athenian hegemony are present — the cultivation by imperial powers of factions within cities they wished to control; the general support of oligarchic constitutions by Sparta and democratic ones by her opponents; the sacrifice, nevertheless, of ideology to political expediency by the great powers; the frequent preference among smaller cities for independence to a political solution imposed from the outside, however desirable. I intend first to survey briefly developments from the point of view of the major powers and then consider the history of some individual cities.

In addition to her dominance of the Peloponnesian League, Sparta by virtue of having defeated Athens in the Peloponnesian War, took over the hegemony of Athens' allies, apart from those cities on the Asiatic mainland which had been ceded to Persia by the treaties of 412-411. Furthermore, in 399 after the defeat and death of Cyrus in Babylonia she was invited by the Greek cities on the mainland, who feared renewed subjection to Persia and reprisals, to support their freedom. Sparta responded and thus found herself in a similar situation to that of Athens in the years following the foundation of the Delian Confederacy. Meanwhile, she attempted to maintain her political dominance in Greece proper. Her handling of Athens may be regarded as a failure in that she was forced to tolerate a democratic regime there. But Athens remained her ally for the time being and in 400 joined in a Spartan punitive expedition against Elis, which led to an unsuccessful *coup* against the Elean democracy. This episode, the first of a series in the history of the

Spartan alliance, provides the only light relief through an incident of black comedy. Oligarchic assassins thought one morning that they had killed the democratic leader Thrasydaios, but he was found by his friends still asleep where he had succumbed dead-drunk the night before.[1]

The Spartans maintained their hegemony by appointing 'harmosts', governors who were both military organisers and political supervisors either of regions or individual cities, as they had done during the Peloponnesian War.[2] Moreover, they imposed oligarchic regimes in Ionia and no doubt elsewhere. Lysander's original policy had been to establish small juntas called dekarchies, based on political associations which he himself had organised. But some time between 403 and 397 this policy was changed by the Spartan ephors, who advised the restoration of ancestral constitutions, *patrioi politeiai*, as had occurred at Athens in 403. This had created some confusion by the time the Spartan King Agesilaos himself arrived in Asia in 396. The ancestral constitutions, that is those current under Athenian hegemony, would usually have been democracies and Sparta's friends would not have thought it proper to re-establish these. The cities may have therefore adopted broad oligarchic governments.[3]

We do not know the immediate result of the political confusion in Ionia, but in any case within a few years the majority of the cities were detached from the Spartan alliance by the Persians and the Athenians.[4] In Greece Sparta came under severe pressure after 395 from both former friends and enemies in the so-called Corinthian War. Her position was secured by military victories and ultimately by the King's Peace negotiated by Antalkidas in 387-386, in which Sparta was commissioned to ensure the autonomy of the Greek cities.[5] This provided her with a pretext for political intervention in a number of cities. Usually this took the form of supporting a particular oligarchic faction, but these were backed by military force when threatened. In 382 a Spartan commander was persuaded by a Theban friend to seize the acropolis at Thebes as a means of coercion. This action provoked first a counter-revolution at Thebes itself in 378, assisted unofficially by Athens, and then a breach between Athens and Sparta through the creation of Athens' second naval confederacy.[6] Athens and Sparta then returned to their fifth-century policies of disputing control over maritime states, especially in the West, while the Spartans attempted to harass the new government in Thebes with support from Orchomenos and Thespiai. This led to Sparta's defeat at Leuctra in 371, which gave the Thebans the opportunity to overturn Spartan hegemony in the Peloponnese.

The decade between the battles of Leuctra and Mantinea (362) was the most fertile of any in revolution. The Messenians were released from their slavery to Sparta; pro-Spartan regimes in Mantinea and Tegea were replaced by democracies, which with Theban approval worked for an Arcadian federation; the oligarchy in Sicyon was replaced for a time by a demagogue tyrant and then perhaps by a democracy; the tyranny of Alexander of Pherai in Thessaly was weakened; there were also abortive democratic revolutions in Elis and Achaia, an attempt at tyranny in Corinth and a pogrom of the wealthy in democratic Argos. The new political trend owed much to the Theban leaders Epaminondas and Pelopidas, but they were able to build on a genuine desire in the Peloponnese to break free from the political limitations imposed by Sparta. The Arcadian movement for federation and independence also initially brought advantages to the poorer Arcadians who served in their federal army, similar to those enjoyed by Athenians during their fifth-century empire.[7]

After the death of Epaminondas at the battle of Mantinea the contest for power between the chief Greek cities abated, nor were there important conflicts between oligarchy and democracy in mainland Greece. However, leading members of Athens' maritime alliance defected, provoking a war of repression — the 'Social War' (357-355) — and in consequence both Chios and Rhodes lost their democratic constitutions. Mytilene and Corcyra also defected about the same time and became oligarchies. Furthermore, the expansion of Macedonian power under Philip II owed as much to diplomacy as to military might and frequently was based on assistance to tyrants or small oligarchic groups. After Philip's victory at Chaeronea (338), constitutions in Greece were in theory protected from subversion from outside by the treaty establishing the League of Corinth, though this was not always observed under the subsequent Macedonian hegemony. In Asia it became Macedonian policy to instal democracies in place of the Persian-supported tyrannies.[8] The rules of the game did not alter very much, only the players and the chosen ground.

What of the political groupings within the cities? These are normally described as the *hetaireiai* of one or more political leaders in the form 'those around Podanemos' or 'those with the same opinions as Ismenias and Androkleidas', whether the group in question is democratic or oligarchic.[9] This implies that in most cities active politics remained the concern of only a limited section of the full citizen-body. When mass action did occur at Argos and Corinth, it was a drastic assault on the upper class. Nevertheless, the political groups involved in civil strife, even those supporting oligarchy, were not necessarily small. The largest number recorded is that of the pro-Spartan faction which joined Agesilaos in his attack on Phleious about 380. This is said to have been more than 1,000 out of a citizen-body of more than 5,000. 800 men are said to have backed the pro-Spartan oligarch Stasippos at Tegea in 370; the Phleiasic exiles and their supporters who tried to seize the acropolis at Phleious in 369 numbered some 600; 500 pro-Spartan Corinthians were driven into exile in 393; a group of 300 is attested on four occasions.[10]

Frequently enmity between rich and poor is at the root of the strife. The classic example is the massacre of 1,200 men at Argos after the discovery that an oligarchic *coup* was planned (c. 370). The other major episode of blood-letting which occurred at Corinth in 393, was a riposte to a move towards peace with Sparta begun by a group whom Xenophon calls tendentiously 'the majority and the best men': they may well have represented the aristocracy but subsequent events do not suggest that they had mass support, but the contrary. At Tegea in 370 those attacking the friends of Sparta expected support from the people as a whole; when Phigaleia became autonomous c. 375, the *demos* seized power and took reprisals on the aristocracy, while at Sicyon Euphron's tyranny in 368 was founded on popular sentiment. Nor was the *demos* always the aggressor. At Mantinea in 386, in spite of its democratic tradition, the Spartan king, though avoiding brutal reprisals against the democratic leaders, broke up the town into villages in the interest of the landed aristocracy. The Spartan expedition to Corcyra in 373 was made to further an oligarchic plan to attack the *demos*.[11]

On the other hand, the division at Phleious between those who had close ties with Sparta and those who did not, may not have been so much on class lines. A Spartan army was admitted to Phleious in response to Iphikrates' raiding in the Corinthian War and, we are told, did not tamper with the form of government nor bring back those who claimed they had been exiled for sympathising with Sparta. Later, about 386, the Spartans did compel the Phleiasians to receive back these exiles, but the latter were unfairly treated, when they sued to recover their property, by the men in power, that is by the wealthy men who had bought it. The conflict thus seems to have lain primarily between two groups of *dunatoi*, as for example earlier in Samos in 412-411. A confirmation of this is provided by Agesilaos' action when Phleious was eventually forced to surrender. A commission of 100 men was set up to decide who should live and who should die, but it was to be drawn half from the returning exiles and half from those who had remained. Nor is it suggested that the constitution was to be changed. Thus, the division of the population of Phleious was at this point less of a conflict of policy and ideology, more a matter of resentment arising from past history, no doubt perpetuated through families and other personal connections.[12]

In general a great deal of *stasis* must have been fuelled by the desire of those previously defeated or their relatives to repair their status. The nature of the Greek *polis* was such that it was not easy to acquire a new citizenship; there was not the space in Greece now, as there was in the West, to create new settlements, and there would have been anyhow powerful emotions urging refugees to recover their birthright. For these reasons the existence of a few hundred political exiles was always a threat to any but the most populous states.

I now turn to some case histories.

Corinth

Conflict arose here as a result of the grand alliance forged against Sparta with Persian backing in 395, in which Corinth was linked with Argos, Boeotia and Athens.[13] After the defeat of the alliance at Coroneia in 394, a considerable group at Corinth, including many of the upper class, were eager for peace with their old ally Sparta. This was opposed by those who had engineered the war, whether through hostility to Sparta or the money they had received from Persia, and they were backed by the Argive democrats, with whose help they were planning to establish a democracy in Corinth. The group organised a massacre of Spartan supporters in the theatre and the *agora* on the last day of the festival of the Eukleia (February/March, 392). They chiefly accounted for the older Spartan sympathisers. The younger ones escaped to Craneion, the area south-east of the *agora*, thence to the citadel Acrocorinth and finally into exile. According to Diodorus they numbered about 500. Some subsequently returned, but, when the new ruling group negotiated the union between Argos and Corinth in order to secure democracy in Corinth and a common front against Sparta, they successfully plotted with the Spartan commander in Sicyon to betray the long walls which connected Corinth with Lechaion on the Corinthian Gulf. This did not lead to the fall of the city, though it assisted Spartan raiding of the territory round the Isthmus, and in fact the political union between Argos and Corinth was completed in 389.[14]

This union, however, was dissolved after the Peace of Antalkidas when the Spartans exploited the provision for the autonomy of the Greek cities to force the Argive garrison to withdraw. Those who had been involved in the massacre and their accomplices, that is the group which favoured democracy and the link with Argos, also retired into exile and the Spartan sympathisers returned. We hear of a war with Argos and Cleonai early in the life of Timoleon, which may have been prompted by the democratic exiles. In 375 a group of exiles were killed after returning secretly with the aim of overthrowing the government. In Plutarch's view the constitution which preceded Timophanes' tyranny was still a democracy, and power subsequently was in the hands of a sovereign assembly. But one may suspect that the constitution was dominated by the pro-Spartan aristocrats. After Leuctra Corinth did not abandon her alliance with Sparta. However, the unsuccessful *coup d'état* by Timophanes, the brother of Timoleon, at the head of a force of 400 mercenaries is evidence of some political strain in the decade following. Whether Timophanes, himself an aristocrat and a cavalry commander, hoped for popular support, we cannot tell. His murder of leading citizens suggests that the effective power base in Corinth was narrow and that their elimination would remove all serious opposition.[15]

Boeotia

We are indebted to the *Hellenica* from Oxyrhyncus for a valuable outline both of the Boeotian federal constitution in the early fourth century and the political divisions of that time. The individual cities had councils, membership of which was permanent and based on a property qualification. Major decisions were taken by a vote of all members, but they were divided into four committees, each of which acted in turn as an executive and prepared business for the full council. Over them was a federal council in Thebes supplied by eleven constituencies, four Theban, two from the Orchomenos area, two from the Thespiai area, and one each from three other groups of towns. Each constituency provided one general (boiotarch) and 60 councillors for the federal assembly from their own register of qualified citizens and paid their daily expenses. The government was thus a broad oligarchy with the central government representative of the various parts of Boeotia – in many ways an impressive constitution. On the other hand, the system was designed to satisfy the Theban aim to hold the Boeotians together in one federation, an aim which had provoked conflict in the mid-fifth century and Athenian intervention on behalf of the dissidents. Thus the chief political issue was not so likely to be one of democracy versus oligarchy as one of federal unity versus local independence, especially

as the latter would have given the best opportunity for the establishment of a narrow oligarchic junta in one of the constituent cities.[16]

Not surprisingly the political leadership rested with the wealthy aristocrats (*beltistoi* and *gnorimōtatoi*), and there were two main groups —
one sympathetic to Spartan leadership, led by Astias, Leontiades and
Coiratadas, which had been dominant during the Peloponnesian War;
the other led by Ismenias, Antitheos and Androkleidas, which had come
to power after the war (perhaps as a result of a quarrel with Sparta over
Boeotia's share of the booty) and had taken an independent line. We
have already noticed Theban assistance to refugees from the Thirty and
their opposition to Pausanias, when he tried to restore an oligarchic
government in Athens after Thrasyboulos seized the Peiraeus. Ismenias'
group were regarded as Athenian sympathisers, but their actions were
not so much governed by a desire to promote Athenian interests as by
self-interest and a wish to damage Sparta. The two factions, or *hetaireiai*,
were influential both in Thebes itself and in the federal assembly, possessing members in the various Boeotian cities. That of Astias and Leontiades had a particularly impressive record in Thebes, since it was under
their leadership during the war that the population of many smaller
towns had been evacuated to Thebes, thereby increasing its size relative
to the remaining Boeotian cities, and later the Thebans had profited
from the occupation of Decelea and the looting of the Attic countryside.[17]

It was Ismenias' group which deliberately provoked a quarrel between
Boeotia's ally Locris and Sparta's ally Phokis in order to furnish a *casus
belli* for themselves. They had received money from the Persian king's
agent, Timokrates of Rhodes but, as among similar groups in Corinth
and Argos, their major motive was a desire for security against their
political opponents, which they hoped to achieve by extracting their
state from Spartan influence and placing it in a new constellation of
allies. In the long run their aim was frustrated at the end of the Corinthian War by the King's Peace, which not only broke up the anti-Spartan
coalition but enabled the Spartans to force the dissolution of the Boeotian League as a condition of the admission of Thebes to the peace
agreement (they claimed that the league offended against the autonomy
principle). The consequences of this for politics within Thebes are not
made plain by our sources, but it must have given a fillip to Astias'
group, especially in view of their reputation within Thebes itself, and
enabled them to dispute the leadership with Ismenias and his friends.[18]

When the Spartan commander Phoibidas arrived at Thebes in the late
summer of 382 on his march north with reinforcements for the Spartan

army fighting Olynthos, the conflict between the two groups was as intense as ever. Leontiades and Ismenias both were polemarchs, that is annually elected military magistrates, who presumably took over the tasks of the boiotarchs when the League was dissolved. Leontiades entertained Phoibidas and persuaded him to occupy the Cadmeia, the Theban acropolis, during the Thesmophoria festival as backing for a *coup* by his own faction. His men arrested Ismenias at a council meeting as an agitator, cowing the latter's supporters, and about 300 of these fled to Athens, including Androkleidas, Pherenikos and Pelopidas. Androkleidas was later murdered there by Theban agents. Ismenias was tried by a jury drawn from Sparta and the other cities of her alliance and executed, the Spartan garrison remained on the Cadmeia, while Leontiades' group became more subservient to the Spartans than they probably had anticipated. Plutarch's description of them as wealthy oligarchs in contrast to the more democratic group of Ismenias seems justified in so far as Leontiades' *coup* brought what once had been a broad oligarchy under the control of a small junta. The same thing was done under Spartan pressure in the other Boeotian cities.[19]

Three years later in the winter of 379-378, a small group of exiles, recorded variously as seven and twelve, were admitted to Thebes with the help of a certain Charon and Phillidas, who was secretary to the two polemarchs, Archias and Philippos. The polemarchs were murdered at a party by conspirators disguised as courtesans or komasts, while Leontiades himself and Hypates, another leading man in his faction, were killed at home, betrayed by their trust in Phillidas. Men were released from prison and hastily given weapons, the citizen-body was called to arms, further exiles returned as reinforcements, while Athenian forces waited on events just over the border. The Spartan harmost on the Cadmeia summoned help from Plataea and Thespiae, but the Plataeans who came were defeated and the Athenians advanced into Boeotia. He therefore agreed to withdraw from the acropolis if the Thebans granted his force immunity. After the Spartan retreat the Thebans killed the Spartan sympathisers and their children, except for some who found sanctuary with the Athenian army.[20]

Sparta's reaction was to maintain her control of the other Boeotian cities and to attempt to defeat the new regime in battle. The details of this struggle, which ended in 371 at Leuctra, need not concern us here. However, the political consequences are of some interest. The Spartans had installed *dunasteiai*, narrow oligarchies, in the cities of Boeotia. The people now began to leave these cities and go to Thebes. We even hear of strife in Thespiai, King Agesilaos' headquarters, where the king had to prevent his supporters in the city massacring their opponents. By the time of Leuctra the federal constitution was apparently restored. One attempt at a counter-revolution about 364 is recorded by Diodorus. A group of Theban exiles wished to restore an aristocratic constitution and enlisted the aid of 300 cavalrymen from Orchomenos, a town which had been one of the centres of Spartan resistance to Thebes during the previous decade. Others joined the conspiracy and a *coup* was planned on the occasion of a military review (the majority of the Theban army was absent on campaign). However, the Theban exiles chose to betray their collaborators to the boiotarchs. Thus, they secured their own readmission to citizenship, but the cavalrymen from Orchomenos were executed, their city destroyed and the rest of its people enslaved. Otherwise the federal constitution remained intact, as far as we know, until the destruction of Thebes by Alexander the Great after its revolt against his leadership in 335.[21]

Arcadia and Elis

When Sparta campaigned against Elis in 400 and 399, a pro-Spartan faction tried unsuccessfully to exploit this, as we have already seen. It became clear that at this time the Spartans did not necessarily want to overthrow an established constitution, when they negotiated a settlement with the democratic leader Thrasydaios. This liberated the cities to the south and east of Elis, which the city had subjected, but allowed her to retain the presidency of the Olympic games in spite of a previous insult to Sparta. In the same spirit the Spartans maintained good relations with the democratic leaders of Mantinea in Arcadia during their 30-year peace with that city from 416 onwards.[22]

After the King's Peace of 387-386, Elis seems to have acquired a more oligarchic constitution but we do not know how and, although some *stasis* is probable, the Spartans may not have been involved. The Eleans joined the anti-Spartan alliance after Leuctra but were most concerned with the towns in Triphylia which they had lost to the Arcadians through Spartan intervention. We are told that shortly before the Arcadians invaded Elis in 365 there was strife between two groups, one favouring oligarchy and the other democracy, and the democratic group led by Charops had been so encouraged by an offer of Arcadian help that they had seized the acropolis. However, they had been expelled and about 300 of them had based themselves at Elean Pylos, where they were joined by a number of the *demos*. The democratic exiles urged further operations by the Arcadians but in 364 they themselves were defeated on a raid and the survivors were besieged and annihilated in Pylos itself.[23]

Mantinea also lost her democracy in 386, after the peace of Antalkidas was sworn and her own treaty with Sparta lapsed. The Mantineans refused to take down their walls as Sparta demanded; they were besieged and forced to surrender, because the river flowing through the city was dammed by the Spartans so that it flooded and undermined the wall. The Spartans demanded not only the removal of the wall but the emasculation of the democracy through the dismemberment of the city into villages. The champions of the people and those who favoured democratic Argos expected death, but their old guest-friend Pausanias, the ex-king of Sparta now in exile in Tegea, obtained the release of 60 democrats in spite of the hatred of their Mantinean opponents. The best men were nevertheless pleased with the break-up of the city since it enabled them to live nearer their own estates in an aristocratic society without harassment by demagogues. We are not informed of the details of constitutional change. There had been anyhow no direct popular election of magistrates in the Mantinean democracy — the magistrates were chosen by an electoral college selected from the whole citizenbody. This feature may have been retained by the oligarchs, and the responsibility of the assembly for political decisions may have been limited. The dispersal into villages would also have cut down *de facto* attendance at assemblies.[24]

In the immediate aftermath of Leuctra the aristocratic Mantinean leaders were ready to join in a Spartan relief expedition under King Archidamos. However, the next year, after Athens had sponsored a renewal of the King's Peace, they were eager to seize the autonomy theoretically contained in that agreement and to reunite in a fortified city. The decision was taken by a meeting of the assembly, but it was the magistrates who conveyed the decision to King Agesilaos. It would seem that there was a new leadership among the upper class. The Mantineans were helped to refortify their town by manpower from other Arcadian cities and money from Elis, then probably oligarchically governed. It was perhaps at this point that Lykomedes, an ambitious and wealthy Mantinean, first proposed an Arcadian federation.[25]

This idea was taken up in neighbouring Tegea, which had been under oligarchic rule during the early fourth century. A faction led by Callibios and Proxenos urged that Tegea should join, but their plan was opposed by the supporters of Sparta under Stasippos (described as 'men of not the least power in the city') and rejected by a majority of the Tegean *thearoi*, who apparently formed an oligarchic council. Callibios' faction thought that they would have a majority of the citizens behind them in an assembly, but resorted to arms, presumably because reference to an assembly was blocked. In the fighting Stasippos' faction were reluctant to follow up an initial victory, and the arrival of the Mantineans led to their defeat and surrender. A number were condemned to death by the Mantineans and Tegeans, but a further 800 escaped to Sparta.[26]

The way was now open for the foundation of the Arcadian League, but it was not created without opposition. According to Diodorus, the total number of exiles was 1,400 and this implies dissent in Arcadian cities other than Tegea. We know little about its constitution, but it pursued a pro-democratic foreign policy and was no doubt influenced by the democratic leaders in Mantinea and Tegea who brought it into being.[27] One of its most important organs was a new federal army (the *eparitoi*), which obviously bulked large in the primary assembly of the federation, the Ten Thousand. The soldiers seem originally to have been drawn from all classes of the citizen-bodies and paid from federal money (perhaps derived from the confiscation of the property of political opponents).[28]

Their maintenance was eventually an issue which divided the federation. After the Arcadians seized much of Elis in 365-364, including the sanctuary at Olympia, they appropriated Olympic funds to maintain their army. The Mantineans objected to this use of sacred money for profane purposes and began to pay their contingent from city funds. The Mantinean example was then followed by other cities and the official policy was then reversed in the Ten Thousand, with the result that pay was no longer automatically provided for the army by the central authority and the army's character changed. The poor dispersed in search of a living, while the wealthy, we are told, enrolled themselves at their own expense in the pursuit of political power — further proof of the political importance of the *eparitoi*. The next year the federal assembly approved a peace with Elis and the surrender of Olympia. The oaths to this were taken at Tegea by the Arcadians and a Boeotian general, Thebaios. But those officials, who had handled Olympic funds and feared prosecution, conspired with sympathetic *eparitoi* and the Boeotians there to arrest the aristocrats assembled from the various Arcadian cities. However, they were forced to release them under pressure from the Mantinean army. This incident produced a schism in the federation: Tegea, Pallantion, Megalopolis and Asea no longer contributed to the *eparitoi*, and the subsequent Theban intervention on behalf of this democratic group led to Epaminondas' death at the battle of Mantinea. The federal assembly was still functioning during Demosthenes' political career some 20 years later, but the dynamism of the federation had been lost.[29]

Sicyon, Achaia and Phleious

About the same time that the Arcadian federation was created, the Thebans and their Peloponnesian allies tried to create democratic constitutions in other states to replace those that had favoured and been favoured by Sparta. In Sicyon after a Theban attack on the city in 369 Euphron, the leading Spartan supporter, changed sides and placed himself at the head of a revolutionary movement with Argive and Arcadian support, promising to make the city a democracy and their ally. Previously, Sicyon had been governed according to a long-established oligarchic constitution with the richest men in control. Euphron's policy, however, was similar to that of Dionysius I: he and four others were elected generals by the assembly with the promise of an egalitarian constitution, but once in power he secured the loyalty of the city's existing mercenaries and attracted new recruits by generous payments from any funds he could find, sacred or profane. He then expelled the old supporters of Sparta (their property was grist to his mill) and either assassinated or exiled his own colleagues.[30]

For about two years his tyranny was accepted by Sicyon's new allies, but in 366 the Arcadian general Aineas of Stymphalos occupied the acropolis and summoned back the exiles. A conflict soon broke out in the city between the aristocracy and the *demos*, and a Theban garrison was sent in. Euphron, meanwhile, after placing the harbour in Spartan hands and trying to ingratiate himself with them once more, acquired mercenaries from Athens and returned in order to exploit the new strife. He was still popular with the *demos* and got control of the city apart from the acropolis. He then went to Thebes to secure recognition as a tyrant but was assassinated there by political opponents. The man who confessed to the crime claimed that Euphron was an enemy of Sicyon and Thebes. He was duly acquitted, but Euphron was buried with honour at Sicyon as a founder of the city. Thus, the Thebans approved the democracy and the overthrow of the old governing class which Euphron had brought about, but they were happy to be rid of the man himself.[31]

The Thebans had also tried to win over the cities of Achaia in 366. Epaminondas was originally satisfied with an alliance without enforcing a change of constitution or the banishment of the aristocracy. However, there were protests at this from the Arcadians and the opponents of those in power in Achaia, and the Thebans decided to send in harmosts of their own. These established democracies with the support of the common people and expelled the old governing class from the cities. But the latter were in total sufficiently numerous to form an army of their own, which recovered the Achaian cities and, when they returned to power, they were stauncher allies of Sparta than before.[32]

We have already studied the earlier struggles in Phleious, which stemmed more from factions among the governing class than conflicts over the constitution. In 369 the exiles driven from the city some 15 years before sought support from Argos and Arcadia for their restoration. They and their supporters numbered 600. Their plan was to enter the city with the aid of friends inside, while the guards were distracted by the appearance of an Argive and Arcadian army. The project succeeded in so far as they managed to enter the acropolis, but they were afterwards expelled in very bitter fighting. At least 80 of the invaders were killed and others maimed. The city population, which apart from the few fifth columnists displayed great unity under stress, were overcome with emotion at their achievement. In the years following there were regular invasions by the Argives and Arcadians and by a mixed force from Thebes, Sicyon and Pellene, but there was no question any longer of betrayal from within the city.[33]

The Allies of Athens

The cities of Athens' fifth-century empire, which had fallen under Spartan domination, were mostly liberated by Persian and Athenian naval operations between 395 and 387. At least two temporarily returned to something like their previous status. An inscription from Athens honours the *demos* of Clazomenai for their loyalty to Athens and deals with taxation and the option of a garrison. At Byzantium democracy was reintroduced by Thrasyboulos of Steiria; the tax on the ships sailing from the Black Sea was reimposed, and a number of Athenians moved into the city on official and private business. We also hear of the secession from Sparta of Cos, Nisyros, Teos, Chios, Ephesus, Erythrai and Mytilene.[34]

Chios was probably a democracy by the time it renewed its alliance with Athens in 384 (it is difficult to see otherwise why close relations between the cities were restored). One may suspect that many of the others who joined the second Athenian confederacy in 377 were also democracies, although the charter specified their autonomy and enjoyment of any constitution they should choose.[35] However, we do not know either their previous constitutions nor whether despite the treaty Athens did in fact try to alter them, especially when they were brought into the alliance by an Athenian military expedition. In the West the Athenian generals, Timotheus and Ctesikles, certainly lent aid to the *demos* of Zacynthus, while Corcyra's entry into the Athenian alliance after Timotheos' expedition stirred the oligarchs there to plan a revolution with Spartan help in 374. The Spartans sent two naval expeditions, which conquered most of the countryside and were close to seizing the city, if the Athenians had not sent further military aid. Later, about 360, there seems to have been another oligarchic *coup*, but this one was supported by the Athenian general Chares.[36]

Although Athens had no consistent policy with regard to the constitutions of her allies, the re-establishment of her hegemony led to a renewal of the tensions which were so familiar in the fifth century. A good example is provided by the testimony of an Athenian decree of 363-362 about the island of Ceos. Here we find first that the Athenian general Chabrias had made a new treaty with the island and restored the (democratic) friends of Athens who had been exiled. Moreover, the Athenian council had condemned to death a certain Antipatros for the murder of the local representative of Athens. However, although the agreement was respected in Carthaia, a coastal town, men from the inland town of Iulis, who had been condemned and driven into exile at this time, returned and conducted reprisals; they overthrew the stones recording the treaty, killed some friends of Athens and condemned to death in their absence the accusers of Antipatros. A further Athenian expedition under Aristophon, assisted by the loyalists in Carthaia, brought back Iulis into the alliance and led to the mild settlement reaffirming the *status quo ante* recorded on the surviving stone.[37]

In 357 there was a major revolt of the members of the Athenian confederacy, led by Chios, Cos, Rhodes and Byzantium and backed by Maussollos, the tyrant of Caria. As a result of this the four leaders of the revolt received recognition of their independence from Athens.[38] By 353 oligarchies were established in Chios, Rhodes and also Mytilene. The latter was followed by the tyranny of Cammes and a restoration of some sort of democracy by 346. At Methymna and Eresos on Lesbos tyrannies are attested in the period after the revolt, though one tyrant received honours from Athens. Even if Athens had not forced democratic constitutions on her allies, it appears that the weakening of her second confederacy led to local revolutions, and many of the ensuing oligarchies or tyrannies were not overthrown until Alexander's expedition to Asia.[39]

Euboea, which had been of such strategic importance in Athens' fifth-century empire, suffered many vicissitudes in the fourth century. After the revolt of 411 the people of Chalcis went so far as to narrow the Euripus channel and construct a movable wooden bridge in order to maintain closer contact with the Boeotians. There seems to have been a Euboean league then under Spartan and Boeotian protection, but later they joined the alliance between Argos, Corinth, Boeotia and Athens, and in 394 Eretria made a separate treaty with Athens. The cities joined individually the second Athenian confederacy.[40] However, about 370 the Euboeans were persuaded to switch their allegiance to the Boeotians — at this time Themison became tyrant in Eretria and Mnesarchos was influential in Chalcis.[41] In 357 there was an outbreak of *stasis*, and both Boeotian and Athenian forces were summoned to help by their respective sympathisers. The Athenians were successful and the cities were readmitted to the confederacy.[42]

In the age of Demosthenes the cities were regularly under the control of tyrants. We hear of Menestratos and Ploutarchos at Eretria. When the latter was threatened by an exile, Cleitarchos, in 348, the Athenians sent help but through dissatisfaction with his loyalty they deposed him in favour of a democracy.[43] In the same period Callias of Chalcis temporarily broke from his alliance with Athens, but by the end of the decade, after flirting with Philip, Callias became the leader of resistance to Philip's political infiltration into the island. Meanwhile about 342-341 both Eretria and Oreus underwent revolutions, which established in power partisans of Philip, the factions of Cleitarchos and Philistides. Both of these groups were expelled by force in 341.[44]

On the whole Athens was concerned, as she had been during the fifth century, to hold the loyalty of the Euboean cities by any means possible, and to this end she supported either tyranny or democracy. The tyrannies may have been popular with the common people, but they seem to have been chiefly maintained by military force. The island suffered from its divided communities and its strategic importance to Athens and her enemies. Any political conflict could lead to immediate foreign intervention, and there was no question of the Euboeans settling their political problems independently and in peace.

Notes

1. Xen., *Hell.* III.1.3ff., 2.25-8. On Athens see Chapter 4, pp. 165ff.

2. Xen. II.2.2, 3.14, 4.28, III.1.4, 2.20, 5.13, VI.4.2 for Spartan harmosts, III.2.11 for an *epimeletes*. Xenophon uses the Spartan term 'harmost' also for governors imposed by the Athenian Conon (IV.8.8) and the Boeotians (VII.1.43, 3.4). On the development of these officials see Chapter 3, p.

3. Plut., *Lys.* 13.3, 23.3; *Ages.* 7.1.; Xen. III.4.2, 7, 5.13; Diod. XIV.3.4, 13.1; Andrewes, 1971(2).

4. Xen. IV.8.25, 27; Diod. XIV.84.3-4, 94; *Hell.*, Oxy. 15; GHI II, 114.

5. Xen. V.1.31-36; Diod. XIV.110.2-4.

6. Xen. V.4; Diod. XV.25-30; GHI II, 123. Cf. p. 229 above.

7. See above, pp. 231ff. Cf. Isoc. 6.64-9 on the troubles that beset the Peloponnese, especially the democrats there, from a Spartan point of view; Plut., *Pelop.* 24; Diod. XV.62.4-5 (Thebans).

8. Arr., *Anab.* I.17.10, 18.2; GHI II, 191, 192.

9. *Hetaireiai* — Xen. V.2.25; *Hell. Oxy.* 17.2; form of words — e.g. *Hell. Oxy.* 6.2, 7.2, 17.1-2, 18.1; Xen. III.5.1, V.2.31, 3.13, 4.5.

10. Phleious (380) — Xen. V.3.16-17; Tegea — VI.5.10; Phleious (369) — Xen. VII.2.5; Diod. XV.40.5; Corinth — Diod. XIV.86.1; see also Xen. V.2.31, 3.22, 4.13, 16.

11. Argos — Diod. XV.57.3-58; Corinth — Xen. IV.4.1-5; Tegea — Xen. VII.5.6; Phigaleia — Diod. XV.40.1-2; Sicyon — Xen. VII.3; Mantinea — Xen. V.2; Corcyra — Diod. XV.46.1-3.

12. Xen. IV.4.15, V.2.8, 3.10-12, 25.

13. Xen. III.5, IV.4.2; *Hell. Oxy.* 7.3-4; Diod. XIV.82. Cf. Plut., *Lys.* 22.2 for obscure Corinthian revolt in Lysander's lifetime. On the Corinthian War and the associated *stasis* see Perlman, 1964; Griffiths, 1950; Kagan, 1962 (less persuasive); on the chronology, Ryder, 1965, 165-9.

14. Xen. IV.4; Diod. XIV.86. According to Diodorus, 500 went into exile (86.1); of these 150 were involved in the counter-attack (Xen. IV.4.9). Union — Xen. IV.8.34; Diod. XIV.92.1, 97.5.

15. Xen. V.1.34, 36; Diod. XV.40.3; Nepos, *Tim.* 1.3-6; Plut., *Tim.* 3-4 (esp. 3.4, 4.1); cf. *Tim.* 5.2 for democracy, 3.1-2 for assembly. Timophanes seized power by killing the leading citizens (*Tim.* 4.4), but such measures, as we have seen, do not imply the existence of an oligarchy rather than a democracy.

16. *Hell. Oxy.* 16.2-4; Bruce, 1967, 102.

17. *Hell.*, Oxy. 17; Xen. III.5 (cf. I.3.15-22 on Coiratadas'·war-service and escape from Athenian captivity); Diod. XIV.6.3; Plut., *Lys.* 27.2-3; *Pelop.* 6.4.

18. *Hell. Oxy.* 18, cf. 7.2; Xen. III.5.1-4; Paus. III.9.8-10; Xen. V.1.32-33. Cf. Lys. 26.23.

19. Xen. V.2.25-36, 4.46; Plut., *Pelop.* 5-6; Diod. XV.20 (alleging that the Spartans had ordered that the Cadmeia should be seized on any conceivable opportunity). For Theban support of Olynthos see OP I.13. Recent discussion by Hack, 1978.

20. Xen. V.4.2-12; Plut., *Pelop.* 7-13; Diod. XV.25-7. For the time of year *Pelop.* 9.1; Xen. V.14-15. Conspirators from Athens named — Melon, Pelopidas, Damokleidas and Theopompos (*Pelop.* 8.2). In Diodorus (26.2) the Athenian army is sent officially after an embassy by the Theban conspirators to Athens. Xenophon by contrast states (V.9-10, 12, 19) that Athenian troops were already on the Theban border at the time of the *coup* and that there was collusion between the conspirators and the Athenian generals, later disowned under Spartan pressure.

21. Xen. V.4.46, 55; federal magistrates – Plut., *Pelop.* 20.2, 23.4, 24.1-2; Arr., *Anab.* I.7.11; cf. IG VII. 2407-8; SEG XV.282; Larsen, 1968, 175; Orchomenos – Diod. XV.79.3-6; cf. Xen. VI.4.10; Plut., *Pelop.* 16.1; *Comp. Pelop. Marc.* 1.1; Dem. 20.109; Paus. IX.15.2.

22. Xen. III.2.25-32; Diod. XIV.17.4-12, 34.1; cf. Xen. V.2.3, 6.

23. Xen. VI.5.2-3, VII.1.26, 28-32, 4.13-26; Plut., *Mor.* 269a; Diod. XV.62, 64.6, 68.1, 77. See Roy, 1971, especially 573-5, 582-4.

24. Xen. V.2.1-7 (on Pausanias, V.2.6, III.5.25); Diod. XV.12.1-2; Ar., *Pol.* 1318b.

25. Xen. VI.4.18, 5.3-5, VII.1.23-4; Diod. XV.59 (stating that Lykomedes came from Tegea); Roy, 570.

26. Xen. VI.5.6-10, 36, cf. 4.18 for the previous power of Stasippòs' faction.

27. Exiles – Diod. XV.59.2; constitution – GHI II, 132; SEG XXII, 339; Larsen, 186; Roy, 571-2. Note also the foundation of Megalopolis out of 20 villages as a bulwark against Sparta – an expression of the new federalist ideology and also of democracy, since it was only by concentration that the *demos* was likely to be influential (Diod. XV.72.4, 94.1-3; Paus. VIII.27).

28. *Eparitoi* – Xen. VII.4.33-6, 5.3; Diod. XV.62.2 (*epilektoi*); 67.2; the Ten Thousand – Xen. VII.4.33; GHI II, 132, 3-4; SEG XXII.339(a), 1. For property confiscated at Tegea cf. the decree of 324 BC restoring the exiles, GHI II, 202.

29. Xen. VII.4.33-5.5; Diod. XV.82; Dem. 19.11; Aeschin. 2.79; Hyp. *Dem.* V., col. 18. Cf. Paus. VIII.32.1. For the new Arcadian league founded after the death of Epaminondas, perhaps under Mantinean leadership, see GHI II, 144.

30. Xen. VII.1.18, 44-6; Diod. XV.70.3; Roy, 577, 579-81; Meloni, 1951.

31. Xen. VII.3.1-12, cf. 2.11 for previous Theban tolerance of Euphron. See VII.3.8 for the allegation that he had enfranchised slaves, VII.3.12 for the honours given to him when dead.

32. Xen. VII.1.42-3, 4.17, 5.1, 18; Diod. XV.75.2.

33. Xen. VII.2.5-9, cf. 10-23; Diod. XV.40.5; Legon, 1967.

34. Xen. IV.8.1-30; Diod. XIV.84.3-4, 94; *Hell., Oxy.* 15; GHI II, 114. Rhodes, Samos and Cnidos seceded but were recovered by Sparta (cf. Diod. XIV.97.1-4, 99.4-5).

35. GHI II, 118 (Chios had apparently been harshly treated by Sparta while under her hegemony – Isoc. 8.98); GHI II, 123, lines 19ff. (autonomy), 97ff. (first cities to join).

36. Xen. VI.2.2-26; Diod. XV.46.1-3, 47.1-7; GHI II, 127; Aeneas, *Pol.* 11.13; Dem. 24.202.

37. GHI II, 142. The secession of Ceos from Athens probably resulted from the voyage of Epaminondas, during which Rhodes, Chios and Byzantium became Theban allies (Diod. VI.79.1-2; Isoc. 5.53). GHI 146 shows cleruchs being sent to bolster the pro-Athenian faction at Potidaea in 361.

38. Diod. XV.7.3-4, 21-2.2; Dem. 15.3; Isoc. 8.16.

39. Dem. 13.8, 15.14-16, 19, 40.37; GHI II, 168, 170, 191; cf. 186; Arr., *Anab.* I.17.10, 18.2.

40. Diod. XIII.47.3-6, XIV.82.3; Xen. IV.2.17, 3.15; GHI II, 103, 123, lines 80, 114, cf. 124 (Chalkis).

41. Diod. XV.76.1; cf. 85.2, 6, 87.3; Xen. VI.5.23, VII.5.4; Dem. 18.99; Aeschin. 2.164, 3.85.

42. Diod. XVI.7.2; Aeschin. 3.85; Dem. 8.74; GHI II, 153, cf. 154 and IG II^2, 149 (though the former may refer to the period c. 340 BC).

43. Dem. 9.57, 21.110, 200; Aeschin. 3.86-8 and schol.; Plut., *Phoc.* 12-13.

44. Dem. 8.36-7, 9.57-66; Aeschin. 3.86-105, Philochorus, FGH 328, F159-60, IG II^2, 230. On the history of Euboea in the fourth century, especially in 343-40 BC see Cawkwell, 1963, and 1978; Brunt, 1969.

7 THE PHILOSOPHERS AND CIVIL CONFLICT — ARISTOTLE'S *POLITICS*

Two general discussions of *stasis* have already been mentioned in this book, those of the fifth-century historians Herodotus and Thucydides. For the latter the conflict between groups representing the 'best men' and the people was a datum of political life and as essential to it as inter-city war. He related how this strife was intensified during the Peloponnesian War when the factions were exploited in the strategic interest of the contending powers and themselves exploited the external backing then available to them. However, he did not try to analyse the origin of *stasis* in Greek political life. By contrast Herodotus in his staged debate between the candidates for the vacant Persian throne was more philosophical and, even if his approach appears naive in points, he can be seen to have laid the foundations of much subsequent Greek political thought on the subject.[1]

Darius argues that in oligarchies, because many strive to prove their excellence in public life and make their policies prevail, the result is violent jealousy, faction and bloodshed, which can only issue into rule by a single man. When a *demos* has power, this means corruption (*kakotes*) in public life, since those who are bad (*kakoi*) in respect of birth and talent get office, but this does not breed faction so much as a conspiracy to damage the public interest while advancing that of the ruling group. Eventually the only answer to this is a demagogue who crushes corruption and through his popularity becomes elevated to the position of a single ruler. We may compare the view taken by 'Xenophon' in the oligarchic essay on the Athenian constitution. This too takes democracy as a conspiracy by the *kakoi* to promote their own interests, but sees no reason why this should damage the city, provided the *kakoi* appreciate properly what is expedient for them. We cannot pursue at length here the question of how far Herodotus' theory about the weakness of democracy had an empirical basis. Was his demagogue who repressed corruption modelled on Pericles? Hardly. Pericles did not rescue Athens from *kakoi*, men of inferior birth and capacity: such men were believed to have succeeded rather than preceded him. It is hard to find any exact parallel. However, the struggles in Croton and Syracuse at the beginning of the fifth century, where democratic movements against oligarchies in fact promoted tyrannies, perhaps suggested this pattern of revolution or he may have been influenced by events in Ionia.

The sophists, whose views were discussed in Chapter 4, viewed society as an arena for a power struggle in which the superior tried to assert themselves, but no detailed analysis of *stasis* by them has survived. The next theory that we find is in Plato's *Republic* VIII, the sketch of the constitutional rake's progress which follows the first slip from the ideal aristocracy Plato has advocated. In this the transition from oligarchy to democracy is apparently peaceful: in an acquisitive society the poor both envy and despise the flabby rich and so take over power. Tyranny, however, arises more violently out of democracy, because under this constitution the poor still require strong leadership from demagogues in order to strip the rich of their property and influence in the state. This portrayal of aggressive demagoguery developing into tyranny may owe something to Plato's view of Athens in the closing stages of the Peloponnesian War but is most clearly grounded in the career of Dionysius I, as Aristotle's restatement makes plain.[2] It is interesting to compare Plato's democratic tyrant with that of Herodotus. The former is the embodiment and spearhead of all the vices of the *demos*; the latter is the strong man brought in to repress these vices. If Plato's villain is Dionysius I, Herodotus' model is nearer Gelon.

Plato in the *Republic* was seeking to describe a society, whose justice, arising from the proper relationship of its class components, in his view entailed stability and freedom from *stasis* and proved the ultimate superiority of justice to injustice in moral worth and the creation of happiness. It is not surprising in the light of this intention that existing constitutions and their vicissitudes are crudely oversimplified to provide an unfavourable comparison. Aristotle's discussion of *stasis* in the *Politics* also arises from an attempt to define the best society and constitutional arrangements but according to a different method. Instead of arguing *a priori* for a certain form of constitution, he set himself to assess the value of the various constitutions that had already been created (including those in Plato's philosophical works) as a guide towards the ideal. He even makes suggestions about making the best of existing constitutions. The picture of how Greek politics actually worked is, as one might expect, fairer and more comprehensive. The work is characterised by references to specific historical episodes and the institutions of individual cities and for this reason has frequently been cited earlier. Nevertheless, this empiricism is deceptive and a possible trap for one who uses Aristotle as a quarry for historical material.

Although the various categories of constitution and the phenomena associated with each are derived from Greek historical experience, the course of Aristotle's argument is determined by certain theoretical tenets about what is desirable in social and political organisation. Prejudice may also be at work, when he selects a particular pattern of behaviour as the norm. The work is most striking for the shrewdness of its broad generalisations about politics. On the other hand, the treatment of specific political changes and their causes is often unsatisfactory. A historical episode is cited as evidence for the importance of a particular factor in *stasis*, without any thorough analysis of how it was important or any account of the other factors which were operative at the same time. Thus, Aristotle takes the secession of Mytilene from Athens in 428 as an example of a revolution caused by a small personal quarrel. Even when the factor he singles out as decisive in a change is in itself convincing, for example the recent victory over the Athenians as the cause of the democratic revolution at Syracuse in 413, the historian may still feel uneasy at his silence over other possible causes.[3]

For Aristotle a city is the largest of the natural communities (the others being the household and the village), whose original purpose was the survival of their members. However, the developed function of the city is to create the good life. The proper organisation of the community is justice. Its constituent elements are households, which are themselves composed of free men and slaves. The despotic management of slaves is natural in a way that the despotic management of free men is not, because slaves are by nature instruments to enable the master of the household to perform the natural task of ensuring its survival. Similarly, it is proper for men to exploit the natural resources of the world to sustain themselves, and this justifies the use of war to acquire goods at the expense of animals and of other men who are naturally subject but do not obey. The essential relationship between master and slave is despotic, even though there may be common interest and friendship between them, but this relationship should not be extended to free men in the management of a city, which is a community of equals regulated by justice.[4]

Granted that a city is a community of free men, how much should in fact be shared? Aristotle rejects the sharing of wives, children and property proposed in Plato's *Republic* both because of practical difficulties and on the theoretical ground that a city is by nature plural, whereas such measures would bring it nearer to being a single household. The nature of the association of men who are free and equal means, moreover, that they should take turns in ruling and thus they should not possess permanently the same status. Aristotle also rejects communism of property on the ground that it produces too many quarrels but believes that the current system of private holdings would be better, if people were encouraged to allow each other the enjoyment of their own possessions. He is anyhow suspicious of acquisition of wealth as an end in itself, believing that economic activity should be directed to the fulfilment by the household of its function, so that the good life may be lived on this basis, not to the unlimited accumulation of money.[5] Aristotle admits that inequality of property is taken with some justification as a cause of *stasis*. Phaleas of Chalcedon had advocated the equalisation of property; Solon of Athens and lawgivers in Leucas and Locri had passed laws which tended to this end. Phaleas had also argued for equality in education. Aristotle suggests not that such policies are wrong but that they are futile and have attendant disadvantages. Men do not do wrong simply for the lack of the necessities of life, but to gain enjoyment and to fulfil their desires. Nor do really serious crimes spring from the lack of necessities.[6]

Aristotle here considers poverty only as something suffered by individuals in isolation. For he declares that if a man through necessity becomes a thief, he will be no great danger to the community, but he does not consider the danger that might arise from a number of starving people acting at once. This must seem to a modern reader somewhat naive, but carries important implications about Aristotle's perception of the class struggle in the classical city. It is true, however, that equalisation of property would not be enough to avert strife without a programme of education to make it acceptable to the people.

He is also right to perceive that inequality of property is not the only major source of strife in existing communities: inferiority in wealth provokes the masses, but the aristocracy are disturbed by equality of political privilege.[7] This would not be a valid objection to Phaleas' proposal, if aristocracies were indeed eliminated by the equalisation of property. However, when a Greek of that period contemplated his own society, he would have found it difficult to imagine the disappearance of those who claimed to be 'beautiful and good', and we may concede that Aristotle would have been justified, if he suspected that even in a state with equal properties there would survive a class of people who believed that they were better than others. The responsibility of the aristocracy for fomenting civil strife in the pursuit of political superiority had, as we have seen, been highlighted by Solon long before and was amply documented by the history of the last two centuries. Aristotle does this justice, but he is equally suspicious of the (as he thinks) insatiable depravity of the common man who, when he is given a two-obol dole, always asks for more. The answer is, in his view, to train reasonable men to refrain from indulging their appetites, and to prevent inferior men from doing so by ensuring first that they are a weaker part of the community and secondly that they are not wronged. Aristotle also argues on a number of occasions that if the common people are totally excluded from government, this will make them hostile to the constitution and lead to *stasis*.[8]

Thus, early in his work Aristotle has enunciated two major factors which may lead to the dissolution of any society and constitution — economic inequality and the ambitions of the governing class. It is assumed that *stasis* of any kind is undesirable, and this is not surprising for two reasons. Aristotle sees the value of the city lying not only in its provision of material support for human life but in its being the essential framework for the good life according to virtue. Furthermore, he envisages an ideal society as something complete in itself and static. When he comes to pass a verdict on a constitution, as he does early in his work on those of Sparta and Crete, he comments on their vulnerability to *stasis*. The Spartans, like the Thessalians, have created a problem for themselves in their subject race of helots; the Cretans create anarchy by faction in their narrow governing class and their refusal to abide by their own laws; the Carthaginians avoid uprisings from their *demos* by making them prosperous through settlement in colonies, but their constitution contains no remedy for a revolt by the masses.[9]

The central part of the *Politics* is devoted to an investigation of the various types of constitution, their merits and demerits both absolutely and as responses to certain types of society. As a rider Aristotle comments on how the legislator may bolster each type of constitution against overthrow. We thus find an alternative programme to the sketch of the ideal constitution in Books VII and VIII, one in which Aristotle, while not disguising his own ultimate preferences for aristocracy or the mixed constitution termed a *politeia* (constitution), considers all existing forms of government from the inside in the role of a political consultant, as it were, rather than a critic.

He accepts that it is inevitable that different cities will have different constitutions depending on the strength of the various social classes in the city and their relative participation in political life.[10] The basic division lies between the rich, the poor and the middle class, but there are also varieties of rich aristocrats, depending on the character and amount of their wealth, and varieties of common people according to their source of livelihood, whether farming, trade or work as artisans. The *mesoi* or middle class are the ideal citizens for Aristotle, because they avoid the major vices which arise either through power and insolence or by contrast through destitution and petty crime. They do not desire others' property, nor do they have enough themselves to provoke envy among those worse off than they are. Thus, they are a force for stability and against *stasis*. Large cities, in which there is not only absolutely but proportionately a larger middle class are better for this reason, and democracies are more stable than oligarchies, because the *mesoi* are allowed greater participation in government there. Who constitute this middle class? Aristotle is vague about this in his central discussion, but it appears from his review of the grades of democracy that it is a class of farmers with moderate estates, who are the ideal group to be dominant in a democracy, since their properties are such that they cannot afford to take much time off work to devote to politics. He probably has in mind those with the minimum qualification to be a hoplite soldier. In one of his definitions of *politeia* (as the good constitution akin to democracy, where the mass direct the city in the common interest) he assumes that the virtue of the mass lies in military valour.[11]

Although Aristotle initially recognised six forms of constitution — monarchy, aristocracy and *politeia* on the one hand and their three deviant counterparts, tyranny, oligarchy and democracy — his discussion centres on the two main forms, democracy and oligarchy, both of which he regards as capable of being corrected to the point that they become tolerable constitutions. Democracy is essentially rule by the free poor citizens, who are the majority; oligarchy rule by the wealthy and noble, who are the minority. Aristotle constructs two spectra of the grades of oligarchy and democracy which more or less overlap at their moderate ends, where the most desirable forms of the two constitutions are to be found. He defines the *politeia* as a mixture of oligarchy and democracy and this too must lie very close to the best types of oligarchy and democracy.[12] However, he has to admit that this sort of blend is rare because of the paucity of the middle class, which enables the dominant class, whether it be the wealthy or the people, to drag the constitution over to their side. This occurs especially when there has been civil strife and the victorious party seizes a controlling position in the community as a prize of victory. Aristotle's language here reminds us of that of Thucydides in his excursus on *stasis* inspired by the civil war in Corcyra.[13]

Aristotle deals both with the methods by which any given constitution may be made stable and then (in Book V) with the causes of the overthrow of certain constitutions. Two points may be made before we look more closely at his analysis of the latter. On the whole, he assumes that he is discussing communities with a given social content — of a certain size with so many wealthy citizens, so many middle class and so many poor. On a few occasions he notes that a spontaneous change in these proportions may be the cause of revolution.[14] However, his discussion is still limited to the political probabilities in the light of a social datum. Accordingly, the revolutions he examines are those which seek to change the relationships and balance of power within a given social structure, not to substitute a different social structure for it. Furthermore, he assumes that everyone accepts the validity of his notion of justice and proportionate equality (whereby the status of any man or group within a society should reflect their worth within that society), but then fails to achieve it in practice through what he seems to consider to be primarily an intellectual error. The common people think that, because they are equal to anyone in freedom, they are equal to anyone in all respects and want equal shares in everything. The few by contrast think that because they are unequal in wealth, they are unequal in all respects and should have a bigger share in everything. Civil strife occurs when men do not obtain the share in the life of the community which they believe that they should have.[15]

A basic distinction is drawn between revolutions, in which one form of constitution is changed to another, and less dramatic upheavals – those in which the constitution remains the same but the ruling group is changed; those where the constitution becomes either more moderate or more extreme; those where certain features of the constitution are changed. Aristotle is not concerned here with whether the changes are violent or peaceful. It is enough that the existing form of government has proved unequal to its function and people have come into conflict over their rightful place in that society.[16]

In principle he thinks democracy less likely to produce civil strife than oligarchy, since democracy only creates conflict with oligarchy, while oligarchy engenders conflicts within itself as well as conflict with democracy. Conflicts are in essence struggles for equality or superiority by those who believe that they have been unjustly deprived of these. Aristotle also gives a long list of the specific contexts which produce such conflicts, the efficient causes of *stasis*, most of which are defined by a state of mind, for example envy, insolence, fear and contempt. Particular instances are the fear of reprisals by men who have done wrong and the oligarch's contempt for disorder and anarchy in a democracy.

A different sort of cause is the one which we have just mentioned – the disproportionate increase of a particular class in the community. Aristotle cites the growth of democracy in Tarentum after many aristocrats had been killed in a war with the Iapygians, the situation in Argos after her defeat by Sparta at Sepeia about 494 and, somewhat puzzlingly, the situation in Athens during the Peloponnesian War when many of the aristocrats were killed in infantry fighting — he seems to believe that this made the Athenian democracy more radical under demagogues like Cleon and Hyperbolos.[17] Aristotle adds later to his list the growth in power or reputation of a particular body or class, such as the Athenian Areopagus after the Persian Wars or the Syracusan *demos* after the defeat of Athens in 413.

Other contextual causes mentioned are racial conflict, a territory geographically divided and a variety of personal quarrels. As a coda to this catalogue Aristotle notes that revolutions take place either through force or deceit or a combination of the two, citing the revolution of the Four Hundred as an example of the latter. This may be intended to make more acceptable his assimilation of peaceful and violent changes in the constitution. He nevertheless gives the impression that he is critical of any such changes, even if they occur as a response to changes in society and do not involve force, for example the constitutional changes in Athens in the mid-fifth century.[18]

Aristotle then proceeds to the specific causes of revolution in different constitutions. Under democracy he maintains that the prime cause is the insolence of demagogues in harassing the nobility. The influence of Plato here is obvious, but Aristotle gives Plato's explanation a new twist. He produces four examples of aristocracies reacting to such pressure and overthrowing the democratic government — in Cos, Rhodes, Megara and Heraclea Pontica — none of which are known to us from other sources. He then points out that in ancient times, when demagogues were also generals, such struggles produced tyranny, citing Peisistratus, Theagenes of Megara and Dionysius I of Syracuse. He does not consider here that, among the demagogues he lists, only Dionysius was in fact active under a truly democratic constitution, nor that it is somewhat odd to consign Dionysius to 'ancient times' (his other examples, including Cypselus and Panaetius of Leontini, mentioned elsewhere, all come from the archaic period). This obscures the fact that Dionysius was an exceptional but a recent phenomenon.[19]

The summary treatment of the threats to democracy is followed by a much more detailed account of strife created by oligarchies. Oligarchies are overthrown on the one hand when they injure the masses and provoke a reaction, often led by a dissident member of the oligarchy itself. In particular an over-exclusive distribution of high office leads to a revolution led by wealthy men left outside. This may simply bring about the broadening of the oligarchy, or the *demos* may take advantage of the confusion to seize power under the leadership of a member of the nobility. On the other hand, the origin of the revolution may lie solely within the oligarchy. Aristocratic rivalries induce men to become demagogues either with their fellow oligarchs or the mass of the people outside. By this Aristotle seems to mean that they deliberately curry favour by proposals to dilute the oligarchy. But cultivation of popular support is also the way men resist an attempt to contract the size of an oligarchy. Apart from this there are personal reasons for oligarchic revolutions. Men get into debt through extravagance and seek tyrannies for themselves, or support others in doing so, or by resorting to embezzlement provoke a conflict. There are feuds over marriages and lawsuits. Factors outside the oligarchy may also be important. The use of soldiers in war, or in peacetime to preserve order, may give a would-be tyrant or faction their chance to seize poewer through military command, whether these troops are mercenaries or armed members of the *demos*. Equally, they may be compelled to give the *demos* a bigger share in political life in return for its military services in order to avoid such a tyranny. Finally, the oligarchy may succumb to a spontaneous change, when its property qualification is attained by many people in a time of prosperity and the city becomes willy nilly more democratic.[20]

Similar causes of revolution are to be found in aristocracies (according to Aristotle's definition, constitutions where the criterion for receiving full political rights is virtue rather than wealth). The fundamental cause of the overthrow of an aristocracy or a *politeia* is a bad mixture in the constitution so that the former becomes too oligarchic and the latter too democratic. In these situations either the imbalance becomes permanent or there is a violent reaction to the opposite. As an afterthought Aristotle notes the danger of small changes in a constitution (a basis for a later revolution), and he repairs what is a major omission in his account by referring to the possibility of foreign interference. The examples he takes are the Athenian destruction of oligarchies and the Spartan destruction of democracies.[21]

The following discussion about the preservation of constitutions not surprisingly does not deal with the multiplicity of threats that Aristotle has detailed. Basically he believes that the chief safeguard is respect for the law. Aristocracies and oligarchies are maintained by diplomacy with all those who are not full citizens and the democratic treatment of all who are. Control must be exercised over the economic balance of a society, so that adjustments must be made to property qualifications during economic success and any excess of wealth and power should be checked by ostracising the individual concerned. The legislator should ensure that there is a built-in majority in his society who desire the continuance of the constitution and should keep his eye above all on the mean and the middle class.[22]

The merits of Aristotle's analysis of *stasis* and its roots are patent. A great many different possible causes are mentioned, and those which are central become the clearer because they are set against the background of the previous analysis of society in the city and the various forms of constitution. The most important of these is the economic factor, the imbalance between rich and poor, which Aristotle recognises as a potential cause of conflict, although he does not believe that it should be eliminated, merely controlled. He also brilliantly picks out the rival ideologies of democrat and oligarch, in his view both mistaken, the one because its aim is universal and absolute equality, the other because it pursues systematic inequality. Thus, he did not see the class struggle as simply a striving by the poor to better themselves at the expense of the rich: he realised that it consisted equally in the rich abusing their privilege of wealth to take more than their proper share in the community. He has no illusions about oligarchs, citing the parody of the democratic oath sworn by some of them, 'I shall be an enemy of the people and devise whatever mischief I can for them.'[23] Thus, the central framework of his theory has balance and coherence, while he understands that in practice a multitude of special factors — constitutional, personal, even geographical — may lead to political divisions.

One major defect of the analysis of *stasis* we have already noticed — the failure to weigh the relative importance of different factors in particular situations. For example, Aristotle never asks how far the conflict between rich and poor was itself sufficient to produce civil strife in a city or if it required the stimulus of intervention by a power like Athens or Sparta or some special, perhaps personal factor, to ignite it. His reply might have been that he was not concerned with the historian's task of explaining past events, but with providing rules and warning examples for legislators. In their work the balance between social classes and the corresponding balance in institutions were critical. They should be aware of the other factors too, but these would usually be outside their control.

A second criticism is that, although he gives an exhaustive and fair account of everything which may go wrong in an oligarchy or aristocracy (and for that matter in a monarchy or tyranny), his treatment of democracy is over-simple. I can do no more than notice here Aristotle's ambivalent treatment of democracy in the *Politics*. We find one of the best analyses of democratic principles in antiquity and an endorsement of the value of majority opinion, but in contrast expressions of regret about the development of Athenian democracy after the Persian Wars as well as the relegation of democracy to the ranks of the deviant constitutions in the main theory.[24]

His chief explanation of the overthrow of democracy is that demagogues brutally attack men of property either by private accusations or by spearheading popular campaigns and force them into a conspiracy. Thus, as in Herodotus, democracy is overthrown by the reaction it provokes. Aristotle also entertains the view put forward by Plato in *Republic* VIII, that the aggressive demagogue may become himself a tyrant. As we have seen, he regards this as ancient history, in spite of the fact that his best instance is Dionysius I, and he does not consider any special factors that may be involved. He implies that a democracy is on the whole tolerated by its oligarchic opponents unless it gets too aggressive, but he does not take into account at this point the occasions when a democracy was overthrown when it was in some way weak. He knows the importance of military success or failure in boosting or depressing the status of a section of the community,[25] but he does not apply this to the anti-democratic revolutions in Athens and Syracuse in the late fifth century. Indeed it is striking how he fails to give an adequate account of the revolutions in Athens about which he was well informed. He ascribes the revolution of 411 to deceit of the *demos* by the Four Hundred, when they alleged that in this way the Persian king would give them money to fight the Spartans. But he does not consider further the origin and methods of the conspiracy, and he says nothing about the revolution of 404.[26] In short the historian's main objection to Aristotle's *Politics* here must be that it is not empirical enough and does not explain some of the most interesting phenomena.

There is no doubt that in general the *Politics*, apart from its philosophical merits, is a valuable historical document in that it epitomises many of the attitudes and values of the citizen of a Greek city and shows an intelligent Greek's appreciation of the problems generated by the city. The importance of the conflict between rich and poor and of faction among the aristocracy in Aristotle's work are fair reflections of their importance in Greek politics, as can be judged by the evidence examined in the present work. I doubt, however, whether we can draw from the *Politics* specific conclusions about the development of *stasis* and the fear of *stasis* in the fourth century BC. Most of Aristotle's themes are not new. The dangers of inequality between rich and poor and of aristocratic ambition were seen by Solon, and oligarchic faction was stressed by Herodotus. In Herodotus also and in Plato can be found the elements of Aristotle's criticism of the instability of democracy. Nor does Aristotle suggest in his text or by his examples that there was a particular crisis facing the Greek city in his own time, as Isocrates does (with deliberate tendentiousness) in his pamphlets.[27]

Moreover, for all his analysis of the various forms of turbulence, there is no sign that Aristotle anticipated a fundamental revolution in the society or the city-state, such as might lead, for example, to the liberation of slaves or the creation of a communist society among its citizens. The poor, led by their demagogues, may attack the rich, while the rich themselves may form a conspiracy against the *demos*, but in the end the assumption is that the basic social structure will remain — the few, who are wealthy, the many, who are poor, and in between them a middle class, which is only likely to be considerable in large cities. Again, Aristotle does not foresee a mass revolt by those who are destitute: such men will merely turn to petty crime.

This may seem a paradox in view of his admission that inequality of property was a fundamental cause of *stasis*. However, he sees the resentment evoked by differences in wealth as a motive force among those who are already equal in liberty to the rich, that is, among citizens, who had at least a minimum status within society and on the whole would have preferred to build on this rather than jeopardise the society which gave it meaning. Moreover, the raids on the wealthy are assumed to take place under the leadership of demagogues as part of the political process. This may lead to revolution, when a demagogue seizes power as a tyrant. But, this situation apart, in his view the danger is that a democracy will collapse, because the threatened aristocrats band together in an oligarchic conspiracy against it, not that the rich will be overthrown in a redistribution of property.

Notes

1. Thuc. III.82-3; Hdt. III.82 (in my view one source for the cycle of constitutions in Polybius VI.7-9).
2. Plato, *Rep.* VIII, esp. 555b ff.; Ar., *Pol.* 1310b, cf. 1305a.
3. *Pol.* 1304a, 1304b.
4. 1252b ff., esp. 1253a, 1255b, 1256b. Cf. 1277b.
5. 1261a-3a. Cf. 1257b-8a.
6. 1266a-7a.
7. 1266b-7a; 67a-b. Cf. 1280a, 1301a.
8. 1267b.
9. 1269a, 1272b, 1273b.
10. Variation according to relative strength of classes — 1289b-90a; middle class — 1295b-6a.

11. 1292b, 1279a-b.
12. 1290bff.; esp. 1291a-b, 1292b. Cf. *Eth. Nic.* 1160a-b on the six forms.
13. 1296b; Thuc. III.83. There is no evidence that the middle class was a force for stability at Athens, when revolution threatened.
14. 1302b, 1303a, 1306b, 1308a-b.
15. 1301a. Cf. 1280a, 1266b-7a; *Eth. Nic.* 1131a.
16. 1301b ff.
17. 1301b-3a.
18. 1303a-4b. Cf. 1274a.
19. 1304b-5a. Cf. 1310b.
20. 1305a-6b.
21. 1306b-7b.
22. 1308a-9b. Aristotle goes on to consider how monarchies and tyrannies are overthrown by *stasis* and conversely preserved, but the discussion of *stasis*, as he himself admits, largely repeats what has been said before in the discussion of oligarchy.
23. 1310a.
24. 1317a ff.; 1281a-2a; 1273b-4a.
25. 1304a.
26. 1304b.
27. Isoc. 6.64-9, 7.31-5, 51-2, 15.159-60. Since Newman (1887, I, 520ff., IV, 275ff.), discussion of Aristotle's views on *stasis* has been inadequate. Wheeler, 1951, breaks the ice, but is weak on history; Aalders, 1965, makes some useful points in his discussion of the 'mixed constitution'; Thomas' unpublished thesis, 1978, chs. 6 and 9, has valuable analysis and criticism of Aristotle's method.

8 THE IMPORTANCE OF CIVIL STRIFE IN THE CLASSICAL CITY

It is almost too easy to draw a moral or deduce a necessity from the history of the Greek cities in the fourth century: their perpetual external and civil wars left them at the mercy of a new power, the ruthless and single-minded Philip of Macedon. Yet it is not immediately clear how far political behaviour in the cities had declined from what it had been in the fifth century, their supposed zenith, nor is it easy to pick out significant changes in their political organisation or their social and economic conditions.

If we set the period 470-400 against 400-330 BC, we can hardly say that there was more war among the Greeks in the latter period than the former. One might argue that the fourth century saw more fighting on the mainland of Greece itself, whereas much of the great Peloponnesian War took place in Athens' overseas empire. Yet there remains a substantial amount of fighting about which we are not very well informed – for example Sparta's struggles with dissident members of the Peloponnesian League between 470 and 464, the land operations of the first Peloponnesian War, and the smaller wars after 431, which Thucydides mentions in passing, such as that between Mantinea and Tegea in winter 423-422.[1] We may get a misleading impression of the quantity of fighting from the fullness of the sources on the fourth century.

When the incidence of *stasis* in these two periods is compared, the result is similar and there are the same reasons for caution. Certainly, we know more about *stasis* in the Athenian Empire in the fifth century and more about *stasis* on the Greek mainland in the fourth. However, in spite of our ignorance of the internal politics of the cities of the Peloponnesian League in the first period and of those of the members of Athens' second confederacy, there are sufficient pointers to indicate what is missing – e.g. the creation of democracy in Elis in the mid-fifth century on the one hand and the changes of government in Chios, Lesbos and Rhodes after the Social War on the other.[2] It would be more reasonable to take the beginning of the Peloponnesian War as a turning-point, inasmuch as Peloponnesian strategy in particular was based on the exploitation of *stasis* among Athens' allies. Yet, as we have seen this policy had precedents before the Persian Wars.

The chief elements in *stasis* in the fourth century were those with which we have already become familiar. First, the struggle for power among wealthy *dunatoi* – the archaic form of *stasis* which survived in the groups surrounding eminent individuals in fourth-century struggles. Secondly, the conflict over constitutions, which had given a new dimension to the conflicts of the *dunatoi* from the time Cleisthenes chose to woo the people with a political programme in order to defeat Isagoras. Thirdly, intervention in both these forms of conflict by foreign powers. In the fifth century BC rivalry between the two great powers polarised the antagonism between democracy on the Athenian model and the oligarchic *isonomia* favoured by Sparta. In the fourth century Athens was not so assiduous in promoting democracy among her confederacy as before, but on the mainland the democratic standard was picked up by the Thebans and their Arcadian allies, both of whom, like the Athenians in 507, acquired a revolutionary fervour in the course of liberating themselves from Spartan domination.

The fourth element – that of class conflict between the *dunatoi* and the *demos* – is perhaps more significant in the fourth century than before, although it was not evoked in every conflict between oligarchs and democrats, for example those in Phleious or that at Mantinea in 370.[3] The *demos* in many cities seems to have been more embittered against the rich than before and more prepared to act ruthlessly in its own interest. During the Peloponnesian War there were comparatively few genuine popular movements, those at Corcyra, Argos and Mytilene, all called forth by extremes of oppression or misery. In the fourth century the common people of Argos once again reacted violently to a plot by the wealthy; that of Corcyra also showed independence (to judge from the support of an Athenian commander for an oligarchic government).[4] Hostility to the upper class as a whole is attested at Phigaleia in 375 and must be inferred from the accounts of Sicyon under Euphron's tyranny (it is hard otherwise to account for Euphron's subsequent consecration as a liberator).[5] The expulsion of the Spartans from Thebes in 379-378 was brought about by an aristocratic plot which kindled a renascent nationalism, but Thebes subsequently became a refuge for the people from the Boeotian cities still controlled by Sparta.[6] At Tegea the faction advocating federation in 370 expected general popular support, and it seems that the original policy of the Arcadian federation was to satisfy the aspirations of the people by providing democratic organs of federal government, which could override the local *dunatoi* of the cities. The brutality at Corinth in 393 may be in part attributable to Argive influence on the city's democratic leaders, but the scale of the attack suggests widespread popular participation in' what amounted to a political revolution.[7] Finally, to look outside Greece proper, we have seen in detail how at Syracuse Dionysius I came to power through exploiting public resentment against the rich, and how even the tyranny of Dion later began as a popular crusade.

It is hardly surprising that socio-economic explanations have been sought by scholars for the intensification of hostility between rich and poor, in particular in worsening conditions of agriculture and greater pressure by landowners on tenants and debtors.[8] The difficulty is the lack of evidence for this, except perhaps in Athens, where in any event there were no significant conflicts between democrats and oligarchs between 403 and the death of Alexander the Great in 323. Certainly, both Aristotle and Demosthenes in their different ways attest the problem of maintaining the poor in the latter half of the fourth century.[9] Again, there is evidence of the concentration of property in fewer hands.[10] However, even if we ascribe the increase in poverty to the concentration of property among the rich (and it is not clear how far the rich had expropriated peasants and ceased to employ free labour), we cannot transfer this conclusion necessarily to other cities at different stages of development.[11] There is a frequently quoted passage in the contemporary writer on siegecraft Aeneas (14.1), to the effect that during a siege one should assure oneself of the loyalty of the poor by liberating debtors from interest, or part of the principal of their debt, and by providing those in need with the necessities of life. This is certainly revealing about the general conditions of life in the Greek world in the fourth century, but it does not follow from this that these were worse than in the preceding century.

The increased participation in civil strife by the common people in their own interest seems to me to have resulted from greater political consciousness, or class consciousness, if we do not interpret that term too strictly. In Corinth, for example, it is evident that the people learnt directly from the experiences of their Argive allies.[12] The fortunes of the Athenian *demos* under the Thirty would have had their effect across the border in Boeotia and contributed to the vigour with which the Spartans were repulsed there after 379. In general, when after 387 Sparta adopted a policy of repressing the moderate democracies among her allies, which she had previously tolerated, this spread throughout southern Greece the acrimony which in the fifth century had characterised Argive and Corcyrean politics. However, it is difficult to detect a positive programme behind most of the outbreaks of violence against the wealthy. On the whole, they were either reprisals for previous oppression or defensive measures against suspected plots. We do not hear of social or economic demands as we do in sources on early Roman history. If anything, the issue was the preservation of the constitutional privileges of the *demos* — in essence a political rather than a socio-economic aim. However, these privileges may have helped to protect the livelihood of the poor by securing their status in the community and ensuring their access to justice, for example in disputes over land and debt. An unusual instance of a political demand with economic overtones was the attempt by the poor *eparitoi* in the Arcadian federal army in 363 to resist the change of policy towards the funding of the army, because it would lead to their unemployment.[13]

In this respect then, the greater political involvement of the common people, we may speak of a progression in the history of civil strife — one which probably owed much to the lead of the Athenian *demos* in 404-403. Yet on the whole there was little new about fourth-century *stasis* and, if Greek political history seems more turbulent, this was caused by the complexity of the conflicts between the cities, which made not only war but civil strife more diffuse and less coherent than they had been, even if their sheer volume had not increased. In the fifth century, politics in Greece were dominated by the attempts of Athens and Sparta to establish hegemony, and this gives a greater appearance of purpose both to inter-city wars and the civil strife associated with them. In the fourth century, on the other hand, the demolition of Spartan hegemony, although it created autonomy and some experiments in federalism, led to no solid power constellation nor a new political direction in Greek affairs, until these were provided by Macedon. The acts of violence in the cities, however important to the participants, do not gain added significance through contributing to a general political movement. As for the inter-city wars that nourished the civil violence, these often seem a habit which might be justified by the pursuit of glory but not by the material gains in prospect.

The provisions for assistance against revolution, which are an interesting feature of some fourth-century peace treaties, are a symptom of the turbulence of the period. They should not, however, be interpreted as evidence of fears of general social upheaval impending. They find their natural place in the context in which they appear — wars and their settlement. Indeed, they emphasise the interdependence of civil violence and war. The decree of the Arcadian federation passed between 365-364 and 363-362,[14] in which such provisions first appear, was made at the end of a decade of revolutions backed by foreign forces, mainly the Boeotians and their allies. Similar clauses appear in the alliance between Athens, Arcadia, Achaia, Elis and Phleious, made in 362-361 after the battle of Mantinea and in the Athenian alliance with Thessaly the following year.[15] The revolutionary actions envisaged by the treaties were not merely matters of personalities or factions but actions against the fundamental constitution of the communities concerned, which would almost certainly have been mounted from outside.[16] The treaties may not have reduced the likelihood of foreign intervention in civil strife but increased it, since a city could call on its allies to repress such challenges. Viewed crudely, they were simply guarantees to the regimes currently in power. When Philip incorporated a clause of this kind into the foundation charter of the League of Corinth,[17] he no doubt foresaw the legitimate opportunities this gave Macedon to protect favoured regimes, but the Greek associates probably by then accepted the stability of internal politics as a *sine qua non* of the maintenance of good international relations. The development of Greek civil strife necessitated that any agreement between cities should entail a restriction on internal autonomy.

One development which has been associated with the decline of the city-state through international warfare and internal violence is the rise in importance of the mercenary soldier. From what I have said earlier it is clear that I do not believe that this led to any growth of civil strife, but the question remains whether it affected the quality of the civil strife that occurred.

Some tyrants – for example the two Dionysii and Dion in Syracuse, Clearchos in Herakleia-on-Pontos[18] and Euphron in Sicyon – owed their positions largely to the backing of mercenary troops. Although a tyrant might seize power through popular support, it is difficult to see how he could have maintained himself in power in a developed city-state without a guard of professional soldiers, and the mercenary was an obvious choice for such a task. Yet if such men were not available, similar guards could be recruited from the citizen-body: indeed Dionysius' guard was in part drawn from Syracusan citizens.[19] It cannot be said therefore that mercenaries were an essential precondition for tyranny. A mercenary force might also be recruited by a prospective tyrant for a *coup d'état*, but it was unlikely to be successful without support either from the citizen-body or abroad, as the careers of Dion and Euphron show.

Nor had mercenaries suddenly become available in the fourth century. Greeks had been serving alien cities or foreign kings, often to earn a living when in exile, sometimes through frustration at home, since the days of Archilochus and the brothers Alcaeus and Antimenidas. The employment by the Athenians of Argives and Mantineans after their cities had made peace with Sparta in 418-417 is an interesting feature of the latter part of the Peloponnesian War. Mercenary helpers (*epi-kouroi*) had been associated with tyrants since the days of Peisistratus and Polycrates; they had also been recruited to assist in civil strife during the Peloponnesian War.[20]

A connection may be made, however, between civil violence and the mercenary in the reverse direction. The outcome of *stasis* was usually the exile of the leading members of the defeated group, perhaps several hundred. Many of these would have been driven to mercenary service for a livelihood. It was such men whom Alexander the Great wished to restore to their cities at the conclusion of his Asiatic campaign (we hear of 20,000 exiles and 6,000-8,000 mercenaries).[21] Yet the vicious circle was not necessarily completed. When exiles embarked on mercenary service, they were likely to become dispersed and less of a threat to the regime which had expelled them. Certainly they swelled the pool of mercenaries available and may be thought on that account to have increased the likelihood of war. However, it is a melancholy fact that there does not seem to have been a shortage of mercenaries before the reign of Alexander the Great. The supply was always there; it was the demand that fluctuated.

The international element in classical civil strife and the struggle over constitutions have their counterparts in more recent and contemporary history. However, on the whole Greek *stasis* seems a much more limited affair, and it is worth considering why several features of more recent civil strife do not figure in this account.

A class struggle in the Marxist sense could not occur for two main reasons. The first is that there was no labour market as such, nor a separate sector of economic activity, in which men could confront one another as employers and employees. There was certainly a conflict between those with and without property, but this was not on the whole one between the owners of the means of production and their labour force, nor even necessarily between landlords and tenants (although this opposition must have occurred on occasions),[22] but rather between two ranks in society whose relationship had to a great extent been sanctioned by the laws of the community. What the poor eventually came to desire was not so much a change in the system but a fresh start in the shape of cancellation of debts or reassignment of land. The free poor preferred not to act as hired labourers for private individuals but as independent peasants and craftsmen. Their aim was not to improve the conditions for selling their labour but to avoid that kind of labour altogether. Their pressure on the wealthy was most profitably exercised through politics in order to secure for themselves advantages embodied in law.[23]

The second obvious explanation for the absence of a class struggle is the schism between free labour and slaves. Occasionally slaves might be summoned to take part in revolutionary activity with promises of freedom. Both oligarchs and the *demos* appealed to the slaves at Corcyra in 427, only the *demos* successfully. We hear that Iphikrates threatened to use the Chian slaves in a revolution c. 388, and the Athenians may have exploited them earlier, when trying to regain control of Chios in 412-411.[24] Yet in the vast majority of civil struggles slaves had no part. One may seek theoretical explanations for this in the distinction drawn between free men and those who were instruments destined to obey their masters. More significant, however, was their lack of shared interests with the free poor. They had neither constitutional rights nor land to fight for. Their only reason for engaging in civil violence was an offer of freedom or some other reward.

Furthermore, slaves rarely, if at all, revolted on their own account, as they did in the Roman world later. The exceptional outbreaks occurred when a great number of slaves were congregated together. In Chios the slaves regularly escaped to the mountains and raided the farms from there. Moreover, there was, perhaps in the fourth century, a slave-king called Drimachos, who received a hero-cult after his death and clearly became a centre of folk-lore.[25] The helots provide a parallel to this. However, they were not chattel-slaves but conquered peoples still tied to the land that they once had owned, so that their resentment of slavery was aggravated by suppressed nationalism. The docility of the majority of slaves may be attributed to their lack of organisation and of homogeneity. They were usually scattered among various households, living under different conditions, and had sprung from different races and backgrounds. The normal reaction of slaves, like that of certain peasants, to ill-treatment was flight to a place where their status did not matter.[26]

If the class struggles characteristic of capitalist industrial society are irrelevant, what about the types of pre-industrial violence, which have recently been studied with such profit by Hobsbawm, Rudé and others?[27] Most of them, I believe, can be documented in the ancient world at a later date. Crowd violence in cities, as portrayed by Rudé, is not, however, a feature of the city-state. On the one hand, as we have seen in Chapter 1, there occurred even in Athens the private violence that one might expect in a community which, however free from major social divisions, had few police and did not attach great weight to enforcing law and order through public authority.[28] On the other hand, when the grievances of larger groups were brought to the surface, they found expression either through the constitutional machinery of the state or through violence under political leadership and usually with specific political aims. Unlike the members of pre-industrial crowds in western Europe, full citizens in classical cities were not kept at a distance from those who controlled their society; when they resorted to violence, it was as the *ultima ratio* of the political life, in which they all had some share, however small. Moreover, those who were wholly or partially disfranchised through the existence of a narrow oligarchy or tyranny, only seem to have used their physical strength in response to a previous attack on them or because of specific pressure from those in power. Thus, in spite of frequent corn shortages we have very little evidence of anything resembling a food riot in this period. The revolt of the *demos* at Mytilene in 427 is the best example, but this happened during a siege and under an oligarchy, where other factors were at work. The alleged attempt at a tyranny by Spurius Maelius at Rome was also associated with a corn shortage, and we may suspect the same of other incidents in the Struggle of the Orders there.[29] Yet these events were part of a more general political conflict.

In explanation I would suggest that the greater social coherence of the city-state, its sense of community and probably also the persistance of some patron-client relations between the *dunatoi* and the *demos* prevented the emergence of the robust forms of social protest characteristic of the eighteenth century AD. If we knew more about the struggle between patricians and plebeians in early Rome, perhaps some parallels would appear. Certainly, the tradition of 'popular justice' seems to have been stronger there than in the Greek world. But on our present evidence the everyday violence in Rome was on a small scale, while the major secessions threatened rather than used violence and, I believe, were characterised by the participation of many of the community's soldiers.[30]

In the countryside we do not find the limited uprisings against food prices, taxes, machines and conditions of employment, typical in eighteenth and nineteenth-century England and France. The large-scale *jacquerie* or peasant revolt is perhaps attested on a few occasions. A good example, if the evidence is trustworthy, is the struggle between the wealthy (*Ploutis*) and the *Cheiromacha* or *Gergithes* at Miletus.[31] This may have had racial overtones, as a movement by those of Asiatic descent against the families of Ionian colonists. Other similar risings are not merely peasant revolts but expressions of racial and nationalist feeling. The Helot revolts were essentially attacks on an occupying power, although they were probably stimulated by pressures on the Helots as agricultural workers. Similar antagonism to exploitation by alien landowners may lie behind the Libyan revolts against the Carthaginians and the emergence of the Bruttians in Italy. In 396-395 a body of Carthaginian allies, both free and slave, numbering 200,000, of mixed origins and without proper leaders, seized Tunis and kept Carthage under siege until their own food ran out (it should be noted that Diodorus later distinguishes between Libyans like these and the Nomads, the herdsmen of the Sahara and its fringes).[32] In the middle of the fourth century the Bruttians appeared in Calabria, a multiracial group said to have been mainly composed of runaway slaves. At first they contented themselves with raiding the Greek cities in the area, which presumably housed many of their former masters. Later they captured whole cities and established a form of federal government of their own.[33]

Banditry was to flourish by land in the Hellenistic and Roman periods. Although the robber on the road was a feature of myth, there is little evidence for such activity in the classical period apart from Thucydides' general comment on the north-west of Greece, and this contrasts with the evidence for piracy.[34] It is possible that in classical Greece the man who in other periods would have become a bandit, regularly took to the sea: he could thus operate further from home and so avoid offence to his own neighbours. However, we may have a misleading impression through the chance selection of our evidence. One fifth-century document certainly, the list of those publicly cursed at Teos, comprises equally the brigand and the pirate.[35] Social banditry, that is banditry deliberately undertaken to redress the balance between the peasants and the richer landowners, may have occurred in some contexts. Indeed, one may classify the actions of the legendary slave-leader Drimachos on Chios under this heading. A striking feature of his leadership was robbery according to fixed weights and measures and the sealing of the storehouse doors afterwards — methods which recall a present-day system of protection.[36]

Nevertheless, within the citizen-body of a classical city antagonisms between the poor peasants and the rich did not reach such a high pitch, even if the city had a large country area (*chōra*) attached to it. In Attica Solon's reforms reduced the pressures on the peasantry for centuries to come. Even though a few decades later men who were poor and in debt joined Peisistratus' faction, there was no question of an uprising throughout the countryside. At Syracuse at the time of Dionysius' *coup* the city poor seem to have had a greater grievance against the wealthy men who were the current leaders of the city, than the rural proletariat. If

the *demos* at Leontini turned into a kind of *jacquerie* in the years before 415, this was because their own aristocracy and the Syracusans had
deliberately thrown them out of their city.[37] On the whole, like the
city proletariat, the peasants seem to have been reconciled to their
betters by membership of a political community, which gave the poor
some, even if indirect, constitutional access to the levers of power. If
they resorted to violence, it was through their involvement with what
went on in the city.

In fact, the family or tribal nature of the classical city,[38] by virtue
of which the citizens felt themselves part of a single organism, gave
much of the violence there its peculiar quality. Whatever the precise
origin of any outbreak of *stasis*, it provided a retort into which all the
existing antagonisms could be poured, whether they derived from class,
political beliefs or personal relationships. In the period before 500 the
demos were frequently spectators; later they were usually drawn into
the struggles of the *dunatoi*. Conversely, any conflict between rich and
poor tended to entail a split among the *dunatoi*, since some of these
would champion the cause of the poor through a mixture of paternalist
altruism, personal ambition and hostility to their fellow aristocrats.
Conflicts which penetrated deep into the citizen-body were not quickly
decided. *En masse* the *demos* had the power to overwhelm oligarchic
opponents, but it was not always so easy, since an oligarchic group
might number up to about 1,000 men, perhaps an eighth of the adult
male citizens, in a medium-sized city, while it was even harder for any
oligarchic group to subdue the *demos* by its own resources. This was
not the first cause of foreign intervention in *stasis*, whose genesis lay
rather in the ambitions of powerful men and states in the Archaic Age.
However, it was a strong motive for the parties in *stasis* to seek help
from abroad, especially when there was always a state whose support
could be expected on ideological grounds.

The importance of foreign intervention is a warning of the limits of
this investigation into civil violence. One cannot treat the internal life
of a city and the strife this caused as a separable category of behaviour,
which contains all the answers to its own problems. The evidence that
we have considered shows that from about 500 onwards it was war
between cities which was the greatest stimulus to fighting inside cities.
The material for political and social conflicts existed there already, but
war ignited them. Thucydides stressed the moral influence of war on
civil conflict, comparing it to that of a violent schoolmaster, but he also
pointed out that it provided a context and support for conflicts which
otherwise might never have occurred. The pressure caused by war might

also bring to a head internal divisions, when there was no foreign intervention in the affairs of a city, as at Syracuse in 405. War was indeed the main cause of political change in the ancient world at this period, especially for the smaller cities. Their inward-looking exclusiveness and solidarity tended to be conservative and only underwent change through convulsions. By contrast, Rome, the city which achieved political maturity in the early centuries of the Republic through flexibility and adapting itself to political pressures, was far more mixed in its population and open to outsiders.

In the Hellenistic world the old patterns of civil strife were to persist and international wars remained one of their chief causes, until Rome brought Greece and the eastern Mediterranean closely under her supervision during the second century BC. The cessation of war between Greek cities then brought to an end *stasis*, as Thucydides knew it. The cities had peace under oligarchic governments, occasionally disturbed by uprisings of their *demos* over a social issue. However, other forms of violence arose among those subjected to the great Hellenistic powers, while Rome, which for centuries had resolved her internal conflicts without serious bloodshed and had found in imperial expansion a substitute for civil conflict, finally generated within herself a violence in which the rivalries and frictions typical of the city were fought to an issue with the resources of the whole Mediterranean.

Notes

1. Thuc. IV.134, V.29.1, 31.3, 32.2.
2. Chapter 3, p. 90, Chapter 6, p. 235. On the Peloponnesian League cf. Thuc. V.33.1 on *stasis* among the Parrasioi in Arcadia.
3. Chapter 6, pp. 225, 231.
4. Diod. XV.57.3-58; Isoc. 5.52; Aeneas, *Pol.* 11. 7-15.
5. Diod. XV.40.1-2; Xen., *Hell.* VII.3.
6. Xen. V.4.46.
7. Xen. VI.5, IV.4.
8. Mossé, 1962, 217.
9. Ar., *Pol.* 1320a-b; Dem. 1.19, 3.1, 10.35; ps. Dem. 13.1-3, 59.4-6; cf. Hyp. 5.26; Mossé, 1962, 158, 308.
10. Xen., *Oec.* 20.22 (Ischomachos); Isaeus, 11.41ff.; Dem. 23.207-8; ps. Dem. 42.5, 31, 43.69. Mossé, 1962, 40.
11. IG XII.5.872 shows a number of small properties on Tenos, although some belong to the same persons. The decree about the return of exiles to Tegea (GHI II.202) likewise implies a number of modest holdings.
12. Xen. IV.4.2-6; cf. V.2.6 for a group of alleged 'argolisers' in power in Mantinea in 386.
13. Xen. VII.4.36-7.
14. SEG XXII.339, b-c.

15. GHI II, 144. 24; 147. 16, 147. 26.

16. It is clear that Thessaly was not particularly concerned with an internal social upheaval, as there is no reference to a revolt of the *penestai*. By contrast in 421 Athens agreed to help Sparta against the Helots (Thuc. V.23.3).

17. GHI II, 177. 11; ps. Dem. 17.10, 15.

18. On Clearchos see Appendix II.

19. Diod. XIII.96.1.

20. Hdt. I.64.1, III.45.3; Thuc. II.33, III.73, 85, IV.52, 56, VI.43, VII.62; see Parke, 1933.

21. Diod. XVII.109.1, 113.3, XVIII.8-9, 21; Curtius X.2.4-7; Justin XIII.5.2-5; cf. Ar. fr. 1.16; GHI II, 201, 202.

22. One example probably is the strife between the *Ploutis* and *Cheiromacha* at Miletus, cf. Chapter 2, p. 55. Landlord-tenant conflict was also one aspect of the strife between the helots, and other groups like them, and their masters.

23. Austin and Vidal-Naquet, 1977, 20-6.

24. Thuc. III.73, VIII.40.2; Polyaen. III.23.

25. Athenaeus VI.265d-6e (Nymphodorus of Syracuse, FGH 572, F4); Laquer, RE XVII.1623-7.

26. See Finley, 1960, 67, citing examples of mass desertion in Thuc. VII.27.5, 75.5, VIII.40.2.

27. See especially Hobsbawm, 1959; Rudé, 1964.

28. On the Scythian archers see Oehler, RE 2.III.692-3. Cf. Chapter 4, p.

29. Thuc. III.27-8. On Maelius see Lintott, 1970.

30. On 'popular justice' see Lintott, 1968, 6. On secessions see above Chapter 2, p. 73.

31. Chapter 2, p. 55.

32. Diod. XIV.77, cf. XX.3.3 for later Libyan hostility to Carthage, XX.55.4 and 57.3-4 for the distinction between Libyans and Nomads.

33. Diod. XVI.15; Justin XXIII.1.3-10; Strabo VI.1.2(253).

34. Thuc. I.5.

35. ML 30, B18 (ATPW 63).

36. See above, note 25.

37. Thuc. V.4.2-4.

38. Argued long ago by Fustel de Coulanges, *La Cité Antique*. Among recent authors see especially Lacey, 1968.

APPENDIX I: PROBLEMS IN THE OLIGARCHIC REVOLUTIONS

1. The Colonos Assembly

There has recently been an exceedingly ingenious attempt by Flach, 1977, to save the credit of Aristotle's account of the 411 revolution. Flach begins from two premisses, neither of which is acceptable to me, that Thucydides was not well informed about events at Athens in 411 and that his and Aristotle's accounts are of sufficiently similar material to be stitched together. In fact, Thucydides describes a brutal *coup d'état* with the minimum of constitutional operations; Aristotle a deliberate and amicable change of constitution, which was essentially a confidence trick by the Four Hundred (compare his judgement on the revolution in *Pol.* 1304b) but later went sour and had to be imposed by force. Flach tries to bridge the gap between the accounts by attributing to the Colonos assembly acts ascribed to it neither by Thucydides nor Aristotle (in order to complete the constitutional jigsaw Aristotle has left behind) – the approval of a detailed constitution for the Four Hundred; the grant of powers for a commission of 100 to draw up a new constitution as well as selecting the Five Thousand. He further postulates a meeting of an assembly, which called itself the Five Thousand and which selected a commission of 100, at some time between the Colonos assembly and the dismissal of the old council. Interestingly, from then on he believes Thucydides' account. Yet he cannot see that, if Thucydides has rightly portrayed the leaders of the Four Hundred, these elaborate manoeuvres are the last thing that they would have tolerated. From the point of view of methodology this sort of interpolation into a coherent and elaborately worked account cannot be sound, because thereby the validity of the rest of the account has been impugned.

2. The Second Oligarchic Conspiracy

The revival of the oligarchic *hetaireiai* is said to have occurred 'while there was still democracy' in Lys. 12.43, and in 13.5-8 the plotting is said to have begun at the time of peace negotiations with Sparta. Against this both Beloch, 1916, II.2.204, and Meyer, 1915, IV.663, argued that the plotting did not in fact occur until after Lysander's arrival in the Peiraeus, and they have been more recently followed by Hignett, 1952, 287, and Sealey, 1976, 379. Beloch's best argument is that Critias could not have returned before the fall of Athens because he was in exile, but *pace* Andokides' interpretation of the Patrokleides decree of 405 (1.80), the decree itself did permit the return of some exiles (And. 1.78; Lys. 12.47). The council described in Lys. 13.20-30 is not an oligarchic council but the democratic council of 500 which had abandoned its proper loyalties through corruption. Nor is the departure of two merchant ships in Lys. 13.25 proof that Lysander's blockade no longer existed (their arrival would have been another matter). Beloch in effect treats the whole of the first part of Lys. 13 against Agoratos as a misrepresentation. For in this it is clearly stated that the resistance of the generals and taxiarchs to the peace proposals and the counter-plot by Theramenes' friends took place before the surrender (Lys. 13.14-17, 34). Now we may admit that the speech has been slanted to heap on Agoratos the chief responsibility for the surrender and the overthrow of the democracy, but the transfer of a plot from after to before the surrender would not have been necessary in order to prove Agoratos' complicity in oligarchic murder and could easily have been refuted. Furthermore, Beloch's thesis involves postulating two visits by Lysander to Athens in 404, separated by an interval in which there was no Spartan presence in the city. This, to be sure, is Diodorus' story (XIV.3.4-5) — a version designed to exculpate Theramenes, in which Lysander is summoned by the hard-liners allegedly opposed to Theramenes. It is not, however, *pace* Beloch, Lysias' story in 12.71. There we are told that Theramenes summoned Lysander from Samos and the enemy army lodged in the town. The context makes it plain that Lysias is simply describing in a tendentious way the original surrender. In his view the assembly did not have a chance to decide its own fate until it met under Spartan military supervision. For what it is worth, there is no trace of two visits by Lysander to Athens in 404 to be found in Plutarch, *Lysander* 15.5. Finally, it is hardly credible that Lysander would have both retired himself and withdrawn the Spartan army before a new regime had been established.

3. The Constitution of the Thirty

Ath. Pol. 35.1 says that the council was of 500, as under the democratic regime; it also refers to a pre-selected body of 1,000 from whom officials were drawn. However, this need not imply a proper register: the term 1,000 may have been simply used by the Thirty for their supporters. In 35.2 we find some legal reforms – the abolition of the laws of Ephialtes and Archestratos about the Areopagos, the elimination of the *dikasterion* as the final court of appeal and the correction of some contentious points in Solon's legislation. However, in practice their legal processes took place before their own council in a summary and arbitrary manner (Xen., *Hell.* II.3.12; Lys. 13.36-8).

APPENDIX II: HERAKLEIA ON THE PONTOS

We have little evidence about civil strife in most of the cities of Asia Minor during the classical era. Herakleia is an exception, thanks to the number of historians and other writers who were its citizens, even though their work mainly survives to us in fragments or indirectly in general histories.

Herakleia was founded as a colony by the Boeotians and Megarians in the sixth century with a democratic constitution. The land for it was seized from an area for the most part occupied by the Maryandynoi, a people of mixed Thracian and Anatolian origin (Justin XVI.3.3-7, cf. Burstein, 1976, 6ff.). Not long after the settlement, the aristocracy were expelled by the popular leaders but returned and established an oligarchy (Arist., *Pol.* 1304b). Meanwhile, the Greeks had come into conflict with the native Maryandynoi and eventually resolved it by reducing them to a servile status — compared to that of the Spartan helots, Cretan *klarotai* and Thessalian *penestai* (Plato, *Laws* VI.776c-d; Strabo XII.3.4; Paus. V.26.7). They seem to have accepted their status as tribute-paying subjects of the city without attempting to rebel — in this respect more like their Thessalian and Cretan counterparts than the Helots.

It is possible that the overthrow of the democracy arose from jealousy over the uneven redistribution of the land captured from the Maryandynoi. At all events the oligarchy which ruled the enlarged territory progressed from a narrow group based on a few heads of families to a wider group including all adult male members of those families, until it reached the number of 600. The common people, moreover, were still allowed to vote in the law courts (Arist., *Pol.* 1305b). This constitution survived perhaps until the late fifth century, when a certain Eurytion was condemned in a public court for adultery and the political conflicts over his punishment led to the collapse of the oligarchy (Arist., *Pol.* 1306a, cf. 1305b). This should probably be placed in a wider context of Herakleia's inclusion among Athens' tribute-paying subjects in the assessment of 425 and Lamachos' expedition to the area (Thuc. IV.65; Justin XVI.3.10; ATL II, A9, IV.127; Burstein, 1976, 34ff.).

The democracy continued to rule at a time of considerable prosperity for Herakleia in the early fourth century, although about 370 it had to suppress an oligarchic military *coup d'état* (Aeneas Tacticus 11.7, 10a). Later there must have been a successful oligarchic plot. For by 364 there was an oligarchic government of 300 (Polyaenus II.30.2). Under pressure from the people who wanted a redivision of land and abolition of debt (Justin XVI.4), they called in Clearchos, an exiled aristocrat, who had studied at Athens under Isocrates and Plato and had been a friend of the Athenian general Timotheus (Memnon, FGH IIIB 434, F1; Suda, s.v. Klearchos; Diod. XV.81.5 for the date). He was summoned with a body of mercenaries to maintain security and supervise a settlement. He had obtained the mercenaries as a loan from a Mithridates (probably the son of Ariobarzanes, the Persian satrap of Hellespontine Phrygia) against a promise to place the city in Persian power, but he double-crossed Mithridates by seizing him and holding him to ransom. Later he betrayed the cause of the oligarchy by an appeal to the people like that of Dionysius I, and was elected *strategos autokrator* (Justin XVI.4.6-16; Polyaenus II.30). He purged the city ruthlessly of its old aristocracy and established a dynastic tyranny, although he himself succumbed to a conspiracy of 50 men led by Chion, another pupil of Plato, in 352 (Justin XVI.4.17-5.18; Diod. XVI.35.3; Memnon, FGH IIIB 434, F3-4; cf. the first century AD novelette in letters, *Chion of Heraclea*). The basic demands of the poor seem to have remained unsatisfied until the accession of Timotheos in 346-345 (ibid.).

Herakleia is an interesting parallel to Syracuse as a city which possessed democratic government for some time, but which found it difficult to subordinate the power of its wealthy citizens to the interests of the state. The lot of the poor at Herakleia was perhaps harsher initially than in fifth-century Syracuse, and the *dunatoi* had more freedom than their Syracusan counterparts. In the end, although the democracy was overthrown by an oligarchy, this too was destroyed by a man who imitated the methods of Dionysius I. Not only did Clearchos make generous promises to the people and exploit his mercenaries to the full to achieve power, but he also followed Dionysius' example when in power, redistributing land in the interest of his supporters and endeavouring to establish a new type of dynastic kingship (see Memnon F1; Suda, s.v.; Justin XVI.5.14-15). He proclaimed his debt to his exemplar by calling his son Dionysius.[1]

Note

1. On the political struggles of the fifth and fourth century see Burstein, 1976; Berve, 1967, I, 315, II, 679.

APPENDIX III: THESSALY

The struggles in Thessaly cannot for the most part be strictly classified as *stasis*, since they were not conflicts inside cities, but conflicts between individual cities belonging to the league (*koinon*). Although in the fourth century BC after the tyranny of Jason of Pherai, this league had for a time an *archon* as chief magistrate and a range of other civil and military officials, usually there was little or no central authority established constitutionally. From time to time the league created a long-term president or *tagos*, and by the fifth century there was a system of military and financial contributions. Socially Thessaly was characterised by its powerful aristocracy, who exploited a class of serfs called *penestai* resembling the helots, especially in so far as they were liable for military service. There were also free dependants of the rich, whom Dionysius of Halicarnassus compared to Roman clients. The cities were normally ruled by *dunasteiai*, narrow oligarchies, which were themselves subject to faction and frequently strove for ascendancy over the other oligarchies in Thessaly.[1]

At the time of Xerxes' expedition the Aleuadai of Larisa were kings in Thessaly (Hdt. VII.6.2, cf. 172), although their rule was not acceptable to all. After the Persian War Aristomedes and Angelos, perhaps the current Aleuad leaders, were deposed by the Spartans (Hdt. VI.72; Plut., *Mor.* 859C). In 455 shortly after their alliance with Thessaly the Athenians tried unsuccessfully to restore to his position Orestes, who is said to have been king of Thessaly (his city of origin is unknown) (Thuc. I.111.1; Diod. XI.83.3-4). In 431 there were two factions in Larisa and both sent their leaders, Polymedes and Aristonous on the expedition to help Athens (Thuc. II.22.3), while Pharsalos sent Menon. But seven years later, when Thessaly was still in theory allied to Athens, Pharsalians befriended the Spartan commander Brasidas and he was guided by a man from Larisa (Thuc. IV.78.1-2).

By the end of the century Thessaly under the Aleuad Aristippos was overshadowed by the powerful centralising king of Macedon, Archelaos, and by Lykophron, tyrant of Pherai. The Athenian exile Critias meanwhile was fomenting a revolution and arming the *penestai*, probably at Larisa (Xen., *Hell.* II.3.36). The Aleuadai planned an alliance with Archelaos, but there was opposition and eventually an alliance with Sparta was proposed instead. In fact, Lykophron defeated Larisa and

269

the other Thessalian cities in a battle at the time of the eclipse of September 404 (Xen., *Hell.* II.3.4). Probably before this battle the narrow oligarchy at Larisa was overthrown through an alliance between the city guard and the common people. The new magistrates, apparently wealthy manufacturers, admitted new citizens, perhaps from the *penestai*, whose elevation was ridiculed by the orator Gorgias (Ar., *Pol.* 1275b, 1305b). The constitution became sufficiently democratic to fear an oligarchy imposed by Sparta.[2] Aristippos meanwhile was loaned 4,000 men by the Persian prince Cyrus to assist him to recover his position, but these were withdrawn when Cyrus was ready for his march to Mesopotamia and Aristippos was told to come to terms with his opponents (Xen., *Anab.* I.1.10, 2.1). Archelaos failed to instal his protégé Hellanokrates in Thessaly and the latter in rancour joined in a plot to assassinate him (Ar., *Pol.* 1311b; Diod. XIV.37.6 makes the killing an accident). Larisa and Pherai remained at war, and in 395 the Larisan commander, Medeios, took Pharsalos from Sparta (Diod. XIV.82.5-6, cf. Xen., *Hell.* IV.3.3), presumably because she was backing Lykophron.

Our sources, which were never very satisfactory, now fail us completely. We must assume that hostilities in Thessaly lessened and that the constitution in Larisa probably slipped back into a more oligarchic form. Relations with Macedon improved. The Thessalians restored Amyntas to the Macedonian throne about 393 after his expulsion by the Illyrians (Diod. XIV.92.3). Subsequently Jason became tyrant of Pherae and about 375 *tagos* of all Thessaly, having persuaded Polydamas of Pharsalos under pressure to become his ally (Xen., *Hell.* VI.1.2ff.; Diod. XV.30.3-4). After Jason's death in 369 there was a dynastic struggle (Xen. VI.4.33ff.). One of his brothers, Polydoros, was murdered by the other, Polyphron, when both were colleagues in the tyranny. Polyphron then killed Polydamas of Pharsalos and eight other leading aristocrats there, presumably a rival faction, but was himself murdered by Polydoros' son, Alexander.

Alexander's domination of Thessaly was also ruthless and unpopular. The dissident Thessalians were backed by Theban expeditionary forces, which enjoyed little success until Alexander was defeated in 364 at Cynoscephalai (in a battle in which the Theban commander Pelopidas also died) and was forced to grant the cities of Thessaly their ancient autonomy (Diod. XV.80; Plut., *Pel.* 31-5.1). Athens, previously allied to Alexander, became the ally of the *koinon* and tore down the *stēlē* with the earlier treaty. In due course Alexander was assassinated by the brothers of his wife Thebe — Lykophron (II), Tisiphonos and Peitholaos (Plut., *Pel.* 35.3; Xen. VI.4.35ff.).

The Aleuadai of Larisa once again tried to recover their influence by appealing to Philip of Macedon. Eventually he campaigned in Thessaly and overthrew Lykophron (II) in spite of Phokian aid to Pherai (Diod. XVI.14, 35, 37-8; Dem. 18.295). However, the profit was to be largely Philip's, since he seized Larisa also and appropriated the revenues of Pagasai and Magnesia. After a period of indirect rule he eliminated tyrants from Larisa and Pherai, became Thessalian archon himself and brought all the cities more closely under his control by reviving the Thessalian regional tetrarchies.[3]

The struggles in Thessaly seem crude and primitive compared with those of southern Greece and the Aegean, since the issue was nearly always the power of a very few men (the only serious attempts to create a broader constitution, which are known to us, occurred at Larisa in the late fifth century). However, what happened in Thessaly was a portent for the future. The politics of their neighbours, the Macedonians, were even simpler — monarchy modified by assassination — and it was Macedonian power which came to dominate Greece.

Notes

1. Constitution — GHI II, 147; Syll[3] 274; Xen., *Hell.* VI.1.8; military contingents and taxes — Ar. fr. 497-8; Xen. VI.1.12, 19; *penestai* — Dem. 13.23, 23.199; Xen. VI.1.11; Ar., *Pol.* 1269a; Athen. VI.263e, 265b; Dion. Hal. II.9.2; *dunasteiai* — Thuc. IV.78.3. See in general on Thessalian politics Meyer, 1909; Westlake, 1935; Morrison, 1942; Sordi, 1958.

2. Thrasymachus, DK B.2; Ps. Herodes, *Peri Politeias* (K. Müller, *Oratores Attici* II, 189), especially §§ 4-6. See Wade-Gery, 1945, for the view that it was composed by Critias. The speaker tries to allay fears of an oligarchy imposed by Sparta, saying that the city had once such an oligarchy, but not long enough to profit from it. The implication is that the city is currently free from a *dunasteia* and can choose its future.

3. Justin VII.6.8-9; Diod. XVI.69.8; Dem. 1.22, 6.22, 9.26, 18.48; Ar., *Pol.* 1306a.

APPENDIX IV: PROFESSOR RUSCHENBUSCH'S VIEW OF GREEK CIVIL STRIFE

I read Ruschenbusch's book (1978) when this work was almost complete and, although I did not wish to develop an argument with him within the text of the book, I felt that I could not let his interpretation of Greek politics pass without explicit comment.

Ruschenbusch believes:

1. In the 'normal city' of c. 450-1,250 adult male citizens there were no tyrannies and, he implies, no *stasis* except perhaps when it was imported from outside through international conflicts. The tyrannies which occurred in the larger cities during the Archaic Age sprang simply from the competition for office among the larger aristocracies.

2. The strife which took place between 550 and 350 BC in the larger cities was caused by international conflicts impinging on the struggles between the aristocrats there. Indeed, there was no domestic issue to divide the governing class, except that of who should be in power.

3. During this period constitutional changes were merely a means by which a great power secured an appropriate political alignment in a subordinate city.

4. The groups involved in civil strife were always essentially small political *hetaireiai*, whether they were oligarchs or *demos*.

5. There was no serious move towards fundamental socio-economic reforms in this period, such as the redistribution of land, at least in the Greek homeland.

6. In so far as members of the *demos* outside the governing class took part in civil strife, it was because in the larger cities the artisans and hired labourers from the towns were drawn into the factional struggles by the leading men. The artisans chose on the whole to support Athens, because they profited from being members of the Athenian alliance through doing military service in the fleet. In consequence Sparta's partisans believed that alliance with Sparta was only possible under oligarchic government.

7. For all these reasons the conflict between rich and poor was not at the centre of internal struggles in the cities, as Aristotle thought. If such a conflict did occur between 550 and 350, it was an accidental

consequence of international politics. In the Archaic Age the resentment of the poor was channelled into the support of faction leaders and tyrants. It only once produced something of a social revolution – in Athens through Solon.

It should be clear from what I have said earlier that in spite of a measure of agreement I find this thesis one-sided and insecurely based on the evidence. My particular comments are:

A. Since on Ruschenbusch's taxonomy the 'normal city' is so small that its activities do not figure in our surviving sources, how can we know that it was never troubled by tyranny or strife?

B. How do we know that domestic issues did not divide the governing class, for example levels of taxation, forms of jurisdiction and of political organisation? Is Athens completely atypical?

C. Thucydides implies (III.82.1) that the conflict between the oligarchs and the leaders of the *demos* existed before the intervention by the great powers. Ruschenbusch himself admits the example of Epidamnus (Thuc. I.24.4). Nor was foreign policy the only cause elsewhere. The conflict at Megara in the early 420s was between oligarchs and democrats who were originally both hostile to Athens. The political revolution at Argos in the 460s did not change the city's hostility to Sparta and its desire to recover hegemony in the Argolid.

D. If we allow that Athens and Sparta had political ideologies, why should not other Greek states have had a preference on principle for oligarchy or democracy? The Argive attachment to democracy was forged before they became allies of Athens and itself was a motive power in politics during the fourth century.

E. Ruschenbusch, like most modern authors, seems to assume that a conflict between rich and poor takes the form of the poor assailing the position of the rich. In practice, the poor only acted in this way in Greece and the Aegean under considerable provocation. Ruschenbusch neglects the occasions when oligarchic groups already in power with foreign support at Corcyra, Samos and Athens, sought to increase their grip on society by further attacks on their opponents.

BIBLIOGRAPHY

I omit works listed under 'Abbreviations' at the front of the book and use the following abbreviations for periodicals:

ABSA   *Annual of the British School at Athens*
AJP   *American Journal of Philology*
CQ   *Classical Quarterly*
JHS   *Journal of Hellenic Studies*
JRS   *Journal of Roman Studies*
PCPS   *Proceedings of the Cambridge Philological Society*
ZPE   *Zeitschrift für Papyrologie und Epigraphik*

Aalders, C.J.D. (1965) 'Die Mischverfassung und ihre historische Dokumentation in den Politica des Aristoteles', *Entretiens Fondation Hardt*, 11, 201-44.

Adamesteanu, D. (1956) 'Osservazioni sulla battaglia di Gela nel 405 a.c.', *Kokalos* 2, 142-57.

— (1963) 'L'ellenizazione della Sicilia ed il momento di Ducezio', *Kokalos* 8, 167-98.

Alföldi, A. (1964) *Early Rome and the Latins*.

Anderson, J.K. (1971) *Ancient Greek Horsemanship*, Berkeley.

Andrewes, A. (1952) 'Sparta and Arcadia in the early fifth century', *Phoenix* 6, 1-5.

— (1953) 'The Generals in the Hellespont', *JHS* 73, 5-9.

— (1956) *The Greek Tyrants*, London.

— (1970) 'Lysias and the Theramenes Papyrus', *ZPE* 6, 35-8.

— (1971)(1) *Greek Society (The Greeks)*, Harmondsworth.

— (1971)(2) 'Two Notes on Lysander', *Phoenix* 25, 202-26.

— (1974) 'The Arginousai Trial', *Phoenix* 28, 112-22.

— (1976) 'Androtion and the Four Hundred', *PCPS*, n.s. 22, 14-25.

— (1978) 'The Opposition to Perikles', *JHS* 98, 1-8.

Asheri, D. (1966) 'Distribuzioni di terre nell'antica Grecia', *Memorie dell' Accademia di Torino*, 4th ser., no. 10.

— (1969) 'Leggi Greche sul problema dei debiti', *Studi Classici e Orientali*, 18, 5-117.

Aurenche, O. (1974) *Les groupes d'Alcibiades, de Leogoras et de Teucros*, Paris.

Austin, M.M. and Vidal-Naquet, P. (1977) *Economic and Social History of Ancient Greece: An Introduction*, London.

Barron, J.P. (1962) 'Milesian Politics and Athenian Propaganda c. 460-440 BC', *JHS* 82, 1-6.

— (1964) 'The Sixth Century Tyranny at Samos', *CQ* n.s. 14, 210-29.

Beloch, K.J. (1916) *Griechische Geschichte* II.2, Berlin/Leipzig.

Berve, H. (1956) *Dion*, Mainz.

— (1967) *Die Tyrannis bei den Griechen*, 2 vols., Munich.

Bòardman, J. (1972) 'Herakles, Peisistratus and sons', *Revue Archéologique*, 57-72.

Bockisch, G. (1965) *'Harmostai (431-387)'*, *Klio* 46, 129-239.

Boehringer, Chr. (1979) 'Zu Finanzpolitik und Munzprägung des Dionysios von Syrakus', in A. Mφrkholm and N. Waggoner (eds.), *Essays in Honor of Margaret Thompson*, Wetterau, 9-33.

Bohannan, P.J. (1957) *Justice and Judgement among the Tiv*, Oxford.

Bradeen, D.W. (1960) 'The Popularity of the Athenian Empire', *Historia* 9, 257-69.

Bruce, I.A. (1967) *Commentary on Hellenica Oxyrhyncia*, Cambridge.

Brunner, H. and Schwerin, C. von (1906) *Deutsche Rechtsgeschichte*, 2nd ed., 1906/1958, Leipzig/Berlin.

Brunnsäker, S. (1955) *The Tyrant-Slayers of Kritias and Nesiotes*, Lund.

Brunt, P.A. (1969) 'Euboea in the Time of Philip II', *CQ*, n.s. 19, 245-65.

Burstein, S.M. (1976) *Outpost of Hellenism: the emergence of Heraclea on the Black Sea*, Berkeley.

Calhoun, C.M. (1913) *Athenian Clubs in Politics and Litigation*, Austin, Texas.

Cartledge, P.A. (1977) 'Hoplites and Heroes', *JHS* 97, 11-27.

— (1979) *Sparta and Lakonia: a regional history 1300-362 BC*, London.

Cawkwell, G.L. (1963) 'Demosthenes' Policy after the Peace of Philokrates' II, *CQ*, n.s. 13, 200-13.

— (1978) 'Euboea in the late 340's', *Phoenix* 32, 42-67.

Christian, J. (1975) 'Mercenaires et partis politiques à Syracuse de 357 à 354', *Revue des Etudes Anciennes*, 77, 63-73.

Cloud, J.D. (1971) *'Parricidium* from the *lex Numae* to the *lex Pompeia de parricidiis'*, *Zeitschrift der Savigny-Stiftung für Rechtsgechichte* (Rom. Abt.) 88, 1-66.

Connor, W R. (1971) *The New Politicians of Fifth Century Athens*, Princeton.

Cook J.M. (1958-9) 'Old Smyrna 1948-1951', *ABSA* 53-4, 1-34.

Cornell, T.J. (1974) 'Notes on the Sources for Campanian History in the Fifth Century BC' *Museum Helveticum* 31, 193-208.

— (1975) 'Etruscan Historiography', *Annali della scuola normale superiore di Pisa* (Scienze Morali), 3rd ser., 6, 411-39.

Cozzoli, U. (1965) 'Aristodemo Malaco', *Miscellanea Greca-Romana. Studi pubblicati dell' istituto italiano per la storia antica* 16, 5-30.

Dover, K.J. (1963) 'Androtion on ostracism', *CR*, n.s. 13, 256-7.

Drews, R. (1972) 'The first tyrants in Greece', *Historia* 21, 129-44.

Dunbabin, T.J. (1948) *The Western Greeks*, Oxford.

Edelstein, L. (1966) *Plato's Seventh Letter*, Leiden.

Ehrenberg, V. (1968) *From Solon to Socrates*, London.

Ferguson, W.S. (1938) 'The Salaminioi of Heptaphylai and Sounion', *Hesperia* 7, 1-74.

Fine, J.V.A. (1951) '*Horoi*', *Hesperia*, Supplement 9.

Finley, M.I. (1952) *Studies in Land and Credit in Ancient Athens 500-200 BC*, New Brunswick.

— (1960) (ed.), *Slavery in Classical Antiquity*, Cambridge.

— (1965) 'La Servitude pour Dettes', *Revue Historique de droit français* et *étranger* 43, 159-84.

— (1968) 'The Alienability of Land in Ancient Greece', *Eirene* 7, 25-32.

— (1971) *The Ancestral Constitution*, An Inaugural Lecture, Cambridge.

— (1974) 'The World of Odysseus Revisited', *Proceedings of the Classical Association* 71, 13-31 (abridged in Appendix I of 1977).

— (1977) *The World of Odysseus*, 2nd ed. London (1956).

Flach, D. (1977) 'Die oligarchische Staatsstreich in Athen von Jahr 411', *Chiron* 7, 9-33.

Forrest, W.G. (1960) 'Themistokles and Argos', *CQ*, n.s. 10, 221-41.

— (1963) 'The Date of the Lykourgan Reforms at Sparta', *Phoenix* 17, 157-79.

— (1966) *The Emergence of Greek Democracy*, London.

— (1968) *A History of Sparta 950-192 BC*, London.

— (1969) 'The Tradition about Hippias' Expulsion from Athens', *Greek, Roman and Byzantine Studies* 10, 277-86.

— (1970) 'The Date of the Pseudo-Xenophontic *Athenaion Politeia*', *Klio* 52, 107-16.

Fowler, B.H. (1957) 'Thucydides I.107-8 and the Tanagra Federal Issues', *Phoenix* 11, 164-70.

Fraenkel, E. (1961) 'Two Poems of Catullus', *JRS* 51, 46-53.

French, A. (1956) 'The Economic Background to Solon's Reforms', *CQ*, n.s. 6, 11-25.

— (1964) *The Growth of the Athenian Economy*, London.

Fritz, K. von (1940) *Pythagorean Politics in Southern Italy*.

Fuks, A. (1953) *The Ancestral Constitution. Four Studies in Athenian Party Politics at the End of the Fifth Century BC*, London.

Gawantka, W. (1975) *Isopoliteia*, Munich.

Gluckman, M. (1967) *Politics, Law and Ritual in Tribal Society*, Oxford.

Greenhalgh, P.A.L. (1973) *Early Greek Warfare: horsemen and chariots in the Homeric and Archaic Ages*, Cambridge.

Griffiths, G.T. (1950) 'The Union of Corinth and Argos, 392-386 BC', *Historia* 1, 236-56.

Guarino, A. (1978) *La Rivoluzione della Plebe*, Naples.

Gulley, N. (1972) 'The Authenticity of the Platonic Epistles', in Pseudepigrapha I, *Entretiens Fondation Hardt* 18, 103-43.

Guthrie, W.K.C. (1971) *The Sophists* (= *A History of Greek Philosophy* II.1, 1969), Cambridge.

Hack, H.M. (1978) 'Thebes and the Spartan Hegemony 386-382 BC', *AJP* 99, 210-27.

Harding, P. (1974) 'The Theramenes Myth', *Phoenix* 28, 101-11.

Harris, W.V. (1971) *Rome in Etruria and Umbria*, Oxford.

Harrison, A.R.W. (1968) *The Law of Athens*, 2 vols., Oxford (1968/1971).

Hatzfeld, J. (1940) *Alcibiade*, Paris.

Helbig, W. (1904) *Les Hippeis Athéniens*, Paris.

Henrichs, A. (1968) 'Zur Interpretation des Michigan-Papyrus über Theramenes', *ZPE* 3, 101-8.

Hereward, D. (1952) 'New Fragments of IG II^2.10', *ABSA* 47, 102-17.

Herrman, P. (1970) 'Zu den Beziehungen zwischen Athen und Milet im 5 Jahrhundert', *Klio* 52, 163-73.

Heurgon, J. (1966) 'The Inscriptions of Pyrgi', *JRS* 56, 1-15.

Hignett, C. (1952) *A History of the Athenian Constitution*, Oxford.

Hobsbawm, E.J. (1959) *Primitive Rebels: Studies in Archaic Forms of Social Movement in the Nineteenth and Twentieth Centuries*, Manchester (3rd ed., 1973).

Hopper, R.J. (1961) 'Plain, Shore and Hill in Early Athens', *ABSA* 56, 189-219.

Hunt, D.W.S. (1947) 'Feudal Survivals in Ionia', *JHS* 67, 68-76.

Huxley, G.L. (1962) *Early Sparta*, London.

Jacoby, F. (1949) *Atthis*, Oxford.

Jenkins, G.K. (1966) *Coins of Greek Sicily*, London.

Kagan, D. (1962) 'Corinthian Politics and the Revolution of 392 BC', *Historia* 11, 447-57.

Keaney, J.J. and Raubitschek, A.E. (1972) 'A late Byzantine Account of Ostracism', *AJP* 93, 87-91.

Kiechle, F. (1963) *Lakonien und Sparta*, Munich.

Kraay, C.M. (1964) 'Hoards, Small Change and the Origin of Coinage', *JHS* 84, 76-91.

— (1969) *Greek Coins and History*, London.

— (1976) *Archaic and Classical Greek Coins*, London.

Lacey, W.K. (1968) *The Family in Classical Greece*, London.

Lang, M. (1968) 'Herodotus and the Ionian Revolt', *Historia* 17, 24-36.

Larsen, J. (1968) *Greek Federal States*, Oxford.

Last, H.M. (1945) 'The Servian Reforms', *JRS* 35, 30-48.

Latte, K. (1931) 'Beiträge zu Griechischen Strafrecht', *Hermes* 66, 30-48 and 129-58 = *Kleine Schriften*, Munich (1968) 252-93.

Lauritano, R. (1957) 'Ricerche su Filisto', *Kokalos* 3, 98-122.

Leahy, D.M. (1955) 'The Bones of Tisamenus', *Historia* 4, 26-38.

— (1955-6) 'Chilon and Aeschines', *Bulletin of the John Rylands Library*, 38, 406-35.

— (1959) 'Chilon and Aeschines again', *Phoenix* 13, 31-7.

Legon, R.P. (1967) 'Phliasian Politics and Policy in the Early Fourth Century BC', *Historia* 16, 324-37.

Lepore, E. (1969) 'Classi e ordini in Magna Grecia', in C. Nicolet (ed.), *Recherches sur les Structures Sociales dans l'Antiquité Classique*, Colloque, Caen, 43-62.

Lévêque, P. and Vidal-Naquet, P. (1964) *Clisthène l'Athénien*, Paris.

Lewis, D.M. (1954) 'Notes on Attic Inscriptions', *ABSA* 49, 17-50.

— (1963) 'Cleisthenes and Attica', *Historia* 12, 22-40.

— (1977) *Sparta and Persia*, Leiden.

Lintott, A.W. (1968) *Violence in Republican Rome*, Oxford.

— (1970) 'The Tradition of Violence in the Annals of the Early Roman Republic', *Historia* 19, 12-29.

Lipsius, J.H. (1905) *Das Attische Recht und Rechtsverfahren*, repr. Hildesheim (1966).

Lloyd-Jones, H. (1975) 'More about Antileon, Tyrant of Chalkis', *Classical Philology* 76, 197.

Lorimer, H.L. (1947) 'The Hoplite Phalanx', *ABSA* 42, 76-138.

Losada, L.A. (1972) 'Fifth Columns in the Peloponnesian War', *Klio* 54, 125-45.

Lungo, C.P. (1980) 'La Bulé e la procedura dell' ostracismo. Considerazioni su Vat.Gr.1149', *Historia* 29, 257-81.

MacCormack, G. (1973) 'Revenge and Compensation in Early Law', *American Journal of Comparative Law*, 21.1, 69-85.

MacDowell, D.M. (1962) *Andokides on the Mysteries*, Oxford.

Mattingly, H.B. (1966) 'Periclean Imperialism', in E. Badian (ed.), *Ancient Society and Institutions: Studies Presented to Victor Ehrenberg*, Oxford, 193-223.

Meiggs, R. (1972) *The Athenian Empire*, Oxford.

Meloni, P. (1951) 'La tirannide di Eufrone I in Sicione', *Rivista di filologia e d'istruzione classica* 29, 10-33.

Mendelsohn, I. (1949) *Slavery in the Ancient Near East*, New York.

Meritt, B.D. (1952) 'Greek Inscriptions', *Hesperia* 21, 340-80.

Merkelbach, R. and Youtie, H.C. (1968) 'Ein Michigan-Papyrus über Theramenes', *ZPE* 2, 161-9.

Meyer, Ed. (1899) *Forschungen zu alten Geschichte*, II, Halle.

— (1909) *Theopomps Hellenika*, Halle.

— (1915) *Geschichte des Altertums*, IV, 2nd ed., Stuttgart/Berlin.

Mitchell, B.M. (1966) 'Cyrene and Persia', *JHS* 86, 99-113.

Momigliano, A. (1963) 'An Interim Report on the Origins of Rome', *JRS* 53, 95-121.

Morrison, J.S. (1942) 'Meno of Pharsalus, Polycrates and Ismenias', *CQ* 36, 57-78.

— (1961) 'Antiphon', *PCPS*, n.s. 7, 49-58.

Mossé, C. (1962) *La fin de la démocratie athénienne*, Paris.

— (1969) *La tyrannie dans la Grèce antique*, Paris.

— (1973) *Athens in Decline*, London.

Newman, W.L. (1887) *The Politics of Aristotle*, Oxford, 1887-1902.

Nicole, J. (1907) *L'Apologie d'Antiphon*, Paris.

Nilsson, M. (1929) 'Die Hoplitentaktik und das Staatswesen', *Klio* 22, 240-9.

Ogilvie, R.M. (1965) *Commentary on Livy I-V*, Oxford.

— (1976) *Early Rome and the Etruscans*, Glasgow.

Oliviero, G., Pugliese-Carratelli, G. and Morelli, D. (1961-2) 'Supplemento epigrafico cirenaico', *Annuario della scuola archeologica di Atene* 39-40, 219-375.

Orth, W. (1979) 'Der Syrakusaner Herakleides', *Historia* 28, 51-64.

Ostwald, M. (1955) 'The Athenian legislation against tyranny and subversion', *Transactions of the American Philological Association* 86, 103-28.

Page, D.L. (1955) *Sappho and Alcaeus*, Oxford.

Parke, H.W. (1930) 'The Development of the Second Spartan Empire', *JHS* 50, 37-79.

— (1933) *Greek Mercenary Soldiers from the Earliest Times to the Battle of Ipsus*, Oxford.

Perlman, S. (1964) 'The Causes and Outbreak of the Corinthian War',

CQ, n.s. 14, 64-81.

Pleket, H.W. (1963) 'Thasos and the Popularity of the Athenian Empire', *Historia* 12, 70-7.

Pollock, F. and Maitland, F.W. (1895) *The History of English Law before the time of Edward I*, 2nd ed., Cambridge.

Pouilloux, J. (1952) *Recherches sur l'histoire et les cultes de Thasos*, Paris.

— (1960) *Choix d'Inscriptions Grecques*, Paris.

Price, M. and Waggoner, N. (1975) *Archaic Greek Coinage: The Asyut Hoard*, London.

Quinn, T.J. (1964) 'Thucydides and the Unpopularity of the Athenian Empire', *Historia* 13, 257-66.

— (1969) 'Political Groups at Chios', *Historia* 18, 22-30.

Reece, D.W. (1962) 'The Fall of Ithome', *JHS* 82, 111-20.

Rhodes, P.J. (1972)(1) *The Athenian Boule*, Oxford.

— (1972)(2) 'The Five Thousand in the Athenian Revolution of 411 BC', *JHS* 92, 115-27.

Richard, J.C. (1978) *Les origines de la plèbe romaine*, Rome.

Rizzo, F.P. (1970) *La repubblica di Siracusa nel momento di Ducezio*, Palermo.

Robert, L. (1949) 'Bergers grecs', *Hellenica* 7, 152-60.

— (1969) *Opera Minora Selecta*, 3 vols., Amsterdam.

Romilly, J. de (1966) 'Thucydides and the Cities of the Athenian Empire', *Bulletin of the Institute of Classical Studies* 13, 1-12.

Rostovtzeff, M. (1923) 'Notes on the Economic Policy of the Pergamene Kings', in W.H. Buckler and W.M. Calder (eds.), *Anatolian Studies Presented to Sir W.M. Ramsay*, London, 359-90.

Roy, J. (1971) 'Arcadia and Boeotia in Peloponnesian Affairs 370-62 BC', *Historia* 20, 569-99.

Rudé, G. (1964) *The Crowd in History 1730-1848*, New York.

Ruschenbusch, E. (1978) *Untersuchungen zu Staat und Politik in Griechenland vom 7.-4. Jh. v. Chr.*, Bamberg.

Rutter, N.K. (1980) *Campanian Coinages 475-380 BC*, Edinburgh.

Ryder, T.T.B. (1965) *Koine Eirene*, Hull/Oxford.

Ste Croix, G.E.M. de (1954) 'The Character of the Athenian Empire', *Historia* 3 (1954-5), 1-41.

— (1972) *The Origins of the Peloponnesian War*, London.

Salmon, J. (1977) 'Political Hoplites?', *JHS* 97, 84-101.

Schapera, I. (1956) *Government, Law and Politics in Tribal Society*, London.

Schreiner, J.H. (1976) 'The Origin of Ostracism Again', *Classica et*

Mediaevalia 31 (1970; appeared 1976), 84-97.

Schulze, W. (1933) 'Beiträge zur Wort- und Sittengeschichte', II, in *Kleine Schriften* (2nd ed., Göttingen 1966), 160-89.

Seager, R. (1967) 'Thrasybulus, Conon and Athenian Imperialism', *JHS* 87, 95-115.

Sealey, R. (1967) *Essays in Greek Politics*, New York.

— (1976) *A History of the Greek States 700-338 BC*, Berkeley.

Shefton, B.R. (1960) 'Some Iconographic Remarks on the Tyrannicides', *American Journal of Archaeology* 64, 173-9.

Snodgrass, A.H. (1964) *Early Greek Armour and Weapons from the End of the Bronze Age to 600 BC*, Edinburgh.

— (1965) 'The Hoplite Reform and History', *JHS* 85, 110-22.

— (1980) *Archaic Greece*, London.

Sordi, M. (1958) *La lega Tessala*, Rome.

— (1961) *Timoleonte*, Palermo.

Stanton, G.R. (1970) 'The Introduction of Ostracism and Alcmeonid Propaganda', *JHS* 90, 180-3.

Stinton, T.C.W. (1976) 'Solon, fragment 25', *JHS* 96, 159-62.

Stroheker, K.F. (1958) *Dionysius I*, Wiesbaden.

Szemerényi, O. (1969) *'Si parentem puer verberit, ast olle plorassit'*, II, in *Festschrift F. Altheim*, 182-91.

Talbert, R.J.A. (1974) *Timoleon and the Revival of Greek Sicily 344-317 BC*, Cambridge.

Thomas, D.H. (1978) 'Aristotle's Treatment of Historical Material in the Politics', unpublished D.Phil. thesis, Oxford.

Thomsen, R. (1972) 'The Origin of Ostracism — a Synthesis', *Humanitas* 4, Copenhagen.

Tomlinson, R.A. (1972) *Argos and the Argolid*, London.

Toynbee, A.J. (1969) *Some Problems of Greek History*, Oxford.

Traill, J.S. (1978) 'Diakris, the inland trittys of Leontis', *Hesperia* 47, 89-104.

Usener, H. (1900) 'Italische Volksjustiz', *Rheinisches Museum* 56, 1-28 = *Kleine Schriften* IV, Leipzig (1912-14), 356-82.

Wade-Gery, H.T. (1945) 'Kritias and Herodes', *CQ* 39, 19-33.

— (1966) 'The Rhianos-Hypothesis', in E. Badian (ed.), *Ancient Society and Institutions*, Oxford, 289-302.

Walcot, P. (1970) *Greek Peasants*, Manchester.

Wallace, W.P. (1954) 'Kleomenes, Marathon, the Helots and Arkadia', *JHS* 74, 32-5.

West, M.L. (1970) 'Melica', *CQ*, n.s. 20, 205-15.

— (1978) *Hesiod, Works and Days*, Oxford.

Westlake, H.D. (1935) *Thessaly in the Fourth Century BC*, London.

— (1952) *Timoleon and his Relations with Tyrants*, Manchester.

Wheeler, M. (1951) Aristotle's Analysis of the Nature of Political Struggle', *AJP* 72, 145-61 = *Articles on Aristotle* (ed. J. Barnes, M. Schofield and R. Sorabji, London, 1977) 159-69.

White, M.E. (1954) 'The Duration of the Samian Tyranny', *JHS* 74, 36-43.

— (1958) 'The Dates of the Orthagorids', *Phoenix* 12, 2-14.

Wilamowitz-Möllendorf, U. von (1893) *Aristoteles und Athen*, 2 vols., Berlin.

Wilhelm, A. (1911) 'Die lokrische Mädscheninschrift', *Jahreshefte des Österreichischen Archäologischen Institutes in Wien* 14, 163-256.

Will, E. (1969) 'Notes sur les régimes politiques de Samos au Ve siècle', *Revue des Etudes Anciennes* 71, 305-19.

Willetts, R.F. (1959) 'The Servile Interregnum at Argos', *Hermes* 87, 495-506.

Wolff, H.J. (1946) 'The Origin of Judicial Litigation among the Greeks', *Traditio* 4, 31-87.

INDEX

Persons, Peoples and Places

283

Topics